OTHELLO

BROADVIEW / INTERNET SHAKESPEARE EDITIONS

Broadview Editions Series Editor
Martin R. Boyne
Internet Shakespeare Editions Coordinating Editors
Michael Best and Janelle Jenstad
Internet Shakespeare Editions Textual Editor
Eric Rasmussen
Internet Shakespeare Editions Textual Editor
James Mardock

OTHELLO

William Shakespeare

EDITED BY
Jessica Slights

BROADVIEW / INTERNET SHAKESPEARE EDITIONS

BROADVIEW PRESS – www.broadviewpress.com
Peterborough, Ontario, Canada

Founded in 1985, Broadview Press remains a wholly independent publishing house. Broadview's focus is on academic publishing; our titles are accessible to university and college students as well as scholars and general readers. With over 600 titles in print, Broadview has become a leading international publisher in the humanities, with world-wide distribution. Broadview is committed to environmentally responsible publishing and fair business practices.

Library and Archives Canada Cataloguing in Publication

Shakespeare, William, 1564–1616, author
    Othello / William Shakespeare ; edited by Jessica Slights.

(Broadview / Internet Shakespeare Editions)
Includes bibliographical references.
ISBN 978-1-55481-326-1 (softcover)

    1. Othello (Fictitious character)—Drama. 2. Muslims—Drama. 3. Jealousy—Drama. 4. Venice (Italy)—Drama. I. Slights, Jessica, 1968–, editor II. Title. III. Series: Broadview / Internet Shakespeare Editions

Broadview Press handles its own distribution in North America
PO Box 1243, Peterborough, Ontario K9J 7H5, Canada
555 Riverwalk Parkway, Tonawanda, NY 14150, USA
Tel: (705) 743-8990; Fax: (705) 743-8353
email: customerservice@broadviewpress.com

Distribution is handled by Eurospan Group in the UK, Europe, Central Asia, Middle East, Africa, India, Southeast Asia, Central America, South America, and the Caribbean. Distribution is handled by Footprint Books in Australia and New Zealand.

Canada

Broadview Press acknowledges the financial support of the Government of Canada through the Canada Book Fund for our publishing activities.

Copy-edited by Denis Johnston
Book design by Michel Vrana
Typeset in MVB Verdigris Pro

PRINTED IN CANADA

CONTENTS

FOREWORD

The Internet Shakespeare Editions (http://internetshakespeare. uvic.ca) and Broadview Press are pleased to collaborate on a series of Shakespeare editions in book form, creating for each volume an "integrated text" designed to meet the needs of today's students.

The texts, introductions, and other materials for these editions are drawn from those prepared by leading scholars for the Internet Shakespeare Editions, modified to suit the demands of publication in book form. The print editions are integrated with the fuller resources and research materials that are available electronically on the site of the Internet Shakespeare Editions. Consistent with other volumes in the Broadview Editions series, each of these Shakespeare editions includes a wide range of background materials, providing information on the play's historical and intellectual context, in addition to the text itself, introduction, chronology, essays on Shakespeare's life and theater, and bibliography; all these will be found in more extensive form on the website.

The Internet Shakespeare Editions, a non-profit organization founded in 1996, creates and publishes works for the student, scholar, actor, and general reader in a form native to the medium of the Internet: scholarly, fully annotated texts of Shakespeare's plays, multimedia explorations of the context of Shakespeare's life and works, and records of his plays in performance. The Internet Shakespeare Editions is affiliated with the University of Victoria.

The Broadview Editions series was founded in 1992 under the title "Broadview Literary Texts." Under the guidance of executive editors Julia Gaunce and Marjorie Mather, of series editors Eugene Benson, Leonard Conolly, and Martin Boyne, and of managing editors Barbara Conolly and Tara Lowes, it has grown to include several hundred volumes—lesser-known works of cultural significance as well as canonical texts. Designed with the needs of undergraduate students in mind, the series has also appealed widely to scholars—and to readers in general.

Janelle Jenstad, Coordinating Editor, University of Victoria
Eric Rasmussen and James Mardock, General Textual Editors,
    University of Nevada, Reno
Don LePan, Company Founder and CEO, Broadview Press

ACKNOWLEDGEMENTS

I am profoundly grateful to Michael Best, Coordinating Editor of the Internet Shakespeare Editions, for his wise and generous counsel throughout my work on this project. James Mardock offered invaluable early feedback, and Jannelle Jenstad has provided vital encouragement and organizational support. Marjorie Mather coordinated publication of the edition for Broadview Press, and Denis Johnston's expert copy editing has improved it significantly. To Joseph Grossi, *gracie mille* for helping me make sense of early modern Italian, and to Sarah Milligan many thanks for making the transcription and editing of supplementary texts so much swifter and more fun than it otherwise would have been. Ed Pechter first encouraged me to work on *Othello*, and his astute thinking about and editing of the play continue to shape my own. Michael Neill's editorial work on *Othello* has also been essential for me. More broadly, I have benefited from smart conversations with John Baxter, Ann Christensen, Anthony Dawson, Marianne Novy, and many other friends and colleagues, particularly at meetings of the Shakespeare Association of America. I am indebted to my home institution, Acadia University, for supporting my research, and I offer particular thanks to the students who have worked with me over the years, including Emily Cann, Quinn MacKenzie, Martha Mahle, Erin Mullen, and Danika Sihota. This volume is dedicated to my family: to my parents, Bill and Camille, who taught me by example about the value of both loving marriage and Shakespeare scholarship; to my children, William and Madeleine, who continue to delight me with their enthusiasm for stories, both old and new; and, above all, to my partner, Stephen, whose practical help and impractical love make everything else possible.

The brief essays on Shakespeare's life and Shakespeare's theater are reprinted from the Broadview edition of *As You Like It*, courtesy of David Bevington. Quotations from Shakespeare's plays other than *Othello* are from David Bevington's *Complete Works*, 7th edition (New York: Pearson Longman, 2014). Biblical quotations are from *The Geneva Bible: A Facsimile of the 1560 Edition* (Madison, Milwaukee, and London: U of Wisconsin P, 1969). The Beinecke Rare Books Library, the Folger Shakespeare Library, the Glasgow University Library, Harvard University's Houghton Library, and the Library of Congress all generously granted permission for the use of images from their collections.

INTRODUCTION

Othello is perhaps Shakespeare's most unsettling play. The story it recounts is a fairly simple one about a general who undertakes a tour of duty abroad accompanied by his military and domestic entourage, and who then falls under the influence of a malevolent subordinate who encourages in him a violent sexual jealousy that results in his killing his wife Desdemona. This is no murder mystery. The general's standard-bearer, Iago, announces his perfidy almost immediately to the audience, who watch with growing horror as he enacts a plot to destroy the loving relationship between Othello and Desdemona. Finally, in the play's brutal closing scene, the audience act as silent witnesses to Desdemona's murder and its bloody aftermath. Although other Shakespeare plays offer higher body counts, more gore, and more plentiful scenes of heartbreak, *Othello* packs an unusually powerful affective punch, stunning us with its depiction of the swiftness and thoroughness with which love can be converted to hatred, and forcing us to confront our complicity with social and political institutions that can put all of us—but especially the most vulnerable among us—at risk.

Othello's emotional power derives in part from its disconcerting insistence on both the participation and the impotence of its audience. Although we observe the play's most secret moments—the Venetian Duke's emergency meeting about a Turkish military threat, the unpinning of Desdemona's dress at bedtime, Cassio's confession that he has no head for alcohol—as well as its public ones, we are often uncertain about exactly what we have seen and what we should make of it. Rather than displaying clearly and methodically the events it depicts, *Othello* creates the persistent illusion that we are peering nearsightedly at its action from around dark corners or through half-closed doors. We stumble into the play's opening scene, coming upon Roderigo and Iago muttering together as though we have almost bumped into them as we ourselves scurry through the night-darkened streets of Venice. The play keeps us off balance as we struggle to determine who these men are, to decipher the nature of their relationship, and to make sense of their oblique references to the unnamed Moorish general who seems to engender such hatred in them. Theatrical convention teaches us to expect the elaboration of plans for political rebellion or perhaps even murder from these conspirators, but in this too we are surprised as we overhear only gossip and the bitter whining of thwarted ambition. Our initial confusion is soon mirrored by the frantic response of Desdemona's father, Brabantio, as he is startled from sleep and riled by Roderigo and Iago into a bitter fury even as the circumstances of his daughter's departure from home and sudden marriage remain unclear.

The impression that, like Brabantio, we are being called upon to participate in events about which we never know quite enough persists throughout the play. We watch as the Venetian Senate receives conflicting reports about the movements of a Turkish fleet in the Mediterranean, and we ready ourselves for battle as Othello and his forces depart for Cyprus prepared to defend the island from the Ottoman armada. Then we too are suddenly pulled up short—"beleed and calmed" as the play would have it (1.1.28, TLN 32)—as we learn with the Venetians that they have arrived on the fortified island with no opposing force to battle because the weather has already defeated the Turkish threat. Nor are we allowed to settle into complacency when the focus shifts back from the potential of foreign quarrels to the domestic broils on which the play opened. Instead, we are repeatedly unsettled by Iago's malign confidences as he soliloquizes with delighted precision his plans to destroy Othello and Desdemona.

Confirming his place as one of literature's most compelling villains, Iago fascinates us with his single-minded focus on converting Othello's rapturous love for Desdemona into murderous jealousy, and he disarms us with the apparent frankness with which he discloses his plans. For all his confidences, however, Iago's motives remain at best indeterminate, seeming sometimes insufficient (surely even intense professional envy cannot adequately account for his extreme cruelty) and in other moments oddly abundant (if he truly believes that Emilia and Othello have had an affair, why does it take him so long to mention this?). Iago's means and aims are never in doubt, however: he tells us precisely how he hopes to exploit and to ruin those around him, and, by confiding his treachery, he enlists us as tacit accessories to his crimes. More than helpless spectators of his manipulations of Othello, we become in Act 3's central temptation scene, with its erotic echoes of both the serpent's seduction of Eve and the ritualized exchange of vows at the heart of the Christian marriage service, unwilling acolytes of Iago's ritual destruction of his superior. A sense of inevitability gradually displaces the surprises and confusions of the play's earlier scenes, and a gothic tension builds with the increasing likelihood that Iago's horrific devices will succeed. We are left to watch with increasing revulsion a relentless progress toward Desdemona's murder.

The inevitability of Desdemona's death at her husband's hands appears to slow the play's progress, and *Othello*'s final scene is one of the most tortuously protracted in Shakespeare. The murder itself, when it finally comes, is agonizingly prolonged, and not until the discovery of Desdemona's body does the pace of the action increase as the characters begin to gather onstage for the tragic finale. Even in its closing minutes *Othello* disrupts expectations, as Desdemona's death prompts not the murderous retribution of grief-stricken and maddened relatives familiar both from the Cinthio source text and from the revenge dramas so popular in the period, but instead a second murder of a wife by her husband, a bloody suicide, and a silent survival as shocking in its way as the deaths that precede it.

If the shape and pace of *Othello*'s narrative create profoundly unsettling effects for readers and audiences, the play's subject matter and thematic preoccupations are another source of productive discomfort. This is a play that forces encounters with the destructive consequences of institutionalized sexism and racism and thereby challenges us to analyze how gender and race inflect the operations of power within our households and our states, an analysis as vital now as it was in Shakespeare's day. But while *Othello* raises tough questions about such disturbing subjects as the causes of violence against women and the mutually reinforcing character of stereotypes based on gender and race, the play also refuses easy answers to these questions. A disruptive doubleness operates, for instance, in the play's depiction of its central female characters, whose moments of defiance of patriarchal authority are key to their appealing liveliness but whose violent deaths have been read by some as the necessary consequence of their resistance and by others as the corollary of a sociopolitical system that devalues women's lives.

In its portrayal of Desdemona's elopement, her defiant determination to accompany her new husband into battle, and the buoyant wit she exhibits as she banters with his subordinates, *Othello* offers a strong female character prepared to defy convention and to assert herself in a world governed by men. Similarly, the figure of Emilia, with her clear-eyed analysis in 4.3 of an institutionalized double standard that grants men the right to play away from home while requiring of women an incorruptible chastity, complicates the notion that all early-modern women were always rendered silent and obedient by patriarchal stricture. At the same time, *Othello* troubles attempts to construct its female characters as proto-feminist icons. Emilia's authority as social critic is undermined when her position as a plain-speaking truth-teller is compromised by her participation in Iago's scheme to steal Desdemona's handkerchief. And even Desdemona, unquestionably a victim of Iago's malicious scheming and then of her husband's murderous brutality, is not an entirely sympathetic character for many modern readers, who find in her commitment to marriage and her meekness in the face of violence signs of weakness rather than virtue.

The sense that Desdemona is a disappointment despite, or even because of, her loyalty gets strong structural support in her death scene. In a move that exploits a sensationalism more often associated with nineteenth-century melodrama, Shakespeare stages the apparently permanent stifling of Desdemona's breath only to revive her almost immediately. Here is the opportunity denied readers and audiences of *Romeo and Juliet*'s closing scene: a resurrection, a wife awakened from near death before her husband's suicide, and, alive with her, the possibility that the play's litany of failure, violence, and misery—in short, its tragedy—will be converted to comedy. But of course Desdemona frustrates this hope when she fails to revive fully, encouraging in viewers a resentment that wanders odiously close to blaming the victim for her own death. And even as she thwarts the conversion of tragedy to comedy, Desdemona impedes the ostensible consolations of justice and of revenge. She asserts both her victimization and her innocence on her deathbed—"Oh, falsely, falsely murdered. / ... / A guiltless death I die"—but refuses to name her murderer. Instead, she takes responsibility for her own death and asserts Othello's "kindness" to the end. "Oh, who hath done this deed?" asks the distraught Emilia, to which Desdemona replies with her final breath, "Nobody—I myself. Farewell— / Commend me to my kind lord—Oh, farewell" (5.2.123–24, TLN 3384–94).

While *Othello*'s final scene problematizes Desdemona's quiescence, the play's insistence on the cultural embeddedness of its characters finally suggests that both her murder and her reaction to the abuse she experiences at her husband's hands are the product of a deeply masculinist culture. Initially, Venice appears responsive to the needs of its female citizens as the Duke calls upon Desdemona to testify in the matter of her elopement and hears her plea to be allowed to accompany Othello to Cyprus. However, the well-being of women is soon dismissed as a matter best "privately determine[d]" (1.3.275, TLN 625) as the Senate turns to the primary "business of the state" (1.2.90, TLN 311): the protection of its commercial and political interests in the Mediterranean. The Venetian institution of marriage proves similarly problematic for women. Although marriage looks at first like a way for Desdemona to secure both her passionate love for Othello and a measure of independence from her father, the play is clear that she is exchanging obligation to her father for duty to her husband.

Venice's martial ethos also proves especially dangerous for women. Othello is evidently enamored of Desdemona, but he is also a leader in a military community that understands the effects of love as potentially destructive for men. Thus when he is determined to prove his professional commitment to his political masters, Othello declares himself invulnerable to an erotic love that he figures as blindness and associates with a loss of masculine control:

> ... when light-winged toys
> Of feathered Cupid seel with wanton dullness
> My speculative and officed instruments ...
> Let housewives make a skillet of my helm.... (1.3.268–72,
> TLN 618–22)

Offering the Senate a comic image of a proud military man charging into battle with a frying pan on his head, Othello implies that falling in love with women makes men vulnerable to domestic coups that put both their physical safety and their dignity at risk. In seeking to distance himself from the ostensibly endangering effects of domesticity, the general gives voice to his culture's anxiety that rather than affirming masculine dominance, heterosexual love enables the effeminization of men and exposes them to ridicule.

The idea that love for women exposes men to mockery appears consistently throughout the play: in Brabantio's public prediction that

Desdemona will be unfaithful to her new husband; in Roderigo's conviction that Desdemona will abandon Othello and take up with him; in Cassio's care not to let his general "see [him] womaned" (3.4.186, TLN 2359) in Bianca's company; and in the pernicious stereotypes about women's self-indulgence, lustfulness, and disloyalty consistently served up by Iago. Nor is resistance to such constructions of femininity much of an option for *Othello*'s female characters. When Emilia eventually figures out the role Iago has played in Desdemona's death, she refuses to obey his commands that she remain quiet: "No, I will speak as liberal as the north," she announces, "Let heaven and men and devils, let them all, / All, all cry shame against me, yet I'll speak" (5.2.217–19, TLN 3510–12). While her brave words offer a momentary model of resistance to patriarchal control, the terms of Emilia's refusal remind us that hers is a culture that silences women by shaming those who speak out of turn. That the play's liveliest representatives of womanliness are brutally murdered by their husbands, that the institution of marriage fails rather than protects them, and that the Venetian state is either unable or unwilling to stop the violence are fictional realities at the heart of the tragedy of *Othello*; that they continue to find analogs in the lives of real women and men reinforces the importance of the difficult conversations they prompt.

Even as it asks readers and audiences to consider challenging questions about gender and power, *Othello* also demands a focus on complex matters of racialized and religious difference. Its setting in the Mediterranean basin locates the play at a key intersection among the continents and cultures of Africa, Asia, and Europe. This physical positioning signals the play's participation in a set of intricate economic, political, and social relationships informed by race, region, and religion, and variations of these relationships have long animated responses to *Othello*. The play's engagement with place and ethnicity as markers of identity is signaled in its full title: *Othello, the Moor of Venice*. For all its apparent specificity, however, the epithet "Moor of Venice" provides little precise detail about the play's titular protagonist, and the rest of the text does little to resolve the ambiguities it raises. Othello announces in the first act that he comes from "men of royal siege" (1.2.22, TLN 226) and later describes himself as black, but these are the only specific references he makes to his origins and appearance.

Evidence from history offers some valuable context for discussions of race and ethnicity in *Othello*, but it provides no definite racial identity for Othello. The term "Moor" was an elastic one in the early-modern period, used variously as a marker of race, geography, nationality, religion, or some combination of these. The term is associated in texts of the period with light-skinned Arabs from North Africa, with dark-skinned sub-Saharan Africans, with Muslims from the Iberian Peninsula, and with the smaller number of men and women of color who lived in England, some as slaves and others as paid workers. For example, in the chronicle of the Wars of the Roses on which Shakespeare leans heavily in his history plays, sixteenth-century historian Edward Hall (c. 1497–1547) refers to "the Moores or Mawritane nacion, being infidels & unchristened people" (xxiiii). For Hall, "Moors" clearly operates as a geopolitical identifier synonymous with "inhabitants of Mauritania," a region of North Africa sometimes called "Barbary" and comprised of much of modern-day Morocco and northwestern Algeria. At the same time, for Hall as for many early modern writers, "Moor" also serves as a religious identifier, a way of naming non-Christian "infidels"—that is,

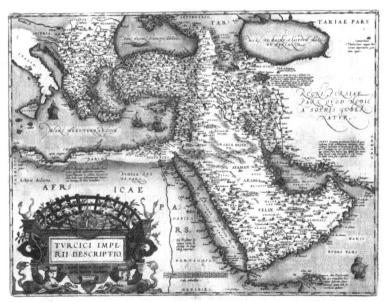

Outline of the Ottoman Empire from Abraham Ortelius, *Theatrum orbis terrarum* (Antwerp, 1570). From the Library of Congress, Geography and Map Division.

Muslims. Such usage suggests that early modern readers and audiences may have understood in Othello's designation as a Moor a connection to the powerful Islamic Ottoman Empire that vied with the Christian forces of Western Europe for military and commercial control of the Mediterranean from the twelfth through the sixteenth centuries—the same Ottoman Empire established in the play's first act as Venice's principal enemy.

Like Hall, physician and travel writer Andrew Boorde (c. 1490–1549), whose *First Book of the Introduction of Knowledge* (1547) describes the customs of various Mediterranean peoples, uses the term "Moor" to identify the racially varied residents of Barbary and to indicate their uniform religious difference from his own Christianity: "Barbary is a great country, and plentyfull of frute, wine, & corne. The inhabytours be Called the Mores: ther be white mores and black moors; they be Infydels and unchristened" (212). As Boorde's description continues, it becomes clear that the word "Moor" was also linked in the period with a specific set of physical features and behavioral characteristics as well as with the practice of slavery:

> There be manye Moores brought into Christendome, in to great cytes & townes, to be sold; and Christenmen do by them, and they wilbe diligent, and wyll do al maner of service; but thei be set most comonli to vile thynges.... they have gret lyppes, and nottyd heare, black and curled; there skyn is soft; and ther is nothing white but their teth and the white of the eye. (212)

The slippage in his account as he moves easily from a description of economic resources such as fruit and corn to a description of human beings emphasizes that, from the perspective of the white Christian European Boorde, Barbary's inhabitants existed primarily as commodities to be bought and sold. A parallel slip occurs in Boorde's description of the characteristics of "Moores," as he veers without comment or change of tone from physical description—noting details about hair and skin texture, for instance—to hasty generalization about morality and behavior: "thei be set most comonli to vile thynges."

In the early modern English theater, too, the term "Moor" was most often connected with blackness and with Islam, and many of the significant number of sixteenth- and seventeenth-century plays that

Abd el-Ouahed ben Messaoud ben Mohammed Anoun, Moorish Ambassador to Queen Elizabeth I, c. 1600. Wikimedia Commons, https://commons.wikimedia.org.

feature Moorish characters depend on similar stereotypes of lustfulness, untrustworthiness, and savagery. The subset of dramas sometimes called the "Turk plays," for instance, took advantage of strong popular interest in and anxiety about the challenge to the military and economic dominance of Europe presented by the Ottoman Empire by offering London theatergoers depictions of Muslim characters and of Turkish history as violent, tyrannical, and treacherous. Robert Greene's *Selimus* (1594), for example, stages the rise to power of Selim I, emphasizing his excessive ambition, his greed, and the glee with which he celebrates his vicious betrayals as he murders his brothers in order to become sultan (see Appendix A4). Shakespeare draws on this theatrical tradition for the character of the Prince of Morocco, a suitor for the wealthy orphan Portia in *The Merchant of Venice* (c. 1596–98). Morocco is not violent, but he is dismissed by Portia before she has even met him for having the "complexion of a devil" (1.2.128, TLN 321), and his performance in the casket test designed to determine whom she will marry marks him as conceited, status-conscious, and materialistic. Aaron, of the revenge tragedy *Titus Andronicus* (1594), is another Shakespearean Moor informed by early modern stereotypes yoking dark skin and moral corruption. A secret lover of the Goth queen who becomes empress of Rome, Aaron engineers the rape and mutilation of a newly married woman, talks her battle-hardened father into chopping off his own hand, confesses to having done "a thousand dreadful things / As willingly as one would kill a fly," and faces public execution repenting only the possibility that he may have done "one good deed" in his life (see Appendix A5). Even as he embodies an almost hyperbolic amorality, however, Aaron is a perversely attractive figure whose two most appealing features—his wit and his powerful love for his infant son—work together to humanize him and to expose the racism of the Goths and the Romans among whom he lives.

We cannot know exactly how Shakespeare imagined Othello would look or precisely which geopolitical, religious, or moral associations his Moorishness might have evoked for the play's first audiences and readers. We can, though, note that a version of the offhand racism that contaminates Boorde's assessment of the inhabitants of Barbary, Portia's reaction to Morocco's suit, and Rome's response to Aaron echoes in the bigoted descriptions of Othello offered by Iago and Roderigo. Roderigo's reference to Othello as "the thick-lips" (1.1.65, TLN 72) may suggest that the general is a black man; the epithet certainly signals the beginning of a string of racist slurs that link his ethnicity with other characters' efforts to discredit him. Iago picks up where Roderigo leaves off, figuring Othello variously as "an old black ram" (1.1.87, TLN 96), "a Barbary horse" (1.1.110, TLN 124), and "the devil" (1.1.90, TLN 99). By systematically associating Othello's racialized difference with the nonhuman—even the inhuman—Iago effects a rhetorical dehumanization of his commander. In a move later aped by Brabantio, Iago also avoids naming Othello, referring to him throughout the opening scene only as "the Moor" and, with ironic reverence, "his Moorship" (1.1.31, TLN 35). By replacing Othello's name with the indeterminate sobriquet "Moor," the general's opponents deny his individuality and insist instead on his role as a potentially threatening outsider.

The ambiguities that inform *Othello*'s explorations of the operations of gender and power are, then, also at work as the play engages issues of race. Although its most unpleasant characters introduce an overtly racist discourse that identifies Othello as a "stranger" (1.1.133, TLN 149), others emphasize his role as a consummate insider. While his enemies foreground his difference and seek to deploy it as a weapon against him, Othello's supporters appear unthreatened by his ethnicity. The Duke of Venice and the Governor of Cyprus, the two primary representatives of state authority in the play, acknowledge Othello's racial difference, but neither man seems concerned by it. In 2.1 Montano, whom Othello replaces as Venice's highest-ranking representative in Cyprus, uses the epithet "the Moor," but he also refers to Othello by name, and his descriptions emphasize Othello's effectiveness as a military commander. The Duke too accentuates Othello's courage and expertise, treating him not as a dangerous outsider but as a trusted leader who can be relied on to defend Venice's claims against the "general enemy Ottoman" (1.3.51, TLN 383). It is worth noting too that while the Duke seems primarily concerned to reconcile Brabantio to Desdemona's marriage because their domestic upheaval risks disrupting state business, his response to the news of the lovers' elopement also suggests that he sees Othello as a reasonable match for a Venetian senator's daughter.

Othello's supportive reception by the state authorities reminds us, then, that he is at once "the Moor" and "of Venice." Indeed, the prepositional force of the play's title emphasizes Othello's belonging in and to Venice, a site best known to Shakespeare's first audiences as a wealthy hub of mercantile activity, a multi-ethnic international port city whose stable republican government, high military spending, and strategic location at the top of a narrow estuary enabled its role as a powerful commercial and cultural nexus linking east and west. Venice also had a reputation in the period as a center for sex tourism, thanks in part to the popularity of travel literature published by English adventurers such as Thomas Coryate (c. 1577–1617). Coryate's 1611 account of a trip through continental Europe purports to offer an eyewitness account of Venice's glamorous courtesans, juxtaposing the ostensible wealth and freedom of their lifestyles with the drab existence of ordinary Venetian wives who are depicted as jealously over-managed by watchful husbands (see Appendix A7). Thus the Venice of which Othello is a part not only provides an evocative physical starting point for the play's action but also is emblematic of its insistence that its characters are the product of the complexly intertwined discourses of race, religion, commerce, militarism, and gender upon which modern civil society is constructed.

The interconnections among *Othello*'s broad preoccupations are elaborated not simply through setting, structure, characterization, and plot, but also stylistically, at the levels of the word, the sentence, and the image. Indeed, much of the play's emotional intensity is generated through its richly textured language and heightened by its depiction of the power of language to shape human experience. The play's preoccupation with duplicity, for instance, is neatly supported by its surfeit of puns. Predictably, wordplay as a marker of the instability of language is often associated with Iago, for whom multiplicity of meaning and ambiguity of interpretation represent disruptive opportunity. When he first lands in Cyprus with Desdemona and Emilia, for example, Iago answers the elaborate gallantry of Cassio's greeting by locating in its ritual language and gestures a licentious undercurrent of which its speaker is apparently unaware. Kissing Emilia in welcome, Cassio speaks politely, if rather pompously, to her husband:

> Let it not gall your patience, good Iago,
> That I extend my manners. 'Tis my breeding
> That gives me this bold show of courtesy.
> (2.1.96–98, TLN 866–68)

Iago's punning comeback—"Sir, would she give you so much of her lips / As of her tongue she oft bestows on me, / You'd have enough"— deliberately elides erotic kissing with scolding, and comes at the expense of both Emilia and Cassio, setting a pattern for Iago's more elaborate and equally self-serving deceptions later in the play.

The connection between punning and deceitfulness is perhaps most clearly displayed in the opening lines of 3.4, a comic exchange between Desdemona and the Clown that turns on multiple meanings of the word "lie." Desdemona's simple inquiry about Cassio's whereabouts—"Do you know, sirrah, where Lieutenant Cassio lies?" (3.4.1, TLN 2139)—elicits from the Clown a circuitous response that plays on various definitions of the verb "to lie": to tell a falsehood, to occupy a dwelling place, to recline in bed. None of this brings Desdemona any closer to locating Cassio, but it does construct a powerful verbal chain linking both characters to deceit and to the bedroom. This is, of course, the linguistic chain to which Othello will, in the following scene, add a fatal final link when he recognizes that "lying" is also a euphemism for "having sex." In an earnest echo of Desdemona's query about Cassio, Othello tries to extract information about the lieutenant from Iago, who proves, like the Clown before him, more interested in diversion and duplicity than in providing a clear response:

> OTHELLO.   What hath he said?
> IAGO. Faith, that he did—I know not what he did.
> OTHELLO. What? What?
> IAGO.   Lie.
> OTHELLO.   With her?
> IAGO. With her, on her—what you will.
> OTHELLO. Lie with her? Lie on her? We say "lie on her" when they belie her. Lie with her? Zounds, that's fulsome! (4.1.31–36, TLN 2406–13)

With Iago's subtle encouragement, Othello extends the interpretive chain linking Desdemona and Cassio all the way to adultery, exchanging his usual confident declarative rhetorical mode for a series of increasingly frantic questions and betraying the extent to which he buys into stereotypes about women's inconstancy by the speed with which he carves his way through multiple meanings of "lie" to the image of Cassio and Desdemona in bed together.

Of course, Iago's machinations exploit not only the instabilities of language but also the limits of sense perception as he stage-manages for Othello dramatic encounters with Cassio and then between Cassio and Bianca. Inviting Othello to "withdraw" to a position that limits his capacity to hear and see the scene before him, Iago ensures that the general overhears only misleading snippets of conversation between the drama's unsuspecting actors. In effect, Iago creates for Othello an interpretive space within which the gestures and objects he spies confirm his worst fears about his wife's alleged infidelity. Iago's theatrical turn is so devastatingly effective because it appears to provide for Othello precisely the "ocular proof" (3.3.358, TLN 2003) of Desdemona's betrayal that he has demanded. The dramatic irony produced by the gap between Othello's certainty that he has seen for himself proof of his wife's treachery and the reader's knowledge that he has instead witnessed Bianca's anger over what she has mistaken for a sign of Cassio's unfaithfulness reinforces an uncomfortable connection between the effects of the play's action on its characters and on its audience. By tracing the shattering effects of Iago's counterfeit dumbshow, the play offers a metatheatrical reminder of our own readerly vulnerability, since, like Othello, we must rely on a language whose multiplicities have been associated with the potential for deception and on a set of five senses that have been exposed repeatedly as dangerously unreliable.

These intellectually and emotionally destabilizing linguistic and visual effects are magnified by *Othello*'s often bizarre and eerie imagery. Animals feature prominently in the play's figurative landscape, usually in disturbing contexts, and images of monstrousness and cannibalism haunt the characters' speech. Iago initiates a grotesque metaphorics just moments into the play when he announces to Roderigo: "I will wear my heart upon my sleeve / For daws to peck at" (1.1.63–64, TLN 70–71). Although we now recognize as proverbial the phrase "to wear one's heart upon one's sleeve," meaning "to show openly how one feels," the *Oxford English Dictionary* records Iago's as the first occurrence of this expression. For the play's earliest audiences the horrific image of an excised heart displayed outside the body and thus vulnerable to preda-tion by carrion eaters—an image not yet blunted by familiarity—must have been particularly disturbing. These first viewers may also have been attuned to the disruptive politics of Iago's metonymic image with its substitution of the heart—the organ most closely linked in the period with private desire—for the livery badge customarily displayed on the sleeve of the household servant as a sign of his submission to the will of a wealthy master. This association of the heart as a signifier of the self with domestic labor supports Iago's attack on the traditional model of service that he blames for Cassio's promotion at his expense. However, it also unleashes a series of animal images that are part of his wider project of dehumanizing both Othello and Desdemona. "[A]n old black ram / Is tupping your white ewe" (1.1.87–88, TLN 96–97), proclaims Iago to Brabantio, "your daughter and the Moor are making the beast with two backs" (1.1.113–14, TLN 128–29).

The connection between the play's language of bestiality and mon-strosity and the racist and sexist stereotyping of Moors and of women as lustful, untrustworthy, and nonhuman spreads throughout the play, eventually contaminating Emilia's account of the birth of jealousy— "It is a monster / Begot upon itself, born on itself" (3.4.152–53, TLN 2318–19)—and Othello's account of his marriage to Desdemona, which he likens to the relationship between the hunter and the bird of prey tamed to do his bidding. The play's monstrous imagery is particularly evident as Othello's terror of cuckoldry corrupts the image of the fairy-tale frog prince by reimagining it as a horrific toad that thrives on poisonous fumes: "I had rather be a toad / And live upon the vapor of a dungeon," the general announces, "Than keep a corner in the thing I love / For others' uses" (3.3.269–72, TLN 1901–04). Othello figuratively dehumanizes not only himself but also Desdemona, leaving her unnamed, a "thing"—a mere possession of her husband, like all married women under early-modern English law—and reifying her imagined role as adulteress by transforming her into a room or a building whose dark corners house illicit behavior inadvertently "kept," that is, maintained, by Othello. Iago's habit of lacing his language with innuendo has also infected Othello's speech by this point in the play, and sexual slang—"corner" = vagina; "thing" = whore; "use" = sexual employment—lends his image a particular gothic horror.

Othello associates such doubling linguistic effects as punning and innuendo with emotional treachery and ultimately with physical violence. However, it also insists that plurality of meaning and the limits to knowing imposed by ambiguity are endemic to language and to human experience. Most of the play's major characters are duplicitous in one way or another, and their duplicity is presented as inextricably tied to the complexities of social self-construction. Iago's famous self-denial "I am not what I am" (1.1.64, TLN 71) identifies him early as the play's primary deceiver, a man prepared to misrepresent himself to the world and thus a threat to social cohesion. Then, as Iago's influence over his commander grows, Othello announces his own public deception, claiming, "I will be found most cunning in my patience" (4.1.89, TLN 2473). But even as it tracks the contagious nature and destructive force of Iago's strategy of misrepresentation, the play recognizes that deceit can be a tool for social cohesion. After all, it is not Iago but Desdemona who announces, "I do beguile / The thing I am by seeming otherwise" (2.1.121–22, TLN 896–97). Recognizing a social obligation to trick those around her into believing that she is cheerful even as she worries that her husband has been lost at sea in a storm, Desdemona falsifies her self-presentation not in order to weaken communal bonds but to strengthen them. Indeed, in its ironic assigning to its Janus-faced antagonist Iago the dictum that "Men should be what they seem" (3.3.129, TLN 1736), the play emphasizes that closing the gap between being and seeming may be neither possible nor desirable in the social realm.

In his final speech, Othello pleads to be remembered as "one that loved not wisely, but too well." His lines are poignant not simply for their heart-rending recognition that in killing Desdemona he has destroyed the thing he most loved, but also for their naive insistence that an unambiguous account of his "deeds" can exist:

> I pray you in your letters,
> When you shall these unlucky deeds relate,
> Speak of me as I am. Nothing extenuate,
> Nor set down aught in malice. Then must you speak
> Of one that loved not wisely, but too well;
> Of one not easily jealous, but, being wrought,
> Perplexed in the extreme; of one whose hand,
> Like the base Indian, threw a pearl away
> Richer than all his tribe; of one whose subdued eyes,
> Albeit unused to the melting mood,
> Drops tears as fast as the Arabian trees
> Their medicinable gum. Set you down this,
> And say besides that in Aleppo once,
> Where a malignant and a turbaned Turk
> Beat a Venetian and traduced the state,
> I took by th'throat the circumcisèd dog
> And smote him—thus.
> [*Othello stabs himself.*] (5.2.336–52, TLN 3650–67)

Even as he acts to end his life, Othello tries to manage his legacy by wrenching control of his narrative from those to whom it will fall to tell his story after his death. Like his titular designation "the Moor of Venice," Othello's closing images link his life and person—his deeds, his hand, his eyes, his tears—both to Venice and to the non-Christian, non-white world beyond its boundaries. "Speak of me as I am," Othello begs, but as the play that bears his name insists from its opening moments in a dark Venetian alley, our ability to know others is necessarily limited and narrative control is always contingent.

Othello has always been a popular play with acting companies and audiences, and over the centuries it has occasioned considerable and varied response among scholars. While many critics have regarded it as one of Shakespeare's most successful plays, there have been vocal detractors, both early in the play's life and more recently. The flashpoint of critical controversy has most often been the race and social status of its title character, but significant debates have also arisen about the play's dramatic structure, its representation of women, and the powerfully disturbing figure of Iago. The following discussion sketches in broad strokes some of the most influential critical approaches to *Othello*, including character criticism, formalism, psychoanalysis, and a range of politically inflected approaches such as feminism and new historicism.

As early as the final decade of the seventeenth century, *Othello* was criticized for depicting a man of color as a tragic hero. Thomas Rymer (c. 1641–1713), whose *A Short View of Tragedy* appeared in 1693, is notable for providing the first major published criticism of the play, and also for the intensity of his dislike of *Othello* and its titular hero. Attacking the play as merely an unfortunate and implausible stage adaptation of the Italian prose tale from which its plot derives, Rymer argues that *Othello* ignores a number of key principles of dramatic composition, specifically the neoclassical prescription that a play ought to trace, in real time and in a focused manner, the events of a single day in a single location.[1] He saves his most virulent attacks, however, for what he presents as the play's violation of the conventions of a natural hierarchy that positions people of color firmly below white Europeans, and non-Christians below Christians. Discussing Othello's rank in the Venetian military, Rymer argues:

> The character of that state [i.e., Venice] is to employ strangers in their wars, but shall a poet thence fancy that they will set a negro to be their general, or trust a Moor to defend them against the Turk? With us, a Blackamoor might rise to be a trumpeter, but Shakespeare would not

---

1 For more about the neoclassical notion of the unities, visit the "Life & Times" section of the Internet Shakespeare Editions website and click on Drama: Classical.

have him less than a lieutenant-general.... Nothing is more odious
in nature than an improbable lie, and, certainly, never was any play
fraught, like this of *Othello*, with improbabilities. (91–92)

Of the many attacks on nature for which Rymer holds *Othello* responsible, he clearly considers its depiction of the marriage of a senator's
daughter to a military commander irksome, and its portrayal of a man
of color in the illustrious rank of general loathsome.

Although Rymer's hostility to *Othello* and his overt racism make
unpleasant reading for modern critics, *A Short View of Tragedy* is not
without valuable perceptions about the play, and it is worth noting
that Rymer is the first published critic to recognize (however disap-
provingly) that language or "talk" is the basis of Othello's courtship
of Desdemona:

> Shakespeare, who is accountable both to the eyes and to the ears, and
> to convince the very heart of an audience, shows that Desdemona
> was won by hearing Othello talk ... This was the charm, this was the
> philtre, the love powder that took the daughter of this noble Venetian
> [i.e., Brabantio]. This was sufficient to make the blackamoor white
> and reconcile all, though there had been a cloven foot into the bargain.
> (89–90)

While Rymer takes Brabantio's part in understanding Othello's rhetorical skill as a kind of devilishness, the critic's insight that language
is presented in the play as equal to the task of reconciling difference,
if not finally of overcoming tragedy, is one that continues to inform
modern readings of the play.

Othello was particularly popular with eighteenth-century critics, few
of whom were convinced either by Rymer's strict views on neoclassical dramatic form or by his claim that the play's plot and characters
were implausible. On the contrary, readers such as Samuel Johnson
(1709–84), one of the most influential essayists and commentators of
the period, defended the play specifically on the basis of its compelling
portrait of human behavior. In this excerpt from the commentary in his
1765 edition of Shakespeare's plays, for instance, Johnson highlights
the aesthetic value of *Othello* and then argues that the play offers crucial
insight into human nature:

The beauties of this play impress themselves so strongly upon the attention of the reader, that they can draw no aid from critical illustration. The fiery openness of Othello, magnanimous, artless, and credulous, boundless in his confidence, ardent in his affection, inflexible in his resolution, and obdurate in his revenge; the cool malignity of Iago, silent in his resentment, subtle in his designs, and studious at once of his interest and his vengeance; the soft simplicity of Desdemona, confident of merit, and conscious of innocence, her artless perseverance in her suit, and her slowness to suspect that she can be suspected, are such proofs of Shakespeare's skill in human nature, as, I suppose, it is vain to seek in any modern writer. (473)

As Johnson's comments suggest, the construction of Shakespeare as a national literary hero that was well underway by this time was firmly tied to the perception that he had a particular skill for creating convincingly human characters.

While critical interest in the dramatic portraits drawn by Shakespeare produced some engaging readings of his work, the developing conviction that literary texts could hold, as Hamlet would have it, "the mirror up to nature," contributed to the problematic assumption that that which is "natural" is at once fully consistent and apparent to everyone. As socially constructed notions about race, religion, nationality, gender, and class came to be presented instead as the product of an unalterable "nature" that recognized the inevitable superiority of a white, Christian, European, male elite, readings of *Othello* as a literary confirmation of this hierarchical view began to gain ground. At the beginning of the nineteenth century, for example, German poet and translator August Wilhelm Schlegel (1767–1845) read Othello's descent into murderous jealousy not as a shocking reversal, but as the inevitable return of an innately barbarous man to his ostensibly uncivilized roots:

We recognize in Othello the wild nature of that glowing zone which generates the most ravenous beasts of prey and the most deadly poisons, tamed only in appearance by the desire of fame, by foreign laws of honour, and by nobler and milder manners. His jealousy is not the jealousy of the heart, which is compatible with the tenderest feeling and adoration of the beloved object; it is of that sensual kind which, in burning climes, has given birth to the disgraceful confinement of women and many other unnatural usages. A drop of this poison flows in his veins, and sets his whole blood in the wildest ferment. The Moor seems noble, frank, confiding, grateful for the love shown him; and he is all this, and, moreover, a hero who spurns at danger, a worthy leader of an army, a faithful servant of the state; but the mere physical force of passion puts to flight in one moment all his acquired and mere habitual virtues, and gives the upper hand to the savage over the moral man. (Lecture 25)

In Schlegel's view, nature dictates that that which is European is civilized and moral, while that which is Moorish is savage and immoral: Othello may have "acquired" a veneer of civilization, but he was born with savagery in his "blood," and it is this "poison" which causes his fall. While this gross oversimplification of the play based on racist stereotypes seems absurdly simple-minded now, its account of the association of Moorish identity with violent sensuality persisted, in various guises, throughout the nineteenth century.

As Romantic poet and critic Samuel Taylor Coleridge's (1772–1834) comments on the play illustrate, the conviction that *Othello* depicts fundamental truths about human nature did not always lead to the sort of condemnation of its central character found in Schlegel. Favoring a view of Othello "not as a negro, but a high and chivalrous Moorish chief"—and thereby providing scholarly support for actor Edmund Kean's so-called "tawny" stage Othello—Coleridge reads the tragic hero's actions as the product not of innate and uncontrollable passions, or even of jealousy, but rather as the consequence of moral indignation and wounded honor, and he argues that by generating an empathetic response in the audience the play is finally sympathetic to Othello (2.350). Coleridge was also fascinated by the figure of Iago, and his assessment of the play's enigmatic villain as a "passionless character, all *will* in intellect" (1.49; emphasis in original) influenced readings of the play for decades. Indeed, Coleridge's claim that Iago's final soliloquy is best understood as "the motive-hunting of motiveless malignity" (1.49) remains one of the most quoted assessments of Iago to this day.

In addition to prompting a reassessment of Iago, the nineteenth-century view of Shakespeare's characters as expressions of fundamental truths about human nature stimulated a growing interest in Desdemona. This attentiveness to the play's tragic heroine intersected with a notable increase in the number of women's voices contributing to public conversations in the realm of literary criticism, as female actors began lecturing and publishing on the roles they performed on stage, and as women slowly began to be admitted to the ranks of professional scholars of Shakespeare. Among the latter category, Anna Jameson (1794–1860) is notable as the author of the first substantial and systematic discussion of Shakespeare's female characters, a volume published first in 1832 as *Characteristics of Women, Moral, Poetical, and Historical*, and later retitled simply *Shakespeare's Heroines*. Jameson challenges boldly many of her contemporaries by locating *Othello*'s tragedy not in the plight of its male hero but rather in the character of its heroine, arguing that "the source of the pathos throughout—of that pathos which at once softens and deepens the tragic effect—lies in the character of Desdemona" (224). Discussing Desdemona at length, Jameson describes her in amusingly patronizing terms as "one in whom the absence of intellectual power is never felt as a deficiency, nor the absence of energy of will as impairing the dignity, nor the most imperturbable serenity as a want of feeling: one in whom thoughts appear mere instincts, the sentiment of rectitude supplies the principle, and virtue itself seems rather a necessary state of being, than an imposed law" (224). Desdemona is, in Jameson's account, a young woman who is neither clever nor dynamic, and whose dominant features—her goodness and gentleness—are both beyond her control and inadequate to ensure her survival: "Desdemona displays at times a transient energy, arising from the power of affection, but gentleness gives the prevailing tone to the character—gentleness in excess—gentleness verging on passivity—gentleness which not only cannot resent—but cannot resist" (218).

Jameson's work on *Othello* is also significant for locating the play's fundamental opposition not in the marriage of Desdemona and Othello, which so many of her contemporaries viewed as a hopeless mismatch, but in the relationship between Desdemona and Iago:

> Had the colours in which [Shakespeare] has arrayed Desdemona been one atom less transparently bright and pure, the charm had been lost; she could not have borne the approximation; some shadow from the overpowering blackness of [Iago's] character must have passed over the sunbright purity of *hers*.... To the brutish coarseness and fiendish

malignity of this man, her gentleness appears only a contemptible weakness; her purity of affection ... only a perversion of taste; her bashful modesty only a cloak for evil propensities; so he represents them with all the force of language and self-conviction, and we are obliged to listen to him. (64; emphasis in original)

Picking up on the play's discourse of color, Jameson argues convincingly that *Othello*'s horror lies not in the affectionate relationship of the white-skinned Desdemona and the black-skinned Othello but rather in the profound clash between the virtuous Desdemona and the malevolent Iago.

Critical interest in *Othello* continued into the early twentieth century, when, thanks to A.C. Bradley's *Shakespearean Tragedy* (1904), the play gained a place alongside *Hamlet*, *King Lear*, and *Macbeth* in the pantheon of Shakespeare's greatest tragedies. Bradley finds *Othello* "the most painfully exciting and the most terrible" of the tragedies, arguing that "the reader's heart and mind are held in a vice, experiencing the extremes of pity and fear, sympathy and repulsion, sickening hope and dreadful expectation" (131). In the midst of this maelstrom Bradley locates a thoroughly romanticized Othello, a noble and mysterious everyman whose destruction results from the cunning Iago's ability to turn his virtues against him and whose ruin speaks to a universal experience of tragedy. Like Othello, Desdemona is not a particularized character in Bradley's account, but a representative figure, "the 'eternal womanly' in its most lovely and adorable form, simple and innocent as a child, ardent with the courage and idealism of a saint," and the story of her love for the "noblest soul on earth" becomes for Bradley the story of anyone who has ever aimed high and been held back: "She met in life with the reward of those who rise too far above our common level" (150). While Bradley's brand of character criticism— his practice of treating the literary text as a "little world of persons" (28) populated by characters whose behavior could be explored just as one might discuss the behavior of one's neighbors—is the defining feature of his approach to Shakespeare's tragedies, he is also attuned to matters of dramatic structure. Of *Othello*, he argues that it was "not only the most masterly of the tragedies in point of construction, but its method of construction is unusual. And this method, by which the conflict begins late, and advances without appreciable pause and with accelerating speed to the catastrophe, is a main cause of the painful tension" (131). This analysis of the structural basis for the feelings of frantic and claustrophobic intensity generated in the play has gone on to shape the insights of many later critics.

Bradley's sympathetic reading of *Othello*, with its emphasis on Othello's nobility, Desdemona's saintliness, and Iago's central role as destroyer of their mutual and admirable love, has been enormously influential, although his approach has been attacked vociferously over the years, mostly notably in the 1930s by G. Wilson Knight, L.C. Knights, and F.R. Leavis, and again more recently by poststructuralist critics. For Knight, Bradley's Romantic reading of the play as an anatomy of generalized human nature misses the point completely. "In *Othello*," Knight claims, "we are faced with the vividly particular rather than the vague and universal," and his own reading of the play focuses on explicating the symbolic function of its characters and celebrating what he calls the play's "formal beauty" (109). L.C. Knights's objection to Bradley, famously articulated in his mockingly titled essay "How Many Children Had Lady Macbeth" (1933), lies in what he sees as Bradley's refusal to acknowledge Shakespearean tragedy's status as poetry. Knights accuses Bradley of treating the plays as novels, an approach he claims leads to an erroneous emphasis on their psychological dimensions at the expense of their verbal constructions. In "Diabolic Intellect and the Noble Hero" (1937), F.R. Leavis contributes to this attack, finding Bradley's reading of *Othello* excessively sentimental and accusing him of an over-identification with Othello that blinds him to what Leavis reads as the general's "self-approving self-dramatization" (142). For Leavis, Othello is not the naive and noble victim of Iago's superior intellect but rather an egoist whose "self-pride becomes stupidity, ferocious stupidity, an insane and self-deceiving passion" (146–47).

Perhaps the most influential close reading of the language of *Othello* remains William Empson's 1951 essay "Honest in *Othello*." Noting that the word "honest" appears so often throughout the play, Empson explores how this key term is used by various characters at significant junctures in the action, locating his discussion within an analysis of shifts in the word's meaning over time. According to Empson, Shakespeare is attentive to this semantic slippage and employs "honest," particularly as it is associated with Iago, as a means of acknowledging a gradual cultural shift toward individualism. Bernard Spivak's reading of *Othello* also afforded Iago particular attention, though his *Shakespeare and the Allegory of Evil* (1958) locates the play not within linguistic history but within the history of dramatic form. Noting that *Othello* shares a number of features with traditional morality plays, Spivak argues that Iago is best understood as a version of the stock character Vice, a personification of evil with a dangerously privileged relationship with the audience.

For critics a generation and more later, the suggestion that *Othello* criticism ought to consist in consideration of the play's generic antecedents, in appreciation and explication of what Knight had earlier called the "music" of its language (109), or in analysis of its thematic preoccupation with jealousy as this relates to a generalizable experience of action, emotion, and moral value began to seem at best naive and at worst politically suspect. In the 1960s, critics on both sides of the Atlantic sought to understand *Othello* not as remote from the social and political effects of its historically specific sites of production and reception but as shaped by them. Influenced by many of the same impulses that propelled the American civil rights movement, many of these critics explored the play's relationship to early-modern representations of race rather than its formal properties. This period produced such groundbreaking work as Eldred Jones's *Othello's Countrymen: The African in English Renaissance Drama* (1965) and G.K. Hunter's "*Othello* and Colour Prejudice" (1967), which offered accounts of medieval and early-modern discussions of blackness, traced the effect of racial prejudice on the reception of literary texts featuring characters of color, and so introduced productive ways of exploring race in/and *Othello*. Although the impact of this early work on race in history and drama was gradual, the trail it laid was developed in the 1980s in a series of influential books, including Elliot Tokson's *The Popular Image of the Black Man in English Drama, 1550–1688* (1982), Anthony Barthelemy's *Black Face, Maligned Race* (1987), and Jack D'Amico's *The Moor in English Renaissance Drama* (1991). The collective effect of these studies was to remind readers of the prominence of black characters on the early-modern stage and literary page, to prompt new thinking about the impact of pernicious stereotypes equating blackness with ugliness, disloyalty, and evil, and to encourage further investigation of the historical realities and enduring legacies of slavery. *Othello* criticism became increasingly politically charged as scholars debated the play's relation to modern conceptions of race and racism. For some the play came to be about "a black man whose humanity is eroded by the cunning and racism of whites" (Cowhig 7), while for others it was an anti-racist polemic that "in its fine scrutiny of the mechanisms underlying Iago's use of racism, and in its rejection of human pigmentation as a means of identifying worth ... continues to oppose racism" (Orkin 188).

Although attempts to carry issues of history and race to the center of the conversation about *Othello* gained ground in the 1960s, the determination persisted to read the play's characters and events as representative of a universal human experience. Bradleyan character criticism had fallen out of favor, but the impulse to address the psychological complexities of Shakespeare's characters found fertile new ground in the insights of psychoanalytic theory. First published in the 1950s and reprinted a decade later, a series of influential psychoanalytic readings of the plays found a readership fascinated with exploring links among Shakespeare, Sigmund Freud, and the psychological dimensions of human sexuality. Martin Wangh's "*Othello*: The Tragedy of Iago," for instance, treats Iago as a case study in repressed homosexuality, arguing that the ensign's stifled erotic desire for Othello causes him to despise, and so to seek the destruction of, his rival for the general's affection, Desdemona. Building on Wangh's analysis of Iago as a paranoiac motivated by hatred for the wife of the man he cannot admit he desires, Gordon Ross Smith makes a more general case for a psychoanalytic approach to Shakespearean drama on the grounds that it provides a "common sense" understanding of tragedy. "One may, if he wish," Ross argues, "continue to consider *Othello* a poetic melodrama creakily hinging upon an inexplicable villain and trivial mischance, but the sense of tragedy cannot be brought about by such elements" (182). Instead, in a move reminiscent of the character criticism that dominated in the previous century, he suggests that it is best to understand "all the major figures" of the play as "possible people caught in a net of circumstance which their characters make them unable to escape" (182).

The influence of psychoanalytic approaches to Shakespeare continued to be felt as feminist criticism and sexuality studies evolved throughout the 1980s and 1990s, and as *Othello* criticism began to consider the play's language, symbols, and characters in relation to such broader social institutions as marriage, religion, and law. In an oft-quoted 1975 article titled "Othello's Handkerchief: 'The Recognizance and Pledge of Love,'" for instance, Lynda Boose argues that the strawberry-spotted handkerchief given to Desdemona by her husband gathers a heavy symbolic burden in the course of the play as it comes to stand for that much larger expanse of fabric, the couple's wedding sheets, and thus for both "the sanctified union promising life and the tragic union culminating in death" (373). Similarly, Edward A. Snow's "Sexual Anxiety and the Male Order of Things in *Othello*" (1980) offers a symptomatic reading of *Othello* in which the "truth" (387) of its determination to expose a "pathological male animus toward sexuality" rooted in "the social institutions with which men keep women and the threat they pose at arm's length" (388) is both revealed and concealed by its theatrical and verbal discourses. Snow notes that the play's language and its "theatrical spectacle" (387) are marked by disavowal, denial, and introversion, and he calls on readers to "look for what resists dramatic foregrounding and listen for what language betrays about its speaker" (387), a process that reveals a world of sexual repression and misogyny in which the superego, the "voice of the father" upon which patriarchal social order is founded, is exposed as the site of "evil and malice" (410). Stephen Greenblatt's *Renaissance Self-Fashioning* (1980) also finds in *Othello* the operations of a patriarchy based in sexual repression and the subordination of women. Reading Desdemona's proud claim "my heart's subdued / Even to the utmost pleasure of my lord"[1] as a "moment of erotic intensity," Greenblatt argues that her forthright display of sexual submission, rather than reassuring Othello of her fidelity, plays into Iago's slanderous account of her as adulterous because it appears to confirm her as a sensual and desirous woman instead of as the sexually reluctant but obedient wife that marriage manuals and church doctrine taught men to expect and to value (250). Coppélia Kahn also accounted men's expectations about women's lustful nature responsible for Desdemona's death in her analysis of the intensity of early modern anxiety about cuckoldry in 1981's *Man's Estate*, while Marianne Novy focused her psychological account of gender relations in *Othello* on the paradoxical subconscious fantasy of "fusion with a woman both

---

1   This is the First Quarto (Q1) reading of the line, which Greenblatt prefers. It differs from the version in this edition, which follows the First Folio (F1) and Second Quarto (Q2). See "A Note on the Text," p. 71, for further information on these versions.

maternal and virginal" (133) that she argues forms the basis of Othello's desire for Desdemona.

Irene Dash's sociological approach to *Othello* in *Wooing, Wedding, and Power: Women in Shakespeare* (1981) marked an important moment in the history of the play's reception as, for the first time, it focused critical attention on its depiction of the potential destructiveness for women of the institution of marriage. According to Dash, *Othello* explores the tragic possibilities for married women trapped within a patriarchal system that condones their subjection and even their abuse. Desdemona experiences "a slow loss of confidence in the strength of the self, always with the aim of adjusting to marriage" (104), and thus her death must be laid at the door of a sexist system that celebrates compliance and self-abnegation in wives rather than mutual respect in marriage. A few years later, Carol Thomas Neely's *Broken Nuptials in Shakespeare's Plays* (1985), with its nuanced understanding of history and its attentiveness to the operations of power within patriarchy, helped feminist criticism develop a more robust account of the role of marriage in the social and dramatic construction of early-modern women. Her reading of *Othello* locates the characters within an early-modern moment that celebrates a newly emerging ideal of companionate marriage even as it continues to advocate for women's subservience to their husbands. Desdemona and Emilia become, on Neely's reading, the victims not of marriage but of male characters who view them through the opposing but mutually reinforcing cultural lenses of romantic idealization and anxious misogyny. The legacy of feminist scholarship committed to exploring both the historical and political dimensions of *Othello* continued throughout the 1990s in the work of critics such as Lisa Jardine, who reads the accusations of adultery levied against Desdemona within the context of defamation cases involving real early-modern women, and in the 2000s by critics such as Sarah Munson Deats, who reads the play within the context of early-modern debates between the religious doctrines of obedience and conscience.

Gradually the discourses of race studies, psychoanalysis, feminism, new historicism, and sex/gender criticism began to coalesce as scholars became increasingly alert to the interplay of sexual politics and race in *Othello* and in history. In 1987's "'And wash the Ethiop white': Femininity and the Monstrous in *Othello*," for instance, Karen Newman argued that Desdemona's love for Othello represents a direct threat to

Venice because it embodies the twin dangers of freely expressed female desire and miscegenation. This take on the play was then developed by Ania Loomba, who argued that "the 'central conflict' of the play ... is neither between white and black alone, nor merely between men and women—it is both a black man and a white woman. But these two are not simply aligned against white patriarchy, since their own relationship cannot be abstracted from sexual or racial tension" ("Sexuality" 172). The work of male critics, too, integrated analysis of the play's psychosexual elements with historically aware discussions of its treatment of race and of gender. For example, picking up on Snow's earlier analysis of Iago's repressed sexuality and employing a similar hermeneutic of suspicion, Michael Neill's "'Unproper Beds'" (1989) finds in the play's curtained bed a potent symbol for an "unutterable" anxiety about interracial love and sex (394). Bruce Smith's pioneering work on homosexuality in early modernity also builds on Snow's insights as it investigates the fraught relationship between masculine friendship and marriage in Shakespeare. Smith's reading of *Othello* suggests that aspects of the relationship between Iago and Othello that might be characterized in modern terms as gay are presented in the play as assertions of masculinity, while love of women is consistently associated with the threat of effeminacy.

The imbrication of scholarly discourses on gender and race found perhaps its clearest material confirmation in Margo Hendricks and Patricia Parker's 1994 volume *Women, "Race," and Writing in the Early Modern Period*, a collection that includes a number of essays that touch on *Othello*. Most notable is Parker's own "Fantasies of 'Race' and 'Gender,'" which interrogates notions of monstrosity, barbarousness, and civility by locating in the play a series of "split chiastic exchanges and divisions" (98) that see Desdemona and Othello trading cultural identities as they assume varied roles within the complexly racialized and gendered narratives of literary teratology and colonialism. From the same year, Ruth Vanita's work on *Othello* addresses directly the vexed issue of its relationship to both sexism and racism, arguing that "the play forcefully combats racism (which posits blacks and whites as essentially different) precisely by its presentation of Othello as not at all different from any white husband" (342). Vanita's article indicts not only the play's male bystanders but also its readers and audiences for silent collusion in Desdemona's murder, claiming that she "is killed not only by Othello and Iago but by all those who see her humiliated and beaten in public, and fail to intervene" (338). Virginia Mason Vaughan's *Othello: A Contextual History* (1994) embodies the scholarly commitment to recognizing literature and history as mutually constitutive modes of discourse, both intimately connected to expressions of, and struggles for, power. Locating the play within both the historical moment that participated in its original production and the multiple pasts within which it was received and reconstructed by successive generations of players, audiences, and readers, Vaughan's wide-ranging study presents *Othello* as an index of changing conceptions of race, religion, and gender, and as itself a powerful producer of cultural meaning. Joyce Green MacDonald's work on burlesques of *Othello* is another important example of the influence of cultural criticism on the practices of stage history. By exploring the vexed relationship of *Othello* to conventions of blackface minstrelsy codified in the first half of the nineteenth century (see Appendix A8), MacDonald demonstrates how Shakespeare's play became part of the complex process of both constructing and challenging ideas about race at a moment in history when "playing race became a deadly serious kind of cultural work" (234).

While work on *Othello* throughout the 1980s and 1990s was dominated by the impulse to contextualize in general and to historicize in particular, Edward Pechter's *Othello and Interpretive Traditions* (1999) offered a productively skeptical consideration of the drive to "embed" literary texts. Though keenly aware of *Othello*'s status as "the tragedy that speaks most directly and powerfully to current interests" (2), Pechter insists, *pace* the cultural critics, that the play must be recognized as distinct from the narrative of its critical and theatrical reproduction, even though the latter will inevitably "contaminate" every reading of the former. Pairing a sustained reading of the formal and affective qualities of *Othello* with analysis alert to both discontinuities and consistencies in almost 400 years of critical and theatrical response to the play, Pechter demonstrates that the interpretive traditions that have grown up around *Othello* often say more about the preoccupations of their creators than about the play they purport to elucidate.

Throughout the 2000s, *Othello* criticism continued to benefit from the development of increasingly sophisticated accounts of the body, the self, race, ethnicity, religion, nationality, and citizenship, while postcolonial theory offered useful frameworks within which questions about

Othello's nature and his relationship to the people and institutions around him could be examined. Ania Loomba's *Shakespeare, Race, and Colonialism* (2002), for instance, maps the complex connections among race, religion, and colonialism in the play, suggesting that *Othello* is best understood as the product of a historical moment that understood ethnic identity as fluid: "Despite being a Christian soldier, Othello cannot shed either his blackness or his 'Turkish' attributes, and it is his sexual and emotional self, expressed through his relationship with Desdemona, which interrupts and finally disrupts his newly acquired Christian and Venetian identity" (96).

Mary Floyd-Wilson's *English Ethnicity and Race in Early Modern Drama* (2003) also understands early-modern notions of ethnicity and race as unstable. Situating *Othello* within the discourse of geohumoralism—the myth that "variations in topography and climate produced variations in national characteristics" (133)—Floyd-Wilson argues that while early in the play Othello matches early-modern constructions of southerners as cool and wise, he is later contaminated by Iago and becomes "hybrid—alienated from his Moorish complexion by an Italianate doubleness" (155). For Julia Reinhard Lupton, *Othello* is best located within a dramatic tradition preoccupied with the intertwining of religion and nation. In *Citizen-Saints: Shakespeare and Political Theology* (2005), she argues that the play models a profound religious ambiguity in the figure of Othello, who seems at once a convert from paganism whose new faith is assumed to be stable and a convert from Islam whose conversion is immediately suspect. In Lupton's reading, Othello becomes increasingly Islamicized in the course of the play, and she presents his self-stabbing as an act of extreme circumcision, what she calls a "death into suicide" that affirms both his commitment to Venetian Christianity and his identity as a Muslim man even as it reveals the tragic cost of early-modern Europe's refusal to allow him this hybrid identity.

Othello's intersections with Islam have also fascinated a number of other critics, including Daniel Vitkus, whose *Turning Turk* (2003) identifies the play as one of a series of early-modern dramas about the rise of the Ottoman Empire and the complex commercial, political, and ideological space of the early-modern Mediterranean. According to Vitkus, *Othello* participates in stereotypes about Muslim men as despotic, lustful, and emotionally undisciplined by presenting Othello as a Christianized Moor so overcome by jealousy that he reverts to "a version of the Islamic tyrant" (99) and then ensures his own damnation by committing suicide. Jonathan Burton's *Traffic and Turning* (2005) also takes up the idea of conversion in *Othello*, arguing that Othello tries to counter the destructive psychological effects of an intense desire to be accepted by Christian Europe with "purple speech, his position at the vanguard of Christendom's forces against the Turks ... and his marriage to Desdemona," all actions that Burton claims authorize the Moor's place in Venice and simultaneously reveal his profound self-doubt (253). For Burton, as Othello begins to believe in "his own irredeemable difference," and to embrace the discourse of misogyny, he loses the ability to "unsettl[e] the meaning of his skin," and this inability becomes proof of his Christian faith (254). For Emily C. Bartels in *Speaking of the Moor* (2008), on the other hand, *Othello* is one of a range of early-modern texts that represent the Moor as a figure not of "racial or cultural difference" but of cultural indeterminacy (194). According to Bartels, "the Moor's story is never exclusively his own—or, rather, is his own, if we understand that story as insistent on the extravagant interplay of cultures here and everywhere" (189). Instead of enlisting *Othello* as evidence of a hostile collision between Islamic East and Christian West, Bartels argues, critics ought to understand the play as a product of a historical moment in which overlapping concerns about race, religion, and nationalism were being negotiated within the militarily and commercially significant space of the Mediterranean, and ought to view its titular Moor as emblematic not of cultural discord but of proto-globalization.

While consensus is building around the notion of *Othello* as a text of the early-modern Mediterranean, new work on connections between early-modern London's black community and the city's playhouses (Habib and Salkeld) and on links between sixteenth-century dyeing practices and the properties of Desdemona's handkerchief (I. Smith) suggests that alternative historical contexts for the play will continue to emerge. The direction of *Othello* criticism will also be affected as literary criticism's longstanding commitment to cultural historicism comes under pressure from those who argue that explorations of context often come at the expense of literature's formal properties and affective registers, and as developments in the digital humanities enable fresh methods of exploring this engaging text.

The first record of a performance of *Othello* is an entry in the Accounts Book of Master of the Revels Edmund Tilney, noting that on 1 November 1604, "the King's Majesty's players ... [acted] a play in the Banqueting House at Whitehall called The Moor of Venice [by] Shaxberd." This performance at the London palace of James I was just one of many early productions of what would become one of Shakespeare's most popular plays. According to the title page of the first quarto edition of the play, *Othello* was performed "diverse times" at both the open-air Globe playhouse and the indoor Blackfriars. Records show that the play was performed by the King's Men in celebration of the 1612 wedding of Princess Elizabeth to Frederick V, Elector Palatine, and that *Othello* continued in the repertory until the early days of the English Civil War when, in 1642, Parliament banned the staging of plays in London theaters.

Although we know little about these first productions, we can state with some certainty that they would have looked and sounded quite different from most modern performances of *Othello*. Acting styles, stage technologies, and even expectations about audience behavior have undergone enormous changes over the last 400 years, and some shifts in theatrical convention—particularly those involving casting practices—have had significant impact on the play. In the early seventeenth century, for instance, the parts of Othello and Desdemona would have been played by white men. Richard Burbage (c. 1567–1619),[1] the foremost tragedian of Shakespeare's acting company, was almost certainly the first Othello, while Desdemona would have been acted by a young male actor from the troupe, since women were banned from the public stage in England until the second half of the century.

Modern readers sometimes assume that such casting decisions would have created a distracting artifice in these early productions, interfering with the play's ability to generate a powerful emotional response in its audience. There is no evidence to suggest that *Othello*'s first viewers felt disengaged from its wrenching story, however. Instead, as the comments of one attentive audience member suggest, cross-dressed

---

1   To read more about the actors in Shakespeare's company, visit the "Life & Times" section of the Internet Shakespeare Editions website and click on Stage: Acting.

male actors were accepted as female characters even under close scrutiny, and the affective force of their performances could be formidable: "Desdemona," he reports, "murdered by her husband in our presence, although she always pled her case excellently, yet when killed moved us more, while stretched out on her bed she begged the spectators' pity with her very facial expression" (Jackson). Detailing the expression on the actor's face while at the same time designating him with the feminine pronouns "her" and "she," this early theater critic demonstrates that early-modern audiences could simultaneously read and read through the bodies of the male actors who took female roles.

When London's theaters reopened after the English Civil War, professional female actors were finally permitted on English stages for the first time. *Othello* was quickly revived, and diarist Samuel Pepys (1633–1703), who attended one of the first performances at the Cockpit Theatre on 11 October 1660, reports seeing Nicholas Burt (c. 1621–c. 1690) in the title role. While Pepys makes no mention of who took the female lead, he does note that "a very pretty lady that sat by me, called out, to see Desdemona smothered," an anecdote that suggests the play continued to generate passionate responses in its audiences. Records indicate that just two months later the King's Company performed *Othello* with Margaret Hughes (c. 1630–1719) as Desdemona.

While it seems plausible that the regular appearance of female actors in productions of *Othello* might have resulted in increased interest in the play's female characters throughout the later seventeenth and into the eighteenth century, the popularity of the play's title role with leading men appears instead to have produced a particular fascination with the figure of Othello at the expense of Desdemona, Emilia, and Bianca. Indeed, scholars have noted that although the play was not so extensively adapted as many of Shakespeare's plays were during the Restoration period, the roles of its female characters were consistently diminished thanks to the removal of ostensibly unseemly sexual references, modifications that may, in turn, have contributed to the growing interest in the figure of Othello.

Although there was a general fascination with Othello and his transformation from eminent general and loving husband to murderer and suicide, there was what many modern readers find to be surprisingly little discussion about Othello's racial identity during these years. Nor was there much variety in the ways in which Othello's Moorishness was staged: Othello was played by white actors who darkened their skin using stage makeup to present him as a sub-Saharan "black Moor." While their understanding of the physical characteristics of Othello's racial identity was fairly consistent, however, the leading men of this period offered varied readings of his temperament. James Quin (1693–1766), for instance, a popular Othello in the first half of the eighteenth century, chose to emphasize the general's dignified professionalism, presenting his lines in a then-stylish declamatory fashion while costumed in full British military uniform and wearing a powdered wig above his heavily blackened face. The celebrated David Garrick (1717–79), on the other hand, challenged the depiction of Othello as a confident leader, playing him instead as a taut, anxious figure topped with an elaborately plumed turban that lent him an isolating exoticism. The tall, deep-voiced Irish actor Spranger Barry (1719–77) also appeared turbaned and in blackface, though his famously electrifying performance—characterized by emotional turmoil and physical vigor—proved far more popular than Garrick's more neurotic one.

Among the most interesting of the late-eighteenth-century Othellos was John Philip Kemble (1757–1823), who took the role several times over his long career. Unlike the tumultuous Othello presented by Barry, Kemble's Othello was majestic and stately, and his restrained performances were not always popular with audiences, especially early in his career. While experience doubtless enriched his approach to the character as the years went by, comments by his contemporaries suggest that at least some of the negative response to his earliest performances resulted from the destabilizing effect of his dignified Othello on widely held assumptions about the inability of Africans to control their ostensibly tempestuous passions. Recalling a 1785 production at Drury Lane, his friend and biographer James Boaden celebrates Kemble's Othello as "grand, and awful, and pathetic" but then qualifies his praise this way: "but he was a European: there seemed to be philosophy in his bearing; there was reason in his rage" (145). There was little room, it seems, for a thoughtful or reasonable Othello on the late-eighteenth-century English stage. However, by the time Kemble revived the play at Covent Garden in 1803–04, playing opposite his famous sister Sarah Siddons (1755–1831), his production was praised as "better than it was ever performed in the memory of the oldest critic" (Shattuck ii).

In 1814, an even more significant shift in performance tradition occurred when Edmund Kean (1787–1833) presented the first of the so-called "tawny" Othellos. Kean gave audiences a light-skinned, North African Othello rather than the black, sub-Saharan Othello they had grown accustomed to seeing. But if Kean's lightened stage makeup challenged established theatrical convention, his reading of Othello did little to destabilize entrenched stereotypes about the savagery of non-Europeans. His was a performance remarkable for its bursts of passion, and writer and critic Leigh Hunt wrote in *The Examiner* on 4 October 1818 that he "never saw anything that so completely held us suspended and heart-stricken." Indeed, rather than opening a dialogue about the politics of race, Kean's radical break with theatrical custom allowed theaters to stage *Othello* even as they avoided engaging with increasingly divisive public debates about the moral viability of a

Edwin Booth as Iago, c. 1870. Wikimedia Commons, https://commons.wikimedia.org.

lucrative trade in black African slaves that had flourished in England for 200 years.

The innovation of the "tawny Othello" at first unsettled audiences familiar with Kemble's dark-skinned version of the role, but eventually the idea of a scimitar-wielding North African Othello at the mercy of his passions caught on and successfully held the stage in England and the United States for the next hundred years. In the 1840s, Edwin Forrest (1806–72), the first notable American Othello, brought to the role an animated physicality that prompted comparisons to wild animals, and, although audiences were reportedly sympathetic to Forrest's proclamation that he was proud to be what his biographer called "the impersonator of oppressed races," his Othello seems to have relied on, rather than to have dislodged, persistent generalizations about the relationship of race to temperament and morality. Starting in 1875, Italian-born Tommaso Salvini (1829–1915) could play into what had become firmly entrenched stereotypes about the inability of African men to control their innate savagery to perform Othello as a barbarian lurking under a veneer of European sophistication, and at the beginning of the twentieth century Herbert Beerbohm Tree (1852–1917) was still playing him as a "stately Arab" whose jealous rage transforms him into a "wild beast" (Hankey 67; quoted in Potter 90).

While the practice of casting white actors who "blacked up" to play Othello continued to dominate throughout the nineteenth and well into the twentieth century, a significant challenge to this convention was initiated in 1825 when an American teenager named Ira Aldridge (1807–67) arrived in London and became the first professional black actor to perform the role. His appearance at East London's Royalty Theatre received mixed reviews, and Aldridge left the city fairly quickly to build his repertoire and his experience in England's provincial theaters. Although he would become one of the nineteenth century's better-known actors, early in his career Aldridge was billed as the "Gentleman of Colour," and his acting skills were often overshadowed by a preoccupation with his skin color. Some critics dismissed his casting as a marketing gimmick, while others argued that his race made him unsuited for major theatrical roles, including those designated as "Moors." Still others acknowledged the emotional power of Aldridge's performances but, relying on the same stereotypes associating black men with excessive displays of emotion that had led eighteenth-century critics to praise

From S. Buhler, *Ira Aldridge as Othello*. Mannheim, Germany, 1854. By permission of the Folger Shakespeare Library.

Spranger Barry for his acting skill, dismissed as "natural" Aldridge's ability to embody an Othello so tempestuous that he could wrench audiences from terror to sympathy over the course of a brief scene.

Rather than trying to downplay his racial difference, Aldridge took advantage of widespread fascination with his background by overwriting his modest beginnings as the son of a New York clerk and claiming instead to be Senegalese royalty. Playbills trumpeting his fictionalized heritage appeared widely and must have resonated especially with those who saw him in the role of Othello, another man of color who claims descent from "men of royal siege." After almost a decade of touring, Aldridge returned to London, where he played Othello opposite Ellen Tree (1805–80) at Covent Garden. Although audiences were mostly enthusiastic, the papers, heavily influenced by a pro-slavery lobby whose financial backing they received in exchange for supportive copy, were hostile to the idea of a black man performing a leading role in a play by the nation's most revered playwright. The *Times* review of 11 April 1833 was marked by a thinly veiled racism that constructed Aldridge's accent as "unpleasantly, and we would say vulgarly, foreign" and found his "manner, generally, drawling and unimpressive." The bigotry of other critics was even more overt. On 13 April of the same year, for instance, the *Athenaeum* reviewer railed against the "blow at respectability" of having a "black servant in the character of *Othello*— *Othello* forsooth!!! Othello, almost the master-work of the mastermind." Though Aldridge did not return to the London stage for some time after this, his exhilarating style proved popular throughout Europe, where he was mostly warmly received, and he continued to perform in the role of Othello until 1865.

It took until 1930 before American singer and civil-rights advocate Paul Robeson (1898–1976) became only the second black man to be cast as Othello in a major London production. Directly challenging pernicious associations between blackness and savagery that continued to dominate in the theater, Robeson moved away from readings of *Othello* as domestic psychological drama and instead presented the play as a tragedy about racial conflict. Robeson's Othello, dignified but finally defenseless in the face of Iago's malignant racism, proved immensely popular with audiences and, increasingly, with critics, and his 1943 taboo- and record-breaking appearance on Broadway opposite Uta Hagen (1919–2004)—which marked the first time a black man kissed a white woman on a major American stage—ran longer than any other Broadway performance of Shakespeare.

Although it became more common for black actors to perform Othello after Robeson's commercial and critical success in the role, the blackface tradition that dominated the first 300 years of Othello's rich performance history proved remarkably resilient. White actors continued to play the part well into the 1960s, including John Gielgud (1904–2000) in a much-derided 1961 Stratford production directed by Franco Zeffirelli, Laurence Oliver (1907–89) in a legendary 1964

Paul Robeson as Othello and Uta Hagen as Desdemona in the Theatre Guild Production on Broadway, 1943–44. Wikimedia Commons, https://commons. wikimedia.org.

National Theatre production that was turned into a film the following year, and Michael Gambon (b. 1940) in a 1968 Birmingham Repertory Company production set during the Crimean War. Since the 1970s, however, black actors have regularly played Othello in England and the United States, with notable performances including those by Tony-award winner James Earl Jones (b. 1931), Jamaican-born opera singer Willard White (b. 1946), television's David Harewood (b. 1965),

BAFTA award–winning actor Chiwetel Ejiofor (b. 1977), British standup comedian Lenny Henry (b. 1958), and, most recently, Adrian Lester (b. 1968), whose performance was broadcast around the world as part of the National Theatre Live project. Other memorable *Othellos* have included an apartheid-era South African production starring John Kani (b. 1943), an American production featuring black actors Avery Brooks (b. 1948) and Andre Braugher (b. 1962) in the roles of Othello and Iago, and a "photo negative" production featuring Patrick Stewart (b. 1940) as a white Othello among a predominantly African American cast.

In addition to a rich and varied history on the stage, *Othello* has had a successful career in film and television. The first English-language film version of the play was Orson Welles's 1952 production. With Welles himself in the title role, Micheál MacLiammóir as Iago, and Suzanne Cloutier as Desdemona, the film presents a psychologically taut exploration of marriage, military life, and racial difference against a starkly shot backdrop of Morocco. Ten years later, the Othello story again found its way onto the big screen, this time as a loose adaptation set in the jazz/beat music world of early 1960s London called *All Night Long* (1962). Featuring black actor Paul Harris in the central role and shot, like the Welles film, in black and white, director Basil Dearden's film follows attempts by jealous drummer Johnnie Cousin (Patrick McGoohan) to destroy the marriage and musical careers of Aurelius Rex (Paul Harris) and his loving wife Delia Lane (Marti Stevens). The film is most notable for musical appearances by jazz greats Dave Brubeck, Charles Mingus, and Johnny Dankworth, but is also of interest for its revision of the play's tragic ending: at the conclusion of *All Night Long*, when Cousin's wife Emily (Betsy Blair) recognizes that her husband's claims about Delia's infidelity are inventions, his machinations are revealed and Aurelius and Delia are reconciled.

The next full-length film of the play, this one featuring Shakespearean language and characters, was Stuart Burge's *Othello* (1965), which recorded a version of John Dexter's National Theatre production of the previous year. Featuring strong performances by Maggie Smith (b. 1934) as Desdemona and Frank Finlay (1926–2016) as Iago, the film is best remembered for Laurence Olivier's legendary blackface presentation of the title character. Olivier's performance, embellished by a wig of kinked dark hair, heavy black stage makeup, and an accent that has been described variously as Nigerian, South

African, or West Indian, now appears as a grotesque impersonation of blackness but was widely praised at the time for its ostensible authenticity and was greeted with enthusiasm by audiences. His Othello dominates the film throughout, grandly controlling in the opening scenes, relentlessly brutal in its closing moments, and always the sensual victim of Iago's eerily gentle manipulations. Identifying in Iago an anxiety based in repressed homosexuality—a reading that would influence later portrayals of the character by such actors as David Suchet (1985), Ian McKellen (1989), and Kenneth Branagh (1995)—Finlay plays him as a man whose angst about his own nature arouses in him a viciously racist revulsion of his commander.

A decade later, another musical *Othello* found its way to the big screen, although this time rock rather than jazz provided the soundscape for a loose adaptation of the play. Based on a stage musical that had had limited tours of the US and the UK a few years earlier, 1974's *Catch My Soul* again involved *All Night Long*'s Patrick McGoohan (1928–2009), this time in his only venture as a director. The film, set in the New Mexico desert, gave singer-songwriter Richie Havens (1941–2013), known to contemporary audiences for his opening performance at 1969's legendary Woodstock Festival, his first acting role as Othello, the pacifist leader of a hippie commune. Lance LeGault (1935–2012), later known for a recurring role on the 1980s TV series *The A-Team*, plays a devilish dropout named Iago. Although the film was panned by critics who found its attempts to integrate Shakespeare's play with contemporary anxieties about race and religion both clumsy and tedious, the soundtrack, which includes memorable tracks by Havens, Tony Joe White, and Jerry Lee Lewis, is now much sought after by collectors.

No big-screen *Othello* was released in the 1980s, but Jonathan Miller's adaptation for BBC TV appeared in 1981. Returning to the tradition of featuring white actors in the play's title role, Miller's production stars Anthony Hopkins (b. 1937) as a stony Othello whose dark side is gradually nurtured by Bob Hoskins's (1942–2014) energetically nasty Iago. Crowded interior shots give this studio production a claustrophobic texture that appears at first to emphasize its personal over its political dimensions, but the film develops a feminist edge as the malevolence of the male characters is increasingly focused on Desdemona (Penelope Wilton) and Emilia (Rosemary Leach), whose love and wit prove woefully inadequate defenses against the forces of patriarchal outrage. Twenty years later, another made-for-TV movie, this time a modern-language adaptation set among senior officers of the London Metropolitan Police, explored the play's intersections of sexism and racism by turning *Othello* into a taut crime thriller about the death of a black drug addict at the hands of three white police officers. Black officer John Othello (Eamonn Walker) is promoted over white Assistant Commissioner Ben Jago (Christopher Eccleston) as scandal rocks a metropolitan police force, and Othello's wife, Dessie Brabant (Keeley Hawes), becomes the target of neo-Nazi thugs. When Dessie's ostensible infidelity is established using falsified DNA evidence, she is murdered by her husband who then commits suicide, clearing the way for Jago to be appointed Commissioner. In a moment of triumphant revisionism, Eccleston's Jago closes the film by peering directly into the camera and insisting that the film's events have had nothing to do with race or politics, but only with love. Directed by Geoffrey Sax for Masterpiece Theatre, this stylish production's explicit confrontation of institutionalized bias and its deep cynicism seem even more apt now than they did when the film first aired.

The years between Miller's and Sax's television *Othellos* produced two Hollywood film adaptations of the play. Oliver Parker's 1995 version stars Laurence Fishburne (b. 1961) in the title role, Kenneth Branagh (b. 1960) as an engagingly scheming Iago, and Irène Jacob (b. 1966) as a beautiful if rather vague Desdemona. This is a visually lush film that emphasizes the stark isolation of its stunning Mediterranean setting and the casual sexism of the masculinist military culture it depicts. Parker draws on the play's lengthy production history, offering knowing nods to memorable moments from earlier stage and film productions, but he also provides innovative touches, adding, for instance, a dream sequence depicting Desdemona's alleged adultery. The film takes full advantage of the camera's ability to approach its subjects unseen and so to draw viewers uncomfortably close to the action. This manufactured voyeurism is then jarringly exposed and exploited by Branagh's Iago as he peers jauntily into the lens to confide his destructive plans to the viewer. This is an Iago disturbing primarily in his ordinariness: while there are private flashes of a sinister and brooding habit, his outward manner is so relaxed, amusing, and temperate that his perfidy seems improbable even as it unfolds. Fishburne's Othello, by contrast, is a commanding physical presence whose unassailable strength—we see him defeat Iago handily as the two fence—foreshadows his eventual descent into violence.

While Parker employs Shakespeare's language and period costumes, Tim Blake Nelson's 2001 film *O* is a considerably freer adaptation that exchanges early-modern poetry and clothes for more modern patterns of speech and fashions. With a twenty-something cast including Mekhi Phifer as Odin (Othello), Josh Hartnett as Hugo (Iago), and Julia Stiles as Desi (Desdemona), *O* targets a young audience by engaging with concerns about violence, drugs, and racism in youth culture, school shootings, and sexual violence on campus. Brad Kaaya's screenplay shifts the action from a Cypriot citadel to a private American boarding school, transforms the play's external threat from an Ottoman armada into a rival basketball team, and effects a generic transformation from tragic romance to contemporary teen thriller.

The most recent English-language film version of *Othello* is Zaib Shaikh's made-for-TV adaptation *Othello, the Tragedy of the Moor* (2008). Produced for the Canadian Broadcasting Corporation and aired both as a radio drama and on television, this self-consciously post-9/11 production presents Italian-Canadian actor Carlo Rota's Othello as a North African Muslim whose ethnic identity determines his relationships in ways that exceed his control. While the film offers some interesting performances, its heavily cut text and short runtime prevent it from analyzing in any depth the ideas about race and religion with which it engages.

SHAKESPEARE'S LIFE

BY DAVID BEVINGTON

The website of the Internet Shakespeare Editions (http://internetshakespeare. uvic.ca), in the section "Life & Times," has further information on many topics mentioned here: Shakespeare's education, his religion, the lives and work of his contemporaries, and the rival acting companies in London.

William Shakespeare was baptized on 26 April 1564, in Holy Trinity Church, Stratford-upon-Avon. He is traditionally assumed to have been born three days earlier, on 23 April, the feast day of St. George, England's patron saint. His father, John Shakespeare, prospering for years as a tanner, glover, and dealer in commodities such as wool and grain, rose to become city chamberlain or treasurer, alderman, and high bailiff, the town's highest municipal position. Beginning in 1577, John Shakespeare encountered financial difficulties, with the result that he was obliged to mortgage his wife's property and miss council meetings. Although some scholars argue that he was secretly a Catholic, absenting himself also from Anglican church services for that reason, the greater likelihood is that he stayed at home for fear of being processed for debt. His wife, Mary, did come from a family with ongoing Catholic connections, but most of the evidence suggests that Shakespeare's parents were respected members of the Established Church. John's civic duties involved him in carrying out practices of the Protestant Reformation. John and Mary baptized all their children at the Anglican Holy Trinity Church and were buried there.

As civic official, John must have sent his son William to the King Edward VI grammar school close by their house on Henley Street. Student records from the period have perished, but information about the program of education is plentifully available. William would have studied Latin grammar and authors, including Ovid, Virgil, Plautus, Seneca, and others that left an indelible print on the plays he wrote in his early years.

Shakespeare did not, however, go to university. The reasons are presumably two: his father's financial difficulties, and, perhaps even more crucially, Shakespeare's own marriage at the age of eighteen to Anne Hathaway, since neither Oxford nor Cambridge would ordinarily admit married students. Anne was eight years older than William. She was also three months pregnant when they were married in November 1582. A special license had to be obtained from the Bishop of Worcester to allow them to marry quickly, without the customary readings on three successive Sundays in church of the banns, or announcements of intent to marry. The couple's first child, Susanna, was born in late May 1583. Twins, named Hamnet and Judith, the last of their children, followed in February 1585. Thereafter, evidence is scarce as to Shakespeare's whereabouts or occupation for about seven years. Perhaps he taught school, or was apprenticed to his father, or joined some company of traveling actors. At any event, he turns up in London in 1592. In that year, he was subjected to a vitriolic printed attack by a fellow dramatist, Robert Greene (1558–92), who seems to have been driven by professional envy to accuse Shakespeare of being an "upstart crow" who had beautified himself with the feathers of other writers for the stage, including Christopher Marlowe (1564–93), George Peele (1556–96), Thomas Nashe (1567–1601), and Greene himself.

Shakespeare was indeed well established as a playwright in London by the time of this incident in 1592. In the same year, Nashe paid tribute to the huge success of the tragic death of Lord Talbot in a play, and the only play we know that includes Talbot is Shakespeare's *1 Henry VI*. We do not know for what acting company or companies Shakespeare wrote in the years before 1594, or just how he got started, but he seems to have been an actor as well as a dramatist. Two other plays about the reign of Henry VI also belong to those early years, along with his triumphantly successful *Richard III*. These four plays, forming his first historical tetralogy, were instrumental in defining the genre of the English history play. Following shortly after the great defeat of the Spanish Armada in 1588, they celebrated England's ascent from a century of devastating civil wars to the accession in 1485 of the Tudor Henry VII, grandfather of Queen Elizabeth I. Shakespeare's early work also includes some fine ventures into comedy, including *A Comedy of Errors*, *The Two Gentlemen of Verona*, *Love's Labor's Lost*, and *The Taming of the Shrew*. He wrote only one tragedy at this time, *Titus Andronicus*, a revenge tragedy based on fictional early Roman history. Shakespeare also turned his hand to narrative poetry in these early years. *Venus and Adonis* in 1593 and *The Rape of Lucrece* in 1594, dedicated to the Earl of Southampton, seem to show Shakespeare's interest in becoming a published poet, though ultimately he chose drama as more fulfilling and lucrative. He probably wrote some of his sonnets in these years, perhaps to the Earl of Southampton, though they were not published until 1609 and then without Shakespeare's authorization.

Shakespeare joined the newly formed Lord Chamberlain's Men, as an actor-sharer and playwright, in 1594, along with Richard Burbage (c. 1567–1619), his leading man. This group quickly became the premier acting company in London, in stiff competition with Edward Alleyn and the Lord Admiral's Men. For the Lord Chamberlain's group, Shakespeare wrote his second and more artistically mature tetralogy of English histories, including *Richard II* and the two *Henry IV* plays, centered on the Prince who then becomes the monarch and victor at Agincourt in *Henry V* (1599). He also wrote another history play, *King John*, in these years. Concurrently, Shakespeare achieved great success in romantic comedy, with *A Midsummer Night's Dream*, *The Merchant of Venice*, and *The Merry Wives of Windsor*. He hit the top of his form in romantic comedy in three plays of 1598–1600 with similar throw-away titles: *Much Ado About Nothing*, *As You Like It*, and *Twelfth Night, or What You Will*. Having fulfilled that amazing task, he set comedy aside until years later.

During these years Shakespeare lived in London, apart from his family in Stratford. He saw to it that they were handsomely housed and provided for; he bought New Place, one of the two finest houses in town. Presumably he went home to Stratford when he could. He was comfortably well off, owning one share among ten in an acting company that enjoyed remarkable artistic and financial success. He suffered a terrible tragedy in 1596 when his only son and heir, Hamnet, died at the age of eleven. In that year, Shakespeare applied successfully for a coat of arms for his father, so that John, and William too, could each style himself as gentleman. John died in 1601, Shakespeare's mother in 1608.

Having set aside romantic comedy and the patriotic English history at the end of the 1590s, Shakespeare turned instead to problematic plays such as *All's Well That Ends Well*, *Measure for Measure*, and *Troilus and Cressida*, the last of which is ambivalently a tragedy (with the death of Hector), a history play about the Trojan War, and a bleak existential drama about a failed love relationship. He also took up writing tragedies in earnest. *Romeo and Juliet*, in 1594–96, is a justly famous play, but in its early acts it is more a comedy than a tragedy, and its central figures are not tragic protagonists of the stature of those he created in plays from 1599 onward: *Julius Caesar*, *Hamlet*, *Othello*, *King Lear*, *Macbeth*, *Timon of Athens*, *Antony and Cleopatra*, and *Coriolanus*, this last play written in about 1608. Whether Shakespeare was moved to write these great tragedies by sad personal experiences, or by a shifting of the national mood in 1603 with the death of Queen Elizabeth and the accession to the throne of James VI of Scotland to become James I of England (when the Lord Chamberlain's Men became the King's Men), or by a growing skepticism and philosophical pessimism on his part, is impossible to say; perhaps he felt invigorated artistically by the challenge of excelling in the relatively new (for him) genre of tragedy.

Equally hard to answer with any certainty is the question of why he then turned, in his late years as a dramatist, to a form of comedy usually called romance, or tragicomedy. The genre was made popular by his contemporaries Francis Beaumont (1584–1616) and John Fletcher (1579–1625), and it is worth noting that the long indigenous tradition of English drama, comprising the cycles of mystery plays and the morality plays, were essentially tragicomic in form. The plays of this phase, from *Pericles* (c. 1606–08) to *Cymbeline*, *The Winter's Tale*, and *The Tempest* in about 1608–11, would seem to overlap somewhat the late tragedies in dates of composition. These romances are like the early romantic comedies in many ways: young heroines in disguise, plots of adventure and separation leading to tearfully joyful reunions, comic highjinks, and so on. Yet these late romances are also tinged with the tragic vision that the dramatist had portrayed so vividly: death threatens or actually occurs in these plays, the emotional struggles of the male protagonists are nearly tragic in their psychic dimensions, and the restored happiness of the endings is apt to seem miraculous.

Shakespeare seems to have retired from London to Stratford-upon-Avon some time around 1611; *The Tempest* may have been designed as his farewell to the theater and his career as dramatist, after which he appears to have collaborated with Fletcher, his successor at the King's Men, in *Henry VIII* and *The Two Noble Kinsmen* (1613–14). His elder daughter, Susanna, had married the successful physician John Hall in 1607. In his last will and testament Shakespeare left various bequests to friends and colleagues, but to Anne, his wife, nothing other than his "second-best bed." Whether this betokens any estrangement between him and the wife, whom he had married under the necessity of her pregnancy and from whom he then lived apart during the two decades or so when he resided and worked in London, is a matter of hot debate. Divorce was impossible, whether contemplated or not. He did take good care of her and his family, and he did retire to Stratford. Anne lived on with Susanna and John until she died in 1623. Shakespeare was buried on 25 April 1616. Tradition assumes that he died on 23 April, since he would have left the world on the very feast day (of St. George, England's patron saint) that had witnessed his baptism some 52 years earlier. He lies buried under the altar of Holy Trinity, next to his wife and other family members. A memorial bust, erected some time before 1623, is mounted on the chancel wall.

SHAKESPEARE'S THEATER

BY DAVID BEVINGTON

The website of the Internet Shakespeare Editions (http://internetshakespeare. uvic.ca) includes an extensive discussion of the theaters of Shakespeare's time, and of the audiences that attended them: click on "Life & Times" and choose the menu item "Stage."

Where Shakespeare's plays of the early 1590s were performed we do not know. When he joined the newly-formed Lord Admiral's Men in 1594, with Richard Burbage as his leading man, most public performances of Shakespeare's plays would have been put on in a building called The Theatre, since, when it was erected in 1576 by Richard Burbage's father James Burbage (c. 1530–97), it was the only structure in London designed specifically for the performance of plays, and indeed the first such building in the history of English theater. Earlier, plays were staged by itinerant companies in inns and innyards, great houses, churchyards, public squares, and any other place that could be commandeered for dramatic presentation. In Shakespeare's time the professional companies still toured, but to a lesser extent, and several of them also derived part of their income from private performances at court.

The Theatre had been erected in Shoreditch (also called Moorfields), a short walking distance north of London's walls, in order to evade the too-often censorious regulations of the city's governing council. There, spectators might have chosen to see *Romeo and Juliet*, *A Midsummer Night's Dream*, *The Merchant of Venice*, *King John*, or *Richard II*. They would also have seen some earlier Shakespeare plays that he had brought with him (perhaps as the price needed to pay for a share in the company) when he joined the Lord Chamberlain's Men: plays such as *Richard III* and *The Taming of the Shrew*. When in the late 1590s the Puritan-leaning owner of the land on which the building stood, Giles Allen, refused to renew their lease because he wished "to pull down the same, and to convert the wood and timber thereof to some better use," the Lord Chamberlain's Men performed for a while in the nearby Curtain Theatre. Eventually, in 1599, they solved their problem with the landlord by moving lock, stock, and barrel across the River Thames to the shore opposite from London, just to the west of London Bridge, where audiences could reach the new theater—the Globe—by bridge or by water taxi, and where the players were still outside the authority of the city of London. At the time of this move, the River Thames was frozen over solid in an especially harsh winter, so possibly they slid the timbers of their theater across on the ice.

At any event, the Globe Theatre that they erected in Southwark, not far from the location of today's reconstructed Globe, was in the main the same building they had acted in before. Because timbers were all hand-hewn and fitted, the best plan was to reassemble them as much as was feasible. No doubt the company decided on some modifications, especially in the acting area, based on their theatrical experience, but the house remained essentially as before.

No pictures exist today of the interiors of the Theatre, the Curtain, or the Globe. We do have Visscher's View of London (1616) and other representations showing the exteriors of some theatrical buildings, but for the important matter of the interior design we have only a drawing of the Swan Theatre, copied by a Dutchman, Arend van Buchel (1565–1641), from a lost original by the Dutch Johannes de Witt when he visited London in about 1596–98. In many respects, the Swan seems to have been typical of such buildings. As seen in the accompanying illustration, the building appears to be circular or polygonal, with a thatched roof (called *tectum* in the illustration's labels) over the galleries containing seats and another roof over the stage, but leaving the space for standing spectators open to the heavens. (In the modern Globe, similarly constructed, spectators intending to stand in the yard for a performance can purchase a plastic rain poncho to ward off England's frequent rain showers.) From other kinds of information about Elizabethan playhouses, we can estimate a diameter of about 70 feet for the interior space. A large rectangular stage labeled the *proscaenium* (literally, "that which stands before the scene"), approximately 43 feet wide and 27 feet deep, juts out from one portion of the wall into the yard, or *planities siue arena* ("the plain place or arena"). The stage stands about 5½ feet above the surface of the yard. Two pillars support the roof over the stage, which in turn is surmounted by a hut. A flag is flying at the top, while a trumpeter at a door in the hut is presumably announcing the performance of a play. The spectators' seats are arrayed in three tiers of galleries. Stairway entrances (*ingressus*) are provided for spectators to gain access from the yard to the seats, labeled *orchestra* on the first level and nearest the stage, and *porticus* above.

ABOVE, LEFT: This sketch of the Swan is the most complete we have of any theater of the time. The Swan was built in 1596; Shakespeare's company, The Chamberlain's Men, played there in the same year. RIGHT: This view of the first Globe by the Dutch engraver J.C. Visscher (1586–1652) was printed in 1625, but must be taken from an earlier drawing, since the first Globe was burnt to the ground in 1613 at the first performance of Shakespeare's *Henry VIII*. There is substantial evidence that Visscher simplified the appearance of the theater by portraying it as octagonal: most scholars now believe that it had twenty sides, thus making it seem more circular than in this engraving.

The stage area is of greatest concern, and here the Swan drawing evidently does not show everything needed for performance in a theater such as the Globe. No trapdoor is provided, though one is needed in a number of Renaissance plays for appearances by ghostly or diabolical visitations from the infernal regions imagined to lie beneath the earth. The underside of the stage roof is not visible in this drawing, but from the plays themselves and other sources of information we gather that this underside above the actors' heads, known as the "heavens," displayed representations of the sun, moon, planets, and stars (as in today's London Globe). The back wall of the stage in the drawing, labeled *mimorum ades* or "housing for the actors," provides a visual barrier between the stage itself and what was commonly known as the "tiring house" or place where the actors could attire themselves and be ready for their entrances. The two doors shown in this wall confirm an arrangement evidently found in other theaters like the Globe, but the absence of any other means of access to the tiring house raises important questions. Many plays, by Shakespeare and others, seem to require some kind of "discovery space," located perhaps between the two doors, to accommodate a London shop, or a place where in *The Tempest* Prospero can pull back a curtain to "discover" Miranda and Ferdinand playing chess, or a place to which Falstaff, in the great tavern scene of *1 Henry IV*, can retire to avoid the Sheriff's visit and then be heard snoring offstage before he exits at scene's end into the tiring house. The modern Globe has such a discovery space.

Above the stage in the Swan drawing is what appears to be a gallery of six bays in which we can see seated figures watching the actors on the main stage, thereby surrounding those actors with spectators on all sides. But did theaters like the Swan or the Globe regularly seat spectators above the stage like this? Were such seats reserved for dignitaries and persons of wealth? Other documents refer to a "lords' room" in such theaters. The problem is complicated by the fact that many Elizabethan plays require some upper acting area for the play itself, as when Juliet, in Act II of *Romeo and Juliet*, appears "above" at her "window" to be heard by Romeo and then converses with him, or later, when Romeo and Juliet are seen together "aloft" at her "window" before Romeo descends, presumably by means of a rope ladder in full view of the audience, to go to banishment (3.5). Richard II appears *"on the walls"* of Flint Castle when he is surrounded by his enemies and is obliged to descend (behind the scenes) and then enter on the main stage to Bolingbroke (*Richard II*, 3.3). Instances are numerous. The gallery above the stage, shown in the Swan drawing, must have provided the necessary acting area "above." On those many occasions when the space was needed for action of this sort, seemingly the acting company would not seat spectators there. It is unclear how spectators sitting above would have seen action in the "discovery space," since it may have been beneath them.

On stage, in the drawing, a well-dressed lady, seated on a bench and accompanied perhaps by her lady-in-waiting, receives the addresses of a courtier or soldier with a long-handled weapon or staff of office. Even though the sketch is rough and imperfect, it does suggest the extent to which the plays of Shakespeare and his contemporaries were acted on this broad, open stage with a minimum of scenic effects. The actors would identify their fictional roles and their location by their dialogue, their costumes, and their gestures. On other occasions, when, for example, a throne was needed for a throne scene, extras could bring on such large objects and then remove them when they were no longer needed. Beds, as in the final scene of *Othello*, were apparently thrust on stage from the tiring house. The building itself was handsomely decorated and picturesque, such that the stage picture was by no means unimpressive, yet the visual effects were not designed to inform the audience about setting or time of the action. The play texts and the actors took care of that.

We have a verbal description of the Globe Theatre by Thomas Platter, a visitor to London in 1599, on the occasion of a performance of *Julius Caesar*. The description unfortunately says little about the stage, but it is otherwise very informative about the London playhouses:

> The playhouses are so constructed that they play on a raised platform, so that everyone has a good view. There are different galleries and places, however, where the seating is better and more comfortable and therefore more expensive. For whoever cares to stand below pays only one English penny, but if he wishes to sit, he enters by another door and pays another penny, while if he desires to sit in the most comfortable seats, which are cushioned, where he not only sees everything well but can also be seen, then he pays yet another English penny at another door. And during the performance food and drink are carried around the audience, so that for what one cares to pay one may also have refreshment.

Shakespeare's company may have included ten or so actor-sharers, who owned the company jointly and distributed important roles among themselves. Richard Burbage was Shakespeare's leading man from 1594 until Shakespeare's retirement from the theater. Other actor-sharers, such as John Heminges (1566–1630) and Henry Condell (d. 1627), who would edit the First Folio collection of Shakespeare's plays in 1623, were his longtime professional associates. The quality of performance appears to have been high. Hired men generally took minor roles of messengers, soldiers, and servants. The women's parts were played by boys, who were trained by the major actors in a kind of apprenticeship and remained as actors of women's parts until their voices changed. Many went on in later years to be adult actors.

WILLIAM SHAKESPEARE AND *OTHELLO*:
A BRIEF CHRONOLOGY

(Composition dates of the plays are approximate.)

1509–47	Reign of Henry VIII
1520–66	Reign of Selim I, Sultan of the Ottoman Empire
1534	Act of Supremacy declares Henry VIII Head of the Church of England
1547–53	Reign of Edward VI
1553–58	Reign of Mary I; England returns to Catholicism
1558–1603	Reign of Elizabeth I; England returns to Protestantism
1564	William Shakespeare born, c. 23 April
1565	Great Siege of Malta
1566–74	Reign of Selim II, Sultan of the Ottoman Empire
1570–73	Ottoman-Venetian War
1573	Venetians cede Cyprus to Ottomans
1574–95	Reign of Murad III, Sultan of the Ottoman Empire
1576	Naval victory by coalition of Catholic states at Battle of Lepanto temporarily halts Ottoman expansion in the Mediterranean
1582	Shakespeare marries Anne Hathaway, late November
1583	Birth of Susanna, Shakespeare's first child, late May
1585	Birth of Shakespeare's twins, Judith and Hamnet, early February
1587	Execution of Mary Queen of Scots, 8 February
1588	War with Spain; Spanish Armada attempts invasion of England and is defeated at sea
1589–94	*Two Gentlemen of Verona, 1 Henry VI, 2 Henry VI, 3 Henry VI, The Taming of the Shrew, Titus Andronicus, Richard III, Venus and Adonis* (poem), *The Rape of Lucrece* (poem), *The Comedy of Errors*
1593–1603	*The Sonnets*
1595–96	*Love's Labour's Lost, Richard II, Romeo and Juliet, A Midsummer Night's Dream, King John*
1595	Shakespeare recorded as sharer in Lord Chamberlain's Men acting company
1595–1603	Reign of Mehmed III, Sultan of the Ottoman Empire

1596	Elizabeth I permits deportation of "blackmoors" from England; death of Shakespeare's son, Hamnet
1596–99	*The Merchant of Venice, 1 Henry IV, 2 Henry IV, Much Ado About Nothing, The Merry Wives of Windsor, Henry V, As You Like It, Julius Caesar*
1599	Lord Chamberlain's Men move to Globe Theatre
1600–02	*Twelfth Night, Hamlet, The Phoenix and the Turtle* (poem), *Troilus and Cressida*
1601	Death of Shakespeare's father, John; Earl of Essex tried for treason and executed for leading rebellion against the crown; Earl of Southampton, Shakespeare's patron, imprisoned
1603	Death of Elizabeth I and coronation of James I (24 March); Lord Chamberlain's Men become King's Men
1603–04	*Othello, All's Well That Ends Well, Measure for Measure*
1604	"The Moore of Venice [by] Shaxberd" performed at the English court; peace with Spain
1605	Gunpowder Plot to blow up the Houses of Parliament foiled, 5 November
1605–11	*King Lear, Macbeth, Timon of Athens, Antony and Cleopatra, Pericles, Coriolanus, Cymbeline, The Winter's Tale, The Tempest*
1613	*Henry VIII, The Two Noble Kinsmen*; Globe Theatre burns during performance of *Henry VIII* and is rebuilt
1616	Death of Shakespeare, 23 April
1621	*Othello* added to the Stationers' Register
1622	Publication of First Quarto of *Othello*
1623	Publication of First Folio
1630	Publication of Second Quarto of *Othello*

While it will probably always be impossible to determine a precise date for *Othello*, we do know that the play must have been written sometime between 1601 and 1604. Confirmation of the latest possible date comes from records maintained by the Master of the Revels, Edmund Tilney (1536–1610), who notes that "The Moor of Venice [by] Shaxberd" was performed at the court of King James I in 1604.[1] Another early-modern publication, this one a translation of a Roman work, marks the play's earliest possible date: *Othello* draws heavily in places on accounts of the natural world derived from Pliny the Elder (23–79 CE), whose encyclopedic *History of the World* was translated into English by Philemon Holland (1552–1637) and published in 1601, two years before the death of Elizabeth I. Attempts at establishing a more specific date for the play by analyzing patterns in its diction and metrics and comparing these to other Shakespeare plays whose dates are sometimes firmer have produced conflicting results.[2] On balance, however, these studies appear to confirm a date near the middle of the possible range. Scholars who favor a Jacobean date for the play note that its Mediterranean setting suggests that *Othello* may have been written to catch the imagination of a newly installed James I, who became King of England upon Elizabeth I's death in 1603. James's fascination with the long conflict between Christian Europe and the Ottomans was established in 1591 when he published a long poem detailing the defeat of the Turkish forces at the 1571 Battle of Lepanto. While a London reprinting of James's *Lepanto* soon after his English coronation may have influenced, or even prompted, the creation of *Othello* later that year, such contextual evidence can never be definitive.

---

1   The authenticity of the records now held in London's Public Records Office and attributed to Tilney, who served as Master of the Revels from 1579 to 1610, has been questioned over the years, but most scholars now appear to accept them.

2   In 1935, Alfred Hart noted verbal echoes of *Othello* in the 1603 quarto of *Hamlet*. His work has since been developed by J.C. Maxwell and Ernst Honigmann. Stanley Wells et al. note that analyses of rare vocabulary link *Othello* most strongly with *Hamlet* (1600–01), *Troilus and Cressida* (1602), and *Henry V* (1598–99), while analyses of metrics suggest a date between *Measure for Measure* (1603) and *All's Well That Ends Well* (1604–05).

The first record we have of a printed text of *Othello* is an entry from 6 October 1621 in the Register of the Company of Stationers, the book in which the guild chartered by the Crown to regulate the nation's burgeoning publishing industry charged publishers a fee to list their right to print and sell plays and other works. *Othello* was added to the Stationers' Register by London publisher and bookseller Thomas Walkley, who then published the play in quarto format the following year, 1622, eighteen years after *Othello*'s first recorded performance. *Othello* appeared in print again in 1623, when it was included among the 36 plays collected by Shakespeare's theater colleagues John Heminges and Henry Condell and published in folio form in a volume titled *Mr. William Shakespeares Comedies, Histories, & Tragedies*, a book we now call the First Folio. Seven years later, in 1630, a second quarto edition of *Othello* was published.

The existence of three substantively different early print editions of *Othello* is good news for scholars, since each text contributes valuable information about seventeenth-century literary, theatrical, and publishing practice, and because together these texts offer compelling evidence of the play's popularity in the period. Their existence complicates matters considerably for editors, however. While the First Quarto of 1622 (Q1), the First Folio of 1623 (F1), and the Second Quarto of 1630 (Q2) all present versions of the same play, their publication did not begin until about two decades after it was written, and there are over a thousand textual variations among the three. While many of these differences are so small that they probably make very little difference to most readers, others are substantive and have the potential to affect our understanding of the play's action and its characters. Where, then, ought a modern editor to start? It might seem desirable to choose as preferred copy-text the oldest of the available editions, on the grounds that chronological proximity to Shakespeare must confer on a text some degree of authenticity. Editorial scholarship has taught us, however, that in the matter of texts, older is not necessarily better. We have learned too over the years that the reassuring concept of authorial authenticity is a notion about which we ought to be healthily skeptical. Such general principles are confirmed by the specifics of the *Othello* situation: Q1 may be the earliest of the texts, but it is also some 160 lines shorter than F1, and many of its omissions appear to weaken rather than strengthen the play. Although scholars are divided over whether the F1 lines are later additions or whether Q1 is a shortened version of a longer text, it is worth noting that among the passages that appear only in F1 there are two from Act 4, scene 2 of particular significance to readings of the play's female characters: Desdemona's lovely willow song and Emilia's lucid opposition to the sexual double standard that predominates in her social world. If in the matter of the play's female characters F1 is clearly the fuller text, in others ways it could be considered the lesser since it includes neither the many oaths nor the more detailed stage directions found in Q1. Nor can Q2, the latest of the early texts, be ignored since it appears to be a careful emendation of Q1 based on F1 and provides a useful resource for editors committed to understanding better the relationship of the two earlier texts.

Since I view the F1-only passages as deliberate additions to an earlier, less complete text from which Q1 was derived, the current edition is based on the text printed in the First Folio, though on certain occasions it incorporates readings from Q1, and, less often, it draws on emendations suggested by the anonymous editor of Q2, and by later editors as well. In broad terms, my editorial approach might best be characterized as pragmatic. In order to produce a genuinely readable and theatrically useful edition of the play, I have dispensed with impractical notions of the inviolability of the copy-text, but instead I favor readings from F1 wherever these are viable, and I draw on the Q texts primarily in order either to correct likely errors in F1 or to regularize the meter of verse lines. While it is not feasible to note every minor change, this edition includes brief comments on issues of scansion and offers details about corrections in instances when additional information seems likely to be of interest to readers. Where editorial decisions about variants affect the sense of the text in substantive ways, I discuss them in the commentary that accompanies the online version of this edition available at the website of the Internet Shakespeare Editions (http://internetshakespeare.uvic.ca). The only consistent intrusions from Q1 that are not detailed in the notes are the many oaths and asseverations that do not appear in F1 but that seem likely to have enlivened the play early in its theatrical life. I have also silently modernized spelling, punctuation, and formatting throughout.

Act, scene, and line numbering follows conventional practice, and the Through Line Numbers (TLNs) used by the Internet Shakespeare Editions have been included at the top of each page in order to facilitate movement between the print and online versions of the text.

THE TRAGEDY OF OTHELLO, THE MOOR OF VENICE

[CHARACTERS IN THE PLAY

OTHELLO, *the Moor*
BRABANTIO, *father to Desdemona*
CASSIO, *an honorable lieutenant*
IAGO, *a villain*
RODERIGO, *a gulled gentleman*
Duke of Venice
Senators
MONTANO, *Governor of Cyprus*
Gentlemen of Cyprus
LODOVICO and GRATIANO, *two noble Venetians*
Sailors
Clown

DESDEMONA, *wife to Othello*
EMILIA, *wife to Iago*
BIANCA, *a courtesan*

Messenger
Herald
Officers
Musicians
Attendants and servants]

[1.1]

Enter Roderigo and Iago.

RODERIGO. Tush,[1] never tell me! I take it much unkindly
   That thou, Iago, who hast had my purse
   As if the strings were thine, shouldst know of this.[2]
IAGO. 'Sblood,[3] but you'll not hear me! If ever I
5   Did dream of such a matter,[4] abhor me.
RODERIGO. Thou told'st me thou didst hold him[5] in thy hate.
IAGO. Despise me if I do not. Three great ones of the city,[6]
   In personal suit to make me his lieutenant,
   Off-capped[7] to him—and by the faith of man
10   I know my price; I am worth no worse a place—
   But he, as loving his own pride and purposes,
   Evades them with a bombast circumstance
   Horribly stuffed with epithets of war,[8]
   Non-suits my mediators.[9] For "Certes,"° says he,   *certainly*
15   "I have already chose my officer."
   And what was he?
   Forsooth,° a great arithmetician,[10]   *in truth*
   One Michael Cassio, a Florentine—
   A fellow almost damned in a fair wife[11]—

---

1   Exclamation of impatience.
2   I.e., Othello's marriage to Desdemona.
3   Contraction of "God's blood," a common oath.
4   Another vague reference to Othello's marriage.
5   I.e., Othello.
6   Influential citizens of Venice.
7   Removed their hats as a sign of respect.
8   Pompous circular talk full of military terminology. *Bombast* = inflated, overelaborate.
9   Forces my supporters to withdraw their case.
10   One who is good with numbers.
11   This apparent non-sequitur has been linked to the Italian proverb *L'hai tolta bella? Tuo danno* = "Have a beautiful wife? You're damned." However, this connection does little to clarify a line which seems to imply that Cassio is either married or on the brink of marriage when he appears to be single later in the play. Neill suggests that Iago may have picked up a rumor, started by Bianca, that Cassio plans to marry her, though it seems at least as likely that Iago is trying to start such gossip in an attempt to damage Cassio's reputation (see 4.1.114, TLN 2502).

"A FLORENTINE" (TLN 22)

When Iago identifies Michael Cassio as "a Florentine," his emphasis is on Cassio's foreignness. Othello's new lieutenant is from Florence, not Venice, a point Iago emphasizes throughout his bitter diatribe against Cassio by claiming that his own unsuccessful candidacy for the position was endorsed by three influential Venetians. Bitterly envious of his rival's promotion, Iago also complains that Cassio is ill-suited for the job because he is a bean counter who deals in numbers rather than an experienced soldier versed in the realities of war. In his Arden edition of the play, Ernst Honigmann notes that since Florence was the birthplace of Italian diplomat and political philosopher Niccolò Machiavelli (1469–1527), *Florentine* became synonymous with "crafty devil" for some early moderns. For a discussion of Machiavelli's controversial approach to government, visit the "Life & Times" section of the Internet Shakespeare Editions website and click on Ideas: New knowledge.

Santi di Tito (1536–1603), *Portrait of Machiavelli*. Wikimedia Commons, https://commons.wikimedia.org.

20   That never set a squadron in the field,
      Nor the division of a battle knows
      More than a spinster,[1] unless° the bookish theoric[2]   *except for*

---

1   Woman who spins fibers into thread; unmarried woman.
2   Theory (as opposed to practice).

1.1.27:   "AT RHODES, AT CYPRUS" (TLN 31)

Rhodes and Cyprus, both islands off the southern coast of Turkey, were important sites of conflict in the battle between the Venetians and the Turks for control of the Mediterranean. Rhodes fell under Turkish administration in 1522 and Cyprus in 1571. In 1.3, as the Duke and his Senators discuss reports that the Turkish fleet is moving toward Rhodes, the canny First Senator argues that the Turks are trying to trick the Venetians by misleading them into believing that the fleet is headed for Rhodes when in fact it is destined for Cyprus, where the Turks stand a better chance of winning a battle since the larger island is not as well defended.

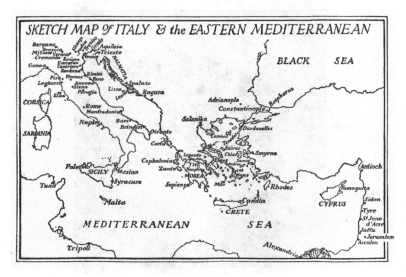

Printed in Thomas Okey, *Venice and Its Story* (London: Dent, 1910). Project Gutenberg, http://www.gutenberg.org.

Wherein the tonguèd[1] consuls[2] can propose
As masterly as he. Mere prattle[3] without practice
Is all his soldiership. But he, sir, had th'election;°   *was chosen*   25
And I—of whom his eyes had seen the proof
At Rhodes, at Cyprus, and on other grounds,
Christened and heathen—must be beleed[4] and calmed
By debitor and creditor. This countercaster,[5]
He, in good time, must his lieutenant be,[6]   30
And I, God bless the mark, his Moorship's ancient.[7]

RODERIGO. By heaven, I rather would have been his hangman.

IAGO. Why, there's no remedy. 'Tis the curse of service;
    Preferment goes by letter and affection,
    And not by old gradation,[8] where each second   35
    Stood heir to th'first. Now sir, be judge yourself
    Whether I in any just term am affined°   *required*
    To love the Moor.

RODERIGO. I would not follow him then.

IAGO. Oh, sir, content you.   40
    I follow him to serve my turn upon° him.   *get my own back at*
    We cannot all be masters, nor all masters
    Cannot be truly followed. You shall mark
    Many a duteous and knee-crooking° knave[9]   *overly submissive*
    That, doting on his own obsequious[10] bondage,   45
    Wears out his time, much like his master's ass,

---

1 Having a tongue; i.e., talkative. Note that here and throughout è indicates that the final *ed* must be pronounced in order for a line of verse to maintain its regular metrical pattern.
2 Elected magistrates who exercised supreme authority in the Roman republic.
3 Inconsequential talk.
4 Cut off from the wind and so becalmed (as a ship).
5 One who calculates figures using counters.
6 The first pronoun in this line refers to Cassio, the second to Othello. The ambiguous pronoun references serve as a reminder that Iago has yet to name Othello.
7 Standard bearer, ensign.
8 I.e., getting ahead is a matter of currying favor not a function of an outmoded seniority system.
9 Servant; dishonest man.
10 Overly servile; dutiful.

For naught but provender,[1] and when he's old—cashiered.[2]
Whip me such honest knaves! Others there are
Who, trimmed in forms and visages[3] of duty,
50   Keep yet their hearts attending on themselves,
And, throwing but shows of service on their lords,
Do well thrive by them—and, when they have lined their coats,

---

1   Fodder, horse food.
2   Dismissed from service, fired.
3   Decked out in external displays.

1.1.48:   "WHIP ME SUCH HONEST KNAVES!"
(TLN 53)

With this abrupt exclamation, Iago contemptuously dismisses a traditional model of service that, to his mind, relies on the compliance of menials in their own exploitation. In his opinion, those foolish enough to bow and scrape in service deserve to be whipped, a punishment usually reserved for those convicted of dishonest behavior. This elision of obedient service with criminality is particularly significant since it is expressed in punning language that is closely associated throughout the play with Iago's own role as untrustworthy servant to Othello. The phrase *honest knaves* sounds complimentary at first, since *honest* could mean "of good moral character" and *knave* was a term for a male servant; however, *honest* was often used as a vague and patronizing term of praise for a social inferior, while *knave* could refer to "an unprincipled man, given to dishonourable and deceitful practices" (*OED* honest *adj.* 3a, 1c; knave *n.* 2a, 3a). Echoes of this scornful attack on conventional ideals of service echo throughout the play as Iago himself is designated repeatedly (and ironically) by the epithet *honest*.

Iago continues his attack on traditional models of service a few lines later when he uses the phrase "Do themselves homage" to mean "serve themselves." *Homage* is the acknowledgement of allegiance by a vassal to the lord from whom he holds land and to whom he owes payment and/ or a debt of service. Iago employs the language of feudal allegiance to reimagine the master/servant relationship as one in which the servant serves himself, thus becoming, in effect, his own master.

Do themselves homage.[1] These fellows have some soul,
And such a one do I profess myself. For, sir,
It is as sure as you are Roderigo,   55
Were I the Moor, I would not be Iago.
In following him, I follow but myself.
Heaven is my judge, not I for love and duty,
But seeming so for my peculiar° end.   *particular; personal*
For when my outward action doth demonstrate   60
The native act and figure of my heart[2]
In complement extern,[3] 'tis not long after
But I will wear my heart upon my sleeve[4]
For daws[5] to peck at: I am not what I am.
RODERIGO. What a full fortune does the thick-lips owe°   *possess* 65
    If he can carry't thus!°   *make this happen*
IAGO.   Call up her father.
    Rouse him, make after him, poison his delight,
    Proclaim° him in the streets. Incense her kinsmen,   *denounce*
    And, though he in a fertile climate dwell,
    Plague him with flies; though that his joy be joy,   70
    Yet throw such chances of vexation on't
    As it may lose some color.
RODERIGO. Here is her father's house. I'll call aloud.
IAGO. Do, with like timorous accent[6] and dire yell
    As when, by night and negligence, the fire   75
    Is spied in populous cities.
RODERIGO. What ho! Brabantio, Signor Brabantio, ho!
IAGO. Awake! What ho, Brabantio! Thieves, thieves!
    Look to your house, your daughter, and your bags!°   *money bags*
    Thieves, thieves!   80

[*Enter Brabantio above at a window.*]
BRABANTIO. What is the reason of this terrible summons?
    What is the matter there?

---

1   Serve themselves.
2   I.e., the way I really am inside (*native act* = natural activity, *figure* = distinctive appearance; image, likeness; emblem, badge).
3   Outward expression.
4   I.e., show openly how I feel.
5   Literally, small crows; figuratively, foolish people.
6   Frightening tone of voice.

RODERIGO. Signor, is all your family within?

IAGO. Are your doors locked?

BRABANTIO.   Why? Wherefore° ask you this?   *why*

85   IAGO. Zounds,¹ sir, you're robbed! For shame, put on your gown!²
     Your heart is burst; you have lost half your soul.
     Even now, now, very now, an old black ram
     Is tupping° your white ewe. Arise, arise!   *copulating with*
     Awake the snorting citizens with the bell,

90   Or else the devil will make a grandsire of you.
     Arise, I say!

BRABANTIO.   What, have you lost your wits?

RODERIGO. Most reverend³ signor, do you know my voice?⁴

BRABANTIO. Not I. What are you?

RODERIGO. My name is Roderigo.

95   BRABANTIO. The worser welcome.
     I have charged thee not to haunt about my doors.
     In honest plainness thou hast heard me say
     My daughter is not for thee. And now in madness,
     Being full of supper and distempering drafts,°   *alcoholic drinks*

100 Upon malicious bravery° dost thou come   *defiance*
     To start my quiet.°   *awake me suddenly*

RODERIGO.   Sir, sir, sir—

BRABANTIO.   But thou must needs be sure
     My spirit and my place⁵ have in their power
     To make this bitter to thee.

RODERIGO.   Patience, good sir.

BRABANTIO. What tell'st thou me of robbing? This is Venice;
     My house is not a grange.°   *barn; country house*

105 RODERIGO.   Most grave Brabantio,
     In simple and pure soul, I come to you.

IAGO. Zounds, sir, you are one of those that will not serve God if
     the devil bid you. Because we come to do you service and you

---

1   Contraction of "God's wounds," a common oath.
2   Get dressed.
3   A courteous form of address, or an adjective meaning "respected."
4   Roderigo's question implies that it is too dark for Brabantio to recognize his
visitors.
5   My character and my social position.

think we are ruffians, you'll have your daughter covered[1] with a
Barbary horse,[2] you'll have your nephews[3] neigh to you, you'll   110
have coursers[4] for cousins and jennets[5] for germans.[6]

---

1   Term used to describe the copulation of horses.
2   Literally, Arabian stallion; figuratively, Othello.
3   Grandsons.
4   Fast horses for racing or for war.
5   Small Spanish horses.
6   Close relatives.

1.1.104:   "THIS IS VENICE" (TLN 118)

Early-modern Venice was a great port city renowned for its wealth, its
cosmopolitan population, and the stability of its republican government. Although the city fathers fought to limit prostitution, Venice
was also famed for its courtesans. (See also Appendix A7.) The image
below shows a pair of gondoliers (1.1.122, TLN 138) navigating a flat-
bottomed gondola through the canals of Venice. The interior of the boat
was originally covered by the flap of paper that could be lifted to reveal
the groping scene hidden beneath.

Niclauss Kippell, *Gondola Ride*, c. 1588. Wikimedia Commons, https://commons.
wikimedia.org.

BRABANTIO. What profane[1] wretch art thou?

IAGO. I am one, sir, that comes to tell you your daughter and the
    Moor are making the beast with two backs.[2]

BRABANTIO. Thou art a villain.°   *unprincipled scoundrel; peasant*

115 IAGO.   You are a senator.

BRABANTIO. This thou shalt answer. I know thee, Roderigo.

RODERIGO. Sir, I will answer anything. But I beseech° you,   *beg*
    If't be your pleasure and most wise consent,
    As partly I find it is, that your fair daughter,
120   At this odd-even[3] and dull° watch o'th'night,   *slow or drowsy*
    Transported with no worse nor better guard
    But with a knave of common hire, a gondolier,[4]
    To the gross clasps[5] of a lascivious Moor—
    If this be known to you and your allowance,[6]
125   We then have done you bold and saucy wrongs.
    But if you know not this, my manners tell me
    We have your wrong rebuke. Do not believe
    That from the sense of all civility
    I thus would play and trifle with your reverence.
130   Your daughter, if you have not given her leave,
    I say again, hath made a gross revolt,°   *flagrant rebellion*
    Tying her duty, beauty, wit, and fortunes
    In an extravagant and wheeling° stranger   *wandering*
    Of here and everywhere. Straight satisfy yourself:
135   If she be in her chamber or your house,
    Let loose on me the justice of the state
    For thus deluding you.

BRABANTIO.   Strike on the tinder,[7] ho!
    Give me a taper.° Call up all my people.   *candle*

---

1   Obscene, foul-mouthed.

2   I.e., having sex.

3   Johnson argues that "the *even* of *night* is *midnight*, the time when night is
divided into *even* parts." Malone goes a step further by arguing that "odd-even"
means "that it was just approaching to, or just past, midnight." Honigmann suggests "neither one thing nor the other, neither night nor day." See also *Macbeth*
3.4.127–28, TLN 1408–09.

4   Oarsman on a gondola, a flat-bottomed boat in use on the canals of Venice.

5   Monstrous embraces.

6   And has your permission.

7   Make a spark to start a flame.

This accident is not unlike my dream;
Belief of it oppresses me already. 140
Light, I say, light!

Exit [Brabantio].

IAGO.   Farewell, for I must leave you.
It seems not meet° nor wholesome to my place   *appropriate*
To be produced[1]—as, if I stay, I shall—
Against the Moor. For I do know the state,
However this may gall him with some check,[2] 145
Cannot with safety cast° him, for he's embarked   *dismiss*
With such loud reason to the Cyprus wars,
Which even now stands in act,[3] that for their souls
Another of his fathom[4] they have none
To lead their business. In which regard, 150
Though I do hate him as I do hell pains,
Yet, for necessity of present life,
I must show out[5] a flag[6] and sign of love—
Which is indeed but sign.[7] That you shall surely find him,
Lead to the Sagittary the raisèd search, 155
And there will I be with him. So farewell.

Exit [Iago].

Enter Brabantio in his nightgown,[8] and servants with torches.
BRABANTIO. It is too true an evil. Gone she is,
And what's to come of my despisèd time[9]
Is naught° but bitterness. Now Roderigo,   *nothing*
Where didst thou see her?—Oh, unhappy girl!— 160
With the Moor sayst thou?—Who would be a father?—
How didst thou know 'twas she?—Oh, she deceives me

---

1   Brought forward to give evidence.
2   Anger him by thwarting him.
3   Is underway.
4   Ability; depth.
5   Display.
6   Piece of cloth attached to a staff or run up a halyard on board ship for use as the distinctive emblem or standard of a military commander.
7   I.e., only for show.
8   A loose gown worn over nightclothes.
9   "(What's left of) my miserable existence."

Past thought!¹—What said she to you? Get more tapers;
Raise all my kindred!° Are they married think you?   *relatives*

---

1 Beyond comprehension.

1.1.155: ·   THE SAGITTARY (TLN 173)

According to Iago, Othello and Desdemona are staying at an inn called
the Sagittary. The sign for Sagittarius, ninth of the twelve houses of the
zodiac, is the archer, and it is most often depicted as a centaur with a
drawn bow. The centaur—a mythical creature with a man's head and chest,
a horse's body and legs, and a warlike temperament—acts in this passage
as a symbolic analog for the conceit that Iago has developed in which
Desdemona's relationship with Othello is figured as bestial. To read more
about Shakespeare and astrology, visit the "Life & Times" section of the
Internet Shakespeare Editions website and click on Ideas: The universe.

Johannes Hevelius, *Sagittarius. Firmamentum Sobiescianum sive Uranographia* (Gdańsk,
1690). Wikimedia Commons, https://commons.wikimedia.org.

RODERIGO. Truly, I think they are.   165

BRABANTIO. O heaven! How got she out? Oh, treason of the
    blood!
Fathers, from hence trust not your daughters' minds
By what you see them act. Is there not charms
By which the property of youth and maidhood
May be abused?° Have you not read, Roderigo,   *deceived*   170
Of some such thing?

RODERIGO.   Yes, sir, I have indeed.

BRABANTIO. Call up my brother.[1]—Oh, would you had had her!—
Some one way, some another.—Do you know
Where we may apprehend her and the Moor?

RODERIGO. I think I can discover° him, if you please   *locate*   175
To get good guard and go along with me.

BRABANTIO. Pray you, lead on. At every house I'll call—
I may command at most. Get weapons, ho,
And raise some special officers of night!
On, good Roderigo; I will deserve your pains.[2]   180

                                      Exeunt.

[1.2]

Enter Othello, Iago, [and] attendants, with torches.

IAGO. Though in the trade of war[3] I have slain men,
Yet do I hold it very stuff o'th'conscience[4]
To do no contrived° murder; I lack iniquity   *planned*
Sometime to do me service. Nine or ten times
I had thought t'have yerked[5] him here under the ribs.   5

OTHELLO. 'Tis better as it is.

IAGO.   Nay, but he prated,[6]
And spoke such scurvy° and provoking terms   *rude*

---

1 I.e., Gratiano.
2 Reward you for the trouble you have taken.
3 Course of war. Honigmann also notes a connection to Othello's occupation.
4 Consider it an essential matter of right and wrong.
5 Struck, usually with a whip or lash. The phrase *under the ribs* suggests that Iago
is thinking of a strike, or an upward thrust, with a dagger.
6 Spoke foolishly or boastfully.

Against your honor
That with the little godliness I have
10   I did full hard forbear him.¹ But I pray you, sir,
Are you fast° married? Be assured of this,   *firmly, securely*
That the magnifico² is much beloved,
And hath in his effect a voice potential
As double as the duke's.³ He will divorce you,
15   Or put upon you what restraint or grievance
The law, with all his might to enforce it on,
Will give him cable.⁴
OTHELLO.   Let him do his spite;
My services, which I have done the signory,⁵
Shall out-tongue° his complaints. 'Tis yet to know—   *out-argue*
20   Which, when I know that boasting is an honor,
I shall promulgate°—I fetch my life and being   *proclaim or publish*
From men of royal siege;⁶ and my demerits°   *merits*
May speak unbonneted⁷ to as proud a fortune
As this that I have reached. For know, Iago,
25   But that I love the gentle Desdemona,
I would not my unhousèd⁸ free condition
Put into circumscription° and confine   *restraint*
For the sea's worth. But look, what lights come yond?

*Enter Cassio [and officers] with torches.*⁹
IAGO. Those are the raisèd° father and his friends;   *awakened*
You were best go in.
30   OTHELLO.   Not I. I must be found.

---

1   I had a difficult time putting up with him.
2   A nobleman of Venice; i.e., Brabantio.
3   I.e., Brabantio's influence in Venice is potentially twice that of the duke.
4   Literally, rope. Iago uses the term figuratively to suggest that Brabantio will contain Othello to the full extent allowed by law.
5   Governing body of Venice.
6   Literally, a seat used by a person of high rank. Othello is apparently claiming descent from a royal line.
7   With head uncovered (as a sign of respect).
8   Without household or family; i.e., without domestic obligations.
9   The early printed texts disagree on the placement of Cassio's entrance, though all allow enough time for Othello and Iago to discuss the arrival before the new-comers are within earshot.

My parts,° my title, and my perfect[1] soul   *abilities; talents*
Shall manifest me rightly.° Is it they?   *show me as I truly am*
IAGO. By Janus,[2] I think no.
OTHELLO. The servants of the duke? And my lieutenant?
The goodness of the night upon you, friends.   35
What is the news?
CASSIO.   The duke does greet you, general,
And he requires your haste-post-haste° appearance,   *immediate*
Even on the instant.
OTHELLO.   What is the matter, think you?

---

1   Virtuous.
2   Two-faced Roman deity of doorways, gates, and beginnings.

1.2.40:   GALLEYS (TLN 249)

Galleys—seagoing vessels propelled by oars and sails—were in common use in the Mediterranean in the sixteenth and seventeenth centuries.

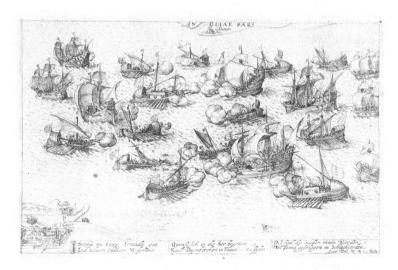

Anonymous etching of battle between Dutch ships and Spanish galleys off the English coast near Dover, 23 October 1602. Wikimedia Commons, https://commons.wikimedia.org.

CASSIO. Something from Cyprus, as I may divine.
40   It is a business of some heat.° The galleys   *urgency*
      Have sent a dozen sequent° messengers   *successive*
      This very night at one another's heels,
      And many of the consuls, raised and met,
      Are at the duke's already. You have been hotly called for,
45   When, being not at your lodging to be found,
      The Senate hath sent about three several° quests   *separate*
      To search you out.
OTHELLO.   'Tis well I am found by you.
      I will but spend a word° here in the house   *speak (to someone)*
      And go with you.
                                                  [*Exit Othello.*]
CASSIO.   Ancient, what makes he here?[1]
50 IAGO. Faith, he tonight hath boarded a land carrack.[2]
      If it prove lawful prize, he's made forever.
CASSIO. I do not understand.
IAGO.   He's married.
CASSIO.   To who?
IAGO. Marry to—

[*Enter Othello.*]
                      Come captain, will you go?
OTHELLO.   Have with you.[3]
CASSIO. Here comes another troop to seek for you.

Enter Brabantio, Roderigo, [and] officers [with] torches [and weapons].
55 IAGO. It is Brabantio. General, be advised;
      He comes to bad intent.°   *with hostile intentions*
OTHELLO.   Holla,[4] stand there.
RODERIGO. Signor, it is the Moor.
BRABANTIO.   Down with him, thief.
                                    [*Both sides draw their swords.*]

---

1   What is he doing here?
2   Literally, gone on board a large ship used to transport goods, usually with
    intent to attack; figuratively, made sexual advances to a desirable woman (i.e.,
    Desdemona).
3   I am ready to go with you.
4   Exclamation meaning "stop."

IAGO. You, Roderigo? Come, sir, I am for you.°   *I will fight you*

OTHELLO. Keep up your bright swords,[1] for the dew will rust them.
  Good signor, you shall more command with years[2] than with   60
  your weapons.

BRABANTIO. O thou foul thief, where hast thou stowed my
      daughter?
  Damned as thou art, thou hast enchanted her;
  For I'll refer me to all things of sense[3]
  If she in chains of magic were not bound,   65
  Whether a maid so tender, fair, and happy,
  So opposite° to marriage that she shunned   *opposed*
  The wealthy curled[4] darlings of our nation,
  Would ever have, t'incur a general mock,
  Run from her guardage° to the sooty bosom   *guardianship* 70
  Of such a thing as thou—to fear, not to delight.
  Judge me the world, if 'tis not gross in sense°   *obvious*
  That thou hast practiced on[5] her with foul charms,
  Abused her delicate youth with drugs or minerals
  That weaken motion.[6] I'll have't disputed on°—   *debated by experts* 75
  'Tis probable and palpable° to thinking.   *likely and plainly observable*
  I therefore apprehend and do attach° thee   *seize and arrest*
  For an abuser of the world, a practicer
  Of arts inhibited and out of warrant.°   *illegal*
  Lay hold upon him; if he do resist,   80
  Subdue him at his peril.

OTHELLO.   Hold° your hands,   *stop*
  Both you of my inclining[7] and the rest.
  Were it my cue to fight, I should have known it
  Without a prompter. Whither will you that I go
  To answer this your charge?

BRABANTIO.   To prison, till fit time   85

---

1 Sheath your unused swords.
2 With the experience of, and respect accorded to, age.
3 Submit my case for judgment to all people with common sense.
4 Literally, adorned with curls or ringlets. Brabantio's point is that Desdemona
has seemed unimpressed by the fashionable dandies of Venice.
5 Acted upon by trickery (so as to induce someone to do or to believe something),
with a suggestion of magical intervention.
6 Inner prompting or inclination.
7 Those of you on my side.

Of law and course of direct session
Call thee to answer.[1]

OTHELLO.　　　　　What if I do obey?
How may the duke be therewith satisfied,
Whose messengers are here about my side
90　Upon some present° business of the state　　　　　*urgent*
To bring me to him?

OFFICER.　　　　　'Tis true, most worthy signor.
The duke's in council, and your noble self
I am sure is sent for.

BRABANTIO.　　　　　How? The duke in council?
In this time of the night? Bring him away!
95　Mine's not an idle° cause. The duke himself,　　　*frivolous*
Or any of my brothers of the state,
Cannot but feel this wrong as 'twere their own;
For if such actions may have passage free,°　　　*are allowed*
Bondslaves and pagans[2] shall our statesmen be.

Exeunt.

[1.3]

Enter Duke [and] Senators [at a table, with lights] and officers.

DUKE. There is no composition° in this news　　　*consistency*
That gives them credit.°　　　　　　　　　　　*credibility*

1 SENATOR.　　　　　Indeed, they are disproportioned;[3]
My letters say a hundred and seven galleys.

DUKE. And mine a hundred forty.

2 SENATOR.　　　　　And mine two hundred.
5　But though they jump not on a just account[4]—
As in these cases where the aim° reports　　　*guesswork*
'Tis oft with difference—yet do they all confirm
A Turkish fleet, and bearing up to° Cyprus.　　*heading for*

DUKE. Nay, it is possible enough to judgment;°　*with careful thought*

1　Until such time as, through the regular proceedings of the law courts, you are summoned to account for yourself.
2　Slaves and non-Christians.
3　Inconsistent.
4　Do not agree on an exact tally.

I do not so secure me in the error,   10
But the main article I do approve
In fearful sense.[1]
SAILOR. (*Within*)° What ho, what ho, what ho!   *i.e., offstage*

Enter Sailor.
OFFICER. A messenger from the galleys.
DUKE. Now, what's the business?   15
SAILOR. The Turkish preparation[2] makes for Rhodes,
    So was I bid report here to the state
    By Signor Angelo.°   *presumably the commander of the Venetian fleet*
DUKE. How say you by° this change?   *what do you think about*
1 SENATOR.   This cannot be,
    By no assay° of reason. 'Tis a pageant°   *test or trial; trick* 20
    To keep us in false gaze.[3] When we consider
    Th'importancy° of Cyprus to the Turk,   *importance*
    And let ourselves again but understand
    That as it more concerns the Turk than Rhodes,
    So may he with more facile question bear it,[4]   25
    For that° it stands not in such warlike brace,[5]   *because*
    But altogether lacks th'abilities
    That Rhodes is dressed in.[6] If we make thought of this,
    We must not think the Turk is so unskillful
    To leave that latest° which concerns him first,   *until last* 30
    Neglecting an attempt of ease and gain
    To wake and wage° a danger profitless.   *provoke and risk*
DUKE. Nay, in all confidence he's not for° Rhodes.   *headed to*
OFFICER. Here is more news.

---

1 I will not let inconsistencies in the reports cause me to underestimate the
powerful threat of which they warn.
2 Fleet prepared for an attack.
3 Looking the other way; distracted.
4 More easily conquer it.
5 State of readiness for war.
6 Equipped with.

"THE OTTOMITES" (TLN 364)

When a Messenger arrives with news that "the Ottomites" are sailing toward Rhodes, he is reporting on the movements of the Ottoman Turks. The Ottoman Empire was established by Osman I (1258–1324) in what is now northern Turkey at the end of the thirteenth century, and it was later expanded by his successors to include all of Asia Minor and much of southeastern Europe. The empire's expansion was halted for several decades after the invasion of the Mongol ruler Tamerlane in 1402, events explored in Christopher Marlowe's play *Tamburlaine the Great* (c. 1587). The expansion later resumed, culminating in the capture of Constantinople in 1453. The power and influence of the Ottoman Empire peaked in the mid-sixteenth century under the leadership of Suleiman I (1494–1566), whose forces presented a constant threat to other nations with political and economic concerns in the Mediterranean.

Antoine Masson (1636–1700), *Sultan Suleyman le Magnifique*. Wikimedia Commons, https://commons.wikimedia.org.

Enter a Messenger.

MESSENGER. The Ottomites, reverend and gracious,   35
  Steering with due course toward the isle of Rhodes,
  Have there injointed° them with an after° fleet.   *united / following*
1 SENATOR. Ay, so I thought. How many, as you guess?
MESSENGER. Of thirty sail; and now they do restem
  Their backward course,¹ bearing with frank appearance   40
  Their purposes toward Cyprus.² Signor Montano,
  Your trusty and most valiant servitor,
  With his free duty, recommends° you thus   *informs*
  And prays you to believe him.
DUKE. 'Tis certain then for Cyprus.   45
  Marcus Luccicos—is not he in town?³
1 SENATOR. He's now in Florence.
DUKE. Write from us to him; post-post-haste, dispatch.⁴
1 SENATOR. Here comes Brabantio and the valiant Moor.

Enter Brabantio, Othello, Cassio, Iago, Roderigo, and officers.

DUKE. Valiant Othello, we must straight° employ you   *immediately*   50
  Against the general⁵ enemy Ottoman.
  [*To Brabantio*] I did not see you. Welcome, gentle signor.
  We lacked your counsel and your help tonight.
BRABANTIO. So did I yours. Good your grace, pardon me.
  Neither my place⁶ nor aught° I heard of business   *anything*   55
  Hath raised me from my bed; nor doth the general care⁷
  Take hold on me, for my particular° grief   *personal*
  Is of so floodgate and o'erbearing nature
  That it engluts° and swallows other sorrows   *consumes*
  And it is still itself.
DUKE.   Why? What's the matter?   60

---

1 Steer back again.
2 Heading openly toward Cyprus.
3 It is unclear who this man is or why the Duke might wish to have him tracked
down.
4 I.e., carry this message at once.
5 "Universal" (Sanders). The implication is that the Turks pose a threat to all
Christians.
6 I.e., office as a senator.
7 Concern for the public good.

BRABANTIO. My daughter! Oh, my daughter!

1 SENATOR.   Dead?

BRABANTIO.   Ay, to me.
    She is abused, stolen from me, and corrupted
    By spells and medicines bought of mountebanks;[1]
    For nature so preposterously to err—
65   Being not deficient, blind, or lame of sense—
    Sans° witchcraft could not.   *without*

DUKE. Whoe'er he be that in this foul proceeding
    Hath thus beguiled your daughter of herself,[2]
    And you of her, the bloody book of law
70   You shall yourself read in the bitter letter
    After your own sense,[3] yea, though our proper[4] son
    Stood in your action.[5]

BRABANTIO.   Humbly I thank your grace.
    Here is the man—this Moor, whom now it seems
    Your special mandate for the state affairs
    Hath hither brought.

75 ALL.   We are very sorry for't.

DUKE. [*To Othello*] What, in your own part, can you say to this?

BRABANTIO. Nothing but "This is so."

OTHELLO. Most potent, grave, and reverend signors,
    My very noble and approved° good masters,   *respected*
80   That I have ta'en away this old man's daughter,
    It is most true; true, I have married her.
    The very head and front of my offending
    Hath this extent,[6] no more. Rude° am I in my speech,   *unrefined*
    And little blessed with the soft phrase of peace—
85   For since these arms of mine had seven year's[7] pith,°   *strength*
    Till now some nine moons wasted,[8] they have used

---

1 Itinerant sellers of supposed medicines; charlatans.
2 Tricked your daughter into uncharacteristic behavior.
3 You will be the one to interpret the law and to determine an appropriately harsh sentence.
4 My own; the duke uses the royal *we*.
5 Were the accused in your legal complaint.
6 This is the limit of my wrongdoing.
7 Since I was seven years old.
8 I.e., nine months ago.

Their dearest° action in the tented field[1]—   *most valuable*
And little of this great world can I speak
More than pertains to feats of broils° and battle,   *quarrels*
And therefore little shall I grace my cause   90
In speaking for myself. Yet, by your gracious patience,
I will a round,[2] unvarnished tale deliver
Of my whole course of love—what drugs, what charms,
What conjuration,° and what mighty magic—   *incantation or spell*
For such proceeding I am charged withal—   95
I won his daughter.

BRABANTIO.   A maiden never bold,
Of spirit so still and quiet that her motion°   *desire*
Blushed at herself, and she—in spite of nature,
Of years, of country, credit,° everything—   *reputation*
To fall in love with what she feared to look on?   100
It is a judgment maimed and most imperfect
That will confess° perfection so could err   *declare*
Against all rules of nature, and must be driven
To find out practices of cunning hell
Why this should be. I therefore vouch again   105
That with some mixtures powerful o'er the blood,
Or with some dram° conjured to this effect,   *dose*
He wrought° upon her.   *worked*

DUKE.   To vouch° this is no proof   *allege*
Without more wider and more overt test
Than these thin habits and poor likelihoods   110
Of modern seeming[3] do prefer° against him.   *advance the case*

1 SENATOR. But, Othello, speak:
Did you by indirect and forcèd courses°   *devious and forcible means*
Subdue and poison this young maid's affections?
Or came it by request and such fair question°   *conversation* 115
As soul to soul affordeth?

---

1 Battlefield (covered with tents).
2 "Expressed in an uncompromising way without omitting or disguising anything"; plain (*OED adj.* 18a; 19).
3 Mere appearances and implausible accusations based on superficial assumptions.

OTHELLO.   I do beseech you,
    Send for the lady to the Sagittary
    And let her speak of me before her father;
    If you do find me foul in her report,
120   The trust, the office I do hold of you
    Not only take away, but let your sentence
    Even fall upon my life.
DUKE.   Fetch Desdemona hither.

                           [*Exeunt two or three officers.*]

OTHELLO. Ancient, conduct them; you best know the place.

                                   [*Exit Iago.*]

    And till she come, as truly as to heaven
125   I do confess the vices of my blood,
    So justly to your grave ears I'll present
    How I did thrive in this fair lady's love,
    And she in mine.
DUKE.   Say it, Othello.
OTHELLO. Her father loved me, oft invited me,
130   Still questioned me the story of my life
    From year to year—the battle, sieges, fortune
    That I have passed.
    I ran it through, even from my boyish days
    To th'very moment that he bade me tell it,
135   Wherein I spoke of most disastrous chances,
    Of moving accidents by flood and field,
    Of hairbreadth scapes i'th'imminent deadly breach;[1]
    Of being taken by the insolent foe
    And sold to slavery, of my redemption thence
140   And portance° in my traveler's history,   *bearing or demeanor*
    Wherein of antars° vast and deserts idle,°   *caves / empty*
    Rough quarries, rocks, hills whose heads touch heaven,
    It was my hint to speak—such was my process—
    And of the cannibals that each other eat,
145   The anthropophagi,[2] and men whose heads
    Do grow beneath their shoulders. These things to hear

---

1   Gap in a fortified wall.
2   *Anthropo-* = human + *phagy* = the eating of; thus, man-eaters.

Would Desdemona seriously incline,
But still the house affairs would draw her thence,
Which ever as she could with haste dispatch,
She'd come again and with a greedy ear   150
Devour up my discourse; which I, observing,
Took once a pliant hour° and found good means   *suitable moment*
To draw from her a prayer of earnest heart
That I would all my pilgrimage dilate,°   *enlarge upon*
Whereof by parcels she had something heard,   155
But not intentively.[1] I did consent,
And often did beguile her of her tears
When I did speak of some distressful stroke°   *blow*
That my youth suffered. My story being done,
She gave me for my pains a world of kisses;   160
She swore in faith 'twas strange, 'twas passing strange;
'Twas pitiful,[2] 'twas wondrous pitiful.
She wished she had not heard it, yet she wished
That heaven had made her such a man. She thanked me,
And bade me, if I had a friend that loved her,   165
I should but teach him how to tell my story
And that would woo her. Upon this hint[3] I spake.°   *spoke*
She loved me for the dangers I had passed,
And I loved her that she did pity them.
This only is the witchcraft I have used.   170
Here comes the lady; let her witness it.°   *attest to what I have told you*

Enter Desdemona, Iago, [and] attendants.
DUKE. I think this tale would win my daughter too.
    Good Brabantio, take up this mangled matter at the best.[4]
    Men do their broken weapons rather use
    Than their bare hands.
BRABANTIO.   I pray you hear her speak.   175
    If she confess that she was half the wooer,
    Destruction on my head if my bad blame

---

1 Intently, with focused attention.
2 Moving, affecting.
3 Opportunity (*OED n.* 1a); slight indication.
4 Make the best of this messy business.

Light° on the man. Come hither, gentle mistress.   *alight, land*
Do you perceive in all this noble company
Where most you owe obedience?
180 DESDEMONA.   My noble father,
I do perceive here a divided duty.
To you I am bound for life and education;
My life and education both do learn° me   *teach*
How to respect you. You are the lord of duty;
185 I am hitherto° your daughter. But here's my husband,   *until now*
And so much duty as my mother showed
To you, preferring you before her father,
So much I challenge that I may profess   `
Due to the Moor my lord.
190 BRABANTIO. God be with you! I have done.
Please it your grace, on to the state affairs.
I had rather to adopt a child than get° it.   *beget*
[*To Othello*] Come hither, Moor.
I here do give thee that with all my heart
195 Which, but thou hast already, with all my heart
I would keep from thee. [*To Desdemona*] For your sake, jewel,[1]
I am glad at soul I have no other child,
For thy escape would teach me tyranny
To hang clogs[2] on them. [*To the Duke*] I have done, my lord.
200 DUKE. Let me speak like yourself and lay a sentence,[3]
Which as a grise° or step may help these lovers   *stair*
Into your favor.
When remedies are past, the griefs are ended
By seeing the worst, which late on hopes depended.
205 To mourn a mischief that is past and gone
Is the next way to draw new mischief on.
What cannot be preserved when fortune takes,
Patience her injury a mockery makes.
The robbed that smiles steals something from the thief;
210 He robs himself that spends a bootless° grief.   *useless; incurable*

---

1 Term of endearment, probably with an ironic edge given Brabantio's anger over
Desdemona's account of her *divided duty* (1.3.181, TLN 528).
2 Heavy pieces of wood shackled to an animal or person to prevent escape.
3 Way of thinking; opinion.

BRABANTIO. So let the Turk of Cyprus us beguile;
We lose it not so long as we can smile.
He bears the sentence well that nothing bears,
But the free comfort which from thence he hears;
But he bears both the sentence and the sorrow   215
That, to pay grief, must of poor patience borrow.

1.3.181:   "DIVIDED DUTY" (TLN 528)

Desdemona's notion of "divided duty" recognizes that, as she is a recently
married woman, her social obligation is shifting from the requirement
that she obey her father to the expectation that she obey her husband; it
thus connects the experiences of Shakespeare's fictional Venetian noble-
woman to those of the real women among the play's first audiences. Like
Desdemona, English women at the turn of the seventeenth century lived
in a patriarchal society dominated by the institution of the family. Power
resided primarily in male heads of households, who were expected both to
govern members of their family at home and to represent them in the outside world. Wives were understood to share in the responsibility for managing the household, but to be subordinate to their husbands. Children were
expected to obey their parents and, when they were grown, to make decisions about marriage in conjunction with them. *The Book of Common Prayer*
rite that bound couples together in marriage required that women vow
obedience and service to their new husbands, and marriage made women
the legal property of their husbands. (See also Appendices B3 and B5.)

   While Desdemona and Othello's elopement could be seen as a challenge
to this patriarchal system, it is worth noting that neither character seems
committed to an agenda of sociopolitical change. Brabantio argues that his
daughter's affection for Othello runs suspiciously strong and against the
fashion, but Desdemona's only other minor rebellion—her refusal to agree
to return to her father's house while Othello is on duty in Cyprus—appears
motivated by love and duty, twin obligations of every new wife confirmed
in the language of the marriage ceremony. Othello too demonstrates a
notable commitment to social obligation as he seeks to address a "divided
duty" of his own by preparing simultaneously to do his political duty to
the Venetian state—taking on a new military command—and to meet his
marital obligations to his wife.

These sentences to sugar or to gall,°   *i.e., to happiness or to bitterness*
Being strong on both sides, are equivocal.
But words are words; I never yet did hear
220   That the bruisèd heart was piercèd through the ears.
I humbly beseech you proceed to th'affairs of state.
DUKE. The Turk with a most mighty preparation makes for Cyprus.
Othello, the fortitude[1] of the place is best known to you, and
though we have there a substitute of most allowed sufficiency,[2]
225   yet opinion, a more sovereign mistress of effects, throws a more
safer voice on you.[3] You must therefore be content to slubber[4] the
gloss[5] of your new fortunes with this more stubborn and boister-
ous expedition.
OTHELLO. The tyrant custom, most grave senators,
230   Hath made the flinty and steel couch of war
My thrice-driven° bed of down. I do agnize°   *very soft / recognize*
A natural and prompt alacrity
I find in hardness, and do undertake
This present war against the Ottomites.
235   Most humbly therefore bending to your state,
I crave fit disposition° for my wife,   *suitable arrangements*
Due reference of place and exhibition,[6]
With such accommodation[7] and besort°   *suitable company*
As levels with[8] her breeding.
DUKE. Why, at her father's.
240 BRABANTIO.   I will not have it so.
OTHELLO. Nor I.
DESDEMONA. Nor would I there reside
To put my father in impatient thoughts
By being in his eye.° Most gracious duke,   *within his sight*
245   To my unfolding lend your prosperous° ear,   *favorable*

---

1   Military strength.
2   Deputy of recognized competence.
3   Reputation, a powerful determinant of results, makes you a more trustworthy
option.
4   Soil.
5   Luster.
6   Assignment of housing and maintenance appropriate to her rank.
7   Room and provision for the reception of people; appropriate care.
8   Is on a par with.

And let me find a charter° in your voice   *permission*
T'assist my simpleness.

DUKE.   What would you, Desdemona?

DESDEMONA. That I did love the Moor to live with him,
  My downright violence and storm[1] of fortunes
  May trumpet to the world. My heart's subdued   250
  Even to the very quality[2] of my lord;
  I saw Othello's visage° in his mind,   *countenance*
  And to his honors and his valiant parts°   *qualities*
  Did I my soul and fortunes consecrate.
  So that, dear lords, if I be left behind,   255
  A moth of peace, and he go to the war,
  The rites for why I love him are bereft me,°   *stolen from me*
  And I a heavy interim[3] shall support°   *endure*
  By his dear absence. Let me go with him.

OTHELLO. Let her have your voice.°   *opinion; judgment* 260
  Vouch with me, heaven; I therefore beg it not
  To please the palate° of my appetite,°   *liking / sexual hunger*
  Nor to comply with heat[4] the young affects°   *raw desires*
  In my defunct[5] and proper satisfaction,
  But to be free and bounteous° to her mind;[6]   *generous* 265
  And heaven defend your good souls that you think
  I will your serious and great business scant
  When she is with me. No, when light-winged toys[7]
  Of feathered Cupid seel[8] with wanton dullness
  My speculative and officed instruments°   *i.e., eyes* 270

---

1 Violent disturbance; "passionate manifestation of feeling" (*OED n.* 3a; b).

2 Profession (as a soldier); character; nature; style, manner.

3 Ponderous period of waiting.

4 Fulfill with erotic ardor.

5 Performed. Cunningham proposes convincingly that *defunct* is a Latinism derived from *defunctus* = "to have done with, acquit oneself of, discharge, perform, finish."

6 A notoriously difficult passage meaning something like "I make this request neither to gratify my lust, nor so that I may fulfill with erotic intensity the raw passions aroused in the performance of consummating my marriage, but rather to generously support Desdemona's wishes."

7 I.e., Cupid's arrows.

8 Sew up (like the eyes of falcons trained to hunt); see extended note, p. 154.

That my disports[1] corrupt and taint my business,
Let housewives make a skillet of my helm°   *helmet*
And all indign° and base adversities   *unworthy, disgraceful*
Make head against° my estimation.°   *attack / reputation*
275 DUKE. Be it as you shall privately determine,
Either for her stay or going. Th'affair cries° haste,   *calls for*
And speed must answer it.
1 SENATOR.   You must away tonight.
DESDEMONA. Tonight, my lord?
DUKE.   This night.
OTHELLO.   With all my heart.
DUKE. At nine i'th'morning here we'll meet again.
280 Othello, leave some officer behind
And he shall our commission bring to you,
And such things else of quality and respect
As doth import you.
OTHELLO.   So please your grace, my ancient—
A man he is of honesty and trust—
285 To his conveyance° I assign my wife,   *escort*
With what else needful your good grace shall think
To be sent after me.
DUKE.   Let it be so.
Goodnight to everyone—and, noble signor,
If virtue no delighted beauty lack,
290 Your son-in-law is far more fair[2] than black.[3]
1 SENATOR. Adieu, brave Moor, use Desdemona well.
BRABANTIO. Look to her,[4] Moor, if thou hast eyes to see;
She has deceived her father, and may thee.
            Exeunt [Duke, Senators, Brabantio, Cassio, Sailor,
            Messenger, officers, and attendants].

---

1   Diversions (with a sexual undertone).
2   Light-skinned, light-haired; beautiful; morally virtuous.
3   Dark-skinned, dark-haired; foul; evil.
4   Keep an eye on her.

OTHELLO. My life upon her faith![1]—Honest[2] Iago,
My Desdemona must I leave to thee.   295
I prithee let thy wife attend on her,
And bring them after in the best advantage.[3]
Come Desdemona, I have but an hour
Of love, of worldly matter and direction
To spend with thee. We must obey the time.   300
                         Exeunt [Othello and Desdemona].
RODERIGO. Iago.
IAGO. What sayst thou, noble heart?
RODERIGO. What will I do, think'st thou?
IAGO. Why, go to bed and sleep.
RODERIGO. I will incontinently[4] drown myself.   305
IAGO. If thou dost, I shall never love thee after. Why, thou silly
gentleman?
RODERIGO. It is silliness to live when to live is torment; and then
have we a prescription to die, when death is our physician.
IAGO. Oh, villainous![5] I have looked upon the world for four times   310
seven years,[6] and, since I could distinguish betwixt a benefit and
an injury, I never found man that knew how to love himself. Ere[7]
I would say I would drown myself for the love of a guinea-hen,[8]
I would change my humanity with a baboon.
RODERIGO. What should I do? I confess it is my shame to be so   315
fond,[9] but it is not in my virtue[10] to amend it.

---

1 I would bet my life on her faithfulness.
2 Respectable; virtuous; truthful; genuine; also, "vague epithet of appreciation
or praise, esp. as used in a patronizing way to an inferior" (*OED adj.* 3c). This is the
first use of the moniker "Honest Iago," by which the ancient is identified so often
in the play.
3 Most favorable opportunity.
4 Immediately.
5 Shameful.
6 I.e., Iago is 28 years old.
7 Before.
8 Literally, female guinea-fowl; common slang for "prostitute."
9 Over-affectionate; foolishly credulous.
10 Ability.

IAGO. Virtue? A fig![1] 'Tis in ourselves that we are thus or thus. Our bodies are our gardens to the which our wills are gardeners, so that if we will plant nettles or sow lettuce, set hyssop and weed
320 up thyme, supply it with one gender[2] of herbs or distract it with many, either to have it sterile with idleness or manured with industry—why, the power and corrigible[3] authority of this lies in our wills. If the beam[4] of our lives had not one scale of reason to poise[5] another of sensuality, the blood[6] and baseness of our
325 natures would conduct us to most preposterous conclusions. But we have reason to cool our raging motions,[7] our carnal stings, our unbitted[8] lusts—whereof I take this that you call love to be a sect or scion.[9]

RODERIGO. It cannot be.

330 IAGO. It is merely a lust of the blood and a permission of the will. Come, be a man! Drown thyself? Drown cats and blind puppies. I have professed me thy friend, and I confess me knit[10] to thy deserving with cables of perdurable[11] toughness. I could never better stead[12] thee than now. Put money in thy purse.[13] Follow
335 thou the wars; defeat thy favor with an usurped beard.[14] I say, put money in thy purse. It cannot be long that Desdemona should continue her love to the Moor—put money in thy purse—nor he his to her. It was a violent commencement[15] in her, and thou shalt see an answerable sequestration[16]—put but money in thy purse.

---

1 Scornful expression of dismissal (*fig* = something small and without value); an obscene gesture which consisted in thrusting the thumb between two of the closed fingers or into the mouth.
2 Variety.
3 Capable of being corrected.
4 The bar from which the scales of a balance are suspended.
5 Balance.
6 Passion.
7 Emotions; impulses.
8 Without a bit (the mouthpiece of a horse's bridle); i.e., unrestrained.
9 Cutting or slip (from a plant).
10 Joined.
11 Eternal.
12 Be useful to, help.
13 "Sell your assets to raise money" (Honigmann).
14 Disguise your appearance with a fake beard.
15 Beginning.
16 Separation.

These Moors are changeable in their wills—fill thy purse with 340
money. The food that to him now is as luscious[1] as locusts[2] shall
be to him shortly as acerb[3] as coloquintida.[4] She must change for[5]
youth; when she is sated with his body, she will find the errors of
her choice. Therefore, put money in thy purse. If thou wilt needs
damn thyself, do it a more delicate way than drowning. Make all 345
the money thou canst. If sanctimony and a frail vow betwixt an
erring barbarian[6] and a super-subtle Venetian be not too hard for
my wits and all the tribe of hell, thou shalt enjoy her. Therefore
make money. A pox of[7] drowning thyself. It is clean out of the
way.[8] Seek thou rather to be hanged in compassing[9] thy joy than 350
to be drowned and go without her.

RODERIGO. Wilt thou be fast[10] to my hopes, if I depend on the issue?

IAGO. Thou art sure of me—go, make money—I have told thee often,
and I retell thee again and again: I hate the Moor. My cause is
hearted;[11] thine hath no less reason. Let us be conjunctive[12] in our 355
revenge against him. If thou canst cuckold him,[13] thou dost thyself
a pleasure, me a sport.[14] There are many events in the womb of
time which will be delivered. Traverse,[15] go, provide thy money.
We will have more of this tomorrow. Adieu.

RODERIGO. Where shall we meet i'th'morning? 360

IAGO. At my lodging.

RODERIGO. I'll be with thee betimes.[16]

---

1 Sweet.
2 Fruits of the carob tree.
3 Sour.
4 Fruit of the colocynth vine (also called bitter-apple), noted for its extreme bitterness and employed as a purgative.
5 Switch to.
6 Foreigner; uncivilized person; native of Barbary. See also 1.1.110, TLN 124, and
note.
7 Exclamation of impatience.
8 Completely inappropriate.
9 Achieving; contriving.
10 Committed to.
11 Fixed or established in the heart.
12 United.
13 I.e., make him a cuckold by seducing his wife.
14 Entertaining pastime.
15 Get moving.
16 At an early hour.

IAGO. Go to, farewell. Do you hear, Roderigo?
RODERIGO. What say you?
365 IAGO. No more of drowning, do you hear?
RODERIGO. I am changed.
IAGO. Go to, farewell. Put money enough in your purse.
RODERIGO. I'll sell all my land.

Exit [Roderigo].

IAGO. Thus do I ever make my fool my purse;
370 For I mine own gained knowledge should profane[1]
If I would time expend with such a snipe[2]
But for my sport and profit. I hate the Moor,
And it is thought abroad° that 'twixt my sheets   *widely*
He's done my office.[3] I know not if't be true,
375 But I, for mere suspicion in that kind,
Will do as if for surety.[4] He holds me well;°   *thinks well of me*
The better shall my purpose work on him.
Cassio's a proper[5] man—let me see now:
To get his place and to plume up[6] my will
380 In double knavery—How? How? Let's see:
After some time to abuse Othello's ears
That he is too familiar with his[7] wife.
He hath a person° and a smooth dispose[8]   *physical appearance*
To be suspected, framed to make women false.
385 The Moor is of a free and open nature
That thinks men honest that but seem to be so,
And will as tenderly be led by'th'nose as asses are.
I have't. It is engendered.° Hell and night   *conceived*
Must bring this monstrous[9] birth to the world's light.

Exit [Iago].

---

1 Violate; desecrate.
2 Literally, a common wading bird with a long slender bill; here, a contemptible person.
3 I.e., he has slept with my wife.
4 Act as though it were a certainty.
5 Suitable; admirable; handsome; respectable.
6 There is no clear reference for this image, but the phrase seems to mean something like "decorate" or "bolster."
7 The first pronoun seems to refer to Cassio, and the second to Othello.
8 Manner.
9 Unnatural; repulsive or frightening (like a monster); immense.

[2.1]

Enter Montano, [Governor of Cyprus, with] two [other] Gentlemen.

MONTANO. What from the cape can you discern at sea?

1 GENTLEMAN. Nothing at all; it is a high-wrought[1] flood.
    I cannot 'twixt the heaven and the main[2]
    Descry° a sail.   *see; observe*

MONTANO. Methinks the wind hath spoke aloud at land.   5
    A fuller blast ne'er shook our battlements;
    If it hath ruffianed° so upon the sea,   *raged; blustered*
    What ribs of oak,[3] when mountains melt on them,
    Can hold the mortise?[4] What shall we hear of this?

2 GENTLEMAN. A segregation[5] of the Turkish fleet—   10
    For do but stand upon the foaming shore,
    The chiding billow° seems to pelt the clouds,   *scolding ocean swell*
    The wind-shaked surge with high and monstrous mane[6]
    Seems to cast water on the burning Bear[7]
    And quench the guards of th'ever-fixèd Pole.[8]   15
    I never did like molestation° view   *such disturbance*
    On the enchafèd flood.°   *frenzied sea*

MONTANO.   If that the Turkish fleet
    Be not ensheltered and embayed,[9] they are drowned;
    It is impossible to bear it out.°   *survive the storm*

Enter a [third] Gentleman.

3 GENTLEMAN. News, lads! Our wars are done.   20
    The desperate[10] tempest hath so banged the Turks
    That their designment° halts.[11] A noble ship of Venice   *plan*

---

1 Very agitated.
2 Between the sky and the open sea.
3 Curved frame-timbers of a ship.
4 Joint holding a ship together.
5 Dividing up (of a collective unity).
6 Long heavy hair growing about the head and neck of such mammals as horses or lions; with puns on *main* = sea, and *main* = physical force (as in "with might and main").
7 The constellation Ursa Minor (Little Bear).
8 Polaris, the North Star or Pole Star.
9 Sheltered in a bay.
10 Extremely dangerous.
11 Moves haltingly; stops.

    Hath seen a grievous wreck and sufferance[1]
    On most part of their fleet.
MONTANO.   How? Is this true?
25 3 GENTLEMAN. The ship is here put in,[2]
    A Veronnesa.[3] Michael Cassio,
    Lieutenant to the warlike Moor, Othello,
    Is come on shore; the Moor himself at sea,
    And is in full commission here for Cyprus.[4]
30 MONTANO. I am glad on't; 'tis a worthy governor.
    3 GENTLEMAN. But this same Cassio, though he speak of comfort
    Touching° the Turkish loss, yet he looks sadly   *on the subject of*
    And prays the Moor be safe, for they were parted
    With foul and violent tempest.
MONTANO.   Pray heavens he be,
35 For I have served him, and the man commands
    Like a full° soldier. Let's to the seaside, ho!   *complete*
    As well to see the vessel that's come in
    As to throw out our eyes° for brave Othello,   *i.e., watch*
    Even till we make the main and th'aerial blue
    An indistinct regard.°   *can no longer distinguish sea from sky*
40 3 GENTLEMAN.   Come, let's do so;
    For every minute is expectancy
    Of more arrivancy.°   *gives expectation of more arrivals*

Enter Cassio.
CASSIO. Thanks, you the valiant of this warlike isle
    That so approve° the Moor. Oh, let the heavens   *commend; esteem*
45 Give him defense against the elements,
    For I have lost him on a dangerous sea.
MONTANO. Is he well shipped?°   *aboard a good vessel*
CASSIO. His bark[5] is stoutly timbered, and his pilot
    Of very expert and approved allowance;°   *skilled and proven ability*
50 Therefore my hopes, not surfeited to death,

---

1   Devastation and damage.
2   Sailed into the harbor.
3   "Either a certain kind of vessel or a ship from Verona" (Pechter).
4   En route to Cyprus with the full authority (of the Venetian Senate).
5   Small sailing ship.

Stand in bold cure.[1]

VOICES WITHIN. A sail! A sail! A sail!

CASSIO.   What noise?

1 GENTLEMAN. The town is empty; on the brow o'th'sea
   Stand ranks of people, and they cry "A sail!"

CASSIO. My hopes do shape him for° the governor.   *make him into*

                                                      [*A shot.*]

2 GENTLEMAN. They do discharge their shot of courtesy;[2]   55
   Our friends at least.

CASSIO.   I pray you sir, go forth
   And give us truth who 'tis that is arrived.

2 GENTLEMAN. I shall.

                                    Exit [*2 Gentleman*].

MONTANO. But good lieutenant, is your general wived?°   *married*

CASSIO. Most fortunately; he hath achieved[3] a maid   60
   That paragons° description and wild fame,   *surpasses*
   One that excels the quirks of blazoning pens[4]
   And in th'essential vesture of creation
   Does tire the ingener.[5]

Enter [*2*] *Gentleman.*

                     How now? Who has put in?

2 GENTLEMAN. 'Tis one Iago, ancient to the general.   65

CASSIO. He's had most favorable and happy speed.
   Tempests themselves, high seas and howling winds,
   The guttered° rocks and congregated sands,[6]   *furrowed*
   Traitors ensteeped° to enclog the guiltless keel,   *immersed*
   As having sense of beauty, do omit   70
   Their mortal° natures, letting go safely by   *neglect their deadly*
   The divine Desdemona.

MONTANO.   What is she?

CASSIO. She that I spake of, our great captain's captain,

---

1   My hopes, not so exaggerated that they are worthless, are for Othello's safe
arrival.
2   Fire a cannon salute in welcome.
3   "To acquire …, esp. through effort, skill, or courage; to gain, win" (*OED v.* 3a).
4   Clever conceits of love poetry.
5   Her natural, unadorned self is so beautiful that any attempt to capture it in
verse would exhaust even the most ingenious poet.
6   "Sandbanks" (Honigmann).

Left in the conduct of[1] the bold Iago,
75   Whose footing here anticipates our thoughts
     A sennight's speed.[2] Great Jove, Othello guard,
     And swell his sail with thine own powerful breath
     That he may bless this bay with his tall ship,
     Make love's quick pants in Desdemona's arms,
80   Give renewed fire to our extincted° spirits   *extinguished*
     And bring all Cyprus comfort—

Enter Desdemona, Iago, Roderigo, and Emilia.
                                   Oh, behold,
     The riches of the ship° is come on shore!   *i.e., Desdemona*
     You men of Cyprus, let her have your knees.°   *i.e., bow to her*
     Hail to thee, lady, and the grace of heaven,
85   Before, behind thee, and on every hand
     Enwheel° thee round.   *encircle*
DESDEMONA.   I thank you, valiant Cassio.
     What tidings can you tell me of my lord?
CASSIO. He is not yet arrived, nor know I aught
     But that he's well and will be shortly here.
90   DESDEMONA. Oh, but I fear—how lost you company?
CASSIO. The great contention of the sea and skies
     Parted our fellowship.
VOICES WITHIN. A sail! A sail!
CASSIO.   But hark, a sail.
                                             [*A shot.*]
     2 GENTLEMAN. They give this greeting[3] to the citadel;°   *fortress*
     This likewise is a friend.
CASSIO.   See for the news.
95   Good ancient, you are welcome. Welcome, mistress.
                                        [*He kisses Emilia.*]
     Let it not gall° your patience, good Iago,   *vex*
     That I extend my manners.[4] 'Tis my breeding

---

1 "To be escorted by" (Neill).
2 Arrival occurs a week earlier than we anticipated.
3 Presumably another *shot of courtesy* (line 55, TLN 814–15) is heard here and
understood as an announcement of the ship's arrival in port.
4 "Take such unusual freedoms in my behaviour" (Neill). This is presumably a
reference to Cassio having kissed Emilia.

That gives me this bold show of courtesy.

IAGO. Sir, would she give you so much of her lips
 As of her tongue she oft bestows on me,   100
 You'd have enough.

DESDEMONA.   Alas, she has no speech![1]

IAGO. In faith, too much;
 I find it still when I have leave° to sleep.   *permission*
 Marry, before your ladyship,° I grant,   *in your ladyship's presence*
 She puts her tongue a little in her heart°   *i.e., stops talking*   105
 And chides with thinking.°   *scolds me with her thoughts*

EMILIA. You have little cause to say so.

IAGO. Come on, come on! You are pictures out of doors, bells in your
 parlors,[2] wildcats in your kitchens, saints in your injuries, devils
 being offended, players in your housewifery,[3] and housewives[4]   110
 in your beds.

DESDEMONA. Oh, fie upon thee, slanderer!

IAGO. Nay, it is true, or else I am a Turk.[5]
 You rise to play and go to bed to work.[6]

EMILIA. You shall not write my praise.

IAGO.   No, let me not.   115

DESDEMONA. What wouldst write of me, if thou shouldst
  praise me?

IAGO. Oh, gentle lady, do not put me to't,
 For I am nothing if not critical.

DESDEMONA. Come on, assay[7]—there's one gone to the harbor?

IAGO. Ay, madam.   120

DESDEMONA. I am not merry, but I do beguile°   *divert attention from*
 The thing I am by seeming otherwise.
 Come, how wouldst thou praise me?

---

1 Either "she's not the chatterbox you make her out to be" or "she's speechless in
the face of your accusations and insinuations."

2 You (i.e., women) are attractive and quiet when you are in public, but raucous
when you are at home.

3 Uninterested in your domestic tasks.

4 Married women with responsibility for managing their households; sexually
loose women.

5 "Anyone having qualities historically attributed to Turks; a cruel, rigorous, or
tyrannical person; any one behaving barbarically or savagely" (*OED n.* 4).

6 I.e., women are interested only in sex.

7 Try.

IAGO. I am about it, but indeed my invention comes from my pate
125   as birdlime does from frieze;[1] it plucks out brains and all. But my
muse labors, and thus she is delivered:
    If she be fair[2] and wise, fairness and wit;°   *cleverness*
    The one's for use, the other useth it.[3]

DESDEMONA. Well praised! How if she be black[4] and witty?
130   IAGO. *If she be black and thereto have a wit,*
    She'll find a white that shall her blackness hit.[5]

DESDEMONA. Worse and worse.

EMILIA.   How if fair and foolish?

IAGO. *She never yet was foolish that was fair,*
    For even her folly[6] helped her to an heir.[7]

135   DESDEMONA. These are old fond[8] paradoxes to make fools laugh
i'th'alehouse. What miserable praise hast thou for her that's foul
and foolish?

IAGO. *There's none so foul and foolish thereunto,*
    But does foul pranks[9] which fair and wise ones do.

140   DESDEMONA. O heavy ignorance! Thou praisest the worst best. But
what praise couldst thou bestow on a deserving woman indeed?
One that in the authority of her merit did justly put on the vouch
of very malice itself.[10]

IAGO. *She that was ever fair and never proud,*
145   *Had tongue at will,[11] and yet was never loud,*

---

1 Iago seems to be comparing the process of thinking up praise for Desdemona
to the challenge of removing a sticky substance from cloth. Wild birds were sometimes trapped using fabric spread with birdlime, a gummy matter that prevented
them from flying away.

2 Blonde and light-skinned; beautiful.

3 I.e., beauty can be a useful asset for an intelligent woman.

4 Dark-haired, dark-skinned; but see also 1.3.290, TLN 643, and note.

5 Iago develops an elaborate conceit comparing sexual intercourse and archery:
while *white* and *black* refer to the central rings of an archery target, *white* also
suggests a pun on *wight* = man (see also line 154, TLN 933), *black* is slang for vagina,
and *hit* figures sexual penetration (Partridge 75, 127). See also extended note at
3.4.120, TLN 2284.

6 Foolishness; sexual promiscuity.

7 Either "assisted her in securing a rich husband" or "resulted in her giving birth
to a child."

8 Silly.

9 Sexual tricks.

10 Was so virtuous that she could withstand the worst possible testimony against
her.

11 I.e., always knew the right thing to say.

Never lacked gold, and yet went never gay,[1]
Fled from her wish, and yet said "now I may."
She that being angered, her revenge being nigh,
Bade her wrong stay and her displeasure fly.
She that in wisdom never was so frail   150
To change the cod's head for the salmon's tail.[2]
She that could think, and ne'er disclose her mind,
See suitors following, and not look behind.
She was a wight,° *if ever such wights were—*   person; man
DESDEMONA. To do what?   155
IAGO. *To suckle fools and chronicle small beer.*[3]
DESDEMONA. O most lame and impotent[4] conclusion! Do not learn
   of him Emilia, though he be thy husband. How say you, Cassio,
   is he not a most profane and liberal[5] counselor?
CASSIO. He speaks home,[6] madam. You may relish him more in the   160
   soldier than in the scholar.[7]

                        [*Cassio takes Desdemona by the hand.*]
IAGO. [*Aside*][8] He takes her by the palm. Ay, well said, whisper!
   With as little a web as this will I ensnare as great a fly as Cassio.
   Ay, smile upon her, do! I will gyve[9] thee in thine own courtship.[10]
   You say true; 'tis so indeed. If such tricks as these strip you out   165
   of your lieutenantry, it had been better you had not kissed your
   three fingers so oft, which now again you are most apt to play
   the sir[11] in. Very good! Well kissed and excellent courtesy! 'Tis

---

1   Dressed in a showy way.
2   Presumably an image of exchanging something of worth for something of
lesser value. Iago achieves a notable density of sexual double-entendres in this
line: *cod* = scrotum, *head* = penis, *tail* = genitals (usually female), and, more generally, *fish* = prostitute.
3   Iago's apparent praise of virtuous women culminates in this dismissive assertion that they are good only for nursing babies and keeping track of trivial matters.
4   Weak; ineffective.
5   "Unrestrained by prudence or decorum" (*OED adj.* 3a).
6   To the point.
7   Appreciate him better as a man of action than as a man of words.
8   Iago's aside is presumably heard only by the audience. He switches back and
forth from discussing Cassio in the third person to pretending to address him
directly, offering both commentary on and encouragement of behavior he knows
will support his plan to undo the lieutenant.
9   Restrain; trap.
10 Courtly behavior.
11 Put on the airs of a gentleman.

so indeed. Yet again, your fingers to your lips? Would they were
170　clysterpipes[1] for your sake.

　　　　　　　　　　　　　　　　　　　　　　[*Trumpet within.*]

　　　[*Aloud*] The Moor. I know his trumpet.
CASSIO. 'Tis truly so.
DESDEMONA. Let's meet him and receive him.
CASSIO. Lo, where he comes.

Enter Othello and attendants.
OTHELLO. O my fair warrior!
175　DESDEMONA.　　　　　　　　　My dear Othello.
OTHELLO. It gives me wonder great as my content
　　To see you here before me. O my soul's joy!
　　If after every tempest come such calms,
　　May the winds blow till they have wakened death,
180　And let the laboring bark climb hills of seas
　　Olympus-high[2] and duck again as low
　　As hell's from heaven. If it were now to die,
　　'Twere now to be most happy, for I fear
　　My soul hath her content so absolute
185　That not another comfort like to this
　　Succeeds in unknown fate.[3]
DESDEMONA.　　　　　　　　The heavens forbid
　　But that our loves and comforts should increase
　　Even as our days do grow.[4]
OTHELLO.　　　　　　　　Amen to that, sweet powers.
　　I cannot speak enough of this content;
190　It stops me here; it is too much of joy.
　　And this, and this—

　　　　　　　　　　　　　　　　　　　　　　[*They kiss.*]

　　　　　　　—the greatest discords be
　　That ere our hearts shall make.

1　Tubes for administering enemas.
2　I.e., very high. Mount Olympus is home to the greater gods and goddesses of
Greek mythology.
3　Will follow in the unpredictable but predetermined future.
4　Both "our time together increases" and "as we get older."

2.1.191:   "THE GREATEST DISCORDS"
             (TLN 979)

Othello employs a common musical metaphor when he puns on the
Latin root of *discord* (*cor* = heart) and imagines his heartstrings joining
Desdemona's in song. Iago further develops the conceit in his sneering
aside, "Oh, you are well tuned now! But I'll set down the pegs that make
this music." Literally, his reference is to putting a stringed instrument
of out of tune by loosening its tuning pegs, though figuratively he refers
to his plan to generate disharmony between Othello and Desdemona.
In his Oxford edition of the play, Michael Neill suggests that Iago may
also be punning on the bawdy use of "music" as a term for sexual intercourse and of "peg" as a word for penis. On this reading he would be
threatening Othello not simply with discord but also with emasculation.
To read more about the ideas of harmony and discord in *Othello* and in
the early-modern period, visit the "Life & Times" section of the Internet
Shakespeare Editions website and click on Literature: Music.

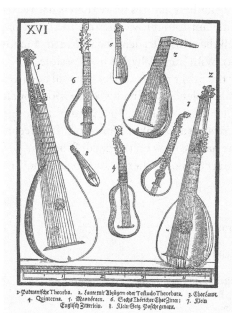

Plate XVI from Michael Praetorius (1571–1621), *Syntagma Musicum Band II, De
Organographia* (Wolfenbüttel, 1618). Wikimedia Commons, https://commons.
wikimedia.org.

IAGO. [*Aside*] Oh, you are well tuned now! But I'll set down the pegs
   that make this music, as honest as I am.
195 OTHELLO. Come, let us to the castle.
   News, friends: our wars are done; the Turks are drowned.
   How does my old acquaintance° of this isle?   *friends*
   Honey, you shall be well desired° in Cyprus;   *greatly sought after*
   I have found great love amongst them. O my sweet,
200 I prattle out of fashion° and I dote   *i.e., in an inappropriate way*
   In mine own comforts. I prithee, good Iago,
   Go to the bay and disembark my coffers.°   *unload my trunks*
   Bring thou the master° to the citadel;   *captain of a ship*
   He is a good one, and his worthiness
205 Does challenge° much respect.—Come, Desdemona,   *demands*
   Once more well met at Cyprus.
                       Exeunt [all but Iago and Roderigo].
IAGO. Do thou meet me presently at the harbor. Come thither, if
   thou be'st valiant—as they say base[1] men being in love have then
   a nobility in their natures more than is native to them—list me:[2]
210 the lieutenant tonight watches on the court of guard.[3] First, I
   must tell thee this: Desdemona is directly[4] in love with him.
RODERIGO. With him? Why, 'tis not possible.
IAGO. Lay thy finger thus,[5] and let thy soul be instructed. Mark me
   with what violence she first loved the Moor, but for bragging and
215 telling her fantastical lies. To love him still for prating?[6] Let not
   thy discreet[7] heart think it. Her eye must be fed. And what delight
   shall she have to look on the devil? When the blood is made dull[8]
   with the act of sport,[9] there should be a game[10] to enflame it, and,

---

1 Low-born; unworthy.
2 Listen to me.
3 "Is on guard duty."
4 Plainly.
5 Put a finger to your lips (in the classic gesture for silence).
6 Speaking foolishly or boastfully.
7 Discerning.
8 Sexual appetite is dampened.
9 Sexual intercourse.
10 Could simply mean "fun," but, given Iago's apparent obsession with
Desdemona's sexuality, more likely means "sexual intrigue."

to give satiety[1] a fresh appetite, loveliness in favor,[2] sympathy in
years,[3] manners, and beauties—all which the Moor is defective   220
in. Now, for want of these required conveniences her delicate ten-
derness will find itself abused,[4] begin to heave the gorge,[5] disrel-
ish[6] and abhor the Moor. Very nature will instruct her in it and
compel her to some second choice. Now sir, this granted (as it
is a most pregnant and unforced[7] position) who stands so emi-   225
nent in the degree of this fortune[8] as Cassio does—a knave very
voluble,[9] no further conscionable[10] than in putting on the mere
form of civil and humane seeming for the better compass[11] of his
salt[12] and most hidden loose affection? Why none, why none! A
slipper and subtle[13] knave, a finder of occasion[14] that has an eye can 230
stamp[15] and counterfeit advantages though true advantage never
present itself. A devilish knave! Besides, the knave is handsome,
young, and hath all those requisites in him that folly and green[16]
minds look after—a pestilent complete[17] knave, and the woman
hath found him already.[18]   235
RODERIGO. I cannot believe that in her; she's full of most blessed
condition.[19]

---

1   Satiation.
2   Beauty.
3   Similarity in age.
4   Deceived; mistaken.
5   Literally, retch or vomit; figuratively, to experience extreme disgust.
6   Dislike.
7   Obvious and natural.
8   Is so well placed to benefit from this opportunity.
9   Inconstant, changeable; with a capacity for fluent speech, glib.
10 Conscientious.
11 Fulfillment.
12 Sexual desire.
13 Deceitful and sly.
14 Opportunist.
15 Manufacture. The image here is of coin making. Iago extends the conceit when
he characterizes Cassio as a counterfeiter.
16 Young and inexperienced.
17 Consummate.
18 The line is unclear, but Iago seems to imply that Desdemona has had sex with
Cassio.
19 Disposition.

IAGO. Blessed fig's-end![1] The wine she drinks is made of grapes. If she had been blessed, she would never have loved the Moor.

240 Blessed pudding![2] Didst thou not see her paddle[3] with the palm of his hand? Didst not mark that?

RODERIGO. Yes, that I did; but that was but courtesy.

IAGO. Lechery, by this hand—an index[4] and obscure prologue to the history[5] of lust and foul thoughts. They met so near with their

---

1 A rude oath.
2 Sausage; slang for penis.
3 Toy with; fondle.
4 Table of contents.
5 Story.

2.1.243: "BY THIS HAND—AN INDEX AND OBSCURE PROLOGUE" (TLN 1039–40)

Iago puns on the pointing index finger, called a manicule, used in early modern books to draw a reader's attention to a particular passage of text, an image reinforced by his use of the phrase "by this hand." References to hands abound throughout *Othello*, and they are associated variously with physical violence, marriage, reconciliation, humoral theory (see extended note, p. 122), and murder.

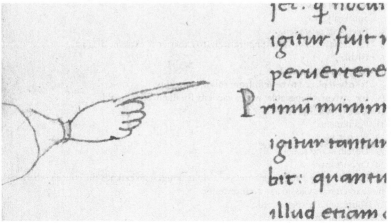

Manicule detail from Cicero, *De Officiis*, 1465. Library Open Repository, University of Tasmania.

lips that their breaths embraced together. Villainous thoughts, 245
Roderigo, when these mutualities[1] so marshal[2] the way, hard
at hand comes the master and main exercise, th'incorporate[3]
conclusion—pish![4] But sir, be you ruled by me. I have brought
you from Venice. Watch you[5] tonight; for the command, I'll lay't
upon you.[6] Cassio knows you not; I'll not be far from you. Do 250
you find some occasion to anger Cassio, either by speaking too
loud, or tainting[7] his discipline, or from what other course you
please which the time shall more favorably minister.

RODERIGO. Well.

IAGO. Sir, he's rash and very sudden in choler,[8] and haply[9] may strike 255
at you. Provoke him that he may, for even out of that will I cause
these of Cyprus to mutiny, whose qualification shall come into
no true taste[10] again but by the displanting[11] of Cassio. So shall
you have a shorter journey to your desires by the means I shall
then have to prefer[12] them, and the impediment most profitably 260
removed without the which there were no expectation of our
prosperity.

RODERIGO. I will do this, if you can bring it to any opportunity.

IAGO. I warrant thee.[13] Meet me by and by at the citadel. I must fetch
his necessaries[14] ashore. Farewell. 265

RODERIGO. Adieu.

Exit [Roderigo].

---

1 Shared intimacies.
2 Guide.
3 Bodily; whole.
4 An interjection expressing contempt or disgust.
5 Serve as a member of the watch.
6 Iago's reassurance to Roderigo seems almost deliberately vague here. He could mean "I will arrange for you to be in charge," or, as Honigmann suggests, "As for taking the lead (in our joint action), I'll leave it to you." Neill offers "I'll give you the orders."
7 Tarnishing.
8 Either "quick to anger" or "impetuous when angry."
9 Perhaps.
10 True nature will not be restored.
11 Supplanting.
12 Promote.
13 I promise.
14 I.e., Othello's possessions.

Humoralism, a theory of human psychophysiology developed by classical physicians that prevailed until the advent of modern medicine, held that a person's health and disposition were determined by a balance of four bodily fluids: blood, phlegm, yellow bile, and black bile. Diseases and disabilities were believed to result from an excess or a deficiency of one or more of these four humors, each of which was identified with a particular temperament. Choler, a distemper resulting from an excess of yellow bile, was said to produce irascibility. For more about choler and other humors, visit the "Life & Times" section of the Internet Shakespeare Editions website and click on Ideas: Ordering nature.

Virgilius Solis, the Elder (1514–62), *Colericus:2*. US National Library of Medicine.

IAGO. That Cassio loves her, I do well believ't;
  That she loves him, 'tis apt and of great credit.°   *entirely plausible*
  The Moor, howbeit that° I endure him not,   *although*
  Is of a constant, loving, noble nature,   270
  And I dare think he'll prove to Desdemona
  A most dear husband. Now I do love her too,
  Not out of absolute lust (though peradventure°   *as it happens*
  I stand accountant° for as great a sin),   *am accountable*
  But partly led to diet° my revenge,   *feed* 275
  For that I do suspect the lusty Moor
  Hath leaped into my seat[1]—the thought whereof
  Doth like a poisonous mineral gnaw my inwards,°   *entrails*
  And nothing can or shall content my soul
  Till I am evened with him, wife for wife;   280
  Or failing so, yet that I put the Moor
  At least into a jealousy so strong
  That judgment cannot cure; which thing to do,
  If this poor trash of Venice,[2] whom I trace
  For his quick hunting,[3] stand the putting on,[4]   285
  I'll have our Michael Cassio on the hip,°   *at a disadvantage*
  Abuse° him to the Moor in the right garb[5]   *malign*
  (For I fear Cassio with my nightcap too),[6]
  Make the Moor thank me, love me, and reward me
  for making him egregiously an ass   290
  And practicing upon[7] his peace and quiet
  Even to madness. 'Tis here, but yet confused;
  Knavery's plain face is never seen till used.

                                 Exit [Iago].

---

1 I.e., had sex with my wife.
2 I.e., Roderigo; *trash* = disreputable or worthless person.
3 Track in order to speed up his chase (of Desdemona, who gets imagined in
Iago's language as Roderigo's prey).
4 Follows through at my incitement.
5 I.e., appropriate manner.
6 I worry that Cassio may have slept with my wife too.
7 Manipulating, with hints of possible magical intervention.

[2.2]

Enter Othello's Herald with a proclamation.

HERALD. [*Reading*] It is Othello's pleasure, our noble and valiant
general, that upon certain tidings now arrived importing[1] the
mere perdition[2] of the Turkish fleet, every man put himself into
triumph:[3] some to dance, some to make bonfires, each man to
5   what sport and revels his addition[4] leads him. For besides these
beneficial news, it is the celebration of his nuptial.[5] So much was
his pleasure should be proclaimed. All offices[6] are open and there
is full liberty of feasting from this present hour of five till the bell
have tolled eleven. Heaven bless the isle of Cyprus and our noble
10   general Othello.

Exit [Herald].

[2.3]

Enter Othello, Desdemona, Cassio, and attendants.

OTHELLO. Good Michael, look you to[7] the guard tonight.
Let's teach ourselves that honorable stop°   *restraint*
Not to outsport discretion.[8]

CASSIO. Iago hath direction what to do;
5   But notwithstanding, with my personal eye
Will I look to't.

OTHELLO.   Iago is most honest.
Michael, goodnight. Tomorrow with your earliest[9]
Let me have speech with you. [*To Desdemona*] Come, my
dear love,
The purchase made, the fruits are to ensue;

---

1 Concerning.
2 Complete destruction.
3 I.e., prepare to celebrate.
4 Rank.
5 Wedding.
6 Parts of a domestic space associated with service, including kitchens, pantries,
and cellars.
7 Keep an eye on.
8 Party beyond the bounds of good judgment.
9 At your earliest convenience.

That profit's yet to come 'tween me and you.[1]   10
Goodnight.

        [Exeunt all but Cassio.]

Enter Iago.

CASSIO. Welcome, Iago. We must to the watch.

IAGO. Not this hour, lieutenant; 'tis not yet ten o'th'clock. Our general cast[2] us thus early for the love of his Desdemona, who let us not therefore blame; he hath not yet made wanton the night[3] with 15 her, and she is sport for Jove.[4]

CASSIO. She's a most exquisite lady.

IAGO. And I'll warrant her full of game.[5]

CASSIO. Indeed she's a most fresh and delicate creature.

IAGO. What an eye she has! Methinks it sounds a parley to 20 provocation.[6]

CASSIO. An inviting eye—and yet methinks right modest.

IAGO. And when she speaks, is it not an alarum[7] to love?

CASSIO. She is indeed perfection.

IAGO. Well, happiness to their sheets. Come, lieutenant, I have a 25 stoup[8] of wine and here without are a brace[9] of Cyprus gallants that would fain have a measure[10] to the health of black Othello.

CASSIO. Not tonight, good Iago. I have very poor and unhappy brains for drinking. I could well wish courtesy would invent some other custom of entertainment. 30

IAGO. Oh, they are our friends—but one cup; I'll drink for you.

---

1   These lines are sometimes read as implying that Othello's marriage to Desdemona has yet to be consummated.

2   Dismissed.

3   Shared a night of sexual pleasure.

4   Jupiter, highest deity in Roman mythology and notorious for sexual escapades with mortal women.

5   Sexual play. Throughout this exchange about Desdemona, Iago works to interject a tone of lewdness while Cassio maintains a respectful, even slightly pompous, decorum.

6   Literally, signals a willingness to cease hostilities in favor of talk; figuratively, announces sexual availability in response to a come-on.

7   Call to arms.

8   Cup.

9   Pair.

10 Be glad to drink.

CASSIO. I have drunk but one cup tonight, and that was craftily
qualified[1] too, and behold what innovation it makes here.[2] I am
infortunate in the infirmity and dare not task my weakness with
35   any more.
IAGO. What, man? 'Tis a night of revels; the gallants desire it.
CASSIO. Where are they?
IAGO. Here at the door. I pray you call them in.
CASSIO. I'll do't, but it dislikes[3] me.

                                                                     Exit [Cassio].

40   IAGO. If I can fasten but one cup upon him[4]
With that which he hath drunk tonight already,
He'll be as full of quarrel and offense
As my young mistress's dog. Now, my sick[5] fool Roderigo,
Whom love hath turned almost the wrong side out,
45   To Desdemona hath tonight caroused[6]
Potations[7] pottle-deep;[8] and he's to watch.
Three else° of Cyprus—noble, swelling° spirits   *others / arrogant*
That hold their honors in a wary distance,[9]
The very elements of this warlike isle[10]—
50   Have I tonight flustered with flowing cups,
And they watch too. Now 'mongst this flock of drunkards
Am I to put our Cassio in some action
That may offend the isle. But here they come.

Enter Cassio, Montano, and Gentlemen [with wine].
If consequence do but approve my dream,°   *things go my way*
55   My boat sails freely, both with wind and stream.

---

1   Diluted.
2   This line presumably operates as a cue for Cassio to demonstrate some sign of
the effect that the alcohol has had on him. Perhaps he struggles to stand steady or
to walk in a straight line.
3   Displeases.
4   Induce him to accept just a single tankard.
5   I.e., lovesick.
6   Has toasted Desdemona repeatedly tonight (i.e., is drunk).
7   Alcoholic drinks.
8   "To the bottom of a half-gallon tankard" (Honigmann).
9   Carefully protect their reputations (and so by implication will defend them
vigorously).
10 Just the sort of men who make Cyprus such a warlike place.

CASSIO. 'Fore God, they have given me a rouse[1] already.

MONTANO. Good faith, a little one—not past a pint, as I am a soldier.

IAGO. Some wine, ho!

    [Singing] And let me the cannikin[2] clink, clink,
    And let me the cannikin clink.   60
    A soldier's a man; Oh, man's life's but a span,[3]
    Why then let a soldier drink.

Some wine, boys!

CASSIO. 'Fore God, an excellent song!

IAGO. I learned it in England, where indeed they are most potent   65
in potting.[4] Your Dane, your German, and your swag-bellied[5]
Hollander—drink, ho!—are nothing to your English.

CASSIO. Is your Englishman so exquisite[6] in his drinking?

IAGO. Why, he drinks you with facility your Dane dead drunk. He
sweats not to overthrow your Almain.[7] He gives your Hollander   70
a vomit ere the next pottle can be filled.

CASSIO. To the health of our general!

MONTANO. I am for it, lieutenant, and I'll do you justice.

IAGO. O sweet England!

    [Singing] King Stephen was and-a worthy peer,   75
    His breeches cost him but a crown;
    He held them sixpence all too dear,
    With that he called the tailor lown.[8]
    He was a wight of high renown,
    And thou art but of low degree;   80
    'Tis pride that pulls the country down,
    And take thy old cloak about thee.

Some wine, ho!

CASSIO. 'Fore God, this is a more exquisite song than the other.

IAGO. Will you hear't again?   85

---

1 Large or full cup of wine.
2 Small can or cup.
3 Short for *handspan*; i.e., short.
4 Very accomplished at heavy drinking.
5 Beer-bellied.
6 Accomplished; refined.
7 German (from the Old French), with a pun on "aleman."
8 "Alternative spelling of the more common *loon* = idler, rogue, base fellow" (Neill).

CASSIO. No, for I hold him to be unworthy of his place that does those things. Well, God's above all, and there be souls must be saved, and there be souls must not be saved.

IAGO. It's true, good lieutenant.

90 CASSIO. For mine own part—no offense to the general nor any man of quality—I hope to be saved.

IAGO. And so do I too, lieutenant.

CASSIO. Ay—but by your leave, not before me. The lieutenant is to be saved before the ancient. Let's have no more of this. Let's to our

95 affairs. God forgive us our sins. Gentlemen, let's look to our business. Do not think, gentlemen, I am drunk. This is my ancient, this is my right hand and this is my left. I am not drunk now. I can stand well enough, and I speak well enough.

GENTLEMAN. Excellent well.

100 CASSIO. Why, very well then—you must not think, then, that I am drunk.

Exit [*Cassio*].

MONTANO. To th'platform,[1] masters; come, let's set the watch.

IAGO. You see this fellow that is gone before:
He's a soldier fit to stand by Caesar

105 And give direction. And do but see his vice:
'Tis to his virtue a just equinox,[2]
The one as long as th'other. 'Tis pity of him;
I fear the trust Othello puts him in
On some odd time of his infirmity
Will shake this island.

110 MONTANO.   But is he often thus?

IAGO. 'Tis evermore° his prologue to his sleep.   *always*
He'll watch the horologe° a double set[3]   *clock*
If drink rock not his cradle.

MONTANO.   It were well
The general were put in mind° of it;   *made aware*

115 Perhaps he sees it not, or his good nature

---

1   Ramparts.
2   Literally, one of the two occasions annually when day and night are of equal length; figuratively, equal counterpart.
3   Two complete rounds; i.e., all day (since twice round the 12-hour clock is 24 hours).

Prizes the virtue that appears in Cassio
And looks not on his evils. Is not this true?

Enter Roderigo.

IAGO. [*Aside to Roderigo*] How now, Roderigo?
 I pray you, after the lieutenant go.

                                           [*Exit Roderigo.*]

MONTANO. And 'tis great pity that the noble Moor   120
 Should hazard such a place° as his own second[1]   *position*
 With one of an ingraft[2] infirmity.
 It were an honest action to say so
 To the Moor.

IAGO.   Not I, for this fair island;
 I do love Cassio well, and would do much   125
 To cure him of this evil—
 (*Voices within*) *Help! Help!*

IAGO.   —but hark, what noise?

Enter Cassio pursuing Roderigo.

CASSIO. Zounds, you rogue! You rascal!
MONTANO. What's the matter, lieutenant?
CASSIO. A knave teach me my duty? I'll beat the knave into a twig-
 gen bottle.[3]   130
RODERIGO. Beat me?
CASSIO. Dost thou prate,° rogue?   *speak foolishly or boastfully*
MONTANO. Nay, good lieutenant! Pray, sir, hold your hand.°   *stop*
CASSIO. Let me go, sir, or I'll knock you o'er the mazard.[4]
MONTANO. Come, come, you're drunk.   135
CASSIO. Drunk?

                                         [*They fight.*]

IAGO. [*Aside to Roderigo*] Away, I say! Go out and cry a mutiny.

                                      [*Exit Roderigo.*]

---

1 Deputy.
2 "Engrafted, ingrained" (Neill).
.3 Literally, wicker covered bottle; i.e., until his back is scored like the pattern of
woven wicker.
4 Cup or other drinking vessel; slang for head.

Nay, good lieutenant. God's will, gentlemen!
Help, ho! Lieutenant! Sir Montano! Sir!
140   Help, masters! Here's a goodly watch indeed.

                                              [A bell rings.]

Who's that which rings the bell? Diablo, ho!
The town will rise. God's will, lieutenant, hold.
You'll be ashamed forever.

Enter Othello and attendants [with weapons].
OTHELLO. What is the matter here?
145 MONTANO. Zounds, I bleed still! I am hurt to th'death.

                                      [Lunging at Cassio.]

He dies!
OTHELLO.   Hold, for your lives![1]
IAGO. Hold, ho! Lieutenant, Sir Montano, gentlemen!
Have you forgot all place of sense and duty?
Hold. The general speaks to you—hold, for shame.
150 OTHELLO. Why, how now, ho? From whence ariseth this?
Are we turned Turks[2] and to ourselves do that
Which heaven hath forbid the Ottomites?[3]
For Christian shame, put by this barbarous brawl.
He that stirs next to carve for his own rage[4]
155 Holds his soul light;[5] he dies upon his motion.[6]
Silence that dreadful bell; it frights the isle
From her propriety. What is the matter, masters?
Honest Iago, that looks dead with grieving,
Speak. Who began this? On thy love, I charge° thee.   command
160 IAGO. I do not know. Friends all, but now, even now,
In quarter and in terms[7] like bride and groom

---

1   Stop fighting, if you know what's good for you.
2   Literally, "converted to Muslim Turks"; colloquially, "become treacherous attackers" (thanks to pervasive cultural stereotypes of Non-Christian "infidels" as disloyal and violent); i.e., become our own worst enemy.
3   Destroy ourselves as God has prevented the Turkish fleet from destroying us (by raising a storm).
4   "Feed his own anger" (Pechter).
5   Values his soul very little.
6   The minute he moves.
7   In action and in words.

Divesting them° for bed; and then, but now,   *undressing*
As if some planet had unwitted° men,   *driven mad*
Swords out and tilting° one at other's breasts   *fighting*
In opposition bloody. I cannot speak   165
Any beginning to this peevish odds.¹
And would in action glorious I had lost
Those legs that brought me to a part of it.
OTHELLO. How comes it, Michael, you are thus forgot?
CASSIO. I pray you pardon me; I cannot speak.   170
OTHELLO. Worthy Montano, you were wont to be² civil;
The gravity and stillness of your youth
The world hath noted, and your name is great
In mouths of wisest censure.³ What's the matter
That you unlace⁴ your reputation thus,   175
And spend your rich opinion for the name
Of a nightbrawler? Give me answer to it.
MONTANO. Worthy Othello, I am hurt to danger.°   *critically injured*
Your officer Iago can inform you—
While I spare⁵ speech, which something now offends me⁶—   180
Of all that I do know; nor know I aught
By me that's said or done amiss this night,
Unless self-charity⁷ be sometimes a vice,
And to defend ourselves it be a sin
When violence assails us.
OTHELLO.   Now, by heaven,   185
My blood begins my safer guides to rule,
And passion, having my best judgment collied,° *begrimed; blackened*
Assays° to lead the way. Zounds, if I stir,   *tries*
Or do but lift this arm, the best of you
Shall sink in my rebuke. Give me to know   190

---

1 Explain how this foolish conflict started.
2 Have always been.
3 Reputation is respected by those of good judgment.
4 Loosen the purse strings of (and thus, risk devaluing). Othello figures
Montano's reputation as currency that the younger man is squandering with his
reckless behavior.
5 Refrain from.
6 Is causing me some pain.
7 Looking out for oneself.

Many works on the emotions were published during the sixteenth and seventeenth centuries. Treatises in fields as disparate as art, medicine, philosophy, political theory, and religious instruction offered accounts of such passions as anger and jealousy, contributing to the general conviction that human emotions were valuable, if volatile, constituents of selfhood. See, for instance, Appendices B3–B6.

Frontispiece to Jean-François Senault, *The Use of Passions*, trans. Henry, Earl of Monmouth (London: Printed for J.L. and Humphrey Moseley, 1649). Wellcome Library, London.

How this foul rout° began, who set it on,   *uproar*
And he that is approved in° this offense,   *proved guilty of*
Though he had twinned with me both at a birth,
Shall lose me. What, in a town of war[1]
Yet wild, the people's hearts brimful of fear,   195
To manage private and domestic quarrel
In night and on the court and guard of safety?[2]
'Tis monstrous! Iago, who began't?
MONTANO. If, partially affined or leagued in office,[3]
  Thou dost deliver more or less than truth,   200
  Thou art no soldier.
IAGO.   Touch me not so near.
  I had rather have this tongue cut from my mouth
  Than it should do offense to Michael Cassio;
  Yet I persuade myself to speak the truth
  Shall nothing wrong him. This it is, general: 205
  Montano and myself being in speech,
  There comes a fellow crying out for help,
  And Cassio following with determined sword
  To execute upon[4] him. Sir, this gentleman°   *i.e., Montano*
  Steps in to Cassio and entreats his pause;°   *begs him to stop* 210
  Myself the crying fellow did pursue,
  Lest by his clamor, as it so fell out,°   *happened*
  The town might fall in fright. He, swift of foot,
  Outran my purpose, and I returned then, rather
  For that I heard the clink and fall of swords,   215
  And Cassio high in oath,° which till tonight   *swearing loudly*
  I ne'er might say before. When I came back—
  For this was brief—I found them close together
  At blow and thrust, even as again they were
  When you yourself did part them.   220
  More of this matter cannot I report,
  But men are men; the best sometimes forget.
  Though Cassio did some little wrong to him,

---

1 Fortified town housing troops.
2 At the very place and by the very people charged with keeping the citadel safe.
3 Biased (in favor of Cassio) because of your personal relationship or your military roles.
4 Attack. Since *execute* can also mean "put to death," Iago implies a serious, even murderous, attack.

As men in rage strike those that wish them best,
225 Yet surely Cassio, I believe, received
From him that fled some strange indignity
Which patience could not pass.°   *let go by*
OTHELLO.   I know, Iago,
Thy honesty and love doth mince° this matter,   *make light of*
Making it light to Cassio.[1]—Cassio, I love thee,
230 But never more be officer of mine.

Enter Desdemona, attended.
Look if my gentle love be not raised up.
I'll make thee an example.
DESDEMONA. What is the matter, dear?
OTHELLO.   All's well, sweeting.
Come away to bed. [*To Montano*] Sir, for your hurts
235 Myself will be your surgeon.° Lead him off.   *doctor*
                              [*Montano is led off.*]
Iago, look with care about the town,
And silence those whom this vile brawl distracted.
Come, Desdemona; 'tis the soldier's life
To have their balmy[2] slumbers waked with strife.
                    Exeunt [*Othello, Desdemona, and attendants*].
240 IAGO. What, are you hurt, lieutenant?
CASSIO. Ay, past all surgery.°   *beyond medical help*
IAGO. Marry, God forbid.
CASSIO. Reputation, reputation, reputation! Oh, I have lost my
    reputation! I have lost the immortal part of myself, and what
245 remains is bestial. My reputation, Iago, my reputation.
IAGO. As I am an honest man, I had thought you had received some
    bodily wound; there is more sense[3] in that than in reputation.
    Reputation is an idle and most false imposition, oft got without
    merit and lost without deserving. You have lost no reputation at
250 all unless you repute yourself such a loser. What, man, there are
    more ways to recover the general again.[4] You are but now cast in

---

1 De-emphasizing Cassio's role.
2 "Deliciously soft and soothing" (*OED adj.* 4).
3 Physical sensation; reason.
4 Regain the general's respect and trust.

his mood,[1] a punishment more in policy than in malice[2]—even so as one would beat his offenseless dog to affright an imperious lion.[3] Sue[4] to him again and he's yours.

CASSIO. I will rather sue to be despised than to deceive so good a   255
commander with so slight, so drunken, and so indiscreet an officer. Drunk? and speak parrot?[5] and squabble? swagger? swear? and discourse fustian[6] with one's own shadow? O thou invisible spirit of wine, if thou hast no name to be known by, let us call thee devil!   260

IAGO. What was he that you followed with your sword? What had he done to you?

CASSIO. I know not.

IAGO. Is't possible?

CASSIO. I remember a mass of things, but nothing distinctly; a   265
quarrel, but nothing wherefore.[7] O God, that men should put an enemy in their mouths to steal away their brains! that we should with joy, pleasance,[8] revel and applause transform ourselves into beasts!

IAGO. Why, but you are now well enough. How came you thus   270
recovered?

CASSIO. It hath pleased the devil drunkenness to give place to the devil wrath; one unperfectness shows me another to make me frankly despise myself.

IAGO. Come, you are too severe a moraler.[9] As the time, the place,   275
and the condition of this country stands, I could heartily wish this had not befallen; but since it is as it is, mend it for your own good.

CASSIO. I will ask him for my place again; he shall tell me I am a drunkard. Had I as many mouths as Hydra, such an answer   280
would stop[10] them all. To be now a sensible man, by and by a

---

1   Dismissed from office because of his temporary bad mood.
2   More a matter of principle than of ill will.
3   I.e., make an example of a guiltless nobody in order to establish one's authority in the eyes of someone more important.
4   Appeal.
5   Talk nonsense.
6   Speak gibberish; rant.
7   About why.
8   Willingness; pleasure.
9   Moralizer.
10 Stopper; plug up.

fool, and presently a beast—Oh, strange! Every inordinate[1] cup is unblessed, and the ingredient is a devil.

---

1   Excessive.

According to Greek mythology, the second labor of Heracles (later renamed Hercules by the Romans) was to kill the Hydra, a monstrous nine-headed sea serpent that terrorized the countryside near Lerna. The beast was particularly difficult to defeat because one of its heads was immortal and the other eight grew back when they were severed. The hero and his nephew Iolaus finally killed the Lernaean Hydra by hacking off its heads one by one and cauterizing the neck stumps with burning torches. Once the eight mortal heads had been removed, Hercules used a sword given him by Athena to chop off the immortal head and then buried it by the roadside. Finally, he sliced open the creature's body and dipped his arrow tips in the monster's venomous blood.

Hans Sebald Beham, "Hercules Slaying the Hydra" (1545). Wikimedia Commons, https://commons.wikimedia.org.

IAGO. Come, come, good wine is a good familiar[1] creature if it be
  well used; exclaim no more against it. And, good lieutenant, I   285
  think you think I love you.

ÇASSIO. I have well approved[2] it, sir—I drunk?

IAGO. You, or any man living, may be drunk at a time,[3] man. I tell
  you what you shall do: our general's wife is now the general. I
  may say so in this respect, for that he hath devoted and given   290
  up himself to the contemplation, mark, and devotement[4] of her
  parts[5] and graces. Confess yourself freely to her; importune[6] her
  help to put you in your place again. She is of so free,[7] so kind, so
  apt, so blessed a disposition she holds it a vice in her goodness
  not to do more than she is requested. This broken joint between   295
  you and her husband entreat her to splinter,[8] and, my fortunes
  against any lay[9] worth naming, this crack of your love shall grow
  stronger than it was before.

CASSIO. You advise me well.

IAGO. I protest in the sincerity of love and honest kindness.   300

CASSIO. I think it freely; and betimes in the morning I will beseech
  the virtuous Desdemona to undertake for me.[10] I am desperate
  of my fortunes if they check[11] me.

IAGO. You are in the right. Goodnight, lieutenant. I must to the
  watch.   305

CASSIO. Goodnight, honest Iago.

                                                      Exit Cassio.

IAGO. And what's he, then, that says I play the villain,
  When this advice is free I give, and honest,
  Probal° to thinking, and, indeed, the course   *plausible*

---

1 Congenial; but, given Cassio's identification of alcohol with the devil, also
"demon or evil spirit" (*OED n.* 3).

2 Proved.

3 Once in a while.

4 The action of devoting.

5 Abilities, talents; but also perhaps her body parts.

6 Petition.

7 Honorable, generous; but also loose, sexually available.

8 Iago casts Desdemona as a doctor who can set (= mend with a splint) the broken relationship between Cassio and Othello.

9 Wager.

10 Take up my cause.

11 I despair for my future if I am blocked.

310   To win the Moor again? For 'tis most easy
      Th'inclining[1] Desdemona to subdue
      In any honest suit. She's framed as fruitful
      As the free elements.[2] And then for her
      To win the Moor were to renounce his baptism,
315   All seals and symbols of redeemèd sin;[3]
      His soul is so enfettered° to her love   *enslaved*
      That she may make, unmake, do what she list°   *likes*
      Even as her appetite° shall play the god   *her desire or inclination*
      With his weak function.[4] How am I then a villain
320   To counsel Cassio to this parallel course
      Directly to his good? Divinity of hell!
      When devils will the blackest sins put on,[5]
      They do suggest° at first with heavenly shows,   *prompt to evil*
      As I do now. For whiles this honest fool
325   Plies Desdemona to repair his fortune,
      And she for him pleads strongly to the Moor,
      I'll pour this pestilence into his ear:
      That she repeals[6] him for her body's lust;
      And by how much she strives to do him good,
330   She shall undo her credit with the Moor.
      So will I turn her virtue into pitch,[7]
      And out of her own goodness make the net
      That shall enmesh them all.

Enter Roderigo.

                          How now, Roderigo?
RODERIGO. I do follow here in the chase, not like a hound that
335   hunts, but one that fills up the cry.[8] My money is almost spent,

---

1   Disposed to favor; the physicality of the image (*incline* = lean toward, submit
to) makes sexual innuendo possible here.
2   Created as generous and productive of good results as the natural world.
3   Proofs of religious redemption (such as baptism).
4   Intellectual or moral powers; performance, with a pun on sexual performance;
"natural instincts" (Ridley).
5   Provoke; but also, figuratively, "dress up in."
6   Argues for his reinstatement.
7   Literally, tar; figuratively, something black and filthy.
8   Pack of hounds.

I have been tonight exceedingly well cudgeled,[1] and I think the
issue[2] will be I shall have so much experience for my pains, and so,
with no money at all and a little more wit, return again to Venice.

IAGO. How poor are they that have not patience?
What wound did ever heal but by degrees? 340
Thou know'st we work by wit and not by witchcraft,
And wit depends on dilatory[3] time.
Does't not go well? Cassio hath beaten thee,
And thou by that small hurt hath cashiered Cassio.
Though other things grow fair against° the sun,   *when exposed to* 345
Yet fruits that blossom first will first be ripe.
Content thyself awhile. By the mass,° 'tis morning;   *an oath*
Pleasure and action make the hours seem short.
Retire thee; go where thou art billeted.
Away, I say; thou shalt know more hereafter. 350
Nay, get thee gone.

Exit Roderigo.

                    Two things are to be done:
My wife must move for[4] Cassio to her mistress;
I'll set her on.
Myself awhile to draw the Moor apart
And bring him jump[5] when he may Cassio find 355
Soliciting his wife. Ay, that's the way;
Dull not device by coldness and delay.[6]

Exit [Iago].

---

1 Badly beaten.
2 Result.
3 "Characterized by delay" (*OED adj.* 2).
4 Plead on behalf of.
5 At the exact moment.
6 I.e., don't ruin a good plan by putting things off.

[3.1]

Enter Cassio, Musicians, and Clown.

CASSIO. Masters, play here—I will content[1] your pains—something
that's brief, and bid "Good morrow, general."[2]

[The musicians play.]

CLOWN. Why, masters, have your instruments been in Naples that
they speak i'th'nose thus?

5 MUSICIAN. How, sir? How?

CLOWN. Are these, I pray you, wind instruments?

MUSICIAN. Ay, marry, are they, sir.

CLOWN. Oh, thereby hangs a tale.

MUSICIAN. Whereby hangs a tale, sir?

10 CLOWN. Marry, sir, by many a wind instrument that I know.[3] But,
masters—here's money for you—and the general so likes your
music that he desires you for love's sake to make no more noise
with it.

MUSICIAN. Well, sir, we will not.

15 CLOWN. If you have any music that may not be heard, to't again.
But, as they say, to hear music the general does not greatly care.

MUSICIAN. We have none such, sir.

CLOWN. Then put up your pipes[4] in your bag, for I'll away. Go, van-
ish into air, away.

Exit Musicians.

20 CASSIO. Dost thou hear, mine honest friend?

CLOWN. No, I hear not your honest friend; I hear you.

---

1 Reward.

2 Although it was customary to play music outside the bridal chamber the morning after a wedding as a means of greeting the newly married couple, Cassio's
decision to hire musicians seems misguided given his role in disturbing Othello
and Desdemona the previous night.

3 The Clown introduces an elaborate series of puns and bawdy jokes during this
exchange. *Instrument* = penis; the references to instruments that *speak i'th'nose* and
to Naples suggest syphilis, a sexually transmitted disease, casually referred to in
the period as "the Neapolitan disease," which produces lesions that destroy the
bridge of the nose; *tale/tail* = penis and *wind* = flatulence, which together produce
quips about bestiality and sodomy.

4 Literally, put away your instruments; figuratively, shut up; with a pun on *pipes* =
penises.

3.1.6: "ARE THESE, I PRAY YOU,
WIND INSTRUMENTS?" (TLN 1524)

Early-modern music featured an array of wind instruments, including the bagpipe, the bladder pipe, the crumhorn, the recorder, the oboe, and the fife. In the course of his conversation with the Musicians, the Clown introduces a series of vulgar quips that pun on the shape of and the sounds produced by such instruments. In addition to an inevitable fart joke, he manages references to sexually transmitted disease, bestiality, and sodomy. To read about early-modern woodwinds and to hear a sample of the music they made, visit the "Life & Times" section of the Internet Shakespeare Editions website and click on Literature: Music.

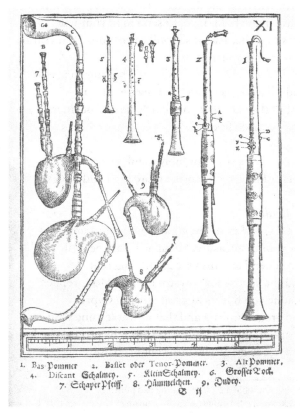

1. Bas Pommer   2. Baſiet oder Tenor-Pommer.   3. Alt Pommer.
4.   Diſcant Schalmey.   5. KleinSchalmey.   6. Groſſer Bock.
7. Schaper Pfeiff.   8. Hümmelchen.   9. Dudey.
B ij

Plate XI from Michael Praetorius (1571–1621), *Theatrum Instrumentorum seu Sciagraphia* (Wolfenbüttel, 1618). Wikimedia Commons, https://commons.wikimedia.org.

CASSIO. Prithee keep up thy quillets.[1] There's a poor piece of gold
for thee. If the gentlewoman that attends the general's wife be
stirring, tell her there's one Cassio entreats her a little favor of
25   speech. Wilt thou do this?
CLOWN. She is stirring,[2] sir. If she will stir hither, I shall seem to
notify unto her.
CASSIO. Do, my good friend.

Exit Clown.

Enter Iago.
CASSIO.   In happy time,[3] Iago.
IAGO. You have not been abed then?
30   CASSIO. Why, no; the day had broke before we parted.
I have made bold, Iago, to send in to your wife.
My suit to her is that she will to virtuous Desdemona
Procure me some access.
IAGO.   I'll send her to you presently,
And I'll devise a mean° to draw the Moor   *way*
35   Out of the way, that your converse and business
May be more free.

Exit [Iago].

CASSIO.   I humbly thank you for't.
I never knew a Florentine more kind and honest.

Enter Emilia.
EMILIA. Good morrow, good lieutenant. I am sorry
For your displeasure, but all will sure be well.
40   The general and his wife are talking of it,
And she speaks for you stoutly. The Moor replies
That he you hurt is of great fame in Cyprus
And great affinity,[4] and that in wholesome wisdom
He might not but[5] refuse you. But he protests he loves you
45   And needs no other suitor but his likings

---

1   *Quillet* = quibble; i.e., stop making bad puns.
2   Awake; moving around; sexually arousing.
3   You have arrived at a good time.
4   Has influential connections.
5   Could do nothing other than.

To take the safest occasion by the front
To bring you in again.

CASSIO.   Yet I beseech you,
If you think fit, or that it may be done,
Give me advantage of some brief discourse
With Desdemon[1] alone.

EMILIA.   Pray you come in.   50
I will bestow you where you shall have time
To speak your bosom° freely.   *voice your innermost thoughts*

CASSIO.   I am much bound to you.

[*Exeunt.*]

[3.2]

Enter Othello, Iago, and Gentlemen.

OTHELLO. These letters give, Iago, to the pilot,
And by him do my duties[2] to the Senate.

[*Othello hands Iago some papers.*]

That done, I will be walking on the works;°   *fortifications*
Repair there to me.°   *meet me there*

IAGO.   Well, my good lord, I'll do't.

OTHELLO. This fortification, gentlemen, shall we see't?   5

GENTLEMEN. We'll wait upon° your lordship.   *accompany*

Exeunt.

[3.3]

Enter Desdemona, Cassio, and Emilia.

DESDEMONA. Be thou assured, good Cassio, I will do
All my abilities in thy behalf.

EMILIA. Good madam, do. I warrant it grieves my husband
As if the cause were his.

---

1 Cassio introduces the shortened version of Desdemona's name, which is used
later by Othello (3.3.53, TLN 1651; 4.2.42, TLN 2735; 5.2.24, TLN 3266; 5.2.277,
TLN 3581). While a play on "demon" is clearly available to readers, it would almost
certainly be lost here on audiences, for whom the *a* beginning "alone" would likely
disguise the missing *a* at the end of "Desdemona."
2 Through him pay my respects.

5 DESDEMONA. Oh, that's an honest fellow. Do not doubt, Cassio,
      But I will have my lord and you again
      As friendly as you were.
    CASSIO.   Bounteous madam,
      Whatever shall become of Michael Cassio,
      He's never anything but your true servant.
10 DESDEMONA. I know't. I thank you. You do love my lord;
      You have known him long, and be you well assured
      He shall in strangeness stand no farther off
      Than in a politic distance.[1]
    CASSIO.   Ay, but, lady,
      That policy may either last so long,
15   Or feed upon such nice and waterish° diet,   *tender and juicy*
      Or breed itself so out of° circumstances   *grow as a result of*
      That I being absent and my place supplied,°   *position filled*
      My general will forget my love and service.
    DESDEMONA. Do not doubt° that. Before Emilia here,   *fear*
20   I give thee warrant° of thy place. Assure thee,   *guarantee*
      If I do vow a friendship, I'll perform it
      To the last article.° My lord shall never rest: *clause in a legal document*
      I'll watch him tame[2] and talk him out of patience;[3]
      His bed shall seem a school, his board a shrift;[4]
25   I'll intermingle everything he does
      With Cassio's suit. Therefore be merry, Cassio,
      For thy solicitor[5] shall rather die
      Than give thy cause away.[6]

Enter Othello and Iago.
    EMILIA.   Madam, here comes my lord.

---

1   Maintain no more than a strategic aloofness from you.
2   I.e., render him tractable by preventing him from sleeping. The phrase refers to falconers' use of sleep deprivation as a means of domesticating birds of prey.
3   Wear out his patience by talking to him.
4   *Board* = table; *shrift* = place of confession; thus, "his dining table will seem like a confessional." There is an echo here of the legal definition of marriage as a contract to share *bed and board*.
5   "One who urges, prompts, or instigates"; "one practising in a court of equity, as distinguished from an attorney" (*OED n.* 1a; 3a).
6   Sacrifice your interests; abandon your case.

CASSIO. Madam, I'll take my leave.

DESDEMONA.   Why stay, and hear me speak.

CASSIO. Madam, not now. I am very ill at ease,   30
Unfit for mine own purposes.

DESDEMONA. Well, do your discretion.°   *what you think is best*
                                                          Exit Cassio.

IAGO. Ha? I like not that.

OTHELLO.   What dost thou say?

IAGO. Nothing, my lord; or if—I know not what.

OTHELLO. Was not that Cassio parted from my wife?   35

IAGO. Cassio, my lord? No sure, I cannot think it
That he would steal away so guilty-like,
Seeing your coming.

OTHELLO.   I do believe 'twas he.

DESDEMONA. How now, my lord?
I have been talking with a suitor[1] here,   40
A man that languishes in your displeasure.

OTHELLO. Who is't you mean?

DESDEMONA. Why, your lieutenant, Cassio. Good my lord,
If I have any grace or power to move you,
His present reconciliation take;[2]   45
For if he be not one that truly loves you,
That errs in ignorance and not in cunning,
I have no judgment in an honest face.
I prithee call him back.

OTHELLO. Went he hence now?

DESDEMONA.   Aye, sooth,° so humbled   *truly*   50
That he hath left part of his grief with me
To suffer with him. Good love, call him back.

OTHELLO. Not now, sweet Desdemon—some other time.

DESDEMONA. But shall't be shortly?

OTHELLO.   The sooner, sweet, for you.

DESDEMONA. Shall't be tonight, at supper?

OTHELLO.   No, not tonight.   55

---

1   Petitioner, one who brings suit; wooer.
2   "Restore him immediately to favor" or "accept the request for reconciliation he
now makes."

DESDEMONA. Tomorrow dinner,° then?   *a noontime meal*

OTHELLO.   I shall not dine at home;

    I meet the captains at the citadel.

DESDEMONA. Why then, tomorrow night, or Tuesday morn,

    On Tuesday noon or night, or Wednesday morn.

60   I prithee name the time, but let it not

    Exceed three days. In faith, he's penitent;

    And yet his trespass, in our common reason[1]—

    Save that they say the wars must make example

    Out of her best—is not almost a fault

65   T'incur a private check.[2] When shall he come?

    Tell me, Othello. I wonder in my soul

    What you would ask me that I should deny

    Or stand so mamm'ring[3] on? What? Michael Cassio,

    That came a-wooing with you, and so many a time

70   When I have spoke of you dispraisingly

    Hath ta'en your part°—to have so much to do   *taken your side*

    To bring him in? By'r Lady, I could do much—

OTHELLO. Prithee, no more. Let him come when he will;

    I will deny thee nothing.

DESDEMONA.   Why, this is not a boon;°   *favor*

75   'Tis as I should entreat you wear your gloves,

    Or feed on nourishing dishes, or keep you warm,

    Or sue to you to do a peculiar profit

    To your own person. Nay, when I have a suit

    Wherein I mean to touch[4] your love indeed,

80   It shall be full of poise and difficult weight,

    And fearful to be granted.[5]

OTHELLO.   I will deny thee nothing.

    Whereon, I do beseech thee, grant me this:

    To leave me but a little to myself.

DESDEMONA. Shall I deny you? No! Farewell, my lord.

---

1 If we consider it commonsensically.

2 Not even an offense worthy of confidential reprimand (much less the public dressing-down that Cassio received).

3 Stammering or muttering in indecision.

4 Test, with a possible pun on *touch* = sexual contact.

5 I.e., a serious matter with grave consequences.

OTHELLO. Farewell, my Desdemona. I'll come to thee straight.[1]   85
DESDEMONA. Emilia, come. [*To Othello*] Be as your fancies[2]
    teach you
  Whate'er you be, I am obedient.
Exeunt [Desdemona and Emilia].
OTHELLO. Excellent wretch![3] Perdition catch my soul[4]
  But I do love thee! And when I love thee not,
  Chaos[5] is come again.   90
IAGO. My noble lord—
OTHELLO.   What dost thou say, Iago?
IAGO. Did Michael Cassio, when you wooed my lady,
  Know of your love?
OTHELLO.   He did, from first to last.
  Why dost thou ask?
IAGO. But for a satisfaction of my thought,   95
  No further harm.
OTHELLO.   Why of thy thought, Iago?
IAGO. I did not think he had been acquainted with her.
OTHELLO. Oh yes, and went between us very oft.
IAGO. Indeed?
OTHELLO. Indeed? Ay, indeed. Discern'st thou aught in that? 100
  Is he not honest?
IAGO. Honest, my lord?
OTHELLO. Honest? Ay, honest.
IAGO. My lord, for aught I know.
OTHELLO. What dost thou think?   105
IAGO. Think, my lord?
OTHELLO. "Think, my lord?" By heaven, thou echo'st me
  As if there were some monster in thy thought
  Too hideous to be shown. Thou dost mean something.
  I heard thee say even now, thou lik'st not that 110
  When Cassio left my wife. What didst not like?

---

1 Right away.
2 Whims.
3 Small person or creature; "a term of playful depreciation" (*OED n.* 2e).
4 I'll be damned.
5 The dark abyss of primordial matter from which the order of the universe evolved; disorder.

And when I told thee he was of my counsel°   *in my confidence*
Of my whole course of wooing, thou cried'st "Indeed?"
And didst contract and purse[1] thy brow together
115   As if thou then hadst shut up in thy brain
Some horrible conceit.° If thou dost love me,   *idea*
Show me thy thought.
IAGO. My lord, you know I love you.
OTHELLO.   I think thou dost;
And for I know thou'rt full of love and honesty,
120   And weigh'st thy words before thou giv'st them breath,
Therefore these stops of thine fright me the more.
For such things in a false disloyal knave
Are tricks of custom,[2] but in a man that's just,
They're close dilations,[3] working from the heart,
That passion cannot rule.
125 IAGO.   For Michael Cassio,
I dare be sworn, I think that he is honest.
OTHELLO. I think so too.
IAGO.   Men should be what they seem,
Or those that be not, would they might seem none.
OTHELLO. Certain, men should be what they seem.
130 IAGO. Why then, I think Cassio's an honest man.
OTHELLO. Nay, yet there's more in this.
I prithee speak to me as to thy thinkings,[4]
As thou dost ruminate, and give thy worst of thoughts
The worst of words.
IAGO.   Good my lord, pardon me.
135 Though I am bound to every act of duty,
I am not bound to that all slaves are free to.°   *free from*
Utter my thoughts? Why, say they are vile and false—
As where's that palace whereinto foul things
Sometimes intrude not? Who has that breast so pure
140 Wherein uncleanly apprehensions

---

1   Draw together, pucker.
2   Characteristic practices.
3   Intimate delays or elaborations.
4   Tell me what is on your mind.

Keep leets[1] and law-days,[2] and in sessions sit
With meditations lawful?

OTHELLO. Thou dost conspire against thy friend, Iago,
If thou but think'st him wronged and mak'st his ear
A stranger to thy thoughts.

IAGO.   I do beseech you,   145
Though I perchance am vicious in my guess—
As I confess it is my nature's plague
To spy into abuses, and oft my jealousy[3]
Shapes° faults that are not—that your wisdom   *creates*
From one that so imperfectly conceits°   *imagines* 150
Would take no notice, nor build yourself a trouble
Out of his scattering and unsure observance.
It were not for your quiet nor your good,
Nor for my manhood, honesty, and wisdom
To let you know my thoughts.

OTHELLO.   What dost thou mean?   155

IAGO. Good name° in man and woman, dear my lord,   *reputation*
Is the immediate jewel° of their souls.   *most valuable possession*
Who steals my purse, steals trash[4]—'tis something, nothing;
'Twas mine, 'tis his, and has been slave to thousands—
But he that filches from me my good name   160
Robs me of that which not enriches him,
And makes me poor indeed.

OTHELLO.   I'll know thy thoughts.

IAGO. You cannot, if my heart were in your hand,[5]
Nor shall not, whilst 'tis in my custody.

OTHELLO. Ha?

IAGO.   Oh, beware, my lord, of jealousy.   165
It is the green-eyed monster, which doth mock

---

1 Special courts of record that the lords of certain manors were empowered to
hold annually or semi-annually.
2 The days on which the court of leet met in session.
3 Vigilance; with an inevitable echo of "distrust of the sexual fidelity ... of a wife"
(*OED n.* 3; 4a).
4 Slang for money.
5 Even if you had the power of life and death over me.

The meat it feeds on.[1] That cuckold[2] lives in bliss
Who, certain of his fate, loves not his wronger;[3]
But oh, what damnèd minutes tells he o'er°   counts
170   Who dotes yet doubts, suspects yet soundly[4] loves?
OTHELLO. Oh, misery!
IAGO. Poor and content is rich, and rich enough,
But riches fineless° is as poor as winter   without end
To him that ever fears he shall be poor.
175   Good God, the souls of all my tribe[5] defend
From jealousy.
OTHELLO.   Why? Why is this?
Think'st thou I'd make a life of jealousy,
To follow still the changes of the moon[6]
With fresh suspicions? No! To be once in doubt
180   Is to be resolved. Exchange me for a goat[7]
When I shall turn the business of my soul
To such exsufflate and blowed surmises[8]
Matching thy inference.° 'Tis not to make me jealous   conclusion
To say my wife is fair, feeds° well, loves company,   eats
185   Is free of speech, sings, plays, and dances;[9]
Where virtue is, these are more virtuous.
Nor from mine own weak merits will I draw
The smallest fear or doubt of her revolt,[10]

---

1   Literally, toys with its prey before devouring it; figuratively, tortures the jealous
lover before destroying him.
2   Derisive term for the husband of an unfaithful wife.
3   I.e., his adulterous wife.
4   Completely; in a healthy manner.
5   I.e., my people. The population of Venice was divided into six tribes in this
period.
6   By becoming so unstable that I imagine new wrongs with each new phase of
the moon.
7   An animal associated with lust, cuckoldry, and—through its cloven hoofs—the
devil.
8   Whispered and exaggerated rumors.
9   Shakespeare's Italian source, *Gli Heccatommithi* (see Appendix A1), opens with
a dialogue featuring an attack on women who tempt men into "dishonourable
lasciviousness" and who "with beauty of body under a semblance of virtue, for
instance in singing, playing, dancing lightly and speaking sweetly, hide an ugly and
abominable soul" (Bullough 7.240).
10   Literally, rebellion; figuratively, infidelity.

For she had eyes and chose me. No, Iago,
I'll see before I doubt; when I doubt, prove;   190
And on the proof, there is no more but this:
Away at once with love or jealousy.

IAGO. I am glad of this, for now I shall have reason
To show the love and duty that I bear you
With franker spirit. Therefore, as I am bound,   195
Receive it from me. I speak not yet of proof.
Look to your wife; observe her well with Cassio.
Wear° your eyes thus, not jealous nor secure.   *use*
I would not have your free° and noble nature   *honorable, generous*
Out of self-bounty° be abused. Look to't.   *personal generosity* 200
I know our country disposition[1] well.
In Venice they° do let God see the pranks   *i.e., women*
They dare not show their husbands; their best conscience[2] ·
Is not to leave't undone, but keep't unknown.

OTHELLO. Dost thou say so?   205

IAGO. She did deceive her father, marrying you;
And when she seemed to shake and fear your looks,
She loved them most.

OTHELLO.   And so she did.

IAGO.   Why, go to then.
She that so young could give out such a seeming°   *deception*
To seel[3] her father's eyes up close as oak[4]   210
He thought 'twas witchcraft—but I am much to blame.
I humbly do beseech you of your pardon
For too much loving you.

OTHELLO.   I am bound to thee forever.

IAGO. I see this hath a little dashed your spirits.

OTHELLO. Not a jot, not a jot.

IAGO.   I'faith, I fear it has.   215
I hope you will consider what is spoke

---

1   Venetian temperament, with a possible pun on *country* = sexual.
2   Most conscientious action.
3   Literally, sew shut the eyelids of; figuratively, trick her father into not noticing.
See also 1.3.269 (TLN 619) and extended note on p. 154.
4   I.e., tightly. Oak is a notably hard, tightly grained wood.

Comes from your love.[1] But I do see you're moved.
I am to pray you not to strain my speech
To grosser issues,[2] nor to larger reach°   *range*
220   Than to suspicion.
OTHELLO. I will not.
IAGO.   Should you do so, my lord,
My speech should fall into such vile success,
Which my thoughts aimed not. Cassio's my worthy friend.
My lord, I see you're moved.
OTHELLO.   No, not much moved.
225   I do not think but Desdemona's honest.°   *chaste; trustworthy*
IAGO. Long live she so, and long live you to think so.
OTHELLO. And yet how nature, erring from itself—
IAGO. Ay, there's the point—as, to be bold with you,
Not to affect[3] many proposed matches
230   Of her own clime,° complexion,[4] and degree,[5]   *region*
Whereto we see in all things nature tends—
Foh![6] One may smell in such a will[7] most rank,
Foul disproportions,[8] thoughts unnatural.
But, pardon me, I do not in position
235   Distinctly speak of her,[9] though I may fear
Her will, recoiling° to her better judgment,   *returning*
May fall to match[10] you with her country forms,[11]
And happily[12] repent.
OTHELLO.   Farewell, farewell.
If more thou dost perceive, let me know more.
240   Set on thy wife to observe. Leave me, Iago.

---

1 My love for you.
2 Force the meaning of my words and thereby draw larger (or more indecent) conclusions from them.
3 Aspire to; show a preference for.
4 Temperament; skin color.
5 Social rank.
6 Expression of disgust.
7 Detect in this sort of willful behavior.
8 Lack of symmetry, thus ugliness.
9 Speak merely of Desdemona.
10 Begin to compare.
11 Habitual Venetian behavior, with a possible pun on *country* = sexual.
12 Perhaps; fortunately; appropriately; in a happy manner.

IAGO. [*Starting to exit*] My lord, I take my leave.

OTHELLO. Why did I marry? This honest creature[1] doubtless
  Sees and knows more, much more, than he unfolds.

IAGO. [*Returning*] My lord, I would I might entreat your honor
  To scan° this thing no farther; leave it to time.   *analyze* 245
  Although 'tis fit that Cassio have his place—
  For sure he fills it up with great ability—
  Yet, if you please to hold him off awhile,
  You shall by that perceive him and his means.°   *methods; intentions*
  Note if your lady strain his entertainment[2]   250
  With any strong or vehement importunity;
  Much will be seen in that. In the meantime,
  Let me be thought too busy in my fears,
  (As worthy cause I have to fear I am),
  And hold her free,° I do beseech your honor.   *innocent* 255

OTHELLO. Fear not my government.°   *self-control*

IAGO.   I once more take my leave.

                          Exit [*Iago*].

OTHELLO. This fellow's of exceeding honesty,
  And knows all qualities with a learned spirit
  Of human dealings. If I do prove her haggard,
  Though that her jesses were my dear heartstrings,   260
  I'd whistle her off and let her down the wind
  To prey at fortune.[3] Haply° for I am black   *perhaps*
  And have not those soft parts of conversation[4]
  That chamberers[5] have, or for I am declined
  Into the vale of years°—yet that's not much[6]—   *i.e., I am older* 265
  She's gone.[7] I am abused and my relief
  Must be to loathe her. Oh, curse of marriage,
  That we can call these delicate creatures° ours   *i.e., our wives*
  And not their appetites!° I had rather be a toad   *sexual urges*

---

1 I.e., Iago (who presumably cannot hear).
2 Push too hard for his reinstatement.
3 To find her own way, to fend for herself.
4 I.e., social niceties.
5 Those who frequent ladies' chambers; gallants.
6 "But that's not important" or, perhaps, "I'm not really that old."
7 "Lost, ruined, undone" (*OED adj.* 1).

3.3.259:   "IF I DO PROVE HER HAGGARD"
                        (TLN 1891)

When Othello uses the word "haggard" to refer to the possibility of Desdemona's unfaithfulness, he is borrowing from the sport of falconry a technical term for an untamed adult female bird. The term "jesses" (the straps used to tether a bird), and the expressions "whistle her off" (hunting birds were sent in pursuit of prey with whistled commands) and "down the wind" (hawks are sent upwind to hunt and downwind for recreation) are also used by falconers, and they help Othello develop an elaborate conceit that figures his marriage to Desdemona as the relationship between an undomesticated bird of prey and its tamer. There are also references in the play to the practice of "seeling," or sewing shut the eyes of a bird of prey to keep it tame during training for the hunt (1.3.269, TLN 619; 3.3.210, TLN 1829). To read more about the popular early-modern sport of falconry or hawking, visit the "Life & Times" section of the Internet Shakespeare Editions website and click on Society: Husbandry.

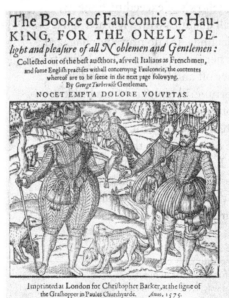

Title page of George Turberville, *The Booke of Faulconrie or Hauking* (London, 1575). With permission of the Internet Shakespeare Editions (http://internetshakespeare.uvic.ca).

And live upon the vapor of a dungeon   270
Than keep a corner in the thing I love
For others' uses. Yet 'tis the plague to great ones,
Prerogatived° are they less than the base;[1]   *privileged*
'Tis destiny unshunnable,° like death.   *unavoidable*
Even then this forkèd[2] plague is fated to us   275
When we do quicken.[3] Look where she comes—

Enter Desdemona and Emilia.
  If she be false, heaven mocked itself;
  I'll not believe't.
DESDEMONA.   How now, my dear Othello?
  Your dinner, and the generous islanders
  By you invited, do attend° your presence.   *wait for*   280
OTHELLO. I am to blame.
DESDEMONA.   Why do you speak so faintly?
  Are you not well?
OTHELLO. I have a pain upon my forehead, here.
DESDEMONA. Why, that's with watching;[4] 'twill away again.
  Let me but bind it hard; within this hour   285
  It will be well.
      [*Desdemona tries to bind Othello's head with her handkerchief.*][5]
OTHELLO.   Your napkin is too little.
                    [*The handkerchief falls.*]
  Let it alone. Come, I'll go in with you.
DESDEMONA. I am very sorry that you are not well.
                Exeunt [*Othello and Desdemona*].

---

1 People of lower status.
2 Horned (like a cuckold); also perhaps an allusion to the forked tongue of a
venomous serpent.
3 The first movement of the fetus felt by a pregnant woman is traditionally called
the quickening, thus "come to life."
4 That comes from staying awake.
5 The movements of Desdemona's handkerchief are of crucial importance
throughout this scene, since the token eventually plays such a crucial role in convincing Othello that his wife has been unfaithful. The early printed editions offer
no stage directions, but Othello's lines provide a basic account of the handkerchief—too small to wrap around his head, but not so small that this wasn't worth
trying—and its travels.

EMILIA. [*Picking up the handkerchief*] I am glad I have found this
    napkin.
290 This was her first remembrance° from the Moor.   *keepsake*
    My wayward husband hath a hundred times
    Wooed me to steal it, but she so loves the token—
    For he conjured[1] her she should ever keep it—
    That she reserves it evermore about her
295 To kiss and talk to. I'll have the work taken out[2]
    And give't Iago. What he will do with it,
    Heaven knows, not I;
    I nothing but to please his fantasy.

Enter Iago.

IAGO. How now? What do you here alone?
300 EMILIA. Do not you chide; I have a thing for you.
IAGO. You have a thing for me? It is a common[3] thing[4]—
EMILIA. Ha?
IAGO. To have a foolish wife.
EMILIA. Oh, is that all? What will you give me now
    For that same handkerchief?
305 IAGO.   What handkerchief?
EMILIA. What handkerchief?
    Why that the Moor first gave to Desdemona,
    That which so often you did bid me steal.
IAGO. Hast stolen it from her?
310 EMILIA. No, but she let it drop by negligence,
    And, to th'advantage,[5] I, being here, took't up.
    Look, here 'tis.
IAGO.   A good wench. Give it me.
EMILIA. What will you do with't, that you have been
    So earnest to have me filch it?
                              [*Iago snatches the handkerchief.*]
IAGO.   Why, what is that to you?

---

1 Elicited a promise from; entreated; charmed, bewitched.
2 Embroidery copied.
3 Slang for whorish, freely available.
4 Slang for vagina.
5 Seizing the opportunity.

EMILIA. If it be not for some purpose of import,   315
   Giv't me again. Poor lady, she'll run mad
   When she shall lack it.°   *notice its absence*
IAGO.   Be not acknown on't;[1]
   I have use for it. Go, leave me.

                                Exit Emilia.

   I will in Cassio's lodging lose this napkin
   And let him find it. Trifles light as air   320
   Are to the jealous confirmations strong
   As proofs of holy writ.[2] This may do something.
   The Moor already changes with my poison.
   Dangerous conceits° are in their natures poisons, .   *ideas*
   Which at the first are scarce found to distaste,[3]   325
   But with a little act upon the blood,[4]
   Burn like the mines of sulfur.[5] I did say so.

Enter Othello.
   Look where he comes. Not poppy, nor mandragora,[6]
   Nor all the drowsy syrups of the world
   Shall ever medicine thee to that sweet sleep   330
   Which thou owedst° yesterday.   *owned*
OTHELLO.   Ha, ha! False to me?
IAGO. Why, how now, general? No more of that.
OTHELLO. Avaunt,[7] be gone! Thou hast set me on the rack.
   I swear 'tis better to be much abused°   *deceived*
   Than but to know't a little.
IAGO.   How now, my lord?   335
OTHELLO. What sense had I in her stolen hours of lust?
   I saw't not, thought it not, it harmed not me.
   I slept the next night well, fed well, was free and merry.
   I found not Cassio's kisses on her lips.

---

1 Do not confess your knowledge about it.
2 I.e., drawn from the Bible.
3 Taste unpleasant; nauseate.
4 "Arouse passion" (Honigmann).
5 I.e., with great heat and forever.
6 Extracts from the opium poppy and mandrake root were used medicinally in
the period as sedatives.
7 Go away.

Tormented by Iago's hints that Desdemona has been unfaithful, Othello figures himself as a prisoner lashed to an instrument of torture. Othello's assertion that knowledge of betrayal is more excruciating than betrayal itself is especially ironic for an audience that knows that "honest Iago's" claims are false, while Desdemona is loyal.

The rack was designed to generate maximum pain by stretching the limbs a little at a time until the muscles are ruined and the joints dislocated. It is closely associated with such concepts as loyalty, faith, knowledge, and truth, due to its role in extracting confessions from political prisoners accused of treason and retractions of faith from religious prisoners accused of heresy. The image below, taken from a history of the Christian Church assembled by Protestant martyrologist John Foxe (c. 1517–87), depicts the interrogation of Cuthbert Simson, deacon of a Protestant congregation in London during the reign of the Catholic queen Mary I. Simson was later burned at the stake, while Mary, half-sister to her successor Elizabeth I, earned the moniker "Bloody Mary" for the large number of religious dissenters executed during her brief reign (1553–58).

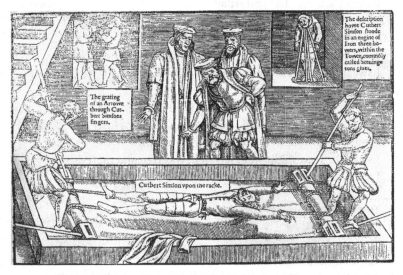

"A true description of the racking and cruell handeling of Cutbert Simson in the Tower" from John Foxe, *The Unabridged Acts and Monuments Online or TAMO* (1583 edition). HRI Online Publications, University of Sheffield, 2011.

He that is robbed, not wanting° what is stolen,   *missing*   340
Let him not know't, and he's not robbed at all.
IAGO. I am sorry to hear this.
OTHELLO. I had been happy if the general camp,[1]
Pioneers[2] and all, had tasted her sweet body,
So I had nothing known. Oh, now, forever   345
Farewell the tranquil mind; farewell content;°   *happiness*
Farewell the plumèd troops and the big wars
That makes ambition virtue! Oh, farewell!
  . Farewell the neighing steed and the shrill trump,°   *trumpet*
The spirit-stirring drum, the ear-piercing fife,   350
The royal banner, and all quality,
Pride,[3] pomp, and circumstance° of glorious war!   *ceremony*
And O you mortal engines° whose rude throats   *deadly weapons*
The immortal Jove's dread clamors° counterfeit,   *i.e., thunder*
Farewell! Othello's occupation's gone.[4]   355
IAGO. Is't possible, my lord?
OTHELLO. Villain, be sure thou prove my love a whore!
Be sure of it. Give me the ocular° proof,   *visual*

                            [*Othello grabs Iago.*]

Or, by the worth of mine eternal soul,
Thou hadst been better have been born a dog   360
Than answer my waked wrath.
IAGO.   Is't come to this?
OTHELLO. Make me to see't, or at the least so prove it
That the probation° bear no hinge[5] nor loop   *proof*
To hang a doubt on, or woe upon thy life!
IAGO. My noble lord—   365
OTHELLO. If thou dost slander her and torture me,
Never pray more; abandon all remorse,
On horror's head horrors accumulate,

---

1 "Whole army" (Neill).
2 Members of an army who provide support to the main troops by performing
the hard labor of digging trenches, making roads, etc.
3 Excessive self-esteem; self-importance; ostentatious display; honor.
4 Career as general (and, perhaps, role as husband) is over.
5 "That on which something is conceived to hang or be supported and to turn; a
pivot, prop" (*OED n.* 3a).

Do deeds to make heaven weep, all earth amazed,
370 For nothing canst thou to damnation add
Greater than that.
IAGO.   O grace! O heaven forgive me!
Are you a man? Have you a soul? or sense?
God b'wi'you,[1] take mine office. O wretched fool
That lov'st to make thine honesty a vice!
375 O monstrous world! Take note, take note, O world,
To be direct and honest is not safe.
I thank you for this profit,° and from hence   *useful lesson*
I'll love no friend sith° love breeds such offense.   *since*
OTHELLO. Nay, stay; thou shouldst be honest.
380 IAGO. I should be wise, for honesty's a fool
And loses that it works for.
OTHELLO.   By the world,
I think my wife be honest,° and think she is not;   *faithful*
I think that thou art just, and think thou art not.
I'll have some proof. Her name,° that was as fresh   *her reputation*
385 As Dian's visage,[2] is now begrimed and black
As mine own face. If there be cords or knives,
Poison, or fire, or suffocating streams,
I'll not endure it. Would I were satisfied.°   *freed from doubt*
IAGO. I see you are eaten up with passion;
390 I do repent me that I put it to you.[3]
You would be satisfied?
OTHELLO.   Would? Nay, and I will.
IAGO. And may—but how? how satisfied, my lord?
Would you, the supervisor,° grossly gape on?   *onlooker*
Behold her topped?[4]
OTHELLO.   Death and damnation! Oh!
395 IAGO. It were a tedious difficulty, I think,
To bring them to that prospect.° Damn them then,   *view*

---

1 Goodbye; i.e., I am done with you.
2 The face of Diana, famously beautiful Roman goddess of women, chastity, and childbirth.
3 Told you about (my suspicions regarding Desdemona and Cassio).
4 Tupped, copulated with. See 1.1.88 (TLN 97), 5.2.135 (TLN 3407), and notes.

If ever mortal eyes do see them bolster[1]
More° than their own. What then? How then?   other
What shall I say? Where's satisfaction?
It is impossible you should see this   400
Were they as prime as goats, as hot as monkeys,
As salt as wolves in pride,[2] and fools as gross
As ignorance made drunk. But yet, I say,
If imputation° and strong circumstances,[3]   accusation
Which lead directly to the door of truth,   405
Will give you satisfaction, you might have't.
OTHELLO. Give me a living° reason she's disloyal.   viable
IAGO. I do not like the office;°   task
But sith I am entered in this cause[4] so far—
Pricked[5] to't by foolish honesty and love—   410
I will go on: I lay° with Cassio lately,   shared a bed
And, being troubled with a raging tooth,°   i.e., painful toothache
I could not sleep. There are a kind of men
So loose of soul[6] that in their sleeps will mutter
Their affairs; one of this kind is Cassio.   415
In sleep I heard him say "Sweet Desdemona,
Let us be wary; let us hide our loves."
And then, sir, would he gripe° and wring my hand,   clutch
Cry "O sweet creature!," then kiss me hard,
As if he plucked up kisses by the roots   420
That grew upon my lips, then laid his leg
O'er my thigh, and sighed, and kissed, and then
Cried "Cursèd fate that gave thee to the Moor!"
OTHELLO. Oh, monstrous! monstrous!
IAGO.   Nay, this was but his dream.
OTHELLO. But this denoted a foregone conclusion;[7]   425

---

1 Literally, a pillow that supports a sleeper's head—thus, to share a bed; figuratively, to have sex.
2 Iago lists examples of animal lust: *Prime* = primitive; lustful; *hot* = sexually aroused; *salt* = lecherous; *pride* = in heat.
3 Powerful circumstantial evidence.
4 Matter; legal case; purpose.
5 Urged on (with the inevitable echo of a pun on *prick* = penis).
6 Free with their innermost secrets; perhaps also, "lacking in virtue."
7 Indicated a previous sexual encounter.

'Tis a shrewd doubt,° though it be but a dream.   *suspicion*
IAGO. And this may help to thicken° other proofs *substantiate*
 That do demonstrate thinly.°   *are less convincing*
OTHELLO.   I'll tear her all to pieces!
IAGO. Nay, yet be wise, yet we see nothing done;
430 She may be honest yet. Tell me but this:
 Have you not sometimes seen a handkerchief
 Spotted with strawberries in your wife's hand?
OTHELLO. I gave her such a one; 'twas my first gift.
IAGO. I know not that, but such a handkerchief—
435 I am sure it was your wife's—did I today
 See Cassio wipe his beard with.
OTHELLO.   If it be that—
IAGO. If it be that, or any, it was hers.
 It speaks against her with the other proofs.
OTHELLO. Oh, that the slave had forty thousand lives!
440 One is too poor, too weak for my revenge.
 Now do I see 'tis true. Look here, Iago:
 All my fond love thus do I blow to heaven—'tis gone!
 Arise, black vengeance from the hollow hell.
 Yield up, O love, thy crown and hearted[1] throne
445 To tyrannous hate. Swell, bosom, with thy fraught,° *freight, load*
 For 'tis of aspics'[2] tongues.
IAGO.   Yet be content.°   *calm*
           [Othello kneels.]
OTHELLO. Oh, blood, blood, blood!
IAGO. Patience, I say. Your mind may change.
OTHELLO. Never, Iago. Like to the Pontic Sea,° *Black Sea*
450 Whose icy current and compulsive course
 Ne'er keeps retiring ebb but keeps due on
 To the Propontic[3] and the Hellespont,[4]
 Even so my bloody thoughts with violent pace
 Shall ne'er look back, ne'er ebb to humble love,

---

1 Located in the heart.
2 Asps; venomous serpents.
3 Sea of Marmara, which lies between the Aegean Sea and the Black Sea.
4 Dardanelles, a strait that connects the Aegean Sea and the Sea of Marmara,
and traditionally separates Europe and Asia.

Till that a capable° and wide revenge   *comprehensive*   455
Swallow them up. Now, by yon marble heaven,[1]
In the due reverence of a sacred vow,
I here engage° my words.   *pledge*
IAGO.   Do not rise yet.
Witness, you ever-burning lights above,°   *i.e., stars*
You elements that clip° us round about,   *embrace*   460

[*Iago kneels.*]

Witness that here Iago doth give up
The execution[2] of his wit,° hands, heart   *intelligence*
To wronged Othello's service. Let him command,
And to obey shall be in me remorse,
What bloody business ever.

[*Othello and Iago rise.*]

OTHELLO.   I greet thy love   465
Not with vain° thanks but with acceptance bounteous,   *worthless*
And will upon the instant put thee to't.
Within these three days let me hear thee say
That Cassio's not alive.
IAGO.   My friend is dead;
'Tis done at your request. But let her live.   470
OTHELLO. Damn her, lewd minx![3] Oh, damn her, damn her!
Come, go with me apart; I will withdraw
To furnish me with some swift means of death
For the fair devil. Now art thou my lieutenant.
IAGO. I am your own forever.   475

Exeunt.

---

1 Presumably a reference to a cold and unforgiving God.
2 Performance; with, in anticipation of Othello's plan to be revenged on Cassio,
echoes of both "enforcement of a judgment" (as in the execution of a court order),
and "putting to death."
3 Wanton woman; whore.

[3.4]

Enter Desdemona, Emilia, and Clown.

DESDEMONA. Do you know, sirrah,[1] where Lieutenant Cassio lies?[2]
CLOWN. I dare not say he lies anywhere.
DESDEMONA. Why, man?
CLOWN. He's a soldier, and for me to say a soldier lies, 'tis stabbing.[3]
5 DESDEMONA. Go to! Where lodges he?
CLOWN. To tell you where he lodges is to tell you where I lie.[4]
DESDEMONA. Can anything be made of this?
CLOWN. I know not where he lodges, and for me to devise a lodging,
     and say he lies here or he lies there, were to lie in mine own throat.
10 DESDEMONA. Can you inquire him out and be edified[5] by report?
CLOWN. I will catechize the world for him[6]—that is, make questions
     and by them answer.[7]
DESDEMONA. Seek him, bid him come hither, tell him I have moved
     my lord on his behalf, and hope all will be well.
15 CLOWN. To do this is within the compass[8] of man's wit, and there-
     fore I will attempt the doing it.

                                                    Exit Clown.

DESDEMONA. Where should I lose[9] the handkerchief, Emilia?
EMILIA. I know not, madam.
DESDEMONA. Believe me, I had rather lose my purse
20 Full of crusadoes;[10] and but° my noble Moor   *were it not that*
     Is true of mind and made of no such baseness
     As jealous creatures are, it were enough
     To put him to ill thinking.
EMILIA.   Is he not jealous?
DESDEMONA. Who, he? I think the sun where he was born

---

1 Term of address to a social inferior, usually expressing contempt.
2 Dwells.
3 Both "is like stabbing him" and "could get me stabbed."
4 Both "reveal myself as a liar" (because I don't know where he lives) and "reveal where I live."
5 Be taught; be morally improved; profit spiritually.
6 Ask around about him.
7 Use the replies to formulate an answer to your query.
8 Limits.
9 Might I have lost.
10 Portuguese coins stamped with an image of the cross.

Drew all such humors from him.[1]
EMILIA.   Look where he comes.   25

Enter Othello.
DESDEMONA. I will not leave him now till Cassio
Be called to him. How is't with you, my lord?
OTHELLO. Well, my good lady. [*Aside*] Oh, hardness to dissemble![2]
How do you, Desdemona?
DESDEMONA.   Well, my good lord.
OTHELLO. Give me your hand.
                          [*Othello takes Desdemona's hand.*]
                          This hand is moist, my lady.   30
DESDEMONA. It hath felt no age, nor known no sorrow.
OTHELLO. This argues[3] fruitfulness° and liberal heart—   *fertility*
Hot, hot and moist. This hand of yours requires
A sequester[4] from liberty—fasting and prayer,
Much castigation,° exercise devout—   *rebuke, scolding* 35
For here's a young and sweating devil here
That commonly rebels. 'Tis a good hand,
A frank one.
DESDEMONA.   You may indeed say so,
For 'twas that hand that gave away my heart.
OTHELLO. A liberal hand. The hearts of old gave hands,   40
But our new heraldry is hands, not hearts.[5]
DESDEMONA. I cannot speak of this. Come, now your promise.
OTHELLO. What promise, chuck?°   *term of endearment*
DESDEMONA. I have sent to bid Cassio come speak with you.
OTHELLO. I have a salt and sorry rheum[6] offends me;   45
Lend me thy handkerchief.
DESDEMONA.   Here, my lord.
OTHELLO. That which I gave you.

---

1 Desdemona imagines a hot African sun with the ability to empty Othello of any
tendency toward jealousy.
2 It is so difficult to pretend that everything is well.
3 I.e., the state of your hand proves that you have.
4 Sequestration, locking apart from (especially in prison or religious seclusion);
banishment; excommunication.
5 These days the giving of hands in marriage does not necessarily signify the giving of hearts in love.
6 I.e., bad head cold.

DESDEMONA.   I have it not about me.

OTHELLO. Not?

DESDEMONA. No, faith, my lord.

50 OTHELLO. That's a fault. That handkerchief
    Did an Egyptian to my mother give.
    She was a charmer° and could almost read   *enchanter*
    The thoughts of people. She told her while she kept it
    'Twould make her amiable[1] and subdue my father
55   Entirely to her love, but if she lost it,
    Or made a gift of it, my father's eye
    Should hold her loathed, and his spirits should hunt
    After new fancies. She, dying, gave it me,
    And bid me, when my fate would have me wived,°   *married*
60   To give it her. I did so; and, take heed on't,
    Make it a darling like your precious eye.
    To lose't or give't away were such perdition°   *damnation*
    As nothing else could match.

DESDEMONA.   Is't possible?

OTHELLO. 'Tis true. There's magic in the web° of it: *woven fabric*
65   A sybil that had numbered in the world
    The sun to course two hundred compasses,[2]
    In her prophetic fury sewed the work;
    The worms were hallowed° that did breed the silk,   *holy*
    And it was dyed in mummy,[3] which the skillful
    Conserved of maidens' hearts.

70 DESDEMONA.   I'faith, is't true?

OTHELLO. Most veritable;° therefore look to't well.   *true*

DESDEMONA. Then would to God that I had never seen't!

OTHELLO. Ha? Wherefore?

DESDEMONA. Why do you speak so startingly and rash?

75 OTHELLO. Is't lost? Is't gone? Speak, is't out o'th'way?

DESDEMONA. Heaven bless us!

OTHELLO. Say you?

---

1   Loveable; desirable.

2   Either "a 200-hundred-year-old prophetess" (Mowat and Werstine) or "a
prophetess who had 'calculated … that the world would end in two hundred years'"
(Honigmann).

3   Tarlike substance prepared from mummified flesh and held to have medicinal
powers.

DESDEMONA. It is not lost; but what and if it were?

OTHELLO. How?

DESDEMONA. I say it is not lost.   80

OTHELLO. Fetch't, let me see't.

DESDEMONA. Why so I can; but I will not now.
  This is a trick to put me from my suit.
  Pray you, let Cassio be received again.

OTHELLO. Fetch me the handkerchief, my mind misgives.[1]   85

DESDEMONA. Come, come!
  You'll never meet a more sufficient° man—   *competent*

OTHELLO. The handkerchief.

DESDEMONA.   A man that all his time
  Hath founded his good fortunes on your love,
  Shared dangers with you—

OTHELLO.   The handkerchief.   90

DESDEMONA. I'faith, you are to blame.

OTHELLO.   Zounds!

Exit Othello.

EMILIA. Is not this man jealous?

DESDEMONA.   I ne'er saw this before.
  Sure there's some wonder in this handkerchief;
  I am most unhappy in the loss.

EMILIA. 'Tis not a year or two shows us a man.   95
  They are all but° stomachs,[2] and we all but food;   *nothing but*
  They eat us hungerly, and when they are full
  They belch° us.   *vomit*

Enter Iago and Cassio.

                      Look you, Cassio and my husband.

IAGO. There is no other way; 'tis she must do't—
  And lo, the happiness![3] Go and importune her.   100

DESDEMONA. How now, good Cassio, what's the news with you?

CASSIO. Madam, my former suit: I do beseech you
  That by your virtuous means I may again
  Exist and be a member of his love,
  Whom I, with all the office of my heart,   105

---

1 Is suspicious.
2 Bellies; appetites; desires.
3 Look, what good luck!

Entirely honor. I would not° be delayed.   *do not want to be*
If my offense be of such mortal° kind   *deadly*
That nor my service past, nor present sorrows,
Nor purposed merit in futurity[1]

110 Can ransom me into his love again,
But to know so must be my benefit;[2]
So shall I clothe me in a forced content
And shut myself up in some other course
To fortune's alms.[3]

DESDEMONA.   Alas, thrice-gentle Cassio,
115 My advocation is not now in tune;[4]
My lord is not my lord,[5] nor should I know him
Were he in favor° as in humor° altered.   *appearance / mood*
So help me every spirit sanctified
As I have spoken for you all my best,
120 And stood within the blank of his displeasure
For my free speech. You must awhile be patient.
What I can do, I will; and more I will
Than for myself I dare. Let that suffice you.

IAGO. Is my lord angry?

EMILIA.   He went hence but now,
125 And certainly in strange unquietness.

IAGO. Can he be angry? I have seen the cannon
When it hath blown his ranks into the air
And, like the devil, from his very arm
Puffed[6] his own brother—and is he angry?
130 Something of moment° then. I will go meet him;   *importance*
There's matter in't indeed if he be angry.

DESDEMONA. I prithee do so.

                            Exit [Iago].
           Something sure of state,
Either from Venice or some unhatched practice

---

1 The worth I plan to demonstrate in the future.
2 Simply knowing the worst must be my only consolation.
3 Limit myself to some other means of earning fortune's charity.
4 This is not a good time for me to advocate on your behalf.
5 Desdemona's warning to Cassio that Othello is out of sorts echoes Iago's
earlier paradoxical pronouncement "I am not what I am" (1.1.64, TLN 71). See also
4.1.258, TLN 2670.
6 Blasted; blew away.

Made demonstrable here in Cyprus to him,
Hath puddled° his clear spirit; and in such cases   *muddied*   135
Men's natures wrangle with inferior things,
Though great ones are their object. 'Tis even so.
For let our finger ache and it endues[1]
Our other healthful members even to a sense

---

1   Teaches; brings to a particular state.

3.4.120:   "THE BLANK OF HIS DISPLEASURE"
(TLN 2284)

In warning that her husband has reacted poorly to her attempts to
restore Cassio to favor, Desdemona draws her image from the sport of
archery, in which competitors took aim at "the blank," a white spot at
the center of a target. Desdemona's figuring of herself as the target of
her husband's anger is complicated by the association between archery
and sexualized violence established by Iago on their arrival in Cyprus
(see note at 2.1.131, TLN 908).

To learn more about early-modern English slang, puns, and proverbs,
see entries in the Bibliography for Dent, Nares, Partridge, and Tilley.

Gilles Corrozet, *Hecatomgraphie* (Paris: Denis Janot, 1540), [A4v]. By permission of
University of Glasgow Library, Special Collections.

140 Of pain. Nay, we must think men are not gods,
Nor of them look for such observancy°   *respectful attention*
As fits the bridal.° Beshrew me¹ much, Emilia.   *wedding day*
I was, unhandsome warrior as I am,
Arraigning° his unkindness with my soul;   *bringing to trial; accusing*
145 But now I find I had suborned° the witness,   *corrupted*
And he's indicted falsely.

EMILIA.   Pray heaven it be
State matters, as you think, and no conception²
Nor no jealous toy° concerning you.   *foolish idea*

DESDEMONA. Alas the day! I never gave him cause.

150 EMILIA. But jealous souls will not be answered so;
They are not ever jealous for the cause,
But jealous for they're jealous. It is a monster
Begot° upon itself, born on itself.   *sired*

DESDEMONA. Heaven keep the monster from Othello's mind.

155 EMILIA. Lady, amen.

DESDEMONA. I will go seek him. Cassio, walk here about.
If I do find him fit, I'll move your suit
And seek to effect it to my uttermost.

CASSIO. I humbly thank your ladyship.

Exeunt Desdemona and Emilia.

Enter Bianca.

BIANCA. 'Save you, friend Cassio.

160 CASSIO.   What make you from home?
How is't with you, my most fair Bianca?
I'faith, sweet love, I was coming to your house.

BIANCA. And I was going to your lodging, Cassio.
What, keep a week away? Seven days and nights?
165 Eight score eight hours?° And lovers' absent hours   *i.e., a week*
More tedious than the dial eight score times?
Oh, weary reckoning!³

CASSIO.   Pardon me, Bianca.

---

1 A playful curse; i.e., shame on me.
2 Idea; "mere fancy" (*OED n.* 7b; only occurrence of this usage cited).
3 Counting; punishment; amount owing.

I have this while with leaden thoughts been pressed,[1]
But I shall in a more continuate[2] time
Strike off this score° of absence. Sweet Bianca,   *pay off this debt*   170
Take me this work out.°   *copy this needlework for me*
             [*Cassio gives Desdemona's handkerchief to Bianca.*]
BIANCA.   O Cassio, whence came this?
   This is some token from a newer friend.
   To the felt absence now I feel a cause.[3]
   Is't come to this? Well, well.
CASSIO.   Go to, woman!
   Throw your vile guesses in the devil's teeth,   175
   From whence you have them. You are jealous now
   That this is from some mistress, some remembrance?°   *keepsake*
   No, by my faith, Bianca.
BIANCA.   Why, whose is it?
CASSIO. I know not neither; I found it in my chamber.
   I like the work well; ere it be demanded,[4]   180
   As like enough it will, I would have it copied.
   Take it and do't, and leave me for this time.
BIANCA. Leave you? Wherefore?
CASSIO. I do attend here on the general,
   And think it no addition° nor my wish   *advantage*   185
   To have him see me womaned.[5]
BIANCA.   Why, I pray you?
CASSIO. Not that I love you not.
BIANCA.   But that you do not love me.
   I pray you bring me on the way a little,
   And say if I shall see you soon at night.
CASSIO. 'Tis but a little way that I can bring you,   190
   For I attend here, but I'll see you soon.
BIANCA. 'Tis very good. I must be circumstanced.[6]
                          Exeunt.

---

1   Been weighed down by heavy thoughts, with a play on "pressing to death," a
form of torture and execution by which the prisoner is crushed beneath weights.
2   Uninterrupted; i.e., less busy.
3   Now I sense a reason for the absence I experienced.
4   Before someone asks for it back.
5   In the company of a woman (with the suggestion that keeping such company is
unprofessional and perhaps even effeminizing).
6   Governed by the circumstances in which I find myself.

[4.1]

Enter Othello and Iago.

IAGO. Will you think so?

OTHELLO.   Think so, Iago?

IAGO.   What,
    To kiss in private?

OTHELLO.   An unauthorized kiss?

IAGO. Or to be naked with her friend in bed
    An hour or more, not meaning any harm?

5 OTHELLO. Naked in bed, Iago, and not mean harm?
    It is hypocrisy against the devil.[1]
    They that mean virtuously and yet do so,
    The devil their virtue tempts, and they tempt heaven.

IAGO. If they do nothing, 'tis a venial slip;[2]

10   But if I give my wife a handkerchief—

OTHELLO. What then?

IAGO. Why then 'tis hers, my lord, and, being hers,
    She may, I think, bestow't on any man.

OTHELLO. She is protectress of her honor too;

15   May she give that?

IAGO. Her honor is an essence that's not seen;
    They have it very oft, that have it not.
    But for the handkerchief—

OTHELLO. By heaven, I would most gladly have forgot it!

20   Thou saidst—Oh, it comes o'er my memory
    As doth the raven o'er the infectious house,
    Boding to all—he had my handkerchief.

IAGO. Ay, what of that?

OTHELLO.   That's not so good now.

IAGO. What if I had said I had seen him do you wrong?

25   Or heard him say—as knaves be such abroad
    Who, having by their own importunate° suit   *persistent*
    Or voluntary dotage° of some mistress   *infatuation*
    Convincèd or supplied° them, cannot choose   *satisfied sexually*
    But they must blab—

OTHELLO.   Hath he said anything?

---

1 Seeming to sin while behaving virtuously.
2 Pardonable error (as opposed to a "mortal" or irredeemable sin).

IAGO. He hath, my lord, but be you well assured,   30
No more than he'll unswear.

OTHELLO.   What hath he said?

IAGO. Faith, that he did—I know not what he did.

OTHELLO. What? What?

IAGO.   Lie.

OTHELLO.   With her?

IAGO. With her, on her—what you will.°   *whatever you wish*

OTHELLO. Lie with her? Lie on her? We say "lie on her" when they   35
belie her. Lie with her?[1] Zounds, that's fulsome![2] Handkerchief!
Confessions! Handkerchief!—To confess and be hanged for his
labor. First to be hanged and then to confess! I tremble at it.
Nature would not invest herself in such shadowing[3] passion without some instruction. It is not words that shakes me thus. Pish!   40
Noses, ears, and lips!—Is't possible? Confess? Handkerchief? O
devil!

                              [*Othello*] *falls in a trance.*

IAGO. Work on,
My medicine works! Thus credulous fools are caught,
And many worthy and chaste dames even thus,   45
All guiltless, meet reproach. What ho! My lord?
My lord, I say! Othello!

Enter Cassio.

                              How now, Cassio?

CASSIO. What's the matter?

IAGO. My lord is fallen into an epilepsy.
This is his second fit; he had one yesterday.   50

CASSIO. Rub him about the temples.

IAGO.   No, forbear.
The lethargy must have his quiet course;
If not, he foams at mouth and by and by
Breaks out to savage madness. Look, he stirs.
Do you withdraw yourself a little while.   55
He will recover straight. When he is gone,

---

1   This passage puns on three different meanings of the word *lie*: to have sex with;
to share a bed with; to tell a falsehood.
2   Lustful; offensive, disgusting.
3   Prefiguring.

I would on great occasion° speak with you.   *about an important issue*
                                                   [*Exit Cassio.*]

How is it, general? Have you not hurt your head?

OTHELLO. Dost thou mock me?

IAGO.   I mock you not, by heaven!

60 Would you would bear your fortune like a man.

OTHELLO. A hornèd man's a monster and a beast.

IAGO. There's many a beast then in a populous city,
    And many a civil monster.

OTHELLO. Did he confess it?

IAGO.   Good sir, be a man.

65 Think every bearded fellow[1] that's but yoked[2]
    May draw with[3] you. There's millions now alive
    That nightly lie in those unproper[4] beds,
    Which they dare swear peculiar.[5] Your case is better.
    Oh, 'tis the spite of hell, the fiend's arch-mock,[6]

70 To lip a wanton in a secure couch[7]
    And to suppose her chaste. No, let me know,
    And, knowing what I am, I know what she shall be.

OTHELLO. Oh, thou art wise, 'tis certain.

IAGO.   Stand you awhile apart;
    Confine yourself but in a patient list:[8]

75 Whilst you were here, o'erwhelmèd with your grief—
    A passion most unsuiting such a man—
    Cassio came hither. I shifted him away
    And laid good 'scuses upon your ecstasy,[9]
    Bade him anon return and here speak with me,

---

1   Man old enough to grow a beard; i.e., adult man.

2   Literally, fastened together to a plough (like oxen); figuratively, married.

3   Literally, pull alongside, like yoked oxen pull the same cart; figuratively, bear the common burden of adulterous wives.

4   A coinage, presumably the opposite of "proper" which indicates both ownership and respectability.

5   Their own personal property.

6   Principal act of derision.

7   Kiss an unchaste woman in a supposedly chaste bed.

8   Stay within the bounds of patience (i.e., be patient).

9   Vague term in the period for "all morbid states characterized by unconsciousness, as swoon, trance, catalepsy, etc." (*OED n.* 2a).

4.1.61: "A HORNÈD MAN'S A MONSTER AND A BEAST" (TLN 2442)

There is a long tradition in visual art and literature of depicting male victims of adultery, or cuckolds, with horns emerging from their heads. This image is invoked by Othello when he complains, "I have a pain upon my forehead" (3.3.283, TLN 1918), reminding early-modern readers and audiences that headaches were said to accompany the emergence of a cuckold's horns.

From the broadside ballad *The Westminster Frolick* (London, 1670–96). EBB65H, Houghton Library, Harvard University.

80   The which he promised. Do but encave[1] yourself,
        And mark the fleers,° the gibes and notable scorns   *sneers*
        That dwell in every region of his face.
        For I will make him tell the tale anew:
        Where, how, how oft, how long ago, and when
85   He hath and is again to cope[2] your wife.
        I say, but mark his gesture—marry, patience!
        Or I shall say you're all in all in spleen[3]
        And nothing of a man.
      OTHELLO.   Dost thou hear, Iago?
        I will be found most cunning in my patience,
        But—dost thou hear?—most bloody.
90 IAGO.   That's not amiss,
        But yet keep time in all.[4] Will you withdraw?
                            [Othello withdraws.]
        Now will I question Cassio of Bianca,
        A huswife[5] that by selling her desires
        Buys herself bread and cloth. It is a creature
95   That dotes on Cassio—as 'tis the strumpet's plague
        To beguile many and be beguiled by one.
        He, when he hears of her, cannot restrain
        From the excess of laughter. Here he comes.

        Enter Cassio.
        As he shall smile, Othello shall go mad;
100   And his unbookish° jealousy must conster° *unlearned / naive; interpret*
        Poor Cassio's smiles, gestures, and light behaviors
        Quite in the wrong. How do you, lieutenant?
      CASSIO. The worser that you give me the addition
        Whose want even kills me.[6]
105 IAGO. Ply° Desdemona well, and you are sure on't.   *keep working on*

---

1 Hide away, as in a cave.
2 Meet (with sexual overtones).
3 Under the influence of an uncontrollable rage.
4 Maintain measured behavior.
5 Prostitute; woman responsible for maintaining a household.
6 I feel worse when you call me by the title (i.e., lieutenant) whose loss is causing me suffering.

Now if this suit lay in Bianca's power,
How quickly should you speed.

CASSIO.   Alas, poor caitiff!°   *wretch*

OTHELLO. [*Aside*] Look how he laughs already.

IAGO. I never knew a woman love man so.

CASSIO. Alas, poor rogue, I think i'faith she loves me.   110

OTHELLO. [*Aside*] Now he denies it faintly and laughs it out.[1]

IAGO. Do you hear, Cassio?

OTHELLO.   [*Aside*] Now he importunes° him   *begs*
To tell it o'er. Go to, well said, well said.

IAGO. She gives it out that you shall marry her.
Do you intend it?   115

CASSIO. Ha, ha, ha!

OTHELLO. [*Aside*] Do you triumph, Roman? Do you triumph?

CASSIO. I marry? What, a customer?[2]
Prithee bear some charity to my wit;[3]
Do not think it so unwholesome. Ha, ha, ha!   120

OTHELLO. [*Aside*] So, so, so, so! They laugh that wins.

IAGO. Faith, the cry goes that you marry her.

CASSIO. Prithee say true.

IAGO. I am a very villain else.

OTHELLO. [*Aside*] Have you scored me?[4] Well.   125

CASSIO. This is the monkey's° own giving out.   *i.e., Bianca's*
She is persuaded I will marry her
Out of her own love and flattery, not out of my promise.

OTHELLO. [*Aside*] Iago beckons[5] me; now he begins the story.

CASSIO. She was here even now; she haunts me in every place. I was   130
the other day talking on the seabank with certain Venetians, and
thither comes the bauble[6] and, by this hand, she falls me thus
about my neck.

---

1   Laughs it off.
2   Companion, familiar associate; buyer.
3   Have some faith in my common sense.
4   Although the exact meaning of the phrase is unclear, it likely draws on a
metaphoric linking of physical violence with financial and sexual exchange.
Score = strike hard enough to leave a mark; brand for public disgrace; settle an
account; make sexual conquest.
5   Signals.
6   Showy ornament or plaything; i.e., Bianca.

OTHELLO. [*Aside*] Crying "O dear Cassio!" as it were; his gesture
135   imports it.
CASSIO. So hangs, and lolls, and weeps upon me; so shakes and pulls
     me. Ha, ha, ha!
OTHELLO. [*Aside*] Now he tells how she plucked him to my chamber.
     Oh, I see that nose[1] of yours, but not that dog I shall throw it to.
140 CASSIO. Well, I must leave her company.
IAGO. Before me![2] Look where she comes.

Enter Bianca.
CASSIO. 'Tis such another[3] fitchew[4]—marry, a perfumed one!
     What do you mean by this haunting of me?
BIANCA. Let the devil and his dam haunt you! What did you mean
145   by that same handkerchief you gave me even now? I was a fine
     fool to take it! I must take out the work? A likely piece of work,[5]
     that you should find it in your chamber and know not who left it
     there. This is some minx's[6] token, and I must take out the work?
     There, give it your hobby-horse![7]
                    [*Bianca throws down the handkerchief.*]
150   Wheresoever you had it, I'll take out no work on't.
CASSIO. How now, my sweet Bianca? How now? How now?
OTHELLO. [*Aside*] By heaven, that should be my handkerchief!
BIANCA. If you'll come[8] to supper tonight, you may; if you will not,
     come when you are next prepared for.[9]
                                    Exit [Bianca].
155 IAGO. After her, after her!
CASSIO. Faith, I must; she'll rail[10] in the streets else.
IAGO. Will you sup there?

---

1   Slang for penis.
2   A mild oath.
3   Another of the same kind.
4   Literally, polecat, a small mammal known for its fetid smell and associated in
    the period with lust; figuratively, a whore.
5   A likely story (with an ironic pun on *work* = needlework).
6   Whore's.
7   Whore.
8   If you wish to come.
9   "The next time I am ready for you" (sarcastically); i.e., never.
10 Rant.

CASSIO. Faith, I intend so.

IAGO. Well, I may chance to see you, for I would very fain speak[1] with you. 160

CASSIO. Prithee come, will you?

IAGO. Go to, say no more.

[*Exit Cassio.*]

OTHELLO. [*Coming forward*] How shall I murder him, Iago?

IAGO. Did you perceive how he laughed at his vice?

OTHELLO. Oh, Iago! 165

IAGO. And did you see the handkerchief?

OTHELLO. Was that mine?

IAGO. Yours, by this hand—and to see how he prizes the foolish woman your wife; she gave it him, and he hath given it his whore.

OTHELLO. I would have him nine years a-killing![2] A fine woman, a 170 fair woman, a sweet woman!

IAGO. Nay, you must forget that.

OTHELLO. Ay, let her rot and perish and be damned tonight, for she shall not live. No, my heart is turned to stone; I strike it and it hurts my hand. Oh, the world hath not a sweeter creature! She 175 might lie by an emperor's side and command him tasks.

IAGO. Nay, that's not your way.[3]

OTHELLO. Hang her, I do but say what she is: so delicate with her needle, an admirable musician—Oh, she will sing the savageness out of a bear—of so high plenteous wit and invention! 180

IAGO. She's the worse for all this.

OTHELLO. Oh, a thousand, a thousand times—and then of so gentle a condition!

IAGO. Ay, too gentle.[4]

OTHELLO. Nay, that's certain—but yet the pity of it, Iago! Oh, Iago, 185 the pity of it, Iago!

1 I would very much like to speak.
2 I.e., slowly tortured to death.
3 The path you should follow.
4 Othello refers to Desdemona's mild temperament (and perhaps also to her social standing as a gentlewoman), but Iago turns his praise into implied criticism of her ostensible failure to resist sexual temptation.

IAGO. If you are so fond over her iniquity, give her patent to offend;[1]
    for if it touch not you, it comes near nobody.

OTHELLO. I will chop her into messes[2]—cuckold me?

190 IAGO. Oh, 'tis foul in her.

OTHELLO. With mine officer?

IAGO. That's fouler.

OTHELLO. Get me some poison, Iago, this night. I'll not expostu-
    late[3] with her lest her body and beauty unprovide[4] my mind again.

195 This night, Iago.

IAGO. Do it not with poison. Strangle her in her bed, even the bed
    she hath contaminated.

OTHELLO. Good, good—the justice of it pleases! Very good.

IAGO. And for Cassio, let me be his undertaker.[5] You shall hear more

200 by midnight.

OTHELLO. Excellent good—

                                   [*A trumpet sounds.*]
                  What trumpet is that same?

IAGO. I warrant something from Venice.

Enter Lodovico, Desdemona, and attendants.

    'Tis Lodovico, this, comes from the duke.

    See, your wife's with him.

205 LODOVICO. God save you, worthy general.

OTHELLO. With all my heart, sir.

LODOVICO. [*Giving Othello a letter*] The Duke and the Senators of
    Venice greet you.

OTHELLO. I kiss the instrument of their pleasures.°   *orders*

DESDEMONA. And what's the news, good cousin Lodovico?[6]

---

1 If you are going to dote on her wickedness, you might as well give her license to
sin.

2 Portions of food.

3 Argue; reason.

4 Unsettle; disarm.

5 Handle him. As Neill points out, while it is tempting to give this word its
modern meaning of "funeral undertaker," that professional designation was not
established until the end of the seventeenth century.

6 *Cousin* could mean "kinsman" in the period, but it was also a general term of
friendly address among those of similar social standing, so no family connection is
necessarily implied between Desdemona and Lodovico.

IAGO. I am very glad to see you, signor.   210
   Welcome to Cyprus.
LODOVICO. I thank you. How does Lieutenant Cassio?
IAGO. Lives, sir.
DESDEMONA. Cousin, there's fallen between him and my lord
   An unkind° breach, but you shall make all well.   *unnatural; cruel* 215
OTHELLO. Are you sure of that?
DESDEMONA.   My lord?
OTHELLO. [*Reading*] "This fail you not to do, as you will—"
LODOVICO. He did not call; he's busy in the paper.
   Is there division 'twixt my lord and Cassio?
DESDEMONA. A most unhappy one. I would do much   220
   T'atone° them, for the love I bear to Cassio.   *to reconcile*
OTHELLO. Fire and brimstone!
DESDEMONA.   My lord?
OTHELLO.   Are you wise?
DESDEMONA. What, is he angry?
LODOVICO.   Maybe the letter moved him.
   For, as I think, they do command him home,
   Deputing Cassio in his government.   225
DESDEMONA. By my troth, I am glad on't.
OTHELLO.   Indeed?
DESDEMONA.   My lord?
OTHELLO. I am glad to see you mad.
DESDEMONA.   Why, sweet Othello?
OTHELLO.   [*Striking her*] Devil!
DESDEMONA. I have not deserved this.
LODOVICO. My lord, this would not be believed in Venice,
   Though I should swear I saw't. 'Tis very much.°   *this is very serious* 230
   Make her amends; she weeps.
OTHELLO.   O devil, devil!
   If that the earth could teem[1] with woman's tears,
   Each drop she falls would prove a crocodile.[2]—
   Out of my sight!

---

1   Be impregnated by; crawl with.
2   Othello's image refers to the crocodile's fabled ability to weep as a means of
deceiving its prey. Proverbially, "crocodile tears" are signs of insincere emotion
(Dent C831).

235 DESDEMONA.   [*Starting to exit*] I will not stay to offend you.
LODOVICO. Truly obedient lady!
       I do beseech your lordship call her back.
OTHELLO. Mistress!
DESDEMONA.   [*Returning*] My lord?
OTHELLO.   What would you with her, sir?
LODOVICO. Who I, my lord?
240 OTHELLO. Ay, you did wish that I would make her turn.[1]
       Sir, she can turn, and turn, and yet go on
       And turn again. And she can weep, sir, weep;
       And she's obedient,[2] as you say, obedient,
       Very obedient.—Proceed you in your tears!—
245   Concerning this, sir—O well-painted passion![3]—
       I am commanded home.—Get you away!
       I'll send for you anon.—Sir, I obey the mandate
       And will return to Venice.—Hence, avaunt!—
                                          [*Exit Desdemona.*]
       Cassio shall have my place.[4] And, sir, tonight
250   I do entreat that we may sup together.
       You are welcome, sir, to Cyprus.—Goats and monkeys![5]
                                          Exit [*Othello*].
LODOVICO. Is this the noble Moor whom our full senate
       Call all in all sufficient?° Is this the nature   *thoroughly competent*
       Whom passion could not shake? Whose solid virtue
255   The shot of accident nor dart of chance
       Could neither graze nor pierce?
IAGO.   He is much changed.
LODOVICO. Are his wits safe? Is he not light of brain?

---

1   Literally, turn around or return, but also, go bad; betray; deceive; undergo
religious conversion; have sex.
2   Dutiful; sexually compliant.
3   Othello identifies Desdemona as an embodiment of false emotion (*painted* =
pretended) and associates her with the artifice of both pictorial representation
(*painted* = represented in paint) and the use of cosmetics (*painted* = "artificially
coloured, as with cosmetics"). See *OED adj.* 1b; 2; 1c.
4   Position as governor; role as husband and sexual partner.
5   As Malone first noted, Othello seems to recall Iago's semi-proverbial *as prime
as goats, as hot as monkeys* (3.3.401, TLN 2051).

IAGO. He's that he is;[1] I may not breathe my censure.
　What he might be—if what he might, he is not—
　I would to heaven he were.
LODOVICO.　　　　　　　What? Strike his wife?　　　　　　260
IAGO. Faith, that was not so well; yet would I knew
　That stroke would prove the worst.
LODOVICO.　　　　　　　　Is it his use?°　　　*usual behavior*
　Or did the letters work upon his blood
　And new-create his fault?
IAGO.　　　　　　　Alas, alas!
　It is not honesty in me to speak　　　　　　　　　　265
　What I have seen and known. You shall observe him
　And his own courses° will denote[2] him so　　　　*habits*
　That I may save my speech; do but go after
　And mark how he continues.
LODOVICO. I am sorry that I am deceived in° him.　　*wrong about*　270
　　　　　　　　　　　　　　Exeunt.

[4.2]

Enter Othello and Emilia.
OTHELLO. You have seen nothing then?
EMILIA. Nor ever heard, nor ever did suspect.
OTHELLO. Yes, you have seen Cassio and she together.
EMILIA. But then I saw no harm; and then I heard
　Each syllable that breath made up between them.　　5
OTHELLO. What? Did they never whisper?
EMILIA. Never, my lord.
OTHELLO. Nor send you out o'th'way?
EMILIA. Never.
OTHELLO. To fetch her fan, her gloves, her mask,[3] nor nothing?　10
EMILIA. Never, my lord.
OTHELLO. That's strange.
EMILIA. I durst,° my lord, to wager she is honest,　　*would dare*

1　He is what he is.
2　Describe; distinguish from others; be the outward sign of.
3　Covering for the face to limit exposure to the sun.

Lay down my soul at stake.[1] If you think other,

15 Remove your thought; it doth abuse your bosom.
If any wretch have put this in your head,
Let heaven requite° it with the serpent's curse,[2]   *repay; retaliate for*
For if she be not honest, chaste, and true,
There's no man happy. The purest of their wives
Is foul as slander.

20 OTHELLO.   Bid her come hither—go.

Exit Emilia.

She says enough; yet she's a simple bawd[3]
That cannot say as much. This is a subtle whore,
A closet° lock and key of villainous secrets,   *private inner chamber*
And yet she'll kneel and pray—I have seen her do't.

Enter Desdemona and Emilia.

DESDEMONA. My lord, what is your will?
OTHELLO.   Pray you, chuck, come hither.
DESDEMONA. What is your pleasure?

25 OTHELLO.   Let me see your eyes;
Look in my face.
DESDEMONA.   What horrible fancy's this?
OTHELLO. [*To Emilia*] Some of your function, mistress,
Leave procreants[4] alone and shut the door,

30 Cough or cry "hem!" if anybody come.[5]
Your mystery,° your mystery—nay, dispatch!   *occupation or trade*

Exit Emilia.

DESDEMONA. [*Kneeling*] Upon my knee, what doth your speech
import?°   *mean*
I understand a fury in your words,
But not the words.
OTHELLO.   Why? What art thou?

35 DESDEMONA. Your wife, my lord, your true and loyal wife.

---

1 That which is risked in a bet; post to which those convicted of crimes were bound for execution (especially by burning).
2 In the Old Testament, God curses the serpent for deceiving Eve.
3 One who provides prostitutes.
4 Procreators; i.e., prostitutes and their clients.
5 I.e., some bawds protect the privacy of prostitutes and their clients.

OTHELLO. Come, swear it; damn thyself,
Lest, being like one of heaven, the devils themselves
Should fear to seize thee. Therefore be double damned:
Swear thou art honest.
DESDEMONA.   Heaven doth truly know it.
OTHELLO. Heaven truly knows that thou art false as hell.   40
DESDEMONA. [*Rising*] To whom, my lord? With whom? How am I
    false?
OTHELLO. Ah Desdemon, away, away, away.
DESDEMONA. Alas the heavy day! Why do you weep?
    Am I the motive of these tears, my lord?
    If haply you my father do suspect   45
    An instrument of this your calling back,[1]
    Lay not your blame on me; if you have lost him,
    I have lost him too.
OTHELLO.   Had it pleased heaven
    To try me with affliction, had they rained
    All kind of sores and shames on my bare head,   50
    Steeped me in poverty to the very lips,
    Given to captivity me and my utmost hopes,
    I should have found in some place of my soul
    A drop of patience. But, alas, to make me
    The fixèd figure for the time of scorn   55
    To point his slow and moving finger at![2]
    Yet could I bear that too, well, very well;
    But there where I have garnered° up my heart,   *stored*
    Where either I must live or bear no life,
    The fountain from the which my current runs   60
    Or else dries up—to be discarded thence—
    Or keep it as a cistern[3] for foul toads
    To knot and gender[4] in! Turn thy complexion there,[5]

---

1   If you suspect that my father was involved in arranging that you be called back
to Venice.
2   "The metaphor is that of a clock, whose slow-moving hand points, as if in
contempt, at the *fixed figure* of Othello" (Neill).
3   Large vessel or basin; reservoir.
4   "Fuck and breed" (Pechter).
5   Face that prospect.

Patience, thou young and rose-lipped cherubin;°   *angel*
65 I here look grim as hell.
DESDEMONA. I hope my noble lord esteems me honest.
OTHELLO. Oh ay, as summer flies[1] are in the shambles,[2]
    That quicken° even with blowing.[3] O thou weed,   *come alive*
    Who art so lovely fair and smell'st so sweet
70 That the sense aches at thee,
    Would thou had'st ne'er been born!
DESDEMONA. Alas, what ignorant sin have I committed?
OTHELLO. Was this fair paper,[4] this most goodly book,
    Made to write "whore" upon? What committed?
75 Committed? O thou public commoner,°   *common prostitute*
    I should make very forges of my cheeks
    That would to cinders burn up modesty
    Did I but speak thy deeds. What committed?
    Heaven stops° the nose at it and the moon[5] winks;[6]   *plugs*
80 The bawdy wind that kisses all it meets
    Is hushed within the hollow mine of earth
    And will not hear't—what committed?—impudent strumpet!
DESDEMONA. By heaven, you do me wrong.
OTHELLO. Are not you a strumpet?
DESDEMONA.   No, as I am a Christian.
85 If to preserve this vessel[7] for my lord
    From any other foul unlawful touch
    Be not to be a strumpet, I am none.
OTHELLO. What, not a whore?
DESDEMONA.   No, as I shall be saved.
OTHELLO. Is't possible?
DESDEMONA.   O heaven, forgive us.
90 OTHELLO. I cry you mercy then.
    I took you for that cunning whore of Venice
    That married with Othello.

---

1 So-called "flesh flies" that deposit their eggs in dead flesh.
2 Slaughterhouse.
3 I.e., as soon as their eggs are laid.
4 I.e., Desdemona's white flesh.
5 A common symbol of female chastity.
6 Winces.
7 I.e., her body.

Enter Emilia.

[*To Emilia*] You, mistress,
That have the office opposite to Saint Peter
And keeps the gate of hell. You, you! Ay, you.
We have done our course.[1] [*Giving her money*] There's money for   95
   your pains.°   *efforts*
I pray you turn the key and keep our counsel.[2]

                                            Exit [*Othello*].

EMILIA. Alas, what does this gentleman conceive?°   *think*
   How do you, madam? How do you, my good lady?
DESDEMONA. Faith, half asleep.
EMILIA. Good madam, what's the matter with my lord?   100
DESDEMONA. With who?
EMILIA.   Why, with my lord, madam.
DESDEMONA. Who is thy lord?
EMILIA.   He that is yours, sweet lady.
DESDEMONA. I have none. Do not talk to me, Emilia.
   I cannot weep, nor answers have I none
   But what should go by water.° Prithee tonight   *i.e., tears* 105
   Lay on my bed my wedding sheets, remember,
   And call thy husband hither.
EMILIA.   Here's a change indeed.

                                            Exit [*Emilia*].

DESDEMONA. 'Tis meet° I should be used so, very meet.   *appropriate*
   How have I been behaved that he might stick
   The smallest opinion on my least misuse?[3]   110

Enter Iago and Emilia.

IAGO. What is your pleasure, madam? How is't with you?
DESDEMONA. I cannot tell. Those that do teach young babes
   Do it with gentle means and easy tasks.
   He might have chid° me so, for in good faith   *scolded*
   I am a child to chiding.°   *i.e., unused to be being rebuked*
IAGO.   What is the matter, lady?   115
EMILIA. Alas, Iago, my lord hath so bewhored her,° *called her a whore*

---

1 Business (with a strong sexual innuendo).
2 Maintain our privacy.
3 Reprimand me for the slightest misconduct.

Thrown such despite[1] and heavy terms upon her
That true hearts cannot bear it.

DESDEMONA. Am I that name, Iago?

IAGO.   What name, fair lady?

120 DESDEMONA. Such as she said my lord did say I was.

EMILIA. He called her whore! A beggar in his drink
Could not have laid such terms upon his callet.°   *whore*

IAGO. Why did he so?

DESDEMONA. I do not know; I am sure I am none such.

125 IAGO. Do not weep, do not weep—alas the day!

EMILIA. Hath she forsook° so many noble matches,[2]   *turned down*
Her father, and her country, and her friends,
To be called whore? Would it not make one weep?

DESDEMONA. It is my wretched fortune.

IAGO.   Beshrew him[3] for't!
How comes this trick° upon him?   *way of behaving*

130 DESDEMONA.   Nay, heaven doth know.

EMILIA. I will be hanged if some eternal villain,
Some busy and insinuating rogue,
Some cogging, cozening[4] slave, to get some office,
Have not devised this slander; I will be hanged else.

135 IAGO. Fie, there is no such man! It is impossible.

DESDEMONA. If any such there be, heaven pardon him.

EMILIA. A halter[5] pardon him and hell gnaw his bones.
Why should he call her whore? Who keeps her company?
What place? What time? What form? What likelihood?

140 The Moor's abused by some most villainous knave,
Some base notorious knave, some scurvy[6] fellow.
O heavens, that such companions[7] thou'd'st unfold
And put in every honest hand a whip
To lash the rascals naked through the world
Even from the east to th'west.

---

1 Contempt or scorn.
2 Marriage or marriage agreements.
3 I.e., shame on him (a common curse).
4 Cheating, deceiving.
5 Noose (as for hanging).
6 Contemptible.
7 A term of contempt.

IAGO.   Speak within door.° *i.e., more quietly* 145
EMILIA. Oh, fie upon them! Some such squire¹ he was
   That turned your wit the seamy side without°   *inside out*
   And made you to suspect me with the Moor.
IAGO. You are a fool; go to.
DESDEMONA.   Alas, Iago,
   What shall I do to win my lord again?   150
   Good friend, go to him; for by this light of heaven,
   I know not how I lost him.

                                            [She kneels.]
                Here I kneel.
   If e'er my will did trespass° 'gainst his love,   *offend*
   Either in discourse of thought or actual deed,
   Or that mine eyes, mine ears, or any sense   155
   Delighted them in any other form,
   Or that I do not yet, and ever did,
   And ever will—though he do shake me off
   To beggarly divorcement—love him dearly,
   Comfort forswear² me. *[She stands.]* Unkindness may do much, 160
   And his unkindness may defeat my life,
   But never taint my love. I cannot say "whore."
   It does abhor me³ now I speak the word;
   To do the act that might the addition° earn,   *title; reputation*
   Not the world's mass of vanity⁴ could make me.   165
IAGO. I pray you be content; 'tis but his humor.
   The business of the state does him offense,
   And he does chide with you.
DESDEMONA. If 'twere no other—
IAGO.   It is but so, I warrant.
                          [Trumpets within.]
   Hark how these instruments summon to supper.   170
   The messengers of Venice stays the meat.°   *await their supper*
   Go in, and weep not; all things shall be well.
                Exeunt Desdemona and Emilia.

---

1 Gentleman (Emilia clearly uses the term ironically).
2 Abandon; renounce.
3 Both "makes me feel horrible" and "renders me detestable," with a pun on "whore."
4 All the riches in the world.

Enter Roderigo.

How now Roderigo?

RODERIGO. I do not find that thou deal'st justly with me.

175 IAGO. What in the contrary?

RODERIGO. Every day thou doff'st me[1] with some device, Iago, and
rather, as it seems to me now, keep'st from me all conveniency,[2]
then suppliest me with the least advantage of hope. I will indeed
no longer endure it. Nor am I yet persuaded to put up in peace[3]

180 what already I have foolishly suffered.

IAGO. Will you hear me, Roderigo?

RODERIGO. Faith, I have heard too much, and your words and performances are no kin together.[4]

IAGO. You charge me most unjustly.

185 RODERIGO. With naught but truth. I have wasted myself out of my
means;[5] the jewels you have had from me to deliver Desdemona
would half have corrupted a votarist.[6] You have told me she hath
received them, and returned me expectations and comforts[7] of
sudden respect and acquaintance, but I find none.

190 IAGO. Well, go to, very well.

RODERIGO. "Very well, go to!" I cannot "go to," man, nor 'tis not
"very well." By this hand, I say 'tis very scurvy, and begin to find
myself fopped[8] in it.

IAGO. Very well.

195 RODERIGO. I tell you, 'tis not very well! I will make myself known to
Desdemona. If she will return me my jewels, I will give over my
suit and repent my unlawful solicitation. If not, assure yourself,
I will seek satisfaction[9] of you.

IAGO. You have said now.

---

1 Put me off.
2 Fitting opportunities.
3 Convinced to tolerate quietly.
4 What you say and what you do are not the same.
5 Spent all my money.
6 Nun.
7 Reassurances.
8 Made a fool of; duped.
9 Repayment; atonement for injury or offence; chance to redeem one's honor in
a duel.

RODERIGO. Ay, and said nothing but what I protest intendment of 200
    doing.[1]

IAGO. Why, now I see there's mettle[2] in thee, and even from this
    instant do build on thee a better opinion than ever before. Give
    me thy hand, Roderigo. Thou hast taken against me a most just
    exception,[3] but yet I protest I have dealt most directly[4] in thy 205
    affair.

RODERIGO. It hath not appeared.

IAGO. I grant indeed it hath not appeared, and your suspicion is
    not without wit and judgment. But, Roderigo, if thou hast that
    in thee indeed which I have greater reason to believe now than 210
    ever—I mean purpose, courage, and valor—this night show it.
    If thou the next night following enjoy not Desdemona, take me
    from this world with treachery and devise engines[5] for my life.

RODERIGO. Well, what is it? Is it within reason and compass?[6]

IAGO. Sir, there is especial commission come from Venice to depute 215
    Cassio in Othello's place.

RODERIGO. Is that true? Why then Othello and Desdemona return
    again to Venice.

IAGO. Oh no, he goes into Mauritania[7] and taketh away with him
    the fair Desdemona, unless his abode be lingered[8] here by some 220
    accident, wherein none can be so determinate[9] as the removing
    of Cassio.

RODERIGO. How do you mean removing him?

IAGO. Why, by making him uncapable of Othello's place—knocking
    out his brains. 225

RODERIGO. And that you would have me to do.

---

1   Assert what I plan to do.
2   Courage.
3   Found justifiable fault in me.
4   Honestly.
5   Plots or traps; instruments of torture.
6   Reasonable limits.
7   Region of North Africa corresponding to the north of present Morocco and
parts of western and central Algeria. "I.e., the land of the Moors" (Neill).
8   Stay be extended.
9   Decisive.

IAGO. Ay, if you dare do yourself a profit and a right. He sups tonight
with a harlotry,[1] and thither will I go to him. He knows not yet of
his honorable fortune. If you will watch his going thence—which
230 I will fashion to fall out[2] between twelve and one—you may take
him at your pleasure. I will be near to second[3] your attempt, and
he shall fall between us. Come, stand not amazed at it, but go
along with me; I will show you such a necessity in his death that
you shall think yourself bound to put it on him. It is now high
235 supper time, and the night grows to waste. About it.
RODERIGO. I will hear further reason for this.
IAGO. And you shall be satisfied.

Exeunt.

[4.3]

Enter Othello, Lodovico, Desdemona, Emilia, and attendants.
LODOVICO. I do beseech you, sir, trouble yourself no further.
OTHELLO. Oh, pardon me; 'twill do me good to walk.
LODOVICO. Madam, good night; I humbly thank your ladyship.
DESDEMONA. Your honor is most welcome.
5 OTHELLO. Will you walk, sir? O Desdemona—
DESDEMONA. My lord.
OTHELLO. Get you to bed on th'instant. I will be returned forth-
with.[4] Dismiss your attendant there; look't be done.
DESDEMONA. I will, my lord.

Exeunt [Othello, Lodovico, and attendants].
10 EMILIA. How goes it now? He looks gentler than he did.
DESDEMONA. He says he will return incontinent,[5]
And hath commanded me to go to bed,
And bid me to dismiss you.
EMILIA.   Dismiss me?
DESDEMONA. It was his bidding; therefore, good Emilia,

---

1 Harlot, whore; i.e., Bianca.
2 Arrange to have happen.
3 Assist.
4 Come back at once.
5 Straight away. As Neill notes, the context of Desdemona's preparations for bed
also suggests the adjectival meaning "lacking sexual restraint."

Give me my nightly wearing,° and adieu.   *nightclothes*   15
We must not now displease him.
EMILIA. I would you had never seen him.
DESDEMONA. So would not I; my love doth so approve him
    That even his stubbornness, his checks,° his frowns—   *reprimands*
    Prithee unpin me[1]—have grace and favor in them.   20
EMILIA. I have laid those sheets you bade me on the bed.
DESDEMONA. All's one.[2] Good faith, how foolish are our minds?
    If I do die before thee, prithee shroud[3] me
    In one of these same sheets.
EMILIA.   Come, come, you talk.[4]
DESDEMONA. My mother had a maid called Barbary;[5]   25
    She was in love, and he she loved proved mad
    And did forsake her. She had a "Song of Willow"—
    An old thing 'twas, but it expressed her fortune,
    And she died singing it. That song tonight
    Will not go from my mind; I have much to do   30
    But to go hang my head all at one side

---

1   Refers to undoing a woman's dress by removing pins.
2   It makes no difference.
3   Prepare a corpse for burial by wrapping it.
4   You are talking nonsense.
5   Form of the woman's name "Barbara," with an echo of Iago's earlier designation of Othello as a *Barbary horse* (1.1.110, TLN 125).

4.3.27:   "SONG OF WILLOW" (TLN 2998)

Although the nickname "weeping willow" did not appear in print until
the eighteenth century, the willow has long been emblematic of the
miseries of love lost or unreciprocated, and it features in numerous
traditional ballads popular in the sixteenth and seventeenth centuries.
Desdemona's song is typical of the many early-modern ballads that set
mourning for a failed relationship amid both water (tears, of course, but
also rivers, streams, and brooks) and willow trees. Hers appears to be
the only one that recounts the lamentations of a female lover, however.
While some such songs were circulated without music, many others
were scored for voice and/or instruments.

And sing it like poor Barbary. Prithee dispatch.°   *hurry*
EMILIA. Shall I go fetch your nightgown?
DESDEMONA.   No, unpin me here.
     This Lodovico is a proper[1] man.
EMILIA. A very handsome man.
35 DESDEMONA.   He speaks well.
EMILIA. I know a lady in Venice would have walked
     Barefoot to Palestine[2] for a touch of his nether° lip.   *lower*
DESDEMONA. [*Singing*]
     The poor soul sat singing by a sycamore tree,[3]
       Sing all a green willow;
40   *Her hand on her bosom, her head on her knee.*
       Sing willow, willow, willow.
     The fresh streams ran by her and murmured her moans,
       Sing willow, willow, willow;
     Her salt tears fell from her and softened the stones.
       Sing willow—
         Lay by these.—
45   [*Singing*] *willow, willow.*—
     Prithee, hie thee;° he'll come anon.   *hurry up*
     [*Singing*] *Sing all a green willow must be my garland.*
     Let nobody blame him, his scorn I approve.
     Nay, that's not next. Hark, who is't that knocks?
50 EMILIA. It's the wind.
DESDEMONA. [*Singing*]
     I called my love false love, but what said he then?
       Sing willow, willow, willow;
     If I court more women, you'll couch[4] *with more men.*
     So get thee gone, goodnight. Mine eyes do itch;
     Doth that bode weeping?
55 EMILIA.   'Tis neither here nor there.
DESDEMONA. I have heard it said so. Oh, these men, these men!

---

1   Good, respectable; good-looking.
2   I.e., gone to great lengths (with echoes of religious pilgrimage and crusade).
3   Probably *Acer pseudoplatanus*, an ornamental shade tree introduced into England from Europe, but perhaps *Ficus sycomorus*, a species of fig tree common in North Africa and the Middle East.
4   Lie down; have sex.

Dost thou in conscience think—tell me, Emilia—
That there be women do abuse° their husbands   *deceive*
In such gross kind?°   *flagrant fashion*
EMILIA.   There be some such, no question.
DESDEMONA. Wouldst thou do such a deed for all the world?   60
EMILIA. Why, would not you?
DESDEMONA.   No, by this heavenly light.
EMILIA. Nor I neither, by this heavenly light;
   I might do't as well i'th'dark.
DESDEMONA. Wouldst thou do such a deed for all the world?
EMILIA. The world's a huge thing; it is a great price   65
   For a small vice.
DESDEMONA.   In troth, I think thou wouldst not.
EMILIA. In troth, I think I should, and undo't when I had done.
   Marry, I would not do such a thing for a joint ring,[1] nor for
   measures of lawn,[2] nor for gowns, petticoats, nor caps, nor any
   petty exhibition.[3] But for all the whole world—'ud's pity![4] —who   70
   would not make her husband a cuckold to make him a monarch?
   I should venture[5] purgatory for't.
DESDEMONA. Beshrew me if I would do such a wrong
   For the whole world.
EMILIA. Why, the wrong is but a wrong i'th'world; and having the   75
   world for your labor[6] 'tis a wrong in your own world, and you
   might quickly make it right.
DESDEMONA. I do not think there is any such woman.
EMILIA. Yes, a dozen—and as many to th'vantage[7] as would store[8]
   the world they played[9] for.   80
   But I do think it is their husbands' faults

---

1 A ring made of two separate hoops linked together and having the same shank
split lengthwise so the hoops can be fitted together; such rings were often used as
engagement or marriage rings in the period.
2 Lengths of fine linen.
3 Minor gift.
4 God's pity (an oath).
5 Risk.
6 As reward for your work (with a pun on *labor* = childbirth).
7 In addition, more.
8 Supply (specifically, with offspring).
9 Gambled; had sex.

If wives do fall.[1] Say that they slack their duties[2]
And pour our treasures into foreign laps;
Or else break out in peevish jealousies,
85   Throwing restraint upon us; or say they strike us,
Or scant our former having in despite.[3]
Why, we have galls;[4] and though we have some grace,
Yet have we some revenge. Let husbands know
Their wives have sense[5] like them; they see, and smell,
90   And have their palates both for sweet and sour,
As husbands have. What is it that they do
When they change us for others? Is it sport?
I think it is. And doth affection[6] breed it?
I think it doth. Is't frailty[7] that thus errs?
95   It is so too. And have not we affections,
Desires for sport, and frailty, as men have?
Then let them use us well; else let them know,
The ills we do, their ills instruct us so.
DESDEMONA. Good night, good night. God me such uses send,
100   Not to pick bad from bad, but by bad, mend.[8]

                                              Exeunt.

[5.1]

Enter Iago and Roderigo.
IAGO. Here, stand behind this bulk;[9] straight will he come.
   Wear thy good rapier[10] bare,° and put it home.[11]   *unsheathed*
   Quick, quick, fear nothing; I'll be at thy elbow.

---

1   Succumb to sexual temptation (i.e., sin against their marriage vows).
2   Neglect their (marital) obligations.
3   Reduce our previous allowance out of spite.
4   Feel resentment.
5   Physical senses; reason; sexual desires; feelings.
6   Lust.
7   Moral or physical weakness.
8   Not to imitate the bad behavior of others, but to learn from their negative
example how to make myself better.
9   Part of a building that projects.
10   Long, thin sword designed for thrusting.
11   Thrust it in as far as it will go.

It makes us or it mars us;[1] think on that,
And fix most firm thy resolution.   5
RODERIGO. Be near at hand; I may miscarry in't.[2]
IAGO. Here, at thy hand. Be bold, and take thy stand.
                                            [*Iago withdraws.*]
RODERIGO. I have no great devotion to the deed,
  And yet he hath given me satisfying reasons.
  'Tis but a man gone. [*Drawing his sword*] Forth my sword: 10
    he dies!
IAGO. [*Aside*] I have rubbed this young quat[3] almost to the sense,[4]
  And he grows angry. Now, whether he kill Cassio,
  Or Cassio him, or each do kill the other,
  Every way makes my gain.[5] Live Roderigo,
  He calls me to a restitution large[6]   15
  Of gold and jewels that I bobbed from him[7]
  As gifts to Desdemona.
  It must not be! If Cassio do remain,
  He hath a daily[8] beauty in his life
  That makes me ugly; and besides, the Moor   20
  May unfold° me to him; there stand I in much peril.   *reveal*
  No, he must die. But so—I hear him coming.

Enter Cassio.
RODERIGO. I know his gait, 'tis he. Villain, thou diest!
                                      [*Roderigo attacks Cassio.*]
CASSIO. That thrust had been mine enemy indeed,
  But that my coat is better than thou know'st.   25
  [*Drawing his sword*] I will make proof of° thine.   *put to the test*
                                      [*Cassio wounds Roderigo.*]
RODERIGO.   Oh, I am slain!
      [*Iago wounds Cassio in the leg from behind and exits.*]

---

1 Leads to our success or causes our downfall; makes us or breaks us.
2 Fail in my purpose.
3 Pimple; derogatory slang term for a young man.
4 Most sensitive spot.
5 Results in profit for me.
6 If Roderigo lives he will demand that I make a substantial repayment.
7 Tricked him out of.
8 "Constant; i.e., manifest in everything he does" (Neill).

CASSIO. I am maimed forever! Help, ho! Murder, murder!

[*Enter Othello above.*]
OTHELLO. [*Aside*] The voice of Cassio. Iago keeps his word.
RODERIGO. Oh, villain that I am!
OTHELLO.   [*Aside*] It is even so.
30 CASSIO. Oh, help ho! Light! A surgeon!°   doctor
OTHELLO. [*Aside*] 'Tis he. O brave Iago, honest and just,
That hast such noble sense of thy friend's wrong,
Thou teachest me. Minion,[1] your dear lies dead,
And your unblest fate hies.° Strumpet, I come.   approaches quickly
35 Forth° of my heart those charms,[2] thine eyes, are blotted.[3]   out
Thy bed, lust-stained, shall with lust's blood be spotted.
                                    Exit Othello.

Enter Lodovico and Gratiano.
CASSIO. What ho! No watch? No passage?[4] Murder, murder!
GRATIANO. 'Tis some mischance; the voice is very direful.[5]
CASSIO. Oh, help!
40 LODOVICO. Hark!
RODERIGO. O wretched villain!
LODOVICO. Two or three groan. 'Tis heavy night.
These may be counterfeits;[6] let's think't unsafe
To come into the cry without more help.
45 RODERIGO. Nobody come? Then shall I bleed to death.

Enter Iago [with a light and sword].
LODOVICO. Hark!
GRATIANO. Here's one comes in his shirt, with light and weapons.
IAGO. Who's there? Whose noise is this that cries on[7] murder?
LODOVICO. We do not know.

---

1 Woman kept for sexual favors, mistress; i.e., an ironic reference to Desdemona.
2 Appealing things; magical objects.
3 Obliterated.
4 Passers-by.
5 Full of dread.
6 I.e., faked calls for assistance.
7 Exclaims against.

IAGO.   Do not you hear a cry?

CASSIO. Here, here! For heaven sake, help me!

IAGO.   What's the matter?   50

GRATIANO. This is Othello's ancient, as I take it.

LODOVICO. The same indeed, a very valiant fellow.

IAGO. What are you here that cry so grievously?

CASSIO. Iago? Oh, I am spoiled,° undone by villains.   *seriously injured*
   Give me some help.   55

IAGO. Oh, me, lieutenant! What villains have done this?

CASSIO. I think that one of them is hereabout
   And cannot make away.°   *escape*

IAGO.   O treacherous villains!
   [*To Lodovico and Gratiano*] What are you there? Come in and
      give some help.

RODERIGO. Oh, help me there!

CASSIO.   That's one of them.[1]   60

IAGO. O murd'rous slave! O villain!

                              [*Iago stabs Roderigo.*]

RODERIGO. O damned Iago! O inhuman dog!

IAGO. Kill men i'th'dark? Where be these bloody thieves?
   How silent is this town? Ho, murder, murder!
   What may you be? Are you of good or evil?   65

LODOVICO. As you shall prove us, praise us.[2]

IAGO. Signor Lodovico?

LODOVICO. He, sir.

IAGO. I cry you mercy[3]—here's Cassio hurt by villains.

GRATIANO. Cassio?   70

IAGO. How is't brother?

CASSIO. My leg is cut in two.

IAGO. Marry, heaven forbid—Light, gentlemen!
   I'll bind it with my shirt.

---

1 I.e., one of those who attacked me.
2 As you find us to be by experience, so you will value us; cf. the proverbial
"Prove ere you praise" (see Dent P614.2).
3 Beg your pardon.

Enter Bianca.

75 BIANCA. What is the matter, ho? Who is't that cried?
IAGO. Who is't that cried?
BIANCA.   O my dear Cassio,
    My sweet Cassio—O Cassio, Cassio, Cassio!
IAGO. O notable strumpet. Cassio, may you suspect
    Who they should be that have thus mangled you?
80 CASSIO. No.
GRATIANO. I am sorry to find you thus;
    I have been to seek you.
IAGO.   Lend me a garter.[1] So—

                    [*Iago binds Cassio's leg.*]

    O for a chair[2] to bear him easily hence!
BIANCA. Alas, he faints. O Cassio, Cassio, Cassio!
85 IAGO. Gentlemen all, I do suspect this trash°   *disreputable person*
    To be a party in this injury.
    Patience awhile, good Cassio. Come, come,
    Lend me a light. Know we this face or no?
    Alas, my friend and my dear countryman
90 Roderigo? No—Yes, sure! O heaven, Roderigo!
GRATIANO. What, of Venice?
IAGO. Even he, sir. Did you know him?
GRATIANO. Know him? Ay.
IAGO. Signor Gratiano? I cry your gentle pardon.
95 These bloody accidents must excuse my manners
    That so neglected you.
GRATIANO.   I am glad to see you.
IAGO. How do you, Cassio?—Oh, a chair, a chair!
GRATIANO. Roderigo?
IAGO. He, he, 'tis he.

[*Enter attendants with a chair.*]
                    Oh, that's well said, the chair.
100 Some good man bear him carefully from hence;
    I'll fetch the general's surgeon. For you, mistress,

---

1 Band worn around the leg or waist.
2 A portable sick-chair carried by the arms or on poles is probably intended here.

Save you your labor. He that lies slain here, Cassio,
Was my dear friend. What malice was between you?
CASSIO. None in the world; nor do I know the man.
IAGO. [*To Bianca*] What? Look you pale? [*To attendants*] Oh, bear   105
    him out o'th'air.°   *i.e., inside*
                        [*Exeunt attendants carrying off Cassio in the chair,*
                                              and Roderigo's body.]
    [*To Lodovico and Gratiano*] Stay you, good gentlemen.
        [*To Bianca*] Look you pale, mistress?
    [*To Lodovico and Gratiano*] Do you perceive the gastness[1]
        of her eye?
    Nay, if you stare, we shall hear more anon. [2]
    Behold her well. I pray you, look upon her.
    Do you see, gentlemen? Nay, guiltiness will speak   110
    Though tongues were out of use.°   *not used*

[*Enter Emilia.*]
EMILIA. Alas, what is the matter? What is the matter, husband?
IAGO. Cassio hath here been set on in the dark
    By Roderigo and fellows that are scaped;
    He's almost slain, and Roderigo quite dead.   115
EMILIA. Alas, good gentleman! Alas, good Cassio!
IAGO. This is the fruits of whoring. Prithee, Emilia,
    Go know of Cassio where he supped tonight.
    What, do you shake at that?
BIANCA. He supped at my house, but I therefore shake not.   120
IAGO. Oh, did he so? I charge you go with me.
EMILIA. O fie upon thee, strumpet!
BIANCA. I am no strumpet, but of life as honest
    As you that thus abuse me.[3]
EMILIA.   As I? Fie upon thee!

---

1   Terrified appearance.
2   "You will soon confess the guilt betrayed by your appearance" (Pechter).
3   The term *honest* resonates powerfully here as Emilia joins *honest* Iago in attacking Bianca, and Bianca, who seems guilty of nothing more than having fallen in
love with Cassio, inadvertently reminds readers and audiences not only of Emilia's
guilt by association with Iago but also of her direct culpability in the removal of
Desdemona's handkerchief.

125 IAGO. Kind gentlemen, let's go see poor Cassio dressed.[1]
Come, mistress, you must tell's another tale.
Emilia, run you to the citadel
And tell my lord and lady what hath happed.
Will you go on afore? [*Aside*] This is the night
130 That either makes me or fordoes[2] me quite.

Exeunt.

[5.2]

Enter Othello [with a light] and Desdemona in her bed.
OTHELLO. It is the cause,[3] it is the cause, my soul.
Let me not name it to you, you chaste stars.
It is the cause. Yet I'll not shed her blood,
Nor scar that whiter skin of hers than snow
5 And smooth as monumental alabaster[4]—
Yet she must die, else she'll betray more men.
Put out the light, and then put out the light[5]—
If I quench thee, thou flaming minister,[6]
I can again thy former light restore
10 Should I repent me.° But once put out thy light,[7]   *feel regret*
Thou cunning'st pattern of excelling nature,[8]
I know not where is that Promethean heat[9]
That can thy light relume.[10] When I have plucked thy rose,
I cannot give it vital growth again;
15 It needs must wither. I'll smell thee on the tree.

[*He kisses her.*]

O balmy[11] breath, that dost almost persuade

---

1 Oversee treatment of Cassio's wounds.
2 Destroys.
3 Reason; ground for legal action.
4 White form of gypsum used for carving funeral monuments.
5 Extinguish the light and then snuff out Desdemona's life.
6 I.e., the light that serves Othello; *minister* = one who waits upon another.
7 I.e., Desdemona's life.
8 Most skillfully created model of nature at her best. However, *cunning* (= sly)
also carries potentially negative connotations here.
9 "Divine spark" (McDonald).
10 Rekindle, light again.
11 Deliciously fragrant.

Justice to break her sword—one more, one more.

[*He kisses her.*]

Be thus when thou art dead, and I will kill thee
And love thee after—one more, and that's the last.

[*He kisses her.*]

So sweet was ne'er so fatal.[1] I must weep,   20
But they are cruel tears. This sorrow's heavenly;
It strikes where it doth love. She wakes.

DESDEMONA. Who's there? Othello?

OTHELLO.   Ay, Desdemona.

DESDEMONA. Will you come to bed, my lord?

OTHELLO. Have you prayed tonight, Desdemon?

DESDEMONA.   Ay, my lord.   25

OTHELLO. If you bethink yourself of any crime
   Unreconciled as yet to heaven and grace,
   Solicit[2] for it straight.

DESDEMONA. Alack, my lord, what may you mean by that?

OTHELLO. Well, do it, and be brief; I will walk by.   30
   I would not kill thy unprepared spirit.
   No, heavens forfend!°—I would not kill thy soul.   *forbid*

DESDEMONA. Talk you of killing?

OTHELLO.   Ay, I do.

DESDEMONA. Then heaven have mercy on me.

OTHELLO.   Amen, with all my heart.

DESDEMONA. If you say so, I hope you will not kill me.   35

OTHELLO. Humh.

DESDEMONA. And yet I fear you, for you're fatal[3] then
   When your eyes roll so. Why I should fear I know not,
   Since guiltiness I know not; but yet I feel I fear.

OTHELLO. Think on thy sins.

DESDEMONA.   They are loves I bear to you.   40

OTHELLO. Ay, and for that thou diest.

DESDEMONA. That death's unnatural that kills for loving.
   Alas, why gnaw you so your nether lip?
   Some bloody passion shakes your very frame.

---

1   Deadly; doomed by fate; ominous; prophetic.
2   Beg forgiveness.
3   Ominous, with a pun on *fatal* = deadly.

45   These are portents;° but yet I hope, I hope,   *omens*
       They do not point on me.°   *foretell my fate*

OTHELLO.   Peace, and be still.

DESDEMONA. I will so. What's the matter?

OTHELLO. That handkerchief which I so loved and gave thee,
       Thou gav'st to Cassio.

DESDEMONA.   No, by my life and soul!
       Send for the man and ask him.

50   OTHELLO.   Sweet soul, take heed;
       Take heed of perjury; thou art on thy deathbed.

DESDEMONA. Ay, but not yet to die.

OTHELLO.   Yes, presently.
       Therefore confess thee freely of thy sin;
       For to deny each article[1] with oath

55   Cannot remove nor choke the strong conception[2]
       That I do groan withal. Thou art to die.

DESDEMONA. O heaven have mercy on me!

OTHELLO.   I say amen.

DESDEMONA. And have you mercy too. I never did
       Offend° you in my life, never loved Cassio   *wrong*

60   But with such general warranty° of heaven   *sanction*
       As I might love. I never gave him token.°   *symbol of affection*

OTHELLO. By heaven, I saw my handkerchief in's hand.
       O perjured woman, thou dost stone° my heart,   *turn to stone*
       And makes me call what I intend to do

65   A murder, which I thought a sacrifice.
       I saw the handkerchief.

DESDEMONA.   He found it then.
       I never gave it him. Send for him hither.
       Let him confess a truth.

OTHELLO.   He hath confessed.

DESDEMONA. What, my lord?

OTHELLO.   That he hath—'ud's death![3]—used thee.

DESDEMONA. How? Unlawfully?

OTHELLO.   Ay.

---

1   Count in a criminal charge.
2   Conviction; plan; offspring.
3   God's death (an oath).

DESDEMONA. He will not say so. 70
OTHELLO. No, his mouth is stopped.
   Honest Iago hath ta'en order for't.
DESDEMONA. Oh, my fear interprets. What, is he dead?
OTHELLO. Had all his hairs been lives, my great revenge
   Had stomach° for them all. *appetite* 75
DESDEMONA. Alas, he is betrayed, and I undone.
OTHELLO. Out, strumpet! Weep'st thou for him to my face?
DESDEMONA. Oh, banish me, my lord, but kill me not.
OTHELLO. Down, strumpet.
DESDEMONA. Kill me tomorrow; let me live tonight. 80
OTHELLO. Nay, if you strive.° *struggle*
DESDEMONA. But half an hour.
OTHELLO. Being done, there is no pause.[1]
DESDEMONA. But while I say one prayer.
OTHELLO. It is too late.

[Othello] smothers her.
Emilia [is heard] at the door.

EMILIA. [*Within*] My lord, my lord? What ho? My lord, my lord!
OTHELLO. What noise is this? Not dead? Not yet quite dead? 85
   I that am cruel am yet merciful;
   I would not have thee linger in thy pain—
   [*Smothering her again*] So, so.
EMILIA. (*Within*) What ho? My lord, my lord?
OTHELLO. Who's there?
EMILIA. O good my lord, I would speak a word with you. 90
OTHELLO. Yes—'Tis Emilia.—By and by!°—She's dead. *in a minute!*
   'Tis like[2] she comes to speak of Cassio's death.
   The noise was high.° Ha, no more moving? *loud*
   Still as the grave. Shall she come in? Were't good?
   I think she stirs again. No. What's best to do? 95
   If she come in, she'll sure speak to my wife—
   My wife, my wife—what wife? I have no wife.
   Oh, insupportable! Oh, heavy hour!
   Methinks it should be now a huge eclipse

---

1   This line seems to suggest that having determined Desdemona's guilt and devised a plan for her murder, Othello will not stop until he has killed her.
2   Likely.

100 Of sun and moon, and that th'affrighted globe
Did yawn at alteration.[1]
EMILIA.   [*Within*] I do beseech you
That I may speak with you. O good my lord.
OTHELLO. I had forgot thee. O come in, Emilia.
Soft,—By and by!—let me the curtains draw. [*He closes the bed curtains.*]
105 Where art thou? What's the matter with thee now?

[*He unlocks the door.*] *Enter Emilia.*
EMILIA. O my good lord, yonder's foul murders done.
OTHELLO. What? Now?
EMILIA.   But now, my lord.
OTHELLO. It is the very error of the moon;
She comes more nearer Earth than she was wont,
And makes men mad.
110 EMILIA.   Cassio, my lord, hath killed
A young Venetian called Roderigo.
OTHELLO. Roderigo killed? And Cassio killed?
EMILIA. No, Cassio is not killed.
OTHELLO. Not Cassio killed? Then murder's out of tune,
115 And sweet revenge grows harsh.
DESDEMONA. Oh, falsely, falsely murdered.
EMILIA. O Lord! What cry is that?
OTHELLO.   That? What?
EMILIA. Out and alas, that was my lady's voice!
                [*She opens the bed curtains.*]
Help, help, ho, help! O lady, speak again.
120 Sweet Desdemona, O sweet mistress, speak.
DESDEMONA. A guiltless death I die.
EMILIA. Oh, who hath done this deed?
DESDEMONA. Nobody—I myself. Farewell—
Commend me to my kind lord—Oh, farewell.
                [*Desdemona dies.*]
OTHELLO. Why, how should she be° murdered?   *has she come to be*
125 EMILIA.   Alas, who knows?

---

1 Open wide or gape at change.

OTHELLO. You heard her say herself, it was not I.

EMILIA. She said so; I must needs report the truth.

OTHELLO. She's like a liar gone to burning hell;
   'Twas I that killed her.

EMILIA. Oh, the more angel she, and you the blacker devil.   130

OTHELLO. She turned to folly,[1] and she was a whore.

EMILIA. Thou dost belie her, and thou art a devil.

OTHELLO. She was false as water.°   *i.e., unfaithful*

EMILIA.   Thou art rash as fire[2]
   To say that she was false. Oh, she was heavenly true.

OTHELLO. Cassio did top° her; ask thy husband else.[3]   *copulate with* 135
   Oh, I were damned beneath all depth in hell,
   But that I did proceed upon just grounds
   To this extremity. Thy husband knew it all.

EMILIA. My husband?

OTHELLO.   Thy husband.

EMILIA.   That she was false to wedlock?

OTHELLO. Ay, with Cassio. Had she been true,   140
   If heaven would make me such another world
   Of one entire and perfect chrysolite,[4]
   I'd not have sold her for it.

EMILIA.   My husband?

OTHELLO. Ay, 'twas he that told me on her first.
   An honest man he is, and hates the slime°   *moral filth; semen* 145
   That sticks on filthy deeds.

EMILIA.   My husband?

OTHELLO. What needs this iterance,[5] woman? I say, thy husband.

EMILIA. O mistress, villainy hath made mocks with love—
   My husband say she was false?

OTHELLO.   He, woman;
   I say thy husband—dost understand the word?—   150
   My friend, thy husband, honest, honest Iago.

EMILIA. If he say so, may his pernicious soul

---

1 Wickedness; wantonness.
2 I.e., reckless or foolhardy.
3 If you don't believe me.
4 Greenish gemstone, probably peridot or topaz.
5 Repetition.

Rot half a grain a day;[1] he lies to th'heart.

She was too fond of her most filthy bargain.[2]

155 OTHELLO. Ha?

EMILIA. Do thy worst.

This deed of thine is no more worthy heaven,

Than thou wast worthy her.

OTHELLO.   Peace, you were best.[3]

EMILIA. Thou hast not half that power to do me harm

160 As I have to be hurt. O gull,° O dolt,   *dupe*

As ignorant as dirt,° thou hast done a deed—   *excrement; filth*

[*Othello threatens Emilia with his sword.*]

I care not for[4] thy sword; I'll make thee known[5]

Though I lost twenty lives. Help, help, ho, help!

The Moor hath killed my mistress. Murder, murder!

Enter Montano, Gratiano, and Iago.

165 MONTANO. What is the matter? How now, general?

EMILIA. Oh, are you come, Iago? You have done well,

That men must lay their murders on your neck.[6]

GRATIANO. What is the matter?

EMILIA. [*To Iago*] Disprove this villain, if thou be'st a man.

170 He says thou told'st him that his wife was false.

I know thou didst not; thou'rt not such a villain.

Speak, for my heart is full.

IAGO. I told him what I thought, and told no more

Than what he found himself was apt and true.

175 EMILIA. But did you ever tell him she was false?

IAGO. I did.

EMILIA. You told a lie, an odious damnèd lie,

Upon my soul, a lie, a wicked lie.

She false with Cassio? Did you say with Cassio?

---

1 *Grain* = particle, thus "very slowly."

2 I.e., foul marriage; *filthy* = foul; morally polluted; disgraceful (*OED adj.* 1a; 3; 4a). It may also suggest the ostensible "dirtiness" of Othello's skin color.

3 You had best be quiet.

4 I am not afraid of.

5 I'll tell everyone what you have done.

6 Blame you for their murders.

IAGO. With Cassio, mistress. Go to, charm your tongue.[1]   180
EMILIA. I will not charm my tongue; I am bound to speak.
    My mistress here lies murdered in her bed.
ALL. O heavens forfend!
EMILIA. And your reports have set the murder on.[2]
OTHELLO. Nay, stare not, masters; it is true indeed.   185
GRATIANO. 'Tis a strange truth.
MONTANO.   O monstrous act!
EMILIA. Villainy, villainy, villainy!
    I think upon't, I think I smell't. O villainy—
    I thought so then—I'll kill myself for grief!
    O villainy! Villainy!   190
IAGO. What, are you mad? I charge you get you home.
EMILIA. Good gentlemen, let me have leave to speak.
    'Tis proper I obey him, but not now.
    Perchance, Iago, I will ne'er go home.
OTHELLO. Oh, Oh, Oh!

                        [*Othello falls on the bed.*]
EMILIA.   Nay, lay thee down and roar,   195
    For thou hast killed the sweetest innocent
    That ere did lift up eye.
OTHELLO.   Oh, she was foul!
    I scarce did know you, uncle.[3] There lies your niece,
    Whose breath, indeed, these hands have newly stopped.
    I know this act shows horrible and grim.   200
GRATIANO. Poor Desdemon, I am glad thy father's dead;
    Thy match was mortal to him, and pure grief
    Shore his old thread in twain. Did he live now,
    This sight would make him do a desperate turn;[4]
    Yea, curse his better angel from his side   205
    And fall to reprobance.[5]
OTHELLO. 'Tis pitiful, but yet Iago knows

---

1 I.e., be quiet.
2 Incited the murder.
3 Gratiano is presumably the brother to whom Brabantio refers at 1.1.172, TLN
193.
4 Act of despair; i.e., suicide.
5 Reprobation; rejection of and by God.

That she with Cassio hath the act of shame
A thousand times committed. Cassio confessed it,
210   And she did gratify° his amorous works   *reward*
    With that recognizance° and pledge of love   *token*

5.2.202–03:   THE THREE FATES (TLN 3495)

When Gratiano mourns his niece Desdemona's death, he claims that grief over her marriage to Othello has killed her father, Brabantio, saying "pure grief / Shore his old thread in twain." Gratiano's reference is the representation in classical mythology of life as a thread that is spun, apportioned, and cut by the three Fates: Clotho, Lachesis, and Atropos.

Jacob Matham, *The Three Fates* (1587). Wikimedia Commons, https://commons.wikimedia.org.

Which I first gave her;—I saw it in his hand—
It was a handkerchief, an antique token
My father gave my mother.
EMILIA. O God, O heavenly God!
IAGO.   Zounds, hold your peace.   215
EMILIA. 'Twill out,[1] 'twill out. I peace?
No, I will speak as liberal as the north;[2]
Let heaven and men and devils, let them all,
All, all cry shame against me, yet I'll speak.
IAGO. Be wise, and get you home.
EMILIA.   I will not.   220
        [*Iago threatens Emilia with his sword.*]
GRATIANO. Fie, your sword upon a woman?
EMILIA. O thou dull[3] Moor, that handkerchief thou speak'st of
I found by fortune,° and did give my husband;   chance
For often, with a solemn earnestness—
More than indeed belonged to such a trifle—   225
He begged of me to steal't.
IAGO.   Villainous whore!
EMILIA. She give it Cassio? No, alas, I found it,
And I did give't my husband.
IAGO.   Filth, thou liest.
EMILIA. By heaven, I do not. I do not, gentlemen.—
O murderous coxcomb,[4] what should such a fool   230
Do with so good a wife?
        [*Othello runs at Iago and is disarmed by Montano. Iago stabs Emilia.*]
OTHELLO.   Are there no stones in heaven
But what serves for the thunder?[5] Precious[6] villain!
GRATIANO. The woman falls; sure he hath killed his wife.
EMILIA. Ay, ay. Oh, lay me by my mistress's side.
                                          [*Exit Iago.*]

---

1   The truth will emerge.
2   As freely as the north wind blows.
3   Obtuse; foolish.
4   Cap worn by jesters; i.e., Emilia is calling Othello a fool.
5   *Stones in heaven* = thunderbolts, sometimes called thunderstones; Othello
wonders here at heaven's apparent inability to spare an extra projectile with which
to destroy Iago.
6   Complete (a mocking intensifier).

235   GRATIANO. He's gone, but his wife's killed.
     MONTANO. 'Tis a notorious villain. Take you this weapon
        Which I have here recovered from the Moor.
        Come guard the door without;° let him not pass,   *from the outside*
        But kill him rather. I'll after that same villain,
        For 'tis a damnèd slave.
                                    Exeunt [Montano and Gratiano].
240   OTHELLO.   I am not valiant neither,
        But every puny[1] whipster[2] gets my sword.
        But why should honor outlive honesty?
        Let it go all.
     EMILIA.   What did thy song bode,° lady?   *foretell*
        Hark, canst thou hear me? I will play the swan,
245   And die in music: [*Singing*] Willow, willow, willow.
        Moor, she was chaste. She loved thee, cruel Moor.
        So come my soul to bliss, as I speak true;
        So speaking as I think, alas, I die.
                                              [Emilia dies.]
     OTHELLO. I have another weapon in this chamber;
250   It was a sword of Spain, the ice-brook's temper—[3]
        Oh, here it is. Uncle, I must come forth.
     GRATIANO. [*Within*] If thou attempt it, it will cost thee dear;
        Thou hast no weapon and perforce must suffer.
     OTHELLO. Look in upon me then, and speak with me,
255   Or naked° as I am I will assault thee.   *unarmed*

     [*Enter Gratiano.*]
     GRATIANO. What is the matter?
     OTHELLO.   Behold, I have a weapon;
        A better never did itself sustain
        Upon a soldier's thigh. I have seen the day
        That with this little arm and this good sword
260   I have made my way through more impediments

---

1   Subordinate; weak; inexperienced.
2   Literally, one who drives horses; figuratively, a contemptible inferior.
3   Spanish swords were considered among the most finely crafted available in the period. Sword blades were tempered (brought to a suitable degree of hardness and flexibility) by being heated and then plunged into cold water.

Than twenty times your stop.¹ But—O vain boast!—
Who can control his fate? 'Tis not so now.
Be not afraid, though you do see me weaponed.
Here is my journey's end, here is my butt²
And very seamark of my utmost sail.°   *boundary of my farthest journey*   265
Do you go back dismayed?³ 'Tis a lost° fear.   *groundless*
Man but a rush against⁴ Othello's breast
And he retires. Where should Othello go?
Now, how dost thou look now? O ill-starred° wench,   *ill-fated*
Pale as thy smock; when we shall meet at compt,⁵   270
This look of thine will hurl my soul from heaven
And fiends will snatch at it. Cold, cold, my girl?
Even like thy chastity. O cursèd, cursèd slave!
Whip me, ye devils, from the possession of this heavenly sight,
Blow me about in winds, roast me in sulfur,   275
Wash me in steep-down° gulfs of liquid fire—   *precipitous*
O Desdemon!⁶ Dead Desdemon! Dead—Oh, Oh!

Enter Lodovico, Cassio [in a chair], Montano, and Iago with officers.
LODOVICO. Where is this rash and most unfortunate man?
OTHELLO. That's he that was Othello; here I am.
LODOVICO. Where is that viper? Bring the villain forth.   280
OTHELLO. I look down toward his feet, but that's a fable;⁷
    If that thou be'st a devil, I cannot kill thee.
                                        [*Othello wounds Iago.*]
LODOVICO. Wrench his sword from him.
IAGO.   I bleed, sir, but not killed.
OTHELLO. I am not sorry neither; I'd have thee live,

---

1   The obstacle you present.
2   Terminal point, goal, destination.
3   Overwhelmed with fear.
4   Attack with only a blade of grass.
5   Reckoning; i.e., the Last Judgment.
6   Othello repeats the punning truncation of Desdemona's name that he first
employs at 3.3.53, TLN 1651. See also 3.1.50, TLN 1574; 4.2.42, TLN 2735; 5.2.24,
TLN 3266).
7   Othello refers to the convention that the devil has cloven feet. He looks to
Iago's feet for confirmation that his evil is inhuman, and then reminds himself
that such proofs are the stuff of stories.

285 For in my sense° 'tis happiness to die.   *opinion*
LODOVICO. O thou Othello, that was once so good,
· Fallen in the practice of a damnèd slave,[1]
What shall be said to thee?
OTHELLO.   Why, anything—
An honorable murderer, if you will,
290 For naught I did in hate, but all in honor.
LODOVICO. This wretch hath part confessed his villainy.
Did you and he consent in° Cassio's death?   *agree on*
OTHELLO. Ay.
CASSIO. Dear general, I never gave you cause.
295 OTHELLO. I do believe it, and I ask your pardon.
Will you, I pray, demand that demi-devil
Why he hath thus ensnared my soul and body?
IAGO. Demand me nothing. What you know, you know.
From this time forth, I never will speak word.
LODOVICO. What, not to pray?
300 GRATIANO.   Torments° will ope your lips.   *torture*
OTHELLO. Well, thou dost best.
LODOVICO. Sir, you shall understand what hath befallen,
Which, as I think, you know not. Here is a letter
Found in the pocket of the slain Roderigo,
305 And here another. The one of them imports°   *communicates*
The death of Cassio, to be undertook
By Roderigo.
OTHELLO. O villain!
CASSIO.   Most heathenish and most gross!
LODOVICO. Now here's another discontented paper[2]
310 Found in his pocket too; and this, it seems,
Roderigo meant t'have sent this damnèd villain,
But that, belike,° Iago in the interim   *probably*
Came in and satisfied him.[3]
OTHELLO. O thou pernicious caitiff!°   *prisoner; wretch; villain*
315 How came you, Cassio, by that handkerchief
That was my wife's?

---

1 I.e., as a result of Iago's scheming.
2 Letter filled with complaints.
3 Provided him with a satisfactory explanation.

CASSIO.   I found it in my chamber,
  And he himself confessed it but even now
  That there he dropped it for a special purpose
  Which wrought to his desire.°   *worked to his advantage*
OTHELLO.   O fool, fool, fool!
CASSIO. There is besides in Roderigo's letter   320
  How he upbraids° Iago that he made him   *reproaches*
  Brave° me upon the watch, whereon it came   *challenge*
  That I was cast;[1] and even but now he spake,
  After long seeming dead, Iago hurt him,
  Iago set him on.   325
LODOVICO. [*To Othello*] You must forsake this room and go with us.
  Your power and your command is taken off,
  And Cassio rules in Cyprus. For this slave,
  If there be any cunning cruelty
  That can torment him much and hold him long,   330
  It shall be his. You shall close[2] prisoner rest,°   *stay*
  Till that the nature of your fault be known
  To the Venetian state. Come, bring away.
OTHELLO. Soft you, a word or two before you go.
  I have done the state some service, and they know't;   335
  No more of that. I pray you in your letters,
  When you shall these unlucky deeds relate,
  Speak of me as I am. Nothing extenuate,[3]
  Nor set down[4] aught in malice. Then must you speak
  Of one that loved not wisely, but too well;   340
  Of one not easily jealous, but, being wrought,[5]
  Perplexed in the extreme; of one whose hand,
  Like the base[6] Indian, threw a pearl away
  Richer than all his tribe; of one whose subdued eyes,
  Albeit unused to the melting mood,[7]   345

---

1 As a result of which I was dismissed.
2 Carefully guarded.
3 Omit; lessen the effect of, mitigate.
4 Write, put on the record; bring low, debase.
5 Worked up (by passion); fashioned.
6 Deep in color; morally low; low-born.
7 I.e., tearfulness.

Drops tears as fast as the Arabian trees
Their medicinable gum. Set you down this,
And say besides that in Aleppo¹ once,
Where a malignant and a turbaned Turk
350   Beat a Venetian and traduced° the state,   *defamed*
I took by th'throat the circumcisèd² dog

---

1   City in early modern Turkey (now in Syria) known as a center for trade
between Europe and Asia.
2   Refers to the surgical removal of the foreskin, a traditional rite in Islam, in
Judaism, and also in some Christian churches.

5.2.343:   "THE BASE INDIAN" (TLN 3658)

The early printed texts of *Othello* disagree over this line: the First Quarto
(Q1) of 1622 and the Second Quarto (Q2) of 1630 both read "Indian,"
while the First Folio (F1) of 1623 offers "Iudean." One reading or the
other is almost certainly an error, as the spelling of the two words is
virtually identical, but this notorious crux is unlikely to be resolved
definitively since the arguments for each are plausible. The textual evidence is fairly straightforward, if ultimately inconclusive: 1) as the letter
i was often substituted for the letter *j* before spelling became regular-
ized, either word might have started with an uppercase *I*; similarly, 2)
as the letters *i* and *e* were often used interchangeably, either word may
have ended -*ian* or -*ean*; also, 3) as the letters *n* and *u* are often impossible to distinguish in the handwriting of the period, the second letters of the words offer no guidance; and finally, 4) even if a compositor
recognized in the manuscript from which he was working a clear *n* or
u as the second letter, either letter could have been accidentally turned
during the typesetting process, resulting in an inadvertent transformation of the word.

Although the textual evidence is inconclusive, the dictionary favors
"Indian." While the words "Indian" (meaning either "aboriginal from the
Americas" or "native of India") and "Judean" (meaning either "inhabit-
ant of Judaea" or "member of the tribe of Judah") were both used in the
period, the former appears in print more often, and the *Oxford English
Dictionary* does not record the first appearance of the latter until 1652,
thirty years after *Othello*'s initial publication. Interpretively, too, the case

And smote° him—thus.   *struck*

[*Othello stabs himself.*]

LODOVICO. O bloody period.°   *end*

GRATIANO.   All that is spoke is marred.°   *ruined*

OTHELLO. I kissed thee ere I killed thee—no way but this,

Killing myself, to die upon a kiss.[1]   355

[*Othello kisses Desdemona and*] *dies.*

---

1 Othello's stage death literalizes the *mors osculi*, or death kiss, the mystic phe-
nomenon said to unite bodily extinction, sexual climax, and spiritual ecstasy.

---

is stronger for "Indian" as Othello compares himself to one who "threw a
pearl away / Richer than all his tribe," a simile that presumably draws on
the claim, featured in numerous seventeenth-century travelers' accounts,
that American Indians were oblivious to the value of precious stones
and so disposed of them or traded them for worthless baubles. There
is also at least one literary reference to Moors being indifferent to the
value of pearls. On this reading, then, Othello is comparing his murder
of Desdemona to the inadvertent casting away of a terribly undervalued
treasure. The Folio reading—"(Like the base Iudean)"—can draw on no
such contextual evidence for support since Judeans are not associated
with a comparable lack of awareness about the value of gems. Instead,
scholars who prefer "Judean" suggest that the phrase evokes either
biblical accounts of Judas's betrayal of Jesus or the story of Herod the
Great's murder of his wife Mariam, available to English readers through
Thomas Lodge's 1602 translation of works by first-century Jewish historian Flavius Josephus and later traced in Elizabeth Cary's closet drama
The Tragedy of Mariam, the Fair Queen of Jewry (published 1613). Although
generally more popular with supporters of the F1 reading, the first of
these options is weakened by the fact that the evidence that Judas was
Judean is not strong. The parallels between Judas and Othello—that
both men answer love with betrayal and both preface their devastating
betrayals with a kiss—are also somewhat tenuous. The suggestion that
the phrase might allude to the famed beauty Mariam and the Judean king
Herod is appealing because of the specificity of its parallels, but finally
it seems unlikely that an early-modern audience would have recognized
such a precise and relatively obscure reference.

CASSIO. This did I fear, but thought he had no weapon,
For he was great of heart.

LODOVICO.   O Spartan dog,°   *i.e., Iago*
More fell° than anguish, hunger, or the sea,   *savage*
Look on the tragic loading of this bed.¹
360   This is thy work. The object poisons sight;
Let it be hid. Gratiano, keep² the house
And seize upon the fortunes of the Moor,
For they succeed on you.³ [*To Cassio*] To you, lord governor,
Remains the censure° of this hellish villain;⁴   *judgment*
365   The time, the place, the torture, oh, enforce it.
Myself will straight aboard, and to the state
This heavy act with heavy heart relate.

                                                    Exeunt.

---

1   Lodovico's image is of the bed weighted down by the dead bodies of
Desdemona, Emilia, and Othello.
2   Take possession of; guard; look after.
3   You inherit them.
4   I.e., Iago.

APPENDIX A: SOURCES AND EARLY ANALOGS

1. FROM CINTHIO, *GLI HECCATOMMITHI*, THIRD DECADE (VENICE, 1565), 317–25; TRANS. JESSICA SLIGHTS, WITH SPECIAL THANKS TO JOSEPH GROSSI

[The main source for Shakespeare's *Othello* is a short prose tale first published in 1565 by Italian author Giovanni Battista Giraldi, nicknamed Cinthio (1504–73).[1] Cinthio's *novella* provided Shakespeare with the basic outlines of his plot as well as prototypes of his central characters: an unnamed military commander referred to throughout as "the Moor"; the wife he has married against her family's wishes, called Disdemona; a demoted Corporal on whose behalf Disdemona pleads; Disdemona's closest confidante, wife of the Moor's Ensign; and, of course, the Ensign himself, a malicious figure who falls in love with Disdemona, persuades her husband that she has been unfaithful with the Corporal, and then, with her husband's help, beats her to death and disguises her murder as an accident. While there are clear similarities between Cinthio's tale and *Othello*, substantive differences in plot, tone, and narrative frame emphasize the texts' distinct approaches to their shared subject matter.]

STORY 7

... it happens sometimes that a blameless, loyal, and loving woman, through traps set by a villainous heart and the weakness of one who is more credulous than he should be, is killed by a faithful husband, as you will clearly see from what I am about to relate.

There once lived in Venice a Moor, a very valiant man, who, because of the advantages of his person, and because he had proven his great judgment and his lively intelligence in matters of war, was dear to those lords who in rewarding virtuous deeds surpass those of all other republics. It happened that a virtuous woman, a marvelous beauty called Disdemona, drawn not by her womanly desire but by the Moor's virtue,

---

1   It is possible that Shakespeare knew the tale through a 1584 French translation by Gabriel Chappuys (c. 1546–1613), but similarities in language strongly suggest that he was familiar with Cinthio's Italian version.

fell in love with him. And he, won over by her beauty and noble mind, was likewise inflamed with passion for her. So agreeably did their love proceed that they were joined in marriage, even though her relatives did what they could to make her wed someone else. And they lived so harmoniously and in such tranquility while they were in Venice that they never exchanged a word that was not sweet and loving.

It happened that the Venetian lords made a change in the men-at-arms that they are wont to maintain in Cyprus, and they sent the Moor to be captain of those soldiers. Though he was delighted by the honor (since such an office is given only to noble, strong, and loyal men who have proven their worth), his joy was nevertheless diminished by the prospect of having to undertake such a long and uncomfortable journey since he believed that Disdemona might take offense at it. The Lady, who had no other love in the world but the Moor and was very pleased to witness the honor that so noble and powerful a republic had bestowed upon her husband for his competence, could not wait to see her husband set out with his aides, and to accompany him in such an honored position; but she was troubled to see that the Moor was worried, and, as she did not know the cause of this, one day while they were dining said to him: "Why is it, Moor, that despite the great honor which the signory[1] have bestowed upon you, you are so sad?" The Moor replied to Disdemona: "My joy at the honor I have received is clouded by the love I feel for you because I see one of two things happening: either I take you with me to the dangers of the sea or, to avoid such hardship, I leave you behind in Venice. The first would be grievous to me because every discomfort you experienced and every danger we encountered would cause me extreme anxiety. The second, leaving you behind, would be even more hateful to me because in being parted from you I would be parting from my own life."

Disdemona, on hearing this, said: "Ah, my husband, what thoughts are these that run through your mind? Why do you allow yourself to be upset by such things? I want to come with you wherever you go, even if it means walking through fire in my nightgown rather than traveling with you by sea in a safe and well-equipped ship as I am about to do, and even if there are dangers and hardships I want to share them with you. I should consider myself little loved by you if, rather than having

---

1   The governing body of Venice.

my company at sea, you were to leave me in Venice, or if you persuaded yourself that I would rather stay safely here than be with you in the same danger you face. So I want you to prepare yourself for the trip with all the joy that befits your high rank." The Moor then joyfully threw his arms around his wife's neck and with a loving kiss said to her: "God preserve us long in this love, my dear wife." And after a short time, having gathered his apparel and prepared himself for the trip, he embarked on the ship with his wife and all his train, and with sails to the wind he set off on the journey, on calm seas, to Cyprus.

In his company he had an Ensign[1] who was very handsome but had the most wicked disposition in the world. He was very dear to the Moor, who had no idea of his wickedness for although he had a very wicked mind he concealed the wickedness that he harbored in his heart with lofty and arrogant words and with his manner to such an extent that he seemed like a Hector or an Achilles.[2] This evil man had also brought his wife, a beautiful and virtuous young woman, to Cyprus, and because she was Italian she was dearly loved by the Moor's wife and spent the greater part of the day with her.

In the same company there was also a Corporal who was very dear to the Moor. He often visited the Moor at home and dined with him and his wife. As the Lady knew him to be so well liked by her husband, she showed him signs of greatest kindness. This was much appreciated by the Moor. The wicked Ensign, disregarding the promise he had made to his wife and the friendship, loyalty, and duty he owed the Moor, fell passionately in love with Disdemona, and he turned all his thoughts to how he might enjoy possession of her, but he did not dare reveal himself, fearful that should the Moor notice he would immediately be put to death. He tried in various ways and as secretively as possible to make the Lady aware of his love, but she, who thought only of the Moor, did not notice the Ensign or any other man, and everything he tried to make her fall in love with him had as little effect as if he had not tried at all. He then imagined that she might have behaved this way because she was in love with the Corporal, and he therefore decided to get rid of him and bent his thoughts to this end. But the love that he

---

1   An ancient or standard-bearer.
2   In Greek mythology, Hector and Achilles are the two greatest fighters—and arch-enemies—of the Trojan War.

bore for the Lady changed to the most bitter hatred, and he focused all his thoughts on how, once the Corporal had been killed, he could, if he should fail to enjoy the Lady, prevent the Moor from enjoying her either. After turning over in his mind various wicked and evil plans, he decided in the end to accuse her of adultery and to make her husband believe that the adulterer was the Corporal. But, as he understood the particular love of the Moor for his wife and his friendship with the Corporal, he realized that unless he could devise a particularly cunning deception he would be unable to convince the Moor of either accusation. Wherefore he began to wait for the right time and place in order to enact his wicked plan.

And not long after, the Moor reduced the Corporal's rank for having drawn his sword and wounded a soldier while on guard duty; this [decision of the Moor's] grieved Disdemona deeply. She tried many times to reconcile her husband and the Corporal. In the meantime, the Moor told the wicked Ensign that his wife pestered him so much about the Corporal that he feared he would be compelled to reinstate him. The evil man took from this the notion of putting his plan into action, and said: "Perhaps Disdemona has reason to look upon him so favourably." "And why is that?" asked the Moor. "I do not want," answered the Ensign, "to come between husband and wife, but if you keep your eyes open, you will see for yourself." Not for all the Moor's entreaties would the Ensign do more. Nonetheless his words remained such a sharp thorn in the Moor's mind that he gave himself over to studying their meaning and became all melancholic.

Wherefore one day, as his wife was trying to moderate his anger towards the Corporal, beseeching him not to ignore his many years of service and friendship for such a small fault—especially as there had been a complete reconciliation between the wounded soldier and the Corporal—the Moor was angered and said to her: "There must be a very good reason, Disdemona, for you to care so much for him. He is not your brother nor your relative that you have him so much in your heart." The Lady, with all courtesy and humility, said: "I do not want you to be angry with me. Nothing moves me but the sadness of seeing you deprived of so dear a friend as you have attested the Corporal has been to you. He has not committed a grave enough fault to deserve such hatred. But you Moors are of such a hot nature that any little matter moves you to anger and revenge."

Made more angry by these words, the Moor replied: "Anyone who does not believe that may easily have proof of it! I shall take revenge for injuries done to me until I am fully satisfied." The Lady was dismayed at these words and, observing her husband's uncustomary fury with her, said humbly: "Nothing but good intentions prompted me to speak, but rather than have you angry with me I shall speak no more of this." The Moor, seeing the insistence with which his wife once again pleaded in favor of the Corporal, guessed that the words spoken by the Ensign were meant to suggest that Disdemona was in love with the Corporal, and in deep melancholy the Moor went to talk to the rascal and tried to convince him to speak more openly of the matter. The Ensign, intent upon harming the poor Lady, after having pretended not to want to say anything that might displease the Moor, seemed to be persuaded by his entreaties and said: "I cannot deny that it vexes me greatly to have to tell you something that must cause you enormous distress, but as you want me to, and because the care I have for your honor as my lord spurs me to it, I do not want to fail now to satisfy your request nor to do my duty to you. Just know, therefore, that it wounds your Lady to see the Corporal in disgrace with you for no other reason than that she takes pleasure in him whenever he comes to your house, as though she had already grown bored of your blackness."

These words went to the core of the Moor's heart, but in order to know more—although he believed what the Ensign had said, for suspicion had already been born in his mind—he said with a proud look: "I do not know what is holding me back from cutting out that very bold tongue of yours, which has dared to speak such infamy against my wife." The Ensign said: "I did not expect any glory, Captain, other than the reward of my loving service, but as my duty and care for your honor have carried me this far, I will reply that the situation stands exactly as you understand it, and if the Lady, with a show of love, has so obscured your eyes that you have not seen what you should have, that does not mean that I am not telling the truth. For the Corporal himself has told me, like one whose happiness is not complete unless he has made another aware of it. And if I had not feared your anger, I would, when he told me, have given him the punishment he deserved by killing him. But since letting you know what concerns you more than anyone else brings me such undeserved reward, I wish I had kept silent so as not to have fallen into your disfavor." The Moor then said furiously, "If you do not help me to see with my own eyes what you have just told me, rest assured I shall make you understand that it would have been better for you to have been born mute." "I could have facilitated this," added the villain, "when he used to come to your house, but now that you have cast him off, not for just cause but for an unimportant reason, it will be difficult for me to prove it, for though I think that he still enjoys Disdemona whenever you give him the opportunity, he has to act much more cautiously now that he knows you have come to hate him. Yet, I do not lose hope of being able to show you that which you do not want to believe from me." And with these words they parted.

The wretched Moor, as if he had been stabbed by the sharpest of arrows, returned home to wait for the day when the Ensign would be able to show him the thing that would make him miserable forever and ever. But the chastity observed by the Lady caused the accursed Ensign no little annoyance, for he seemed unable to find a way to make the Moor believe the truth of what he had falsely told him, and, turning over various ideas in his mind, the wicked man came up with a new piece of maliciousness. Often the wife of the Moor, as I have said, visited the home of the Ensign's wife and stayed with her a great part of the day, and because the Ensign saw that the Lady often took with her a handkerchief which he knew was a gift from the Moor that was most delicately worked in the Moorish fashion and was very dear to the Lady and likewise to the Moor, he planned to steal it from her and to prepare her final destruction. He had a three-year-old daughter who was much loved by Disdemona, so he took the child in his arms one day when the wretched Lady had gone to the rogue's house and placed her in the arms of the Lady, who drew her to her bosom. This deceitful scoundrel, who was very deft of hand, lifted the handkerchief from her belt so carefully that her suspicion was not raised, and cheerfully departed from her. Disdemona, knowing nothing, went home, and, busy with other thoughts, did not miss the handkerchief. But then several days later, searching for it and not finding it, she became worried lest the Moor ask her about it, as he often did. The wicked Ensign, seizing a convenient opportunity, went to the Corporal's house and with clever spite left the handkerchief at the head of the bed. The Corporal did not notice it until the following day when as he got out of bed he put his foot on it since it had fallen to the ground. Unable to imagine how it came to be in his house and recognizing it as Disdemona's, he determined to give it to her. Waiting for the Moor to leave the house, he went to the back door and knocked. It appeared as though Fortune had conspired with the Ensign to bring about the death of the poor Lady, since at that very moment the Moor came home and, hearing a knock at the door, he went to the window and angrily demanded "Who is knocking?" The Corporal heard the Moor's voice and, fearing that he might come down and hurt him, ran away without answering. The Moor went downstairs, opened the door, and went out into the street and searched around but saw no one. Going back into the house full of hatred, he asked his wife who had been knocking at the door. The Lady replied honestly that she did not know. But the Moor said, "It looked to me like the Corporal." "I do not know," she responded, "if it was he or another."

The Moor controlled his rage although he was burning with anger. He decided not to act until he had first talked to the Ensign, to whom he went right away, telling him what had happened and begging him to find out from the Corporal all he could about it. The Ensign, delighted by what had occurred, promised to do so. And so one day he spoke to the Corporal when the Moor was in a place where he could see them as they conversed. And talking to him of everything but the Lady, the Ensign burst into the loudest laughter in the world and, with a show of astonishment, he gestured with his head and hands as though he were hearing extraordinary things. The Moor, as soon as he saw them part ways, went to the Ensign to learn what the other man had told him. The Ensign, after making the Moor beg him for a long time, finally said: "He hid nothing from me, and told me that he enjoyed your wife every time you gave them the opportunity with your absence, and that the last time he was with her she gave him the handkerchief that you had given her as a gift when you married her." The Moor thanked the Ensign and thought that if the Lady no longer had the handkerchief, then it was clear that things must be as the Ensign said. Wherefore one day, after dinner, while discussing various matters with his wife, he asked her for the handkerchief. The poor woman, who had greatly feared this, grew red in the face at the request, and, to conceal her blushing, which the Moor noted well, she ran to the chest pretending to look for it. And after much searching, she said, "I do not know why I cannot find it. Perhaps you have had it." "If I had it," said he, "why would I ask you for it? But you will try again with more success."

When he had left, he began thinking how he might murder both his wife and the Corporal such that he was not faulted for their deaths. And since he thought about this day and night, the Lady necessarily noticed that he did not act toward her as he had before. She said several times, "What is bothering you? What is disturbing you? You that used to be the most joyful man in the world are now the gloomiest man that ever lived!" The Moor found various excuses with which to respond to the Lady, but she remained completely unsatisfied. And, while she knew of no action of hers that could have so troubled the Moor, she nonetheless worried that because of the excessive number of times he had had her he had become bored. Sometimes she would tell the Ensign's wife: "I do not know what to make of the Moor. He used to be all loving towards me, but over the last few days he has become another man; and I very much fear that I shall become a warning to your girls not to marry against their parents' wishes, and Italian ladies will learn from me not to match with a man from whom Nature, Heaven, and way of life separates us. But, because I know that he is very friendly with your husband and communicates with him about his affairs, please, if you have learned anything from him of which you can advise me, do not fail to help me." She cried bitterly as she spoke. The Ensign's wife, who knew everything (as her husband had wanted to use her as an assistant in the death of the Lady though she had not been willing to agree) feared her husband and did not dare to tell her anything. She said only: "Be careful not to arouse your husband's suspicion, and try your hardest to make him know your love and loyalty." "That is exactly what I do," said she, "but to no avail."

The Moor, in the meantime, tried every way to get more proof of that which he did not want to uncover, and he begged the Ensign to work it so that he could see the handkerchief in the Corporal's possession, and, although that was difficult for the villain, he promised nonetheless to use all diligence to get him this proof. The Corporal had a woman at home who worked marvelous embroidery on linen, and when she saw the handkerchief and that it belonged to the Moor's wife, she agreed to make a copy before it was to be returned. And while she worked, the Ensign observed that she was near a window and could be seen by passersby on the street, so he caused her to be seen by the Moor who was now convinced that the virtuous Lady was in fact an adulteress. Then he arranged with the Ensign to kill her and the Corporal, treating them as it appeared they deserved. The Moor begged the Ensign to kill the Corporal, promising to remain eternally beholden to him. The Ensign refused to do this as it was very difficult and dangerous because the Corporal was as skillful as he was courageous, but after the Moor had begged him insistently, and given him a large sum of money, he made him promise that he would try to tempt Fortune.

This having been resolved upon, one evening the Corporal left the home of a prostitute with whom he was amusing himself. The night being dark, he was accosted by the Ensign with his sword in his hand, who stabbed at his leg to make him fall; and it happened that he cut his right thigh through so that the poor man fell and the Ensign was on him to finish him off. But the Corporal, who was courageous and accustomed to blood and death, had drawn his sword and, wounded as he was, began to defend himself, shouting: "I am being murdered!" As a result, the Ensign, hearing some people and soldiers who were housed thereabouts come running, began to flee so as not to be caught; then, turning around, he pretended to have run up upon hearing the uproar. And standing among the others looking at the severed leg, he judged that although the Corporal was not dead he would eventually die of his wound. And although he was delighted, nevertheless he commiserated with the Corporal as though he had been his brother.

In the morning the news had spread throughout the city and likewise reached Disdemona's ears; whereupon, she, being kind and not thinking that harm would come to her from it, showed the greatest sorrow at what had happened, from which the Moor drew the worst possible conclusions. And he went to find the Ensign, and said to him: "You know well that my ass of a wife is in such a state about the Corporal's accident that she has gone mad!" "And how could you expect otherwise," the Ensign said, "as he is her life and soul?" "Her soul, eh?" replied the Moor, "I shall pull the soul from her body; I would not be a man if I did not kill such an evil one." As they were discussing whether poison or a knife should slay the Lady, and not settling on one or the other, the Ensign said, "A way has come into my mind that will satisfy you and that will not draw any suspicion. It is this: the house where you have been staying is very old and the ceiling of your room has many cracks; I propose we beat Disdemona with a stocking full of sand so badly that she dies but without showing any sign of the beating on her body. When she is dead we will smash the Lady's head, pretending that a beam killed her as it fell, and in this way no one will suspect you as everyone will judge her death to be accidental." This cruel advice pleased the Moor, and they awaited a fitting time.

One night he was in bed with her and, having already hidden the Ensign in a dressing room that opened into the bedroom according to their plan, the Ensign made a noise in the dressing room, and hearing it the Moor immediately said to his wife, "Did you hear that noise?" "I heard it," she said. "Get up," added the Moor, "and see what it is." The unfortunate Disdemona got up and as soon as she approached the dressing room the Ensign emerged and, being strong and muscular, hit her with the stocking he had ready, giving her a cruel blow in the middle of the back so that she immediately fell down unable to breathe. But with the little voice she had, she called on the Moor to help her, and he, leaping from bed, said to her, "Wicked woman, this is the reward for your dishonesty; this is how such women are treated when, pretending to love their husbands, they put horns on their heads."[1] The wretched Lady, hearing this and feeling the end was near (for the Ensign had given her another blow), called on divine justice to witness her honor since earthly justice had failed her, and called on God to help her; upon receiving a third blow, she was killed by the wicked Ensign. Afterwards, placing her in bed and smashing her skull, he and the Moor brought down the ceiling as they had planned and the Moor began to call for help, that the house was collapsing. Hearing his voice, the neighbors ran in and discovered the bed, and found the Lady dead under the beams, wherefore everyone grieved for the good life led by the Lady.

The next day Disdemona was buried amid the universal mourning of the people. But God, the just observer of souls, did not want such great wickedness to go without the punishment it deserved. Thus the Moor, who had loved the Lady as much as his eyes, finding himself free, began to have so much desire for her that he went about looking for her in every part of the house; seeing that the Ensign had caused him to lose his wife and all love of life he hated the villain so much that he could not stand to see him and, if he had not been afraid of the inviolable justice of the Venetian signory, would have killed him. As he could not do this with safety, he deprived him of his rank and no longer accepted him in his company, whereupon was born such an

---

1 I.e., make cuckolds of their husbands by committing adultery.

animosity between them that no one could imagine a greater or more serious. Consequently, the Ensign, the worst of all villains, turned all of his thoughts to injuring the Moor, and, seeking out the Corporal, who had already recovered and went about with a wooden leg instead of the one that had been severed, said to him: "The time has come for you to take revenge for your lost leg, and, if you wish to come with me to Venice, I shall tell you who the wrongdoer was as here I dare not say for many reasons, and I shall testify for you in court."

The Corporal, who knew himself greatly wronged but did not know why, thanked the Ensign and went to Venice with him. When they got there the Ensign told him that it was the Moor who had cut off his leg because he had developed a suspicion that he had slept with Disdemona, and that for the same reason he had murdered her and afterwards claimed that the collapsed ceiling had killed her. The Corporal, hearing this, denounced the Moor to the signory both for cutting off his leg and for causing the Lady's death, and he called as a witness the Ensign, who said that both were true because the Moor had wanted him to commit both crimes, and that, having killed his wife out of an inhuman jealousy that had taken root in his mind, he had recounted to him how he had brought about her death. The Venetian signory, learning of the cruelty inflicted by the man from Barbary[1] in their town, ordered that the Moor be arrested in Cyprus and brought to Venice, and they tried through torture to extract the truth. But overcoming with courage of spirit every torment, he denied all so staunchly that nothing could be drawn from him. Although by his resoluteness he escaped death, he was, after being many days in prison, condemned to perpetual exile where he was finally killed by relatives of the Lady as he deserved.

The Ensign traveled to his homeland and, not wishing to give up his customary behavior, he accused one of his companions, saying he had sought to have him kill his enemy who was a nobleman, for which reason the man was arrested and tortured, and when he denied the truth of what his accuser said the Ensign was likewise tortured for comparison, where he was given such a blow that his innards ruptured. Whereupon he was released from prison and taken home where he died in misery. Thus did God avenge the innocence of Disdemona. And the Ensign's

---

1 The Saracen countries on the north and northwestern coast of Africa.

wife, who was aware of what had happened, recounted this entire series of events after he had died, just as I have told it to you.

STORY 8

It seemed astonishing to everyone that such malice had been discovered in the human heart, and they grieved the case of the poor Lady, blaming her father for giving her an unlucky name.[1] And the group determined that as a name is the first gift of the father to the daughter he should provide one that arouses admiration and splendor and luck, as though he wished to foresee good fortune and greatness. No less was the Moor blamed, who had been foolishly credulous, but all praised God as the criminals had received fitting punishment.

2. FROM GEOFFREY FENTON, *CERTAIN TRAGICAL DISCOURSES* (LONDON, 1567), FOL. 79–94; EDITED IN MODERN SPELLING BY SARAH MILLIGAN AND JESSICA SLIGHTS

[*Certain tragical discourses written out of French and Latin, by Geoffrey Fenton, no less profitable than pleasant and of like necessity to all degrees that take pleasure in antiquities or foreign reports* is a 1567 English translation of a collection of short prose tales written by Italian author Matteo Bandello (1485–1561) and published in 1554. Working closely with French translations of the tales made by François de Belleforest (1530–83) and Pierre Boaistuau (1517–66), Fenton (1539–1608), an English writer who later became a privy councilor in Ireland, added his own rhetorical turns and moral interventions to Bandello's stories and offered them to an eager Elizabethan reading public with the suggestion that they be read not merely as entertainment but as moral exempla, illustrating in some cases virtuous conduct to be emulated, and

---

1 Pairing the prefix "dis-" meaning "not" with a feminized root reminiscent of "demone," Italian for demon, fiend, or devil, the name "Disdemona" identifies the Lady as the antithesis of evil. Also, the first syllable of her name recalls "Dis," the ancient Roman god of the Underworld whose hellish realm features in both Virgil's *Aeneid* and Dante's *Divine Comedy* as the haunt of adulterers after death, an association that doubles Disdemona's connection with the demonic and may help to explain the listeners' claim that her name is an "unlucky" one.

in others immoral actions and their calamitous effects. Shakespeare could have had access to the tales in all three versions, and he appears to have drawn on them in developing several of his plays, including *Romeo and Juliet*, *Much Ado About Nothing*, and *Othello*. The fourth tale or "discourse" in Fenton's collection, excerpted here, tells the story of an Albanian captain so overcome by jealousy that he violently murders his wife. There are a number of interesting similarities between this tale and Shakespeare's *Othello*, and Fenton's moralizing digressions about the obligations of marriage offer a fascinating perspective on the relationship of literary fiction to real life.]

The argument

It may seem to some that delight in the report of other men's faults, with respect rather to take occasion of sinister exclamation than be warned by their evils to eschew the like harms in themselves, that I have been too prodigal in noting the doings and lives of divers ladies and gentlewomen declining by misfortune from the path of virtue and honor, only to stir up cause of reproach and leave argument to confirm their fond opinion. Albeit, as their error appeareth sufficiently in the integrity of my meaning, so I hope the indifferent sort will give another judgment of my intent, the rather for that I have preferred[1] these discourses both for the profit of the present glory of them that be past, and instruction of such as be to come. Seeing which all, they discover more cause of rebuke and vices more heinous in men than any we find committed by women. And albeit the history last recited hath set forth in lively colors the fury and mad disposition of a woman forced by disloyalty, yet if a man may any way excuse sin, it may in some sort be dispensed withal, or at least with more reason than the tyrannous execution following, committed by a man without occasion, where a certain jealousy sprung of an unjust mislike—as she thought— is ready to cover the fault of Pandora.[2] For what is he so ignorant in the passions of love that will not confess that jealousy is an evil exceeding

---

1 Presented for approval or acceptance; introduced.
2 In Greek mythology, Pandora is the first woman created by the gods. When Prometheus steals fire from gods, Zeus takes vengeance by presenting Pandora to Prometheus's brother, and with her a box that she is forbidden to open. When she is driven by curiosity to open the box, evil escapes into the world.

all the torments of the world, supplanting oftentimes both wit and reason in the most wise that be, specially when appeareth the like treason that Pandora persuaded herself to receive him that forsook her. But for the other, how can he be acquitted from an humor of a frantic man, who, without any cause of offense in the world, commits cruel execution upon his innocent wife, no less fair and furnished in all perfections than chaste and virtuous without comparison? Neither is jealousy the cause of murder considering that the opinion is no sooner conceived than there followeth, as it were, a distrust of the party that thinks to receive the wrong with an indifferent desire to them both to stand upon their guard in sort like two enemies working the mutual destruction the one of the other. Whereof leaving the judgment to them that be of good stomach to digest all kinds of meats or can carry a brain to buckle[1] with the fumes of every broth that is offered them, I have here to expose unto you a miserable accident happening in our time, which shall serve as a bloody scaffold or theater wherein are presented such as play no parts but in mortal and furious tragedies.

An Albanian captain, being at the point to die, killed his wife because no man should enjoy her beauty after his death.

During the siege and miserable sack of Modone,[2] a city of the Moors confining upon the Sea Peloponnese not far from the Strait of Isthmian, by the which the Venetians convey their great traffic and trade of merchandise, Baia-Zeth,[3] the emperor of the Turks and great-grandfather to Sultan Solyman[4] who this day governeth the state of the Orient, used so many sorts of inordinate cruelties in the persecution of those wretches whom fate, with extreme force of his war, had not only abandoned from the soil of their ancient and natural bode,[5] but also, as people full of desolation and void of succor[6] every way,

---

1 Cope, engage.
2 Italian name for Methoni, Greece.
3 Bayezid II (1447–1512) was sultan of the Ottoman Empire from 1481 to 1512.
4 Suleiman the Magnificent (1494–1566) was sultan of the Ottoman Empire from 1520 to 1566. Suleiman was actually the grandson of Bayezid II.
5 Abode.
6 Help.

forced them to crave harbor of the limitrophal[1] towns adjoining their country, to shroud their weary bodies bleeding still with the wounds of their late war, and overcome besides with the violence of hunger and cold, two common enemies that never fail to follow the camp of misery. And, as in a general calamity every man hath his fortune, so, amongst the unhappy crew of these fugitives and creatures full of care, there was one gentleman no less noble by descent than worthily renowned by the glory of his own acts, who, accounting it a chief and principal virtue to withstand the malice of fortune with magnanimity of mind, thought it not also the office of a noble heart to yield to the sentence of adversity or give any place to the injury of present time, considering that in every distress fortune beareth the greatest sway, whose malice is neither of perpetuity nor yet to be feared of such as have their hearts armed with assurance in virtue. For as she is no less uncertain of herself than her doings full of mutability, so, according to the advice of the philosopher, she is to be used with such indifference of all estates that we need neither laugh when she smiles, nor fear when she threats; neither hath she any to follow the chariot of her victory but the caitiff[2] or coward, and such as are denied the assistance and benefit of true virtue.

This gentleman, whom my author termeth by the name of Pierro Barzo, weary even now with drawing the heavy yoke of hard exile, left the rest of his countrymen and companions of care complaining their mutual miseries together, and retired to the rich and populous city of Mantua,[3] where his civil government and prudent behavior, accompanied with a singular dexterity in exploits of arms and other exercises of chivalry, arguing the unfeigned nobleness of his mind, gave such a show of his virtue that he was not only in short time entertained of the marquis and governor there, but also made general of the whole army of footmen; where, enjoying thus the benefit of his virtue, who commonly yields no less success to such as embrace her with true imitation and tread the path of her lore with semblable[4] sincerity of mind, he had there with him at the same instant his wife, being also of Modone, derived of no less nobility than he, and nothing inferior in all gifts of

---

1 Situated on the frontier.
2 Villain.
3 City in northern Italy.
4 Similar.

nature and ornaments of virtue, for, touching her beauty, seeming of such wonderful perfection that it was thought nature was driven to the end of her wits in framing a piece of so great excellency, they doubted not to give her thereby the title of the fair Helen of Greece.[1] Neither was she less meritorious for her virtues being blessed therewith so plentifully at the hands of the Almighty, that it was doubted to the writers of that time whether God or nature deserved the greatest praise in forming so perfect a creature. If this were a consolation and singular contentment of the poor Modonese, weighing erst[2] in the balance of his unhappy fortune, denied any more to enjoy the freedom of his country, driven by force from the ancient succors and solace of his friends, wandering in woods and desert places unknown, and, that which worse is, left only to the mercy of hunger and cold, with expectation to fall eftsoons[3] into the hands of his enemies, and now to be taken from the malice of all these miseries and restored to a place of abode, richesse,[4] and entertainment sufficient for sustentation,[5] to bear office and authority amongst the best, and rampired[6] besides within the assured good will and opinion of the chief governor of a country. I appeal to the opinions of those who erst have changed their miserable condition or state of adversity with the benefit and goodness of the like fortune, or if again he had cause to rejoice and make sacrifice to his fortune that had given him a wife noted to be the odd[7] image of the world for beauty, behavior, courtesy, and upright dealing, constant without cause or argument of dishonesty, and, that which is the chiefest ornament and decoration of the beauty of a woman, to be of disposition ready to obey her husband, yielding him sovereignty with a dutiful obedience, with other virtues that made her an admiration to the whole multitude, and her life a spectacle[8] to the ladies of our age to behold and imitate the like virtues—I leave it to the judgment of that small number of happy men, who, by a special grace from above, are

---

1   Helen of Troy, considered in Greek mythology the most beautiful woman in the world.
2   Already.
3   Again.
4   Wealth.
5   "The action of bearing or enduring an affliction" (*OED n.* 2a).
6   Fortified, strengthened.
7   Singular.
8   An example.

ordained to enjoy the benefit of so rare and precious a gift. This couple, thus rejoicing the return of happy life, resigned with all their tears of ancient dole[1] and embraced the gift of present time with intent to spend the remainder of their years in mutual consolation and contentment of mind. Wherein they were assisted with a second blessing of God, who, for the increase of their new comfort, sent them a daughter who in beauty, virtue, and all other gifts of grace did nothing degenerate from the pattern and mold from whence she was derived, whereof she gave great shows as nature seemed to increase her years and confirm her in discretion.

But what assurance is there in the pleasure of people, seeing the world itself is appointed his date, which he cannot pass; or why should we repose a perpetuity in our worldly affairs, seeing that both their continuance and confidence ends with the length of time? And fortune, who is always jealous of the ease of man and not content to let us live long in quiet, is always laying her ambush, devising how to interrupt our felicity; and, as she is blind of herself and less certainty in her doings, so she forgets not to discover her conspiracies when we least think of her and invade us when we account us most sure of her friendship. Whereof she gave a manifest declaration in the person of this fair lady from whom she took her dear husband in the flower of his years, and she not yet confirmed in age and discretion able to bear and withstand the ordinary assaults of the world, which she found also of more uneasy toleration, as well for the fervent zeal and affiance[2] which law of kind did bind her to bear to her late spouse and loyal husband, as also for that she saw herself left amongst the hands of strangers, far from her parents and friends, void of refuge in her own country, and without a head to defend her from the malice of men, which commonly rageth with more extremity against weak and desolate widows and poor fatherless orphans than against them that are able to withstand their malice and repress their violence with equal power. And albeit she was left to her own liberty to live as she list,[3] as you have heard, and not yet feeling the burden of twenty winters, an age fit to engender suspicion of the evil disposed, yet having no less care to prevent the malice of slander than to keep in entire the small revenue left unto her by her husband, she took order

---

1 Grief.
2 Allegiance.
3 Pleased.

with her domestical[1] affairs according to her present fortune; and so, dismissing her ordinary train of servants, retired to a brother of hers which dwelt also in the same town, where, after the funerals of her dead husband were performed with sufficient tears and duties appertaining, she qualifieth somewhat her dole for him that was dead with the daily view of her young daughter, the lively image of her father, sometime also exercising the endeavor of the needle—a recreation most convenient for widows and all honest matrons—never being seen abroad but of holy and great festival days, when she went in devout manner to the church to hear the divine service of God.

Being unhappily espied, for all that, of an Albanian captain, a noble gentleman thereabout, having for the credit of his virtue and valiantness in arms, the charge of certain troops of horsemen, who, glancing at unawares upon the glistering beams of her beauty, became so desirous eftsoons to encounter the same that with the often view of her stately personage and general fame of her many virtues he became so in love with her that for speedy ease of his present grief he was driven to put his request upon terms, making first his sighs and sad countenance, his solitary complexion of face often given to change his dolorous state and pitiful regards of the eye when he was in her company, forced now and then to abandon the same because he could not keep him from tears, his often greeting her with salutations in amorous order, courting her now and then with letters, ditties, and presents of great price, with a thousand other vain importunities which love doth imagine to animate his soldiers, his chiefest ministers to bewray[2] his intent and solicit his cause. Whereof the effect returned no less frustrate than the device itself ought to seem vain in the eye of all wise men, for she whose heart could not be erst pierced with the malice of her former fortune, nor be brought to stoop to the lure of adversity, thought it a great fault to let love or folly make any breach where so many hot assaults and causes of despair had been valiantly resisted and utterly repulsed; for proof whereof, being wholly wed as yet to the remembrance of her dead husband, she would neither admit his clients nor give audience to his ambassadors, but dismissed both the one and the other with semblable hope, which brought the captain in such case that it seemed to him a

---

1 Domestic.
2 Reveal.

harder matter to compass the good will of his lady than to govern an army or plant a battery with the advantage of the ground and place.

Neither was he able to withdraw his affection or mortify the fire newly burst out to flame because the remembrance of her beauty, the often view of her virtue enlarged by the general fame of all men, together with the nobleness of her race enrolled in the records of antiquity, presented a more desire in him with care to obtain her, and aggravated his grief in being repulsed of that which his heart had already vowed to honor till the extreme date of his days; neither had he the face eftsoons to attempt her of himself, and much less to desist from the pursuit of his desire, but, being at the point to incur the hazard of despair, behold love preferred a new and most sure mean, willing him to crave the assistance of her brother, who, being his dear friend and companion in arms in the service of divers[1] princes afore time, he made no less account of his furtherance than if he had already gotten his friendship. Wherefore, delaying no moment of time, but plying the wax whilst the water was warm, he accosted the young man at a convenient time and roved[2] at him in this short sort: "It is, my dear friend and companion, a virtuous disposition to be ready in well doing and easy to assist honest requests, which to your nature hath been always no less peculiar than to me now a courage in so honest a case to crave your aid; neither can the virtue of true friendship more lively appear, or the office of assured friends more amply be discerned than in making the grief of the one common to both, and bear the gift of time and fortune indifferently with mutual affection and like zeal on both parts. Wherein, for my part, I would I had as good mean to make declaration of my true heart towards you, as of long time I have vowed to be yours to the uttermost of my power, and you no less desire to do me good than your diligence and assistance of friendship is most able to stand me instead in my present case of no less importance than the very safeguard of my life."

Which last words made the Modonese reply with like frank offer of mind, protesting unto him by the faith of a soldier that if ever he felt any motion in himself to do him the least good of the world, his desire was double to requite it proffering herewith, for a further show of his good meaning and declaration of faith, to rack[3] his power on his behalf so far forth as either life, living, or honor would bear him; but he

---

1 Various.
2 Raved; spoke boisterously.
3 Extend.

whose desire tended not to things impossible nor sought to maintain war against the heavens reposing much for himself in the offer of his friend, thought the conquest was half won when he had promised his assistance, and, because there lacked nothing but to utter his grief, he told him that the thing he desired would bring advancement to them both. "And because," saith he, "I will clear the doubt which seems to trouble you, you shall understand that the beauty, gifts of grace, and other honest parts in your sister have so enchanted my senses, that, having already lost the use of my former liberty, I cannot eftsoons be restored without the speedy assistance of her good will; neither have I other power of myself or consolation in my present extremity than such as is derived of the hope which I have hereafter to enjoy her as my lawful wife. For otherwise, I am as void of foul meaning to work her dishonor for the fervent love I bear her, as free from intent to procure so great a spot of infamy to the house which nourished you both in so great honor. And to be plain with you, the glimmering glances of her twinkling eyes, together with a princely majesty which nature hath lent her above the rest of the dames of our days, hath made my heart more assaultable and apt to admit parley[1] than either the noise of the cannon or terror of the enemy, how great soever they have appeared, have heretofore feared me; which makes me think that there is either some celestial or divine mystery shrouded under the veil of her beauty making me thereby yield her honor in hope of preferment, or else, by the angry consent of my cursed destinies, it is she that is appointed to pay the interest of my former liberty in transforming my ancient quiet into a thousand annoys[2] of uneasy toleration. And albeit I have hitherto reserved the maidenhead of my affection and lived no less free from the amorous delights or desires of women, yet being now overtaken and tied in the chains of true affection, I had rather become captive and yield myself prisoner in the pursuit of so fair a lady than to have the honor of the greatest victory that ever happened to captain by prowess, or policy, or dint of cruel sword of his valiant soldiers. Wherefore, as your authority with your sister is rather to command than entreat, and by

---

1 Discuss terms.
2 "A mental state akin to pain arising from the involuntary reception of impressions, or subjection to circumstances, which one dislikes; disturbed or ruffled feeling; discomfort, vexation, trouble" (OED n. 1a).

the friendship which hath remained indissoluble between us from the beginning, never giving place to any peril whatsoever it were, I conjure you, and as my last request beseech you, to aid me herein so far forth as your diligence may seem to work my desire to effect."

Whereunto the Modonese replied with great thanks for the honor he offered him and his sister, whom he half promised already to frame according to his expectation, promising himself a great good hap[1] not only in entering into alliance with so noble a gentleman, but also that he should be the worker of the same. Whereupon, embracing each other, the one glad to see so happy a success like to follow his business, the other no less joyful to have so fit a mean to manifest his friendship towards his friend, departed with semblable contentment, the one to his lodging with a thousand hammers in his head till he saw the effect of his drift,[2] the other with no less grief of mind till he had performed the expectation of his charge. Wherein he began immediately to practice with his sister, whom he found of a contrary opinion, excusing herself with the care she had of her daughter, whom she said she would neither leave alone nor commit herself to the order and government of strangers at whose hands there is as great doubt of good entreaty as small help or hope of amendment being once made their vassal and subject by law of marriage. "Besides, sir," saith she, not without some tears, "it is not yet a year since I lost him whom, if I loved by awe being alive,[3] I ought with no less duty to honor after his death. Neither could I avoid the just murmur and ordinary suspicion of the peoples; yet I should seem more hasty to yield my affection to another than ready to perform my duty and ceremonies of dole to him that is dead, and that within the year afore the funeral be fully ended. The widow's life is also pure of itself, bound to no care nor controlment of any, and so acceptable before God that the apostle doubteth not to account her among the number of the religious if, after she have once tasted of marriage and restored again to her liberty, she content herself with the first clog or burden of bondage, living after in imitation of true virtue. Besides, the holy man Saint Augustine dissuadeth all widows eftsoons to marry, advising them to mortify such motions as the flesh is apt to stir up, and nourish by contemplation, and prayer, and true sincerity of life, saying further

---

1 Luck; success.
2 Scheme.
3 I.e., because I was in awe of him when he was alive.

that they are accounted afore God amongst the number of chaste and pure virgins. And because it may be peradventure the opinion of some that the burden of widowhood is grievous and almost intolerable unto me, presuming the same rather by the greenness of my youth not yet confirmed in ripeness of years and discretion than upon any good or assured ground to justify their opinion, I assure you, I feel myself so plentifully assisted with the spirit of grace that I doubt no more to withstand all temptations and vain assaults, which the wicked instigations of the flesh may hereafter minister unto me, than heretofore in tender years, when nature denied any such motion to stir in me, I lived free and void of such provocation. And for end, good brother, my heart, divining diversely of the success of this marriage, threateneth a further mischief to fall upon me, and too late a repentance for you that is the unfortunate causer of the same."

Here, her brother, knowing it a fault in all women to hear themselves well spoken of, and yet a chief mean to win them to feed their humor with flattering praise, began to join with her in commendation of her honesty, affirming her chaste conversation to be no less meritorious since she was widow than her pure virginity generally allowed and praised of all men afore she was married. "Which is the chiefest cause," said he, "that the captain desireth in honest sort to possess you." But touching any sinister success that might follow this sacred league of lawful matrimony, as she seemed to predestinate within herself, he ministered persuasions to the contrary, alleging the same to be a superstitious folly attributed to the ancients of old time, to calculate their good or ill success by the tunes or charm of birds, or sometime by the sudden encounter of beasts or such men as they looked not for, arguing the same to be such absolute signs of ill luck, yet commonly they would refrain from their affairs as the day. "And touching the murmur and suspicion of the people whose tongues although they be naturally tipped with the metal of slander, yet ought you as little," saith he, "fear their malice as care for their grudge, considering your act is no less acceptable afore God than tolerable by the positive laws of man. Neither can they but judge well of your doings, and like better of your choice, saying you are wooed with great importunities and won by one that is of your own quality and nothing inferior to you in virtue or nobleness of race. But if you stick of any ceremonies which you have yet to perform to him that is dead, your error is greater than you may justify, and your wisdom less than is necessary in such a case; neither is the voice of the multitude in that respect of such continuance, but time can take it away and a wonder lasteth not forever. And for my part, I hope you will confer my present meaning in this matter with the long experienced faith and affection which heretofore you have noted in me. Besides, I could not avoid the imputation of a monster and enemy to nature if I should not be as careful of your quiet as of my own life, praying you for end, and, as my last request, to repose yourself wholly upon my faith, and friendship, and fidelity of him who honoreth you with no less than his life and all that he hath." Wherewith he so much prevailed over his obedient sister that she, being unhappily overcome with his vehement importunities, condescended very willingly to his unfortunate request, which after became the peremptory destruction of the poor widow, leaving too late and miserable a repentance to her brother.

Albeit afore I proceed to the ceremonies of her unfortunate marriage, I thought good to tell unto you in this place the opinion of mine author touching the divination of the spirit of man, who, saith he, albeit by a secret instinct and virtue of the mind, is able sometimes to presage that will fall, and the soul—being divine of itself—doth also prognosticate diversely of the future chances and changes of things, yet the body—being the house or harborer of the mind, framed of the substance of clay, or a thing of more corruption—doth so prevail and overcome the qualities and gifts of the mind, in casting a mist of darkness afore our understanding that the soul is not only barred to expose the fruits of revelation, but also it is not believed when she prognosticates a truth. Neither is it in the power of man to shun or shrink from that which the foreknowledge of the highest hath already determined upon us, and much less to prevent or withstand the sentence of him whose doom is as certain as himself is truth. Wherein, because I am sufficiently satisfied by the authorities of diverse histories, as well sacred as profane, I will not stand here to enlarge the proof with copy of examples, but refer you to the reading of the sequel[1] of this woeful lady who although her fate was revealed unto her afore, yet was she denied to shun the destiny and sharp judgment which the heavens were resolved to thunder upon her.

---

1   I.e., the story that follows.

But now to our purpose: the agreement thus made between the fair Greek lady and Don Spado, the valiant captain, there lacked nothing for consummation of the marriage but the assistance of the rites and ancient ceremonies appointed by order of holy church, which the captain forgot not to procure with all expedition of time; and for the more honor and decoration of the feast he had there the presence of the Marquis of Mantua, being there not so much for the honor of the bridegroom, as to testify to the open face of the world the earnest affection he bore to her first husband, Barzo, whom he accounted no less dear unto him for credit and trust than the nearest friend of his blood. But now this Albanian, enjoying thus the fruits of his desire, could not so well bridle[1] his present pleasure, nor conceal the singular contentment he conceived by the encounter of his new mistress, but in public show began to prate of his present felicity, arguing the same to be of greater moment than if he had been frankly restored to the title and dignity of a kingdom, giving Fortune also her peculiar thanks, that had kept this good turn in store for him, saying yet she could not have honored him with a greater preferment than to put him into the possession of her who was without a second in all Europe. But as in everything excess is hurtful, bringing with it a double discommodity—I mean both a surfeit to the stomach by the pleasure we delight in, and a jealous loathing of the thing we chiefly love and hold most dear—so the extreme and superfluity of hot love of this fond husband towards his wife began within the very month of the marriage to convert itself into a contrary disposition, not much unlike the loving rage of the she-ape towards her young ones, who, as the poets do affirm, doth use to choose among her whelps one whom she loves best, and, keeping it always in her arms, doth cherish and loll it in such rude sort that ere she is ware[2] she breaketh the bones and smothereth it to death, killing by this means with overmuch love the thing which yet would live if it were not for the excess of her affection. In like sort this Albanian, doting without discretion upon the desire of his new lady, and rather drowned beastly in the superfluity of her love than weighing rightly the merit and virtue of true affection, entered into such terms of fervent jealousy that every flea that wasteth afore her made him sweat at the

---

1 Restrain.
2 Aware.

brows with the suspicion he had of her beauty.[1] Wherein he suffereth himself to be so much subject and overcome with the rage of this folly that, according to the jealous humor of the Italian, he thought every man that looked in her face went about to graft horns in his forehead.[2] O small discretion and less wisdom in one that ought with the shape and form to merit the name and virtue of a man! What sudden change and alteration of fortune seems now to assail this valiant captain, who erst loved loyally within the compass of reason, and now, doting without discretion, thinketh himself one of the forked ministers of Cornwall.[3]

And albeit I must confess unto you that the more rare and precious a thing is of itself the more diligence and regard ought we to use to preserve and keep it in good estate, yet a wise and chaste woman being one of the rarest things of the world and special gift of God ought not to be kept in the mew,[4] nor guarded with curious and continual watch, and much less attended upon with the jealous eyes of Argus.[5] For like as she that weigheth her honor and life in indifferent balance, not meaning to exchange the one but with the loss of the other, is not easily corrupted by any sugared train of flattering love, so the restraint of the liberty of women, together with a distrust proceeding of none occasion, is the chiefest mean to seduce her that else hath vowed an honest and integrity of life even until the end of her natural days. And in vain goeth he about to make his wife honest that either locks her in his chamber or fills his house full of spies to note her doings, considering the just cause he gives her hereby to be revenged of the distrust he hath of her without occasion, seeing withal the nature of some women is to enlarge their liberty that is abridged them in doing the thing they are forbidden, more in despite of the distrust of their foolish husbands than for any appetite or expectation of other contentment to themselves. Neither hath this foolish humor of jealousy so much power to enter into the heart of the virtuous and wise man who neither will give his wife such cause to abuse herself towards him, nor suspect her without great occasion,

---

1 I.e., he was jealous of even the most insignificant creatures with which she came into contact.

2 A man whose wife has committed adultery was commonly depicted with horns on his head.

3 Reference unclear.

4 In hiding or confinement; cooped up.

5 Argus Panoptes, a hundred-eyed giant in Greek mythology. *Panoptes* means all-seeing.

nor yet give judgment of any evil in her without a sure ground and manifest proof. And yet is he of such government for the correction of such a fault that he had rather cloak and digest it with wisdom than make publication with open punishment in the eye of the slanderous world, by which rare patience and secret dissimulation he doth not only choke the mouth of the slanderer, burying the fault with the forgetfulness of the fact, but also reclaims her to an assured honesty and faith hereafter, that erst had abused him by negligence and ill fortune. But he which pens his wife in the highest vault of his house, or tieth a bell at her sleeve because he may hear whether she goeth, or when he takes a long journey paints a lamb of her belly[1] to know if she play false in his absence, these slights, I say, do not only deceive him that deviseth them, but also gives him for his travail[2] the true title of cuckold.[3]

In like sort, what greater sign or argument can a man give of his own folly than to believe that to be true which is but doubtful, and, yielding rashly to the resolution and sentence of his own conceits, thinks his wife as light of the fear and apt to deceive him as he is ready to admit sinister suspicion, which proceeds but of an imperfection in himself, judging the disposition of another by his own complexion, which was one of the greatest faults in this valiant Albanian who, fearing even now that which he need not to doubt, began to stand in awe of his own shadow, persuading himself that his wife was no less liberal of her love towards others than to him, and that the benefit of her beauty was common to strangers as to himself. Albeit the good lady, espying well enough the grief of her husband, was not idle for her part to study the means to please him, and also to frame her life in such wise every way that her chaste and discreet[4] government towards him might not only remove the veil of his late suspicion, but also take away the thick mist

---

1   A folk tale circulated throughout Europe in the fourteenth to eighteenth centuries that tells of a painter who, suspecting his wife of adultery, paints a lamb on her belly when he leaves home, assuming that any illicit sexual activity on her part will cause the painting to rub away. In most versions of the story the man returns to find that the lamb has been replaced by an image confirming his cuckoldry, such as a fullgrown horned ram or a man with horns on his head (Donald McGrady, "The Story of the Painter and his Little Lamb," *Thesaurus: Boletin del Instituto Caro y Cuervo* 33.3 [1978]: 357–406).
2   Work.
3   A man whose wife has been unfaithful.
4   Prudent, sound.

of frantic jealousy that put him in such disquiet and made him so far exceed the limits and bonds of discretion. Albeit her honest endeavor herein received a contrary effect, and, as one born under a crabbed constellation,[1] or ordained rather to bear the malice of a froward[2] destiny, she could not devise a remedy for his disease nor any herb to purge his suspicious humor; but the more she sought to prefer a show of sincerity and honesty of life, the more grew the fury and rage of his perverse fancy, thinking the company and fellowship of his wife to be as indifferent to others as peculiar to himself.

What life were like to the married man's state or pleasures semblable to the joys of the bed if either the one or the other might be dispensed withal from the fury of frantic jealousy, or amongst a thousand inconveniences which only the married man doth find? What greater mischief may be more for the dissolution of the mutual tranquility of them both than where the one loves unfeignedly and the other is doubtful without cause but the ease and quiet of men are of so small a moment, and their common pleasures so interlarded with an ordinary mishap, that there is as small hold of the one slipping away with the shortness of time as undoubted assurance to have the other a common guest and haunt us in all our doings, not leaving us till he hath seen us laid in the pit and long bed of rest. Whereof I have here presented you a little proof in the picture and person of this selly[3] Albanian, who, beginning as you have heard to enter into some terms of jealousy with his wife with whom notwithstanding he had consumed certain months in such pleasures as marriage doth allow, began to grow more fervent in that fury than either his cause did require or wisdom ought to suffer. Wherewith, setting abroach[4] the vessel of that poison, forgot not for his first endeavor to dog[5] the doings of his wife with secret spies in every corner, to abridge her liberty in going abroad, and bar the access of any to come to her, keeping, notwithstanding, no less watch and ward about her chamber than the good soldier upon his trench or circumspect captain upon the walls of his fortress, which brought the selly lady into such sorrow that the state of the caitiff and slave of the galley bound to his oar with

---

1 I.e., unlucky stars.
2 Ungovernable.
3 Strange.
4 Pierced so as to allow to flow.
5 To follow closely.

a chain of unreasonable bigness, or he that by hard sentence of the law doth lie miserably in the bottom of a prison all the days of his life seemed of more easy regard than the hard condition of her present state.

Albeit true virtue hath such operation and effect of herself that how grievously soever the world doth persecute her, or seek to crucify her with the malice of men, yet can they not so keep her under by any force they can devise, but certain streams and sparks will burst out now and then, and show herself at last, as she is able, to withstand the violence of any mortal affliction. Whereof an effect appears here in the sequel of this Greek lady, who, noting the disposition of her husband overcharged with a mad humor of wrong conceits,[1] gave judgment immediately of his disease, and, being not able utterly to expulse his new fever, studied by her endeavor to infer a moderation of his passion. Wherein, for her part, she forgot not to make patience her chiefest defense against the foolish assaults of his willful follies, not only requiting his extraordinary rage and fits of fury with a dutiful humility and obedience of a wife, but also ceased not to love him no less than her honor and duty bound her thereunto, hoping, with the assistance of some convenient time and her discreet behavior towards him, both to take away the disease and mortify the cause of his evil. She seemed neither to reprehend his fault openly, nor with other terms than argued her great humility, and, for herself, how evil soever he entreated her, she gave an outward show of thankful contentment, and, when it was his pleasure to shut her close in a chamber as a bird in the cage, she refused not his sentence, but, embracing the gift of her present fortune, took such consolation as the hard condition of her case would admit, giving God thanks for his visitation and craving with like intercession to have her husband restored to the use of his former wits.

Albeit all these dutiful shows of obedience and patient digesting[2] of his unnatural discourtesies, together with a rare and ready disposition in her to frame herself wholly to the appetite of his will, prevailed no more to enlarge her liberty or redeem her from the servile yoke of close imprisonment than to reclaim his haggard mind to the understanding of reason or restore the trance of his frantic humor, raging the more, as it seemed, by the incredible constancy he noted in this mirror of

---

1 Misconceptions.
2 Bearing up without resistance.

modesty, obedience, wisdom, and chastity, whose example in them all deserves certainly to be graven in pillars of eternity and hung up in tables of gold in every palace and place of estate to the end that you ladies of our time may learn, by imitation of her order and government, to attain to the like perfection of virtue, which she left as a special pattern to you all. To the end also that if any of you, by like misfortune, do fall into the danger of semblable accidents, you may learn here the order of your government, in the like affairs, and also to suppress the rage of jealousy rather by virtue than force, which commonly is the foundation of scandal and slander, divorcement and violation of marriage, whereupon doth consequently ensue civil dissensions and utter subversion of houses of antiquity.

But now to the place of our history: This frantic Albanian and jealous captain, being one of the train of the Lord James Trivulso,[1] a great favorer of the faction of Gebalino in Italy, and at that time governor of the Duchy of Milan under the French king Louis, the third of that name, whether it were to make a further proof of the patience of his wife, or by absence to mortify and forget his fond opinion conceived without cause, retired upon a sudden to Newcastle,[2] the court and ordinary place of abode of the said Lord Trivulso. Which, albeit, was of hard digestion to the lady for a time; yet, being not unacquainted with such chances, and no prentice[3] in the practice of her husband, retired to her ancient patience and contentment by force, dissimuling[4] with a new grief and secret sorrow this new discourtesy to the end that her waspish husband should take no exceptions to her in any respect, but find her in this, as the former storms, bent wholly to obey the appetite of his will and not to mislike with that which he finds necessary to be done.

This Trivulso had not spent many months in France but there was commenced information against him to the king that he was revolted from the French and become friend to the Switzers,[5] and sworn to their seigneurie[6] and faction. Wherewith immediately fame, the common

---

1 Possibly Gian Giacomo Trivulzio (1440/41–1518), a Milanese aristocrat and mercenary military captain.
2 Reference unclear; perhaps Neuchâtel, a city in Switzerland.
3 Apprentice.
4 Concealing one's feelings.
5 The Swiss.
6 Governors.

carrier of tales, filled all ears of Milan and the province thereabout with this further addition: that the king for that cause had sent him headless to his grave. Albeit as fame is rather a messenger of lies than a treasure of truth, and rather to be heard than believed, so this brute, being not true in the last, did import a certain credit in the first, for Trivulso, not liking to live in the displeasure of his prince, abandoned his charge and came into Lombardy, where, being summoned by the messenger of death, gave place to nature and died, who being the only master and maintainer of the Albanian captain whilst he lived, could not easily be forgotten of him after his death. For after his departure was past the general doubt of the people, and each voice resolved that he was laid in his grave, Don Captain Spado, resolved wholly into tears, seemed here to pass the mystery of a new trance, which, with the fresh remembrance of his ancient harm and green wound of unworthy jealousy bleeding yet in his mind, brought him in that case that he neither desired to live nor doubted to die, and yet in despair of them both his solace of the day was converted into tears, and the hours of the night went away in visions and hollow dreams. He loathed the company of his friends and hated the things that should sustain nature. Neither was he contented with the present, nor cared for the chance of future time. Which sudden alteration in strange manner drove his careful wife into no less astonishment than she had cause, and, being ignorant of the occasion, she was also void of consolation, which doubled her grief, till time opened her at last a mean to communicate familiarly with him in this sort:

"Alas, sir," saith she, "to what end serve these pining conceits, forcing a general debility thorough all your parts? Or why do you languish in grief without discovering the cause of your sorrow to such as hold your health no less dear than the sweet and pleasant taste of their own life? From whence comes this often change of complexion, accompanied with a disposition of melancholic dumps[1] arguing your inward and fretting care of mind? Why stay you not in time the source of your scorching sighs that have already drained your body of his wholesome humors appointed by nature to give suck[2] to the entrails and inward parts of you? And to what end serveth this whole river of tears, flowing by such abundance from your watery eyes almost worn away with weeping? Is

---

1 Fits of abstraction or musing.
2 Succor, assistance.

your grief grown great by continuance of time or have you conceived some mislike of new? If your house be out of order in any sort, or that want of duty or diligence in me procureth your grudge, declare the cause to the end the fault may be reformed in me and you restored to your ancient order of quiet, and we both enjoy a mutual tranquility as appertaineth."

But he that labored of another disease than is incident commonly to men of good government absolved her of all faults or other mislikes he found in the state of his house, or other his affaires committed to her order, and less lack of her diligence to make declaration of her duty to the uttermost. "But alas," saith he, with a deep sigh derived of the fretting dolor of his mind and doubled twice or thrice within his stomach afore he could utter it, "what cause of comfort or consolation hath he to live in this world from whom the malice of destiny hath taken the chiefest pillar of his life? Or to what end serveth the fruition or interest of longer years in this vale of unquietness when the body abhorreth already the long date of his abode here? Or why should not this soma[1] or mass of corruption which I received of the world be dismissed to earth and my soul have leave to pass into the other world, to shun this double passion of present torment which I feel by the death of my dear friend? Ah, my dear lady and loyal wife, my grief is so great that I die to tell you the cause, and yet the very remembrance presents me with treble torments. Wherein I must confess unto you that since the death of the late Lord John Trivulso[2] I have had so little desire to live that all my felicity is in thinking to die. Neither can there be anything in the world more acceptable to me than death, whose hour and time, if they were as certain as himself, is most sure to come in the end, I could somewhat satisfy the great desire I have to die, and moderate the rage of my passion in thinking of the shortness of the doom that should give end to my dying ghost and unruly sorrows together. Besides weighing the infinite miseries of our time, accompanying us ever from the womb of conception, with the rest and repose which dead men do find, and knowing withal how much I am in the debt of him that is dead, I cannot wish a more acceptable thing than the speedy approach and end of my

---

1 Greek word for "body."
2 The switch of Trivulso's first name from James to John could be explained if the character is based on the historical figure Gian (John) Giacomo (James) Trivulzio.

days, to the end that, being denied the view of his presence here, I may follow him in the other world, where, participating indifferently such good and evil as falleth to his share, I may witness with what dutiful zeal and affectioned heart I sought to honor and serve him in all respects."

But the lady that saw as far into the disease of her husband as his physician into his urine,[1] knowing well enough that he did not languish so much for the desire of him that was dead as the ticklish humor of jealousy troubled him, was content to admit his cholers, how fine[2] so ever they were, as well to prefer her duty to the uttermost, as also to avoid imputation or cause of suspicion on her part, wherewith, entering into terms of persuasion, she added also this kind of consolation following: "More do I grieve, sir," saith she, "with the small care you seem to take of yourself than the terms of your disease do trouble me, considering the same proceeds of so slender occasion that the very remembrance of so great an oversight ought to remove the force and cause of your accident. Admit your grief were great indeed, and your disease of no less importance, yet ought you so to bridle this willful rage and desire to die that, in eschewing to prevent the will and set hour of the Lord, you seek not to further your fatal end by using unnatural force against yourself, making your beastly will the bloody sacrifice of your body, whereby you shall be sure to leave to the remainder of your house a crown of infamy in the judgment of the world to come and put your soul in hazard of grace afore the throne of justice above. You know, sir, I am sure, that in this transitory and painful pilgrimage there is nothing more certain than death, whom albeit we are forbidden to fear yet ought we to make a certain account of his coming. Neither is it any other thing, according to the scripture, than the minister and messenger of God, executing his infallible will upon us wretches, sparing neither age, condition, nor state. It is he that gives end to our misery here, and safe conduit to pass into the other world, and as soon as we have taken possession of the house of rest he shooteth[3] the gates of all annoy against us, feeding us, as it were, with a sweet slumber or pleasant sleep until the last summons of general resurrection. So that, sir, methinks they are of the happy sort whom the great God vouchsafeth to call to his kingdom, exchanging

---

1   It was common practice for doctors to examine a patient's urine when diagnosing illness.

2   "Egregious" (*OED adj.* 5b).

3   Locks.

the toils and manifold cares incident to the creatures of this world, with the pleasures of his paradise and place of repose that never hath end. And touching your devotion to him that was dead, with vain desire to visit his ghost in the other world, persuading the same to proceed of a debt and dutiful desire you have to make yet a further declaration of your unfeigned mind towards him, I assure you, sir, I am more sorry to see you subject to so great a folly than I fear or expect the effect of your dream, for as it seems but a riddle proceeding of the vehemence of your sickness. So I hope you will direct the sequel by sage advice, converting the circumstance into air without further remembrance of so foolish a matter. Wherein also I hope you will suffer the words of the scripture to direct you, who, allowing small ceremonies to the dead, forbids us to yield any debt or duty at all to such as be already passed out of the world, and much less to sacrifice ourselves for their sakes upon their tombs according to the superstitious order of the barbarians in old time, remaining at this day in no less use among the people of the west world, but rather to have their virtues in due veneration and treading in the steps of their examples, to imitate their order with like integrity of life."

"And for my part," saith she, dyeing her garments with the drops of her watery eyes, "proving too late what it is to lose a husband, and to forget him whom both the law of God and nature hath given me as a second part of myself, to live with mutual contentment until the dissolution of our sacred bond by the heavy hand of God, am thus far resolved in myself, protesting to perform no less by him that liveth, that if the fury of your passion prevail above your resistance, or your disease grow to such extreme terms that death will not be otherwise answered but that you must yield to his summons and die, I will not live to lament the loss of my second husband, nor use other dole[1] in the funeral of your corpse than to accompany it to the grave in a sheet or shroud of like attire. For your eyes shall no sooner close their lids or lose the light of this world than these hands shall be ready to perform the effect of my promise, and the bell that giveth warning of your last hour shall not cease his doleful knell till he have published with like sound the semblable end of your dear and loving wife."—Whose simple and frank offer here, opening a most convenient occasion for her willful husband to disclose the true cause of his disease prevailed so much over his doubtful and wavering

---

1   Mourning garments.

mind that dismissing even then his former dissimulation, he embraced her, not without such abundance of tears and unruly sighs that for the time they took away the use of his tongue.

Albeit being delivered of his trance and restored to the benefit of his speech, he disclosed unto her the true cause and circumstance of his grief in this sort: "Albeit since the time of my sickness," saith he, "you have seen what distress and desolation have passed me with fits of strange and diverse disposition, marveling no less, I am sure, from what fountain have flowed the symptoms of so rare a passion, wherein also your continual presence and view of my weak state is sufficiently able to record the whole discourse of my disease. Yet are you neither partaker of my pain nor privy to the principal causes of so strange an evil; neither have I been so hardy to discover them unto you because I have been hitherto doubtful of that whereof your last words have fully absolved me. And now, being weakened with the weariness of time and sickness, in such sort as nature hath rid her hands of me and given me over to the order of death who is to spare me no longer but to utter these last words unto you, I account it a special felicity in my hard fortune that, in the opening of the true causes of my grief, I may close and seal up the last and extreme term of my life. And, because I will clear in few words the mystery which seems to amaze you, you shall note that there be three only ministers and occasions of my disease, whereof the first, and of least importance, is for the death of my late lord and master, Don John Trivulso, whereof you are not ignorant. The second, exceeding the first in greatness of grief and force against me, is to think that the rigor of my destinies and violence of sickness, yielding me into the hands of death, will dissolve and break by that means the league of long and loyal love which from the beginning my heart hath vowed unto you. But the third and last, of a more strange quality than either of the rest, is to think that when I am dead and by time worn out of your mind, another shall enjoy the sweet and pleasant benefit of that divine beauty of yours, which ought to serve but for the diet of the gods. The simple view whereof seems able, if it were possible, to make me suffer the martyrdom of two deaths."

Whereunto she replied with persuasions to drive him from his fond[1] device, proffering herself eftsoons to die for company. Wherein—calling

---

1   Foolish.

the majesty of the highest to witness—she protested again that if he would not be reclaimed from his desire to die within a very short moment of time, she would be as ready to yield death his tribute as he. All which she inferred, I think, rather to feed the time than of intent to perform the effect of her offer, having the like opinion of her husband whom she thought always to have such power to repress the evil spirit that possessed him that he would not become the unnatural murderer of himself, and much less execute the like rage on her.

But, alas, the unfortunate lady brewed here the broth of her own bane[1] and spun the thread of her own destruction. For falling now unhappily into the malice of her destiny, thinking nothing less than of the secret ambush of mortal treason her husband had laid for her, went unhappily to bed with him the same night. Where, for his part, preferring in his face a show of feigned contentment and consolation to the eye, he forced a further quiet of mind by the joy he imagined in the act he meant to do, but chiefly for that he had devised how the innocent lady, through the rage of his villainy, should be forced to an effect of her promise. For the speedy execution whereof, they had not been long in bed together but he rose from her feigning a desire to perform the necessity of nature in the closet or chamber of secrets; his errand indeed being to fetch his dagger, which, without making her privy, he conveyed under the bolster[2] of his bed, beginning even then to prefer a preamble afore the part he meant to play, for, falling from his former complaints of sickness, he retired into terms of extreme frenzy and madness, braying out such groans and sighs of hideous disposition with howling, crying, and foaming at the mouth like one possessed with an evil spirit, that who had seen his often change of color and complexion in his face, his ghastly regards arguing intents of desperation, and his eyes flaming with fury sunk into his head with the order of his passion every way might easily have judged the desire of his heart to be of no small importance, and the thing he went about neither common nor commendable. Wherein he was assisted with three enemies of diverse dispositions: love, jealousy, and death, the least of the which is sufficient of himself to make a man chafe in his harness and take away the

---

1 Poison.
2 "A long stuffed pillow or cushion used to support the sleeper's head in bed" (*OED* *n.1* 1a).

courage of his heart in the midst of the combat; for the one presented a certain fear by reason of the horror of the act, the other sued, as it were, for an abstinence—or at least a moderation—of the cruelty he had commenced against his innocent wife, but the third, being the beginner of all and exceeding the rest in power would not dismiss him from the stage till he had played the uttermost act of his malicious tragedy.

Mark here, good ladies, the desolation of this unfortunate gentlewoman and dispose yourselves to tears on the behalf of her distress. Wherein certainly you have no less reason to help to bewail her wretched chance than just occasion to join in general exclamation against the detestable act of her tyrannous husband, who, disclaiming even now his former state and condition of a man, retires into the habit of a monster and cruel enemy to nature, and, in converting the virtue of his former love and remembrance of the sundry pleasures he had heretofore received of his dear and loving wife into present rage and unnatural fury far exceeding the savage and brutish manner of the tiger, lion, or leopards bred in the deserts of Africa—the common nurse of monsters and creatures cruel without reason—whetting his teeth for the terrible suggestion of the devil, who at the instant put into his hand the dagger. Wherewith, after he had embraced and kissed her in such sort as Judas kissed our Lord the same night he betrayed him, he saluted her with ten or twelve estockados,[1] one in the neck of[2] another, in diverse parts of her body, renewing the conflict with no less number of blows in her head and arms, and, because no part should escape free from the stroke of his malice, he visited her white and tender legs with no less rage and fury than the rest. Wherewith, beholding in her diverse undoubted arguments of death, began the like war with himself, using the same mean and ministers with his own hands, imbrued yet with the blood of his innocent wife, showing, notwithstanding this horrible part and act of despair, diverse and sundry signs of special gladness and pleasure in his face. Wherein he continued till the last and extreme gasp of life, chiefly for that he saw him accompanied to death with her whom he was not able to leave behind him alive, and who, being overcharged, as you have heard, with the number of wounds, the violence whereof, prevailing far above the resistance of life, did press her so much with

---

1 Thrusts with an estoc, a sword with a straight, edgeless, sharply pointed blade.
2 On top of.

the hasty approach of death that the want of breath abridged her secret shrift and confession to God, with less leisure to yield her innocent soul with humble prayer into the hands of her redeemer, and commend the forgiveness of her sins to the benefit of his mercy.

Only she had respite, with great ado to speak, to give order that her body might be laid in the tomb of her first husband, Seigneur Barzo. But the cursed and execrable[1] Albanian, so wholly possessed with the devil that the gift of grace was denied him, abhorred to the last minute of his life the remembrance of repentance, for laughing as it were at the foulness of the fact even until life left him senseless and void of breath, he commended his carcass to the greedy jaws of ravenous wolves, serving also as a fit prey for the venomous serpents and other creeping worms of the earth, and his soul to the reprobate society of Judas and Cain, with other of the infernal crew.

The worthy end of this wicked wretch argueth the just reward of the evil disposed and such as are unhappily dropped out of the favor of God, the ordinary success of those enterprises that are begun without the consent of wisdom or reason, but chiefly the effects and fortune of such as, blinded with the veil of their own will and dimmed with the mist of folly, do repose so much for themselves in the opinion of their own wit that, detesting good counsel and the advice of the wise, do credit only the conceit of their own fancy, which, as a blind guide, doth lead them into infinite miseries and labyrinth of endless annoy, where there is no dispense of their folly but loss of liberty, perpetual infamy, and sometime punishment by untimely death. Which, as they be worthy rewards for such as dote so much in their own wisdom that they account the same able of itself to comprehend the whole globe or compass the world, so the wise man afore he entereth into any enterprise of weight, being careful for the convey of the same, doth not only compare the end with the beginning and cast the sequel and circumstance every way, but also, entering as it were into himself, he makes a view of that which is in him, and for his better assistance he will not refuse the advice of his friends by which means he is sure to reap the reward of his travail[2] with treble contentment, and seldom is he punished with too late a repentance.

---

1   Deserving to be execrated, that is, driven out with a curse.
2   Labor.

Herewith also the example of the wise mariner doth in like sort advise us, who, coming by fortune or violence of weather upon an unknown coast, doth straightaway sound and try the depth of the river by his plummet and line;[1] neither will he let fall his anchor unless he be sure of the firmness of the ground, which, if it do fail him, yet is he to withstand the malice of danger by keeping the channel which yields him water enough. So, if this wretched Albanian had made a view of himself and his forces afore he became subject to the humor of jealous suspicion, or if he had given correction to his fault in time and suffered reason to suppress the rage of his folly afore he was grown to terms of madness, he had enjoyed his lady at pleasure, lived yet in quiet, and prevented the foul note of infamy wherewith the gates and posterns of his house will be painted till the extreme date of the world, and eschewed the peril of damnable despair in killing himself, with like violation and bloody slaughter of his innocent lady, whose death, with the strangeness in execution, being once known to the multitude, it is to be wondered what general dole and desolation were in all parts of the city, how all estates and degrees of people spared no sorts of tears, nor other dolorous tunes, bewailing her misfortune, with several grudges at the malice of her destinies that in such cruel manner took from amongst them the person of her whose virtues and other ornaments of God and nature served as a special mirror or looking glass to all ages. Wherein certainly they had great reason, for a lady or gentlewoman equal with her in conversation every way—I mean chaste without argument of dishonesty, devout and yet hating superstition, bountiful without wasteful prodigality, wise without vain vaunting, so obedient towards her husband as was necessary, and, lastly, lacking the furniture of no good virtue—cannot be too much honored in her life nor worthily renowned after her death, as well for the such rare gifts are no less meritorious for the virtues that be in them than that they serve as special allurements to provoke young ladies and gentlewomen desirous of like glory to imitate the example and virtues of them whose due fame is able to exceed the length of time and live after death; who hath no power but over our corrupt soma or mass of flesh, being barred to meddle with the felicity of the mind to whom only the title of perpetuity is due without exception. And as her life and

---

1 I.e., a plumb line, used to measure depth of water.

death import several virtues and deserve semblable commendation, the one for that she never made show of mislike what wrong soever he wrought her, the other in that she failed not to honor him till the last hour of his life, so may you also discern therein two several examples: the one, to warn the light and harebrained husbands not easily or for small occasions to enter into suspicion with their wives whom they ought to love and honor no less than themselves; the other, to present unto the ladies of our time the due reward of wisdom, obedience, and chastity, which be the things that make this Greek live after her death, being worthily invested with the wreathes of honor among all the ladies of that country.

3. FROM GEORGE PEELE, *THE BATTLE OF ALCAZAR*, *FOUGHT IN BARBARY, BETWEEN SEBASTIAN, KING OF PORTUGAL, AND ABDELMELEC, KING OF MOROCCO* (1588–89; LONDON, 1594); SPELLING MODERNIZED

[George Peele's *The Battle of Alcazar* is one of the earliest plays to stage multiple characters who are both non-white and Muslim, and it is often seen as the inaugurator of the stereotypical figure of the villainous Moor. The play recounts a series of internecine struggles for political control of Morocco that culminated, in the summer of 1578, in an historic battle that killed two claimants to the Moroccan sultanate, as well as the king of Portugal. Peele (1556–96) focusses the action on the ruthless manipulator Mulai Hamet (Abu Abdallah Mohammed), who tricks the play's rather limp hero, the king of Portugal, into sending troops into Alcazar in an attempt to oust his rival Mulai Molocco (Abd Al-Malik). While Hamet's perfidy is associated persistently with his blackness, the play's representation of race, religion, and nationality is considerably more complex than a simple equation of blackness with evil, and, despite its shambling plot and its emphasis on pageantry over subtlety, *The Battle of Alcazar* provides a useful window onto the racialized intricacies of political, economic, and cultural exchange in the Mediterranean region in the sixteenth century. The play's opening moments, excerpted below, set up its main plot, showing Hamet enact in dumbshow the murder of his two younger brothers and his uncle, thus establishing himself firmly as the play's central villain. Peele was a poet and dramatist whose other plays include *The Arraignment of Paris* (1584), *The Old Wives' Tale* (1595), and *David and Fair Bethsabe* (1599).]

Enter the Presenter

Honor, the spur that pricks the princely mind
To follow rule and climb the stately chair,
With great desire inflames the Portingall,[1]
An honorable and courageous king,
5   To undertake a dangerous, dreadful war
And aid with Christian arms the barbarous Moor,
The Negro[2] Mulai[3] Hamet[4] that withholds
The kingdom from his uncle Abdelmelec,
Whom proud Abdallas wronged,
10   And in his throne installs his cruel son,
That now usurps upon this prince,
This brave barbarian lord Mulai Molocco.
The passage to the crown by murder made,
Abdallas dies, and designs[5] this tyrant king
15   Of whom we treat, sprung from the Arabian Moor,
Black in his look and bloody in his deeds,
And in his shirt, stained with a cloud of gore,
Presents himself with naked sword in hand,
Accompanied, as now you may behold,
20   With devils coated in the shapes of men.

The first dumbshow
Enter Mulai Mohammed and his son, and his two young brethren. The Moor showeth them the bed and then takes his leave of them, and they betake them to their rest. And then the presenter speaketh:

Like those that were by kind of murder mummed,[6]
Sit down and see what heinous stratagems

---

1   Person from Portugal.
2   *Negro* is often synonymous with *Moor* in early use, and applied to any dark-skinned native of North Africa.
3   Title used by the rulers of Morocco.
4   Mohammed.
5   Designates.
6   Silenced.

These damnèd wits contrive. And lo, alas,
How like poor lambs prepared for sacrifice
This traitor king hales[1] to their longest home   5
These tender lords his younger brethren both.

The second dumbshow
Enter the Moor and two murderers bringing in his uncle Abdelmunen. Then
they draw the curtains and smother the young princes in the bed. Which done,
in sight of the uncle, they strangle him in his chair and then go forth. And then
the Presenter saith:

His brethren thus in fatal bed behearst,
His father's brother of too light belief
This Negro puts to death by proud command.
Say not these things are feigned, for true they are,
And understand how eager to enjoy   5
His father's crown this unbelieving Moor,
Murdering his uncle and his brethren,
Triumphs in his ambitious tyranny
Till Nemesis, high mistress of revenge,
That with her scourge keeps all the world in awe,   10
With thundering drums awakes the god of war
And calls the furies from Avernus's[2] crags
To range and rage, and vengeance to inflict,
Vengeance on this accursed Moor for sin.
And now behold how Abdelmelec comes,   15
Uncle to this unhappy traitor king,
Armed with great aid that Amurath[3] had sent,
Great Amurath, Emperor of the East,
For service done to Sultan Solomon,
Under whose colors he had served in field,   20
Flying the fury of this Negro's father
That wronged his brethren to install his son.
Sit you and see this true and tragic war,

---

1   Pushes.
2   Ancient name for a crater in present-day Italy thought to be the entrance to the
underworld.
3   Murad I, sultan of the Ottoman Empire (1362–89).

A modern matter full of blood and ruth[1]
25 Where three bold kings,[2] confounded in their height,
Fell to the earth contending for a crown,
And call this war The Battle of Alcazar.   *Exit*

4. FROM ROBERT GREENE, *THE FIRST PART*
OF THE TRAGICAL REIGN OF SELIMUS, SOMETIME
EMPEROR OF THE TURKS (LONDON, 1594);
SPELLING MODERNIZED

[*Selimus* is a fictional dramatization of the rise to power of Selim I (1470–1520), who deposed his father and murdered his older brothers in order to become sultan of the Ottoman Empire in 1512. *Selimus* became part of the repertoire of the Queen's Men acting company in 1588 and is one of a number of so-called "Turk plays" that offer an English perspective on the increasing military and economic dominance of the Ottomans in Europe around the turn of the seventeenth century. While they vary considerably in quality, tone, and historical argument, these plays rely heavily on stereotypes of violent, power-hungry, and untrustworthy Turks. In this excerpt from Scene 2, Selimus, Iago-like, talks aloud about his wicked plans to betray those who trust him most, and in the process he reveals his own lack of faith, contempt for virtue, and ruthless ambition. Greene (1558–92) was a prolific writer whose works include the romances *Pandosto* (1588) and *Menaphon* (1589) and the play *Orlando Furioso* (1594).]

Now Selimus, consider who thou art.
Long hast thou marchèd in disguised attire,
But now unmask thyself and play thy part,
And manifest the heat of thy desire;
5   Nourish the coals of thine ambitious fire,
And think that then thy empire is most sure
When men for fear thy tyranny endure.
Think that to thee there is no worse reproach
Than filial duty in so high a place.

---

1 Calamity; ruin; sorrow, distress.
2 I.e., Sebastian, king of Portugal; Mulai Hamet; and Abdelmelec.

Thou oughtst to set barrels of blood abroach,[1]   10
And seek with sword whole kingdoms to displace.
Let Mahound's[2] laws be locked up in their case,
And meaner[3] men and of a baser spirit
In virtuous actions seek for glorious merit.
I count it sacrilege for to be holy   15
Or reverence this threadbare name of good.
Leave to old men and babes that kind of folly;
Count it of equal value with the mud.
Make thou a passage for thy gushing flood
By slaughter, treason, or what else thou can,   20
And scorn religion—it disgraces man.
My father Bayazet[4] is weak and old,
And hath not much above[5] two years to live.
The Turkish crown of pearl and Ophir[6] gold
He means to his dear Acomat[7] to give,   25
But ere his ship can to her haven drive,
I'll send abroad my tempests in such sort
That she shall sink before she get[8] the port.
Alas, alas, his highness's agèd head
Is not sufficient to support a crown.   30
Then Selimus, take thou it in his stead,
And if at this thy boldness he dare frown
Or but resist thy will, then pull him down—
For since he hath so short a time t'enjoy it,
I'll make it shorter or I will destroy it.   35
Nor pass I what our holy votaries[9]
Shall here object against my forward mind;
I reck[10] not of their foolish ceremonies,

---

1   Pierce and thereby spill the contents.
2   The prophet Muhammed.
3   Inferior.
4   Bayezid II (1481–1512).
5   Little more than.
6   Biblical port famed as a source of wealth.
7   Older brother of Selimus.
8   Reach.
9   I.e., devout supporters of the current sultan.
10 Care.

But mean to take my fortune as I find.
40 Wisdom commands to follow tide and wind,
And catch front of swift Occasion
Before she be too quickly overgone.
Some man will say I am too impious
Thus to lay siege against my father's life,
45 And that I ought to follow virtuous
And godly sons, that virtue is a glass[1]
Wherein I may my errant[2] life behold
And frame myself by it in ancient mould.

Avaunt[3] such glasses! Let them view in me
The perfect picture of right tyranny.
55 Aye, like a lion's look—not worth a leek
When every dog deprives him of his prey—
These honest terms are far enough to seek.
When angry Fortune menaceth[4] decay,
My resolution treads a nearer way.
60 Give me the heart conspiring with the hand,
In such a cause my father to withstand.
Is he my father? Why, I am his son.
I owe no more to him than he to me.
If he proceed as he hath now begun
65 And pass from me the Turkish signory[5]
To Acomat, then Selimus is free.
And if he injure me that am his son,
Faith, all the love 'twixt him and me is done.

5. FROM WILLIAM SHAKESPEARE, *TITUS ANDRONICUS* (LONDON, 1594); SPELLING MODERNIZED

[Like *Othello*, Shakespeare's revenge drama *Titus Andronicus* features a character identified as a Moor. Aaron arrives in Rome with his lover

---

1 Mirror.
2 Straying from the proper course.
3 Away with.
4 Threatens.
5 Rule.

Tamora, the defeated queen of the Goths, and together they plot to destroy the general who has captured them. Although Aaron has sometimes been dismissed as a stereotype of the villainous Moor, he is a complex character whose wit, defiant pride in his blackness, and love for his infant son provide some of the play's most intriguing moments. The first excerpt below, from 4.2, depicts events immediately after Tamora, now married to the Roman Emperor Saturninus, has given birth to a son who is brought to meet his half-brothers, the Empress's adult sons Chiron and Demetrius.]

DEMETRIUS. Soft, who comes here?

Enter Nurse, with a blackamoor child.
NURSE. Good morrow, lords.
　　Oh, tell me, did you see Aaron the Moor?
AARON. Well, more or less, or ne'er a whit at all,
　　Here Aaron is. And what with Aaron now?　　　　　　　　55
NURSE. O gentle Aaron, we are all undone!
　　Now help, or woe betide thee evermore.
AARON. Why what a caterwauling dost thou keep!
　　What dost thou wrap and fumble in thy arms?
NURSE. Oh, that which I would hide from heaven's eye,　　60
　　Our empress's shame, and stately Rome's disgrace.
　　She is delivered, lords, she is delivered.
AARON. To whom?
NURSE. I mean, she is brought abed.[1]
AARON. Well, God give her good rest. What hath he sent her?　　65
NURSE. A devil.
AARON. Why then she is the devil's dam.[2] A joyful issue!
NURSE. A joyless, dismal, black, and sorrowful issue!
　　Here is the babe, as loathsome as a toad
　　Amongst the fair-faced breeders of our clime.　　　　　　70
　　The empress sends it thee, thy stamp, thy seal,
　　And bids thee christen it with thy dagger's point.
AARON. Zounds, you whore, is black so base a hue?

1　Has had a baby; has been put to bed. The Nurse assumes the first meaning, while Aaron puns on the second.
2　Mother.

[*To the baby*] Sweet blowse,[1] you are a beauteous blossom, sure.

75 DEMETRIUS. Villain, what hast thou done?

AARON. That which thou canst not undo.

CHIRON. Thou hast undone[2] our mother.

AARON. Villain, I have done[3] thy mother.

DEMETRIUS. And therein, hellish dog, thou hast undone her.

80   Woe to her chance, and damned her loathèd choice!

    Accursed the offspring of so foul a fiend!

CHIRON. It shall not live.

AARON. It shall not die.

NURSE. Aaron, it must. The mother wills it so.

85 AARON. What, must it, nurse? Then let no man but I

    Do execution on my flesh and blood.

DEMETRIUS. I'll broach[4] the tadpole on my rapier's point.

    Nurse, give it me. My sword shall soon dispatch it.

AARON. [*Taking the baby*] Sooner this sword shall plough thy

    bowels up.

90   Stay, murderous villains, will you kill your brother?

    Now, by the burning tapers of the sky

    That shone so brightly when this boy was got,

    He dies upon my scimitar's sharp point

    That touches this, my firstborn son and heir.

95   I tell you, younglings, not Enceladus[5]

    With all his threat'ning band of Typhon's brood,[6]

    Nor great Alcides,[7] nor the god of war[8]

    Shall seize this prey out of his father's hands—

    What, what, ye sanguine,[9] shallow-hearted boys,

---

1 Literally, red-faced wench.

2 Ruined, destroyed.

3 Had sex with.

4 Impale.

5 One of the giants who waged war against the Olympian gods and was imprisoned under volcanic Mount Etna.

6 The largest and most terrifying of the mythic giants, Typhon is said to have fathered such creatures as the Sphinx, the Nemean Lion, Cerberus, and Chimera.

7 Better known as Heracles (and as Hercules by the Romans), this son of Zeus is famed in mythology for his phenomenal strength.

8 I.e., Ares (known as Mars by the Romans).

9 Red-faced; lustful.

You white-limed[1] walls, you alehouse painted signs![2] 100
Coal black is better than another hue
In that it scorns to bear another hue,
For all the water in the ocean
Can never turn the swan's black legs to white,
Although she lave[3] them hourly in the flood. 105
DEMETRIUS. Wilt thou betray thy noble mistress thus?
AARON. My mistress is my mistress, this myself,
The vigor and the picture of my youth.
This before all the world do I prefer;
This maugre[4] all the world will I keep safe, 110
Or some of you shall smoke[5] for it in Rome.
DEMETRIUS. By this our mother is forever shamed.
CHIRON. Rome will despise her for this foul escape.
NURSE. The emperor in his rage will doom her death.
CHIRON. I blush to think upon this ignomy.[6] 115
AARON. Why, there's the privilege your beauty bears.
Fie, treacherous hue, that will betray with blushing
The close enacts[7] and counsels of thy heart.
Here's a young lad framed of another leer.[8]
Look how the black slave smiles upon the father, 120
As who should say "Old lad, I am thine own."
He is your brother, lords, sensibly fed
Of that self[9] blood that first gave life to you,
And from your womb where you imprisoned were
He is enfranchisèd and come to light. 125
Nay, he is your brother by the surer side,
Although my seal be stampèd in his face.

---

1   White-washed.
2   As their faces reveal their emotional turmoil, Aaron compares Tamora's fair-
skinned sons to white buildings fronted by garishly colored signs advertising the
businesses they contain.
3   Wash.
4   Despite.
5   Suffer.
6   Disgrace.
7   Secret plans.
8   Complexion.
9   Same.

NURSE. Aaron, what shall I say unto the empress?

DEMETRIUS. Advise thee, Aaron, what is to be done,

130 And we will all subscribe to thy advice.

Save thou the child, so[1] we may all be safe.

AARON. Then sit we down and let us all consult.

My son and I will have the wind of you.[2]

Keep there. Now talk at pleasure of your safety.

135 DEMETRIUS. [To the Nurse] How many women saw this child of his?

AARON. Why, so, brave lords! When we join in league

I am a lamb, but if you brave the Moor,

The chafèd[3] boar, the mountain lioness,

The ocean swells not so as Aaron storms.

140 But say again, how many saw the child?

NURSE. Cornelia the midwife and myself.

And no one else but the delivered empress.

AARON. The empress, the midwife, and yourself.

Two may keep counsel when the third's away.

145 Go to the empress; tell her this I said.

He kills [the Nurse].

"Week, week!" So cries a pig preparèd to the spit.

DEMETRIUS. What mean'st thou, Aaron? Wherefore didst thou this?

AARON. O Lord, sir, 'tis a deed of policy.[4]

Shall she live to betray this guilt of ours,

150 A long-tongued babbling gossip? No, lords, no.

And now be it known to you my full intent:

Not far one Muliteus my countryman,

His wife but yesternight was brought to bed.

His child is like to her, fair as you are.

155 Go pack[5] with him and give the mother gold,

And tell them both the circumstance of all,

And how by this their child shall be advanced

And be received for the emperor's heir,

---

1 "So long as" (Bevington).

2 I.e., will sit where we can watch you carefully, as a hunter stays downwind of his prey in order to maintain his advantage.

3 Angered.

4 Expedience; craftiness.

5 Scheme.

And substituted in the place of mine
To calm this tempest whirling in the court,   160
And let the emperor dandle him for his own.
Hark you, lords, you see I have given her[1] physic,[2]
And you must needs bestow her funeral.
The fields are near and you are gallant grooms.[3]
This done, see that you take no longer days   165
But send the midwife presently to me.
The midwife and the nurse well made away,[4]
Then let the ladies tattle what they please.
CHIRON. Aaron, I see thou wilt not trust the air
With secrets.
DEMETRIUS.   For this care of Tamora,   170
Herself and hers are highly bound to thee.
            Exeunt [Demetrius and Chiron, carrying the Nurse's body].
AARON. Now to the Goths, as swift as swallow flies,
There to dispose this treasure in mine arms
And secretly to greet the empress' friends.
Come on, you thick-lipped slave, I'll bear you hence,   175
For it is you that puts us to our shifts.[5]
I'll make you feed on berries and on roots,
And feed on curds and whey, and suck the goat,
And cabin[6] in a cave, and bring you up
To be a warrior and command a camp.   180
                        Exit [with the baby].

[In the following excerpt, from 5.1, Titus's eldest son, Lucius, is preparing to lead an army of Goths, Rome's long-standing enemy, into
battle against Saturninus when Aaron and his baby are captured and
brought before him. Even as he strikes a bargain to save the infant's
life Aaron displays a remorseless villainy that allies him with the stock
figure of Vice in early English morality plays.]

---

1 I.e., the Nurse.
2 Medicine.
3 Boys.
4 Killed.
5 Brings us to this extremity.
6 Shelter.

Enter Lucius with an army of Goths, with drums and soldiers.
LUCIUS. Approvèd warriors and my faithful friends,
   I have receivèd letters from great Rome
   Which signifies what hate they bear their emperor
   And how desirous of our sight they are.
5   Therefore, great lords, be as your titles witness,
   Imperious and impatient of your wrongs,
   And wherein Rome hath done you any scathe,[1]
   Let him[2] make treble satisfaction.
   1 GOTH. Brave slip[3] sprung from the great Andronicus,
10   Whose name was once our terror, now our comfort,
   Whose high exploits and honorable deeds
   Ingrateful Rome requites with foul contempt,
   Be bold in us. We'll follow where thou leadst,
   Like stinging bees in hottest summer's day
15   Led by their master to the flowered fields,
   And be avenged on cursèd Tamora.
   ALL GOTHS. And as he saith, so say we all with him.
   LUCIUS. I humbly thank him, and I thank you all.
   But who comes here, led by a lusty Goth?

Enter a Goth, leading of Aaron with his child in his arms.
20   2 GOTH. Renownèd Lucius, from our troops I strayed
   To gaze upon a ruinous monastery,
   And as I earnestly did fix mine eye
   Upon the wasted building, suddenly
   I heard a child cry underneath a wall.
25   I made unto the noise when soon I heard
   The crying babe controlled with this discourse:
   "Peace, tawny slave, half me and half thy dame.[4]
   Did not thy hue bewray[5] whose brat thou art,
   Had nature lent thee but thy mother's look,
30   Villain, thou mightst have been an emperor.
   But where the bull and cow are both milk white,

---

1   Harm.
2   I.e., the emperor Saturninus.
3   Literally, a small shoot from a plant; figuratively, son.
4   Mother.
5   Reveal.

They never do beget a coal-black calf.
Peace, villain, peace!"—even thus he rates[1] the babe—
"For I must bear thee to a trusty Goth
Who, when he knows thou art the empress' babe,   35
Will hold thee dearly for thy mother's sake."
With this, my weapon drawn, I rushed upon him,
Surprised him suddenly, and brought him hither
To use as you think needful of the man.
LUCIUS. O worthy Goth, this is the incarnate devil   40
  That robbed Andronicus of his good hand;
  This is the pearl that pleased your empress' eye,
  And here's the base fruit of his burning lust.—
  Say, wall-eyed slave, whither wouldst thou convey
  This growing image of thy fiendlike face?   45
  Why dost not speak? What, deaf? Not a word?—
  A halter, soldiers! Hang him on this tree,
  And by his side his fruit of bastardy.
AARON. Touch not the boy; he is of royal blood.
LUCIUS. Too like the sire for ever being good.   50
  First hang the child, that he may see it sprawl,
  A sight to vex the father's soul withal.
  Get me a ladder.
AARON.   Lucius, save the child,
  And bear it from me to the empress.
  If thou do this, I'll show thee wondrous things   55
  That highly may advantage thee to hear.
  If thou wilt not, befall what may befall,
  I'll speak no more but "Vengeance rot you all!"
LUCIUS. Say on, and if it please me which thou speak'st
  Thy child shall live and I will see it nourished.   60
AARON. And if it please thee? Why assure thee, Lucius,
  'Twill vex thy soul to hear what I shall speak;
  For I must talk of murders, rapes, and massacres,
  Acts of black night, abominable deeds,
  Complots of mischief, treason, villainies,   65
  Ruthful[2] to hear, yet piteously performed.
  And this shall all be buried by my death

---

1 Scolds.
2 Dreadful.

Unless thou swear to me my child shall live.
LUCIUS. Tell on thy mind; I say thy child shall live.
70 AARON. Swear that he shall, and then I will begin.
LUCIUS. Who should I swear by? Thou believest no god.
    That granted, how canst thou believe an oath?
AARON. What if I do not? As indeed I do not.
    Yet, for I know thou art religious
75 And hast a thing within thee callèd conscience,
    With twenty popish tricks and ceremonies
    Which I have seen thee careful to observe,
    Therefore I urge thy oath; for that I know
    An idiot holds his bauble for a god
80 And keeps the oath which by that god he swears,
    To that I'll urge him. Therefore thou shalt vow
    By that same god, what god soe'er it be
    That thou adorest and hast in reverence,
    To save my boy, to nourish and bring him up,
85 Or else I will discover naught to thee.
LUCIUS. Even by my god I swear to thee I will.
AARON. First know thou, I begot him on the empress.
LUCIUS. O most insatiate and luxurious woman!
AARON. Tut, Lucius, this was but a deed of charity
90 To that which thou shalt hear of me anon.
    'Twas her two sons that murdered Bassianus.
    They cut thy sister's tongue, and ravished her,
    And cut her hands and trimmed her as thou sawest.
LUCIUS. O detestable villain, call'st thou that trimming?
95 AARON. Why, she was washed, and cut, and trimmed, and 'twas
    Trim sport for them that had the doing of it.
LUCIUS. O barbarous, beastly villains, like thyself!
AARON. Indeed, I was their tutor to instruct them.
    That codding[1] spirit had they from their mother,
100 As sure a card as ever won the set;
    That bloody mind, I think, they learned of me,
    As true a dog as ever fought at head.
    Well, let my deeds be witness of my worth.

---

1 "? Lecherous, lustful" (*OED*).

I trained[1] thy brethren to that guileful hole
Where the dead corpse of Bassianus lay.   105
I wrote the letter that thy father found,
And hid the gold within the letter mentioned,
Confederate with the queen and her two sons.
And what not done, that thou hast cause to rue,
Wherein I had no stroke of mischief in it?   110
I played the cheater for thy father's hand,
And, when I had it, drew myself apart
And almost broke my heart with extreme laughter.
I pried me through the crevice of a wall
When, for his hand, he had his two sons' heads,   115
Beheld his tears, and laughed so heartily
That both mine eyes were rainy like to his.
And when I told the empress of this sport,
She sounded[2] almost at my pleasing tale,
And for my tidings gave me twenty kisses.   120
1 GOTH. What, canst thou say all this and never blush?
AARON. Ay, like a black dog, as the saying is.[3]
LUCIUS. Art thou not sorry for these heinous deeds?
AARON. Ay, that I had not done a thousand more.
Even now I curse the day—and yet, I think,   125
Few come within the compass of my curse,—
Wherein I did not some notorious ill
As kill a man or else devise his death,
Ravish a maid or plot the way to do it,
Accuse some innocent and forswear myself,   130
Set deadly enmity between two friends,
Make poor men's cattle break their necks;
Set fire on barns and haystacks in the night,
And bid the owners quench them with their tears.
Oft have I digged up dead men from their graves   135
And set them upright at their dear friends' door
Even when their sorrows almost were forgot,
And on their skins, as on the bark of trees,
Have with my knife carved in Roman letters

---

1 Lured.
2 Swooned, fainted.
3 "To blush like a black dog" was a common proverb in the period.

140   "Let not your sorrow die, though I am dead."
       But I have done a thousand dreadful things
       As willingly as one would kill a fly,
       And nothing grieves me heartily indeed
       But that I cannot do ten thousand more.
145   LUCIUS. Bring down the devil, for he must not die
       So sweet a death as hanging presently.
       AARON. If there be devils, would I were a devil
       To live and burn in everlasting fire,
       So I might have your company in hell
150   But to torment you with my bitter tongue.
       LUCIUS. Sirs, stop his mouth, and let him speak no more.

[In the closing moments of the play, Titus's only surviving son and the
state's new governor, Lucius, passes judgment on Aaron. The Moor's
final speech enacts his resolute resistance to Rome by parodically
inverting the forms of repentance long associated with condemned
prisoners.]

       [*Enter Aaron, under guard.*]
       ROMAN. You sad Andronici, have done with woes.
       Give sentence on this execrable wretch
       That hath been breeder of these dire events.
       LUCIUS. Set him breast deep in earth and famish him.
180   There let him stand and rave and cry for food.
       If anyone relieves or pities him,
       For the offense he dies. This is our doom.
       Some stay to see him fastened in the earth.
       AARON. Ah, why should wrath be mute and fury dumb?
185   I am no baby, I, that with base prayers
       I should repent the evils I have done.
       Ten thousand worse than ever yet I did
       Would I perform if I might have my will.
       If one good deed in all my life I did,
190   I do repent it from my very soul.
       LUCIUS. Some loving friends convey the Emperor hence,
       And give him burial in his fathers' grave.
       My father and Lavinia shall forthwith
       Be closèd in our household's monument.

As for that ravenous tiger Tamora, 195
No funeral rite, nor man in mourning weed,[1]
Nor mournful bell shall ring her burial,
But throw her forth to beasts and birds to prey.[2]
Her life was beastly and devoid of pity,
And being dead, let birds on her take pity. 200

[*Exeunt.*]

6. FROM WILLIAM SHAKESPEARE, *SHAKESPEARE'S SONNETS* (LONDON, 1609); SPELLING MODERNIZED

[Sonnets 57 and 58 trace in lyric form some of the complex interactions of love, jealousy, and obligation that Shakespeare explores in dramatic form in *Othello*. The speaker of this emotionally and rhetorically intricate pair of poems presents himself variously as his beloved's slave, his vassal, and his servant, and he characterizes the demands of spiritual and erotic bondage as both painful and inevitable. It is worth noting that in sonnet 57 the distinction between speaker and poet is elided when the speaker identifies himself as "your will," a pun on his own name that insists on an intimate link between his sense of self and the desires of his "sovereign" lover. Sonnet 58 uses the language of religious suffering and of legal rights and obligations to trace the speaker's barely controlled jealousy as it threatens to break through into bitter reproach.]

57

Being your slave, what should I do but tend[3]
Upon the hours and times of your desire?
I have no precious time at all to spend,
Nor services to do till you require.
Nor dare I chide[4] the world-without-end[5] hour
Whilst I (my sovereign) watch the clock for you,
Nor think the bitterness of absence sour

---

1   Apparel.
2   I.e., to prey upon.
3   Attend; wait for; look after.
4   Scold; complain about.
5   Endless-seeming.

When you have bid your servant once adieu.
Nor dare I question with my jealous thought
Where you may be, or your affairs[1] suppose,[2]
But like a sad slave stay and think of naught
Save where you are how happy you make those.[3]
   So true a fool is love that in your will,[4]
   Though you do any thing, he thinks no ill.

58

That god forbid, that made me first your slave,
I should in thought control your times of pleasure,
Or at your hand th'account[5] of hours to crave,
Being your vassal[6] bound to stay[7] your leisure.
O let me suffer (being at your beck)[8]
Th' imprisoned absence of your liberty,
And patience tame, to sufferance[9] bide[10] each check,[11]
Without accusing you of injury,[12]
Be where you list,[13] your charter[14] is so strong,
That you yourself may privilege[15] your time
To what you will; to you it doth belong
Yourself to pardon of self-doing[16] crime.
   I am to wait, though waiting so be hell,
   Nor blame your pleasure, be it ill or well.

---

1 Concerns and activities; personal engagements (though the meaning of sexual relationships was not established until the eighteenth century).
2 Imagine.
3 I.e., those who are with you.
4 What you want; perhaps also a pun on the author's name.
5 The explanation; the itemized list; that which is owed.
6 One who owes feudal homage to a lord.
7 Wait for.
8 Command.
9 Patient waiting; suffering.
10 Endure; wait for.
11 Rebuff; block; rebuke; restraint; attack.
12 Wrongdoing.
13 Wish.
14 Right.
15 Freely use.
16 Done by yourself; done to yourself; perhaps also done to me (because we are one).

[Thomas Coryate (1577–1617) was an English travel writer best known for publishing accounts of his expeditions to Europe and Asia. *Coryats Crudities* recounts his five-month tour of numerous European towns and cities and includes vivid descriptions of landscape, local history, and notable residents. Metaphorizing his travelogue as a series of crudities—that is, raw or unrefined foods—the title page of Coryate's lengthy volume presents his experiences as "newly digested ... and now dispersed to the nourishment of the traveling members of this kingdom." Coryate's canny assessment of the appetites of the English reading public are evident in the following excerpts from his account of Venice, which include detailed descriptions of the city's architecture, the fashions favored by its female residents, and the habits of its notorious courtesans. To readers of *Othello*, this near-contemporary picture of the city and its inhabitants is perhaps of most interest for its characterization of Venetian women as either wives kept "always within the walls" by jealous husbands, or as "famoused" prostitutes.]

Such is the rareness of the situation of Venice that it doth even amaze and drive into admiration all strangers that upon their first arrival behold the same. For it is built altogether upon the water in the innermost gulf of the Adriatic Sea, which is commonly called *Golfo di Venezia*, and is distant from the main sea about the space of three miles. From the which it is divided by a certain great bank called *lido maggiore*,[1] which is at the least fifty miles in length. This bank is so necessary a defense for the city that it serveth instead of a strong wall to repulse and reverberate the violence of the furious waves of the sea. For were not this bank interposed like a bulwark betwixt the city and the sea, the waves would utterly overwhelm and deface the city in a moment. The form of this foresaid bank is very strange to behold. For nature herself, the most cunning mistress and architect of all things, hath framed it crooked in the form of a bow, and by the art of man there are five *ostia*, which is mouths or gaps, made therein, whereof

---

1 Greater beach.

Il Signior Tomaso Odcombiano

Margarita Emiliana bella
Cortesana di Venetia

Gu: Hole sculp

Illustration from Thomas Coryate, *Coryats Crudities* (London: Printed by W[illiam] S[tansby for the author], anno Domini 1611). Beinecke Rare Book and Manuscript Library, Yale University.

each maketh a haven and yieldeth passage to the ships to sail forth and back to Venice. (160–61)

The city is divided in the midst by a goodly fair channel, which they call *Canal il grande*.[1] The same is crooked, and made in the form of a Roman S. It is in length a thousand and three hundred paces, and in breadth at the least forty, in some places more. The six parts of the city whereof Venice consisteth are situate on both sides of this *Canal il grande*.... Also, both sides of this channel are adorned with many sumptuous and magnificent palaces that stand very near to the water, and make a very glorious and beautiful show. For many of them are of a great height, three or four stories high, most being built with brick, and some few with fair freestone.[2] Besides, they are adorned with a great multitude of stately pillars made partly of white stone and partly of Istrian marble.[3] (163)

Most women when they walk abroad, especially to church, are veiled with long veils, whereof some do reach almost to the ground behind. These veils are either black, or white, or yellowish. The black, either wives or widows do wear; the white, maids, and so the yellowish also, but they wear more white than yellowish. It is the custom of these maids when they walk in the streets to cover their faces with their veils, *verecundiae causa*,[4] the stuff being so thin and slight that they may easily look through it. For it is made of a pretty slender silk, and very finely curled, so that because she thus hoodwinketh herself you can very seldom see her face at full when she walketh abroad, though perhaps you earnestly desire it, but only a little glimpse thereof. Now whereas as I said before that only maids do wear white veils and none else, I mean these white silk curled veils, which, as they told me, none do wear but maids. But other white veils wives do much wear, such as

---

1   The Grand Canal.
2   A fine-grained, soft stone used for molding and tracery.
3   A dense and impermeable limestone from Istria, the largest peninsula in the Adriatic Sea.
4   For the sake of modesty.

are made of Holland,[1] whereof the greatest part is handsomely edged with great and fair bonelace.[2]

Almost all the wives, widows, and maids do walk abroad with their breasts all naked, and many of them have their backs also naked even almost to the middle, which some do cover with a slight linen—as cobweb lawn[3] or such other thin stuff—a fashion methinks very uncivil and unseemly, especially if the beholder might plainly see them. For I believe unto many that have *prurientem libidinem*,[4] they would minister a great incentive and fomentation of luxurious desires. Howbeit, it is much used both in Venice and Padua, for very few of them do wear bands[5] but only gentlewomen, and those do wear little lawn or cambric[6] ruffs.

There is one thing used of the Venetian women and some others dwelling in the cities and towns subject to the Signory of Venice that is not observed, I think, amongst any other women in Christendom, which is so common in Venice that no women whatsoever goeth without it, either in her house or abroad—a thing made of wood and covered with leather of sundry colors, some with white, some red, some yellow. It is called a "chapiney,"[7] which they wear under their shoes. Many of them are curiously painted, some also I have seen fairly gilt—so uncomely a thing, in my opinion, that it is pity this foolish custom is not clean banished and exterminated out of the city. There are many of these chapineys of a great height, even half a yard high, which maketh many of the women that are very short seem much taller than the tallest women we have in England. Also, I have heard that this is observed amongst them, that by how much the nobler a woman is, by so much the higher are her chapineys. All their gentlewomen, and most of their wives and widows that are of any wealth, are assisted and supported either by men or women when they walk abroad, to the end they may

---

1   A plain-woven linen fabric produced throughout Europe, but particularly in the Netherlands.

2   "Lace, usually of linen thread, made by knitting upon a pattern marked by pins, with bobbins originally made of bone" (*OED, n.* 1).

3   Also called "cobweb lace," a very finely woven, gauzy fabric.

4   Itching lust.

5   Collars.

6   "A kind of fine white linen, originally made at Cambray in Flanders" (*OED n.* a).

7   Also called "chopine," a type of platform shoe. One pair of sixteenth-century Venetian chopines on display at the city's Museo Correr is 20 inches (50 cm) high.

not fall. They are borne up most commonly by the left arm, otherwise they might quickly take a fall. For I saw a women fall a very dangerous fall, as she was going down the stairs of one of the little stony bridges with her high chapineys along by herself; but I did nothing pity her, because she wore such frivolous and, as I may truly term them, ridiculous instruments, which were the occasion of her fall. For both I myself, and many other strangers, as I have observed in Venice, have often laughed at them for their vain chapineys.

All the women of Venice every Saturday in the afternoon do use to anoint their hair with oil or some other drugs,[1] to the end to make it look fair, that is whitish, for that color is most affected of the Venetian dames and lasses. And in this manner they do it: first, they put on a reeden[2] hat without any crown at all but brims of exceeding breadth and largeness; then, they sit in some sun-shining place in a chamber or some other secret[3] room, where, having a looking-glass before them, they sophisticate[4] and dye their hair with the foresaid drugs, and after cast it back round upon the brims of the hat till it be thoroughly dried with the heat of the sun; and, last of all, they curl it up in curious locks with a frizzling or crisping pin of iron, which we call in Latin *Calamistrum*,[5] the top of which on both sides above their forehead is acuminated[6] in two peaks. That this is true, I know by mine own experience, for it was my chance one day when I was in Venice to stand by an Englishman's wife, who was a Venetian woman born, while she was thus trimming of her hair, a favor not afforded to every stranger.

But since I have taken occasion to mention some notable particulars of their women, I will insist farther upon that matter and make relation of their courtesans also, as being a thing incident and very proper to this discourse, especially because the name of a courtesan of Venice is famoused over all Christendom. And I have here inserted a picture of one of their nobler courtesans, according to her Venetian habits, with my own near unto her, made in that form as we saluted

---

1 [Coryate's note:] These kind of ointments wherewith women were wont to anoint their hair were heretofore called *Capillaria unguéta*. Turnebus Adversari. Lib. I ca. 7.
2 Made of reeds.
3 Private.
4 "To deal with in some artificial way"; "to render less genuine or honest"; "to corrupt, pervert, mislead" (*OED v.* 1b, 2, 3).
5 Curling iron.
6 Drawn to a point.

each other. Surely by so much the more willing I am to treat something of them because I perceive it is so rare a matter to find a description of the Venetian courtesans in any author, that all writers that I could ever see which have described the city have altogether excluded them out of their writings. Therefore seeing the history of these famous gallants is omitted by all others that have written just commentaries of the Venetian state, as I know it is not impertinent to this present discourse to write of them, so I hope it will not be ungrateful to the reader to read that of these notable persons which no author whatsoever doth impart unto him but myself, only I fear lest I shall expose myself to the severe censure and scandalous imputations of many carping critics who I think will tax me for luxury[1] and wantonness to insert so lascivious a matter into this treatise of Venice. Wherefore at the end of this discourse of the courtesans, I will add some apology for myself, which I hope will in some sort satisfy them if they are not too captious.[2]

The woman that professeth this trade is called in the Italian tongue *Cortezana*, which word is derived from the Italian word *cortesia* that signifieth courtesy, because these kind of women are said to receive courtesies of their favorites. Which word hath some kind of *affinity* with the Greek word ἑταίρα, which signifieth properly a sociable woman, and is by Demosthenes,[3] Athenaeus,[4] and divers other prose writers often taken for a woman of a dissolute conversation.

As for the number of these Venetian courtesans, it is very great. For it is thought there are of them in the whole city and other adjacent places as Murano, Malomocco, etc. at the least twenty thousand,[5] whereof many are esteemed so loose that they are said to open their quivers to every arrow. A most ungodly thing without doubt that there should be a toleration of such licentious wantons in so glorious, so potent, so renowned a city. For methinks that the Venetians should be daily afraid lest their winking at such uncleanness should be an occasion to draw down upon them God's curses and vengeance from heaven, and to consume their city with fire and brimstone as in times past he did Sodom

---

1 Censure me for lustfulness.
2 Inclined to find fault.
3 Greek orator of Athens (fl. fourth century BCE).
4 Greek rhetorician and grammarian (fl. late second and early third centuries CE).
5 This figure is suspiciously high, since estimates put the total population of Venice at less than 200,000 in this period.

and Gomorrah. But they, not fearing any such thing, do grant large dispensation and indulgence unto them, and that for these two causes.

First, *ad vitanda maiormala*,[1] for they think that the chastity of their wives would be the sooner assaulted, and so consequently they should be capricornified[2]—which of all the indignities in the world the Venetian cannot patiently endure—were it not for these places of evacuation. But I marvel how that should be true, though these courtesans were utterly rooted out of the city, for the gentlemen do even coop up their wives always within the walls of their houses for fear of these inconveniences, as much as if there were no courtesans at all in the city. So that you shall very seldom see a Venetian gentleman's wife but either at the solemnization of a great marriage, or at the christening of a Jew, or late in the evening rowing in a gondola.

The second cause is for that the revenues which they pay unto the Senate for their toleration do maintain a dozen of their galleys,[3] as many reported unto me in Venice, and so save them a great charge. The consideration of these two things hath moved them to tolerate for the space of these many hundred years these kind of Laides and Thaides who may be as fitly termed the stales[4] of Christendom as those were heretofore of Greece. For so infinite are the allurements of these amorous Calypsos,[5] that the fame of them hath drawn many to Venice from some of the remotest parts of Christendom to contemplate their beauties and enjoy their pleasing dalliances.

And indeed such is the variety of the delicious objects they minister to their lovers that they want nothing tending to delight. For when you come into one of their palaces—as indeed some few of the principalest of them live in very magnificent and portly[6] buildings fit for the entertainment of a great prince—you seem to enter into the paradise

---

1   To avoid greater evils.
2   To be fitted with horns. A husband whose wife committed adultery was often described as wearing horns.
3   Seagoing vessels propelled by oars and sails, in common use in the Mediterranean in the period.
4   Prostitutes. Laides and Thaides were evidently loose women of ancient Greece, though the precise reference is obscure.
5   In Homer's *Odyssey*, Calypso is a nymph who detains Odysseus for several years on the island of Ogygia and does not allow him to return home to his wife Penelope.
6   Stately.

of Venus.[1] For their fairest rooms are most glorious and glittering to behold, the walls round about being adorned with most sumptuous tapestry and gilt leather such as I have spoken of in my treatise of Padua. Besides you may see the picture of the noble courtesan most exquisitely drawn. As for herself, she comes to thee decked like the queen and goddess of love—in so much that thou wilt think she made a late transmigration from Paphos,[2] Cnidos,[3] or Cythera,[4] the ancient habitations of Dame Venus—for her face is adorned with the quintessence of beauty. In her cheeks thou shalt see the lily and the rose strive for the supremacy, and the silver trammels[5] of her hair displayed in that curious manner besides her two frizzled peaks standing up like pretty pyramids that they give thee the true *cos amoris*.[6] But if thou has an exact judgment, thou mayst easily discern the effects of those famous apothecary drugs heretofore used amongst the noble ladies of Rome, even *stibium*,[7] *cerussa*,[8] and *purpurissum*.[9] For few of the courtesans are so much beholding to nature but that they adulterate their faces and supply her defect with one of these three. A thing so common amongst them that many of them which have an elegant natural beauty do varnish their faces, the observation whereof made me not a little pity their vanities, with these kind of sordid trumperies. Wherein methinks they seem *ebur atramento candefacere*, according to that excellent proverb of Plautus,[10] that is, to make ivory white with ink.

---

1   Roman name for Aphrodite, the Greek goddess of love.
2   Coastal city in Cyprus; mythical birthplace of Aphrodite and her chief center of worship.
3   Ancient Greek city, also spelled Knidos, located in modern-day Turkey. The famous statue *Aphrodite of Cnidos* was made there in the fourth century BCE.
4   Greek island associated with Aphrodite, who was also known as the Lady of Cythera.
5   Braids or tresses.
6   Literally, grindstone of love. See also John Lyly, *Euphues* (1578): "Venus had her mole in her cheek which made her more amiable, Helen her scar on her chin which Paris called *cos amoris*, the whetstone of love"; John Josselyn, *New England's Rarities* (1671): "seldom without a Comes-to-Me, or 'Cos Amoris,' in their Countenance."
7   Known in English as "Black antimony," a powdered drug used as a cosmetic for darkening eyelids and eyebrows.
8   Ceruse, a white lead mixture used as a cosmetic.
9   A reddish cosmetic paint.
10   Roman comic playwright, c. 254–184 BCE.

Also, the ornaments of her body are so rich that except thou dost even geld[1] thy affections—a thing hardly to be done—or carry the Ulysses herb called moly, which is mentioned by Homer,[2] that is some antidote against venerous[3] titillations, she will very near benumb and captivate thy senses and make reason vail bonnet to affection.[4] For thou shalt see her decked with many chains of gold and orient pearl like a second Cleopatra—but they are very little—divers gold rings beautified with diamonds and other costly stones, jewels in both her ears of great worth. A gown of damask[5]—I speak this of the nobler courtesans—either decked with a deep gold fringe—according as I have expressed it in the picture of the courtesan that I have placed about the beginning of this discourse—or laced with five or six gold laces each two inches broad. Her petticoat of red camlet[6] edged with rich gold fringe, stockings of carnation[7] silk, her breath and her whole body, the more to enamor thee, most fragrantly perfumed. Though these things will at the first sight seem unto thee most delectable allurements, yet if thou shalt rightly weigh them in the scales of a mature judgment, thou wilt say with the wise man, and that very truly, that they are like a golden ring in a swine's snout.

Moreover, she will endeavor to enchant thee, partly with her melodious notes that she warbles out upon her lute, which she fingers with as laudable a stroke as many men that are excellent professors in the noble science of music, and partly with that heart-tempting harmony of her voice. Also thou wilt find the Venetian courtesan, if she be a selected woman indeed, a good rhetorician and a most elegant discourser, so that if she cannot move thee with all these foresaid delights, she will assay thy constancy with her rhetorical tongue. And to the end she may minister unto thee the stronger temptations to come to her lure, she will show thee her chamber of recreation, where thou shalt see all

---

1 Literally, castrate; figuratively, weaken.
2 In Homer's *Odyssey*, Odysseus uses the herb moly to protect himself from Circe's potion, which has turned all of his men into swine. Ulysses is the Roman name for Odysseus.
3 Lustful.
4 I.e., make reason defer to desire.
5 Elaborately patterned silk fabric.
6 An elegant and costly fabric claimed by some to have been spun originally from camel hair, but made in the early modern period from Angora goat hair.
7 "A light rosy pink" (*OED n.* 1b).

manner of pleasing objects, as many fair-painted coffers wherewith it is garnished round about, a curious milk-white canopy of needle work, a silk quilt embroidered with gold, and generally all her bedding sweetly perfumed. And amongst other amiable ornaments she will show thee one thing only in her chamber tending to mortification, a matter strange amongst so many *irritamenta malorum*[1]—even the picture of our Lady[2] by her bedside, with Christ in her arms, placed with a crystal glass.[3] But beware not withstanding all these *illecebra et lenocinia amoris*[4] that thou enter not into terms of private conversation with her. For then thou shalt find her such a one as Lipsius[5] truly calls her, *calli dam et calidam solis filiam*, that is, the crafty and hot daughter of the sun.

Moreover, I will tell thee this news which is most true, that if thou shouldst wantonly converse with her and not give her that *salarium iniquitatis*[6] which thou hast promised her but perhaps cunningly escape from her company, she will either cause thy throat to be cut by her *ruffiano*[7] if he can after catch thee in the city, or procure thee to be arrested if thou art to be found, and clapped up in the prison, where thou shalt remain till thou hast paid her all thou didst promise her.

Therefore, for avoiding of these inconveniences, I will give thee the same counsel that Lipsius did to a friend of his that was to travel into Italy: even to furnish thyself with a double armor, the one for thine eyes, the other for thine ears. As for thine eyes, shut them and turn them aside from these venerous Venetian objects. For they are the double windows that convey them to thy heart. Also thou must fortify thine ears against the attractive enchantments of their plausible speeches. Therefore, even as wrestlers were wont heretofore to fence their ears against all exterior annoyances by putting to them certain instruments

---

1   Incentives of evil. See Ovid's *Metamorphoses* I, 140: *Effodiuntur opes irritamenta malorum* (Riches, the incentives to vice, are dug out of the earth).
2   The Virgin Mary.
3   I.e., behind glass in a picture frame.
4   Enticements and allurements of love.
5   Justus Lipsius (1547–1606), philologist and humanist.
6   Payment of iniquity; see also "wages of sin" (Romans 6:23).
7   Pimp.

called ἀμφῶτιδες,[1] so do thou take unto thyself this firm foundation against the amorous wounds of the Venetian courtesans to hear none of their wanton toys; or if thou wilt needs both see and hear them, do thou only cast thy breath upon them in that manner as we do upon steel, which is no sooner on but incontinent it falleth off again. So do thou only breathe a few words upon them and presently be gone from them, for if thou dost linger with them thou wilt find their poison to be more pernicious than that of the scorpion, asp, or cockatrice.[2] (261–68)

8. FROM MAURICE G. DOWLING, *OTHELLO TRAVESTIE: AN OPERATIC BURLESQUE BURLETTA* (LONDON: THOMAS HAILES LACY, 1836), 9–13

[*Othello Travestie* is one of a series of parodies of Shakespeare plays that attracted enthusiastic audiences in the heyday of minstrelsy, a form of burlesque featuring comic dramas, singing, and dancing performed by white entertainers wearing dark makeup called blackface. Enormously popular on both sides of the Atlantic in the nineteenth century, minstrel shows traded in grotesque caricatures of black women and men as they lampooned what had come to be seen as elitist celebration of all things Shakespearean. Dowling's *Travestie*, which was first performed in the former slave-trading port of Liverpool in 1834, closely follows the plot of *Othello*, though it swaps the play's poetry for rhyming couplets, sets some of its most famous speeches to popular tunes of the day, and features a dim-witted Othello whose failure to murder his wife enables the play's brashly comic ending. Critics are divided over the appropriate response to the now-unperformable texts of the minstrel tradition, some arguing they are best left to gather dust in the archive, others suggesting they be treated as cultural artifacts that enrich understanding of a racist past, and still others defending them as viable instruments of populist subversion.]

---

1   *Amphotide*: covering worn by ancient Greek wrestlers to protect their ears. Later, the early Christian theologian Clement of Alexandria (150–215) reportedly recommended that such devices be used by the faithful to stop their ears against licentious songs (*Dizionario Universale Logico-Artistico-Technologico*).
2   Mythic serpent able to kill with a glance.

SCENE 3

Council chamber of the palace. Duke and Senators discovered sitting,
drinking, and smoking. Enter Ludovico, stage right. Enter Othello,
Brabantio, Policemen, Iago, and Cassio, stage left.

DUKE. [*Smoking a pipe, a pot of porter before him.*]
    Valiant Othello, we're very glad you're come;
    There'll be a precious row—there will by gum!
    Would you believe it, sirs, the galley-slaves
    Are playing "Meg's Diversion"[1] on the waves—
5   Here's one good gentleman—defend us, heaven!
    Says there's a hundred and terwenty-seven.
    And this, my letter, says—the slaves that's naughty,
    Amounts to full two hundred and forty.
    The other gentleman has got a letter,
10   Which says two hundred, and something better.
    What's to be done, Othello? Try and whack 'em!
    Take all the troops; soldiers—you shall not lack 'em.
    Haste, then, away! commence your work of slaughter.
BRABANTIO. Stop, good Sir Duke—he's stole away my daughter.
15   He is a wizard, sir—a very elf!
    I do believe he is the devil himself.
    He has dissolved my daughter into air.
    Or has her spell-bound—heaven alone knows where.
    A rogue and vagabond! I could his head mill—
20   Commit him, I beseech you, to the treadmill.
DUKE. There must be some mistake—come, speak, Othello;
    What say you to the charge, my noble fellow?
OTHELLO. Massa, him neber do de ting dat wrong;
    Him tell him all about it—in him song.

    [*Singing, to the tune of "Yankee Doodle"*]
25   Potent, grave, and rev'rend sir,
    Very noble massa—
    When de maid a man prefer

---

1 Behaving boisterously.

Den him no can pass her.
Yes, it is most werry true
Him take dis old man's daughter,   30
But no by spell, him promise you.
But by fair means him caught her.
'Tis true she lub him berry much,
'Tis true dat off him carry her,
And dat him lub for her is such,   35
'Tis werry true him marry her.
All dis be true—and till him dead,
Him lub her widout ending—
And dis, my massa, is the head
And tail of him offending.   40

Dis old man once him lub me too,
Do' now in rage before ye.
And often say, "Come, Othello,
And tell us pretty story,
About der time when you young child,   45
(You naughty lilly child ye,)
And when you 'bout de wood run wild,
And when you sold for slavey."

Den ebery day him tell all dis,
And sometimes lilly lie, too,   50
And him look in de eye of miss,
And den him hear her sigh, too.
Den missee meet him all alone,
And den him ax her wedder
Him make de both two hearts in one,   55
Den off dey run togedder.

BRABANTIO. 'Tis all a lie! told to defraud the bench;
   Please you to order someone fetch the wench.
                                        Exit Iago and Roderigo, stage left.
   And if she shall confess she first began
   To throw sheep's eyes, and ogle at the man,   60
   If, as he says, she took these means to woo him,
   Why, blow me tight, if I don't give her to him.

Enter Desdemona, Iago, and Roderigo, stage left.
    Oh! here she comes. My cheyld! my darling cheyld!
    Your poor old father has been almost wild.
65 But tell me—since you lost your poor dear mother,
    Don't you love me, dear, more than any other?
DESDEMONA. Why, dear papa, as I must answer candid,
    You've loved your child as much as ever man did,
    And, as in duty bound, I loved, or rather,
70 Worshipped my parent—but then you're my father;
    I've followed the example of my mother,
    Who loved her father, but left him for another.
BRABANTIO. Hussey! Your mother never left her home.
DESDEMONA. Pshaw! Pshaw!
75 Did not she give up all with you to roam?
    I've only done as folks have done before;
    I've cut you all—for this, my blackamoor.
    He is my husband.
OTHELLO. Yes, one and one make one.
DESDEMONA.

    [*Singing to the tune of "Bonnie Laddie"*]
80 I'll tell you why I loved the black, Too ral, etc.
    'Cause ev'ry night I had a knock. Too ral, etc.
    Of list'ning to his tales bewitchin',
    My hair while curling in the kitchen. Too ral, etc.

    Once while darning father's stocking, Too ral, etc.
85 Oh! he told a tale so shocking; Too ral, etc.
    So romantic—yet so tender,
    That I fell fainting 'cross the fender. Too ral, etc.

    When I came about—ah, me! Too ral, etc.
    I was sitting on his knee— Too ral, etc.
90 Grateful for the scrape I'd missed—
    I thanked him—and he welcome kissed. Too ral, etc.

    Listen, ladies, if you please— Too ral, etc.
    Never sit on young men's knees. Too ral, etc.

For though I got a husband by it,
The plan's not good—so pray don't try it. Too ral, etc.   95

BRABANTIO. Well, heaven be with you both, for now I've done.
                                                    He joins their hands.
A word, Othello—watch her—mind you do—
She's cheated me you know, and may cheat you.
DUKE. Now then, Othello, that affair's put right,
And you must toddle off this very night.   100
OTHELLO. Tonight! Good massa duke, me just now married.
DUKE. I don't care—you must go; too long you've tarried.
I shall be robbed and murdered by these chaps,
If you don't go and whack 'em for me, p'rhaps.
OTHELLO. Where shall him leave him wife?   105
DESDEMONA. Oh, you said leave me?
DUKE. Go to your father, dear.
DESDEMONA. I shan't.
DUKE. Oh, fie!
OTHELLO. I wouldn't have it so.   110
BRABANTIO. Nor I.
DESDEMONA. Nor I.
I won't go anywhere but with Othello.
That's what I won't.
BRABANTIO. Well, don't begin to bellow.   115
DESDEMONA. I will—I'll cry for ever—all my life—
What's the use of being made a wife?
I will go with him.
OTHELLO. Massa Duke, oh, pray—
DUKE. That's a brave lass! and so you shall, I say.   120
        Exeunt Duke, Brabantio, Ludovico, Senator, and Policemen, stage left.
OTHELLO. (*to Iago*) Ensign, him werry sure you much good fellow,
Mind you take care of my wife, Mrs. Otello,
If she get cold, mind give her gruel, or sago,[1]
And him be grateful to Iago.
                                    Exit Othello and Desdemona, stage left.
RODERIGO. (*from stage right*) Iago!   125

_____

1   Pudding made from the pith of the sago palm.

IAGO. [*from stage left*] What's the matter with the man?

RODERIGO. I'll drown myself!

IAGO. Thou silly gentleman!

RODERIGO. Silly, indeed! answer me this one query—

130   I'm bound to whine, when done out of my deary?

IAGO. Pshaw! Don't talk nonsense, man—she loves you still,

     Or if she does not, I'll engage she will.

     Put money in thy purse, and cut a dash

     There's nothing to be done now without cash.

135   If you would win her, sport the ready rhino[1]—

     Put money in thy purse, and she's yours, I know

     Drown thyself, eh? Why, what a chap to funk!

     Hark ye! Go drown thy care—get jolly drunk.

RODERIGO. It must be so—I'm really tired of thinking.

140   And I'm determined on't. I'll take to drinking.

IAGO. Meet me tonight—a thought has crossed my nob.

     I'll serve this black chap out, or my name's Bob.

     [*Singing to the tune of "Meet Me by Moonlight"*]

     Meet me tonight on the sly,

     And then I will tell you my mind.

145   For I'm told that my wife, Mrs. I.,

     To Othello's been rather too kind.

     You'll be sure to come—for I swear,

     I will tickle the Moor's dirty back,

     Though I may lose my place, I don't care,

150   If I am but revenged on the black.

     So meet me tonight on the sly,

     Meet me tonight on the sly.

                            Exit waltzing, stage left.

---

1 I.e., money.

APPENDIX B: CULTURAL CONTEXTS

1. PRAYERS FOR PROTECTION AGAINST OTTOMAN ATTACKS; SPELLING MODERNIZED

a. *A form to be used in common prayer every Wednesday and Friday, within the City and Diocese of London: to excite all godly people to pray unto God for the delivery of those Christians that are now invaded by the Turk* (London, 1565)

[The small island of Malta lies in the middle of the Mediterranean between the southernmost tip of Italy and the north coast of Africa. Like Cyprus, where most of the action in *Othello* takes place, Malta was recognized as a strategically important base in a politically, economically, and militarily significant region. In the spring of 1565, a large Ottoman fleet and army attacked Malta, which was then held by the Sovereign Military Hospitaller Order of Saint John of Jerusalem of Rhodes and of Malta (also known as the Knights Hospitaller or the Knights of Malta). There followed a lengthy and brutal siege from which the Knights and their small group of local supporters eventually emerged victorious. The Turks suffered enormous casualties during the summer-long campaign, while the much smaller Maltese contingent lost a third of their number and saw the destruction of much of the island's infrastructure. The Great Siege of Malta, as it came to be known, became one of the most celebrated events in sixteenth-century Europe. In England, the Ottoman siege was cast as an act of religious aggression, and forms distributed to "Pastors and Curates" across the country called on ordinary people to pray for the destruction of their "most deadly enemies the Turks." Virtually identical versions of the following prayer prepared for use in London were published for the dioceses of Salisbury and Norwich.]

Forasmuch as the Isle of Malta (in old time called Melite, where Saint Paul arrived when he was sent to Rome) lying near unto Sicily and Italy, and being as it were the key of that part of Christendom, is presently invaded with a great army and navy of Turks, infidels, and sworn enemies of Christian religion, not only to the extreme danger and peril of those Christians that are besieged and daily assaulted in the holds and forts of the said island, but also of all the rest of the countries of Christendom adjoining. It is our parts which for distance of place cannot succor them with temporal relief to assist them with spiritual aid; that is to say, with earnest, hearty, and fervent prayer to almighty God for them, desiring him, after the examples of Moses, Josaphat, Ezechias, and other godly men, in his great mercy to defend and deliver Christians professing his holy name, and in his justice to repress the rage and violence of infidels who by all tyranny and cruelty labor utterly to root out not only true religion, but also the very name and memory of Christ our only savior, and all Christianity. And if they should prevail against the Isle of Malta, it is uncertain what further peril might follow to the rest of Christendom. And although it is every Christian man's duty of his own devotion to pray at all times, yet for that the corrupt nature of man is so slothful and negligent in this his duty, he hath need by often and sundry means to be stirred up and put in remembrance of his duty. For the effectual accomplishment whereof it is ordered and appointed as followeth.

[...]

THE PRAYER

O almighty and everlasting God, our heavenly father, we thy disobedient and rebellious children, now by thy just judgment sore afflicted and in great danger to be oppressed by thine and our sworn and most deadly enemies the Turks, infidels, and miscreants, do make humble suit to the throne of thy grace for thy mercy and aid against the same our mortal enemies. For though we do profess the name of thy only son Christ, our savior, yet through our manifold sins and wickedness we have most justly deserved so much of thy wrath and indignation that we cannot but say, O Lord correct us in thy mercy and not in thy fury.

Better it is for us to fall into thy hands than into the hands of men, and especially into the hands of Turks and infidels thy professed enemies who now invade thine inheritance. Against thee, O Lord, have we sinned and transgressed thy commandments. Against Turks, infidels, and other enemies of the gospel of thy dear son Jesus Christ have we not offended but only in this: that we acknowledge thee, the eternal father, and thy only son our redeemer, with the holy ghost the comforter, to be one only true almighty and everliving God. For if we would deny and blaspheme thy most holy name, forsake the gospel of thy dear son, embrace false religion, commit horrible idolatries, and give ourselves to all impure, wicked, and abominable life as they do, the devil, the world, the Turk, and all other thine enemies would be at peace with us, according to the saying of thy son Christ, if you were of the world the world would love his own. But therefore hate they us, because we love thee; therefore persecute they us, because we acknowledge thee, God the father, and Jesus Christ thy son, whom thou hast sent.

The Turk goeth about to set up, to extol, and to magnify that wicked monster and damned soul Mahomet above thy dearly beloved son Jesus Christ, whom we in heart believe and with mouth confess to be our only savior and redeemer. Wherefore awake, O Lord, our God and heavenly father, look upon us thy children and all such Christians as now be besieged and afflicted with thy fatherly and merciful countenance, and overthrow and destroy thine and our enemies, sanctify thy blessed name among us which they blaspheme, establish thy kingdom which they labor to overthrow. Suffer not thine enemies to prevail against those that now call upon thy name and put their trust in thee, lest the heathen and infidels say "Where is now their god?" but in thy great mercy save, defend, and deliver all thy afflicted Christians in this and all other invasions of these infidels that we and they that delight to be named Christians may continually laud, praise, and magnify thy holy name, with thy only son Jesus Christ, and the holy ghost to whom be all laud, praise, glory, and empire forever and ever. Amen.

b. Matthew Parker, Archbishop of Canterbury, *A form to be used in common prayer, every Sunday, Wednesday, and Friday, through the whole realm, to excite and stir all godly people to pray unto God for the preservation of those Christians and their countries that are now invaded by the Turk in Hungary or elsewhere* (London, 1566)

[In the spring of 1566, less than a year after the siege at Malta, Suleiman I, sultan of the Ottoman Empire (r. 1520–66), led his forces from Constantinople toward Vienna. As they crossed Hungary, the Ottomans besieged the fortress at Szigeth (Szigetvar), which was held by the defending forces of the Austrian Habsburg monarchy under the command of Miklos Zrinyi (1508–66). Both sides sustained enormous losses, including their leaders: Zrinyi was shot during a final desperate sortie, while Suleiman, then aged 72, died of natural causes just as the castle fell. The following form exhorting English parishioners to pray for God's aid in protecting Hungary from invasion uses the language of sexual violence to characterize the Ottoman forces as "savage and most cruel" rapists planning to attack a virtuous and defenseless "Christendom ... as it were naked and open to ... incursions and invasions." Matthew Parker (1504–75), Archbishop of Canterbury from 1559 until his death, had a significant influence on the character of the Church of England in the early years of Elizabeth's reign and made numerous important contributions to Anglican theology.]

Whereas the Turks the last year most fiercely assailing the Isle of Malta with a great army and navy, by the grace and assistance of almighty God—for the which we with other Christians at that time by our hearty prayers made most humble suit—were from thence repelled and driven, with their great loss, shame, and confusion, they, being inflamed with malice and desire of vengeance, do now by land invade the kingdom of Hungary, which hath of long time been as a most strong wall and defense to all Christendom, far more terribly and dreadfully, and with greater force and violence, than they did either the last year, or at any time within the remembrance of man. It is our parts, which for distance of place cannot succor them with temporal aid of men, to assist them at the least with spiritual aid; that is to say, with earnest, hearty, and fervent prayer to almighty God for them, desiring him, after the examples of Moses, Josaphat, Ezechias, and other godly men, in his great mercy, to defend, preserve, and deliver Christians professing his holy name, and to give sufficient might and power to the Emperor's excellent Majesty, as God's principal minister, to repress the rage and violence of these infidels who, by all tyranny and cruelty, labor utterly to root out not only true religion, but also the very name and memory of Christ our only savior, and all Christianity. And for so much as if the infidels, who have already a great part of that most goodly and strong kingdom in their possession, should prevail wholly against the same—which God forbid—all the rest of Christendom should lie as it were naked and open to the incursions and invasions of the said savage and most cruel enemies the Turks, to the most dreadful danger of whole Christendom, all diligence, heartiness, and fervency is so much the more now to be used in our prayers for God's aid, how far greater the danger and peril is now than before it was. And although it is every Christian man's duty of his own devotion to pray at all times, yet, for that the corrupt nature of man is so slothful and negligent in this his duty, he hath need by often and sundry means to be stirred up and put in remembrance of his duty. For the effectual accomplishment whereof, it is ordered and appointed as followeth.

[...]

THE PRAYER

Almighty and ever-living God, our heavenly father, we, thy disobedient and rebellious children, now by thy just judgment sore afflicted and in great danger to be oppressed by thine and our sworn and most deadly enemies the Turks, infidels, and miscreants, do make humble suit to the throne of thy grace for thy mercy and aid against the same our mortal enemies. For though we do profess the name of thy only son Christ our Savior, yet through our manifold sins and wickedness we have most justly deserved so much of thy wrath and indignation that we cannot but say, O Lord, correct us in thy mercy and not in thy fury. And better it is for us to fall into thy hands than into the hands of men, and especially into the hands of Turks and infidels, thy professed enemies, who now invade thine inheritance. Against thee, O Lord, have we sinned and transgressed thy commandments. Against Turks, infidels, and other enemies of the Gospel of thy dear son Jesus Christ have we not offended, but only in this, that we acknowledge thee, the eternal father, and thy only son our redeemer, with the holy ghost, the comforter, to be one only true, almighty, and ever-living God. For if we would deny and blaspheme thy most holy name, forsake the gospel of thy dear son, embrace false religion, commit horrible idolatries, and give ourselves to all impure, wicked, and abominable life as they do, the devil, the world, the Turk, and all other thine enemies would be at peace with us, according to the saying of thy son Christ, if you were of the world, the world would love his own. But therefore hate they us, because we love thee; therefore persecute they us, because we acknowledge thee God the father, and

Jesus Christ thy son, whom thou hast sent. The Turk goeth about to set up, to extol, and to magnify that wicked monster and damned soul Mahomet, above thy dearly beloved son Jesus Christ, whom we in heart believe, and with mouth confess to be our only savior and redeemer. Wherefore, awake, O Lord, our God and heavenly father, and with thy fatherly and merciful countenance look upon us thy children, and all such Christians as are now by those most cruel enemies invaded and assaulted. Overthrow and destroy thine and our enemies; sanctify thy blessed name among us, which they blaspheme; establish thy kingdom, which they labor to overthrow. Suffer not thine enemies to prevail against those that now call upon thy name and put their trust in thee, lest the heathen and infidels say "Where is now their God?" But in thy great mercy save, defend, and deliver all thy afflicted Christians in this and all other invasions of these infidels, and give to the emperor thy servant, and all the Christian army now assembled with him, thy comfortable might and courage that we and they that delight to be named Christians, may enjoy both outward peace, and inwardly laud, praise, and magnify thy holy name forever, with thy only son Jesus Christ, and the holy Ghost, to whom be all laud, praise, glory and empire forever and ever. Amen.

This prayer to be said at evening prayer, immediately after the collect[1] of the day

O Lord, God of hosts, most righteous judge, and most merciful father, these dreadful dangers and distresses wherein other Christian men our brethren and neighbors do now stand by reason of the terrible invasions of most cruel and deadly enemies the Turks, infidels, and miscreants do set before our eyes a terrible example of our own worthy deserts by our continual sinning and offending against thy great majesty and most severe justice, and do also put us in remembrance, here in this our realm of England, of our most deserved thanks for our great tranquility, peace, and quietness which we, by thy high benefit and preservation of our peaceable prince, whom thou hast given us, do enjoy whiles others in the like or less offenses than ours are against thy majesty are by thy righteous judgments so terribly

---

1 A short prayer.

scourged. These thy fatherly mercies do set forth thy unspeakable patience which thou usest towards us, thy ingrate children, as well in the same thy gracious benefits of such our peace and tranquility, as in thy wholesome warnings of us by thy just punishments of others, less offenders than we be. For the which thy great benefits bestowed upon us without all our deserving, as we praise thy fatherly goodness towards us. So being stricken in our minds with great dread of thy just vengeance for that we do so little regard the great riches of thy fatherly goodness and patience towards us, we most humbly beseech thee to grant us thy heavenly grace, that we continue no longer in the taking of thy manifold graces and goodness in vain. And upon deep compassion of the dreadful distresses of our brethren and neighbors the Christians, by the cruel and most terrible invasions of these most deadly enemies the Turks, we do make and offer up our most humble and hearty prayers before the throne of thy grace for the mitigation of thy wrath and purchase of thy pity and fatherly favor towards them; and not only towards them, but to us also by them, for so much as our danger or safety doth follow upon success of them. Grant them and us thy grace, most merciful father, that we may rightly understand, and unfeignedly confess, our sins against thy majesty, to be the very causes of this thy just scourge and our misery. Grant us true and hearty repentance of all our sins against thee that, the causes of thy just offense being removed, the effects of these our deserved miseries may withal be taken away. Give to thy poor Christians, O Lord God of hosts, strength from heaven, that they, neither respecting their own weakness and paucity, nor fearing the multitude and fierceness of their enemies or their dreadful cruelty, but setting their eyes and only hope and trust upon thee, and calling upon thy name, who art the giver of all victory, may by thy power obtain victory against the infinite multitudes and fierceness of thine enemies, that all men understanding the same to be the act of thy grace, and not the deed of man's might and power, may give unto thee all the praise and glory; and specially thy poor Christians, by thy strong hand being delivered out of the hands of their enemies, we for their and our own safety with them, may yield and render unto thee all lauds, praises, and thanks, through thy son our savior Jesus Christ, to whom, with thee and the holy ghost, one eternal God of most sacred majesty, be all praise, honor and glory, world without end. Amen.

2. ELIZABETH I, LETTERS PERMITTING DEPORTATION OF BLACKAMOORS FROM ENGLAND, *ACTS OF THE PRIVY COUNCIL*, VOL. 26 (1596–97), ED. JOHN ROCHE DASENT (LONDON: EYRE AND SPOTTISWOODE, 1902)

[This pair of letters granting Queen Elizabeth I's (r. 1558–1603) permission for the deportation of "blackmoors" from her realm reminds readers of *Othello* both that early-modern England was home to many people of color and that at least some of these people faced the threat of royally sanctioned displacement as some of the most vulnerable members of a political economy prepared to scapegoat and to commodify them. There is no evidence to support the letters' claim that immigration, either through slavery or otherwise, contributed to joblessness among those born in England, but the highly profitable trade in human merchandise that saw the first African slaves brought into the country in the middle of the sixteenth century was certainly on the increase in this period. Although the second letter suggests that deportation of blackamoors in service should occur "with consent of their masters," neither letter mentions compensation, presumably assuming that English masters will prefer to be served "by their own countrymen" rather than by "those kind of people." This appears to have been a miscalculation, however, as a royal proclamation less than four years later compelled the masters of "negroes and blackamoors" to hand them over to a Lübeck merchant named Casper van Senden—implying that most if not all failed to accede to the original request.]

a. 11 July 1596

An open letter to the lord mayor of London and the aldermen and his brethren, and to all other mayors, sheriffs, etc. Her majesty, understanding that there are of late divers[1] blackmoors brought into this realm, of which kind of people there are already here too many, considering how God hath blessed this land with great increase of people of our own nation as any country in the world, whereof many for want of service and means to set them on work fall to idleness and to great

---

1 Several.

extremity.[1] Her majesty's pleasure therefore is that those kind of people should be sent forth of the land, and for that purpose there is direction given to this bearer Edward Banes to take of those blackmoors that in this last voyage under Sir Thomas Baskerville[2] were brought into this realm the number of ten, to be transported by him out of the realm. Wherein we require you to be aiding and assisting unto him as he shall have occasion, and thereof not to fail. (16–17)

b. 18 July 1596

An open warrant to the lord mayor of London and to all other vice-admirals, mayors, and other public officers whatsoever to whom it may appertain. Whereas Casper van Senden, a merchant of Lubeck[3] did by his labor and travel procure eighty-nine of her majesty's subjects that were detained prisoners in Spain and Portugal to be released, and brought them hither into this realm at his own cost and charges, for the which his expenses and declaration of his honest mind towards those prisoners he only desireth to have license to take up so many blackamoors here in this realm and to transport them into Spain and Portugal. Her majesty, in regard of the charitable affection the suppliant hath showed being a stranger to work the delivery of our countrymen that were there in great misery and thraldom[4] and to bring them home to their native country, and that the same could not be done without great expense, and also considering the reasonableness of his requests to transport so many blackamoors from hence, doth think it a very good exchange and that those kind of people may be well spared in this realm being so populous and numbers of able persons the subjects of the land and Christian people that perish for want of service, whereby through their labor they might be maintained. They are, therefore, in their lordships' name required to aid and assist him

---

1   "A condition of extreme urgency or need" (*OED n.* 7a).
2   English general (d. 1597) in charge of the land forces accompanying Sir John Hawkins (1532–95) and Sir Francis Drake (1540–96) on their last expedition to the Indies in 1595. When both Hawkins and Drake grew ill and died, Baskerville succeeded to the command and brought the expedition home.
3   Lübeck, a port city in Northern Germany, served throughout the early-modern period as the de facto capital of the Hanseatic League, the confederation of merchant guilds and market towns that dominated trade along the northern coast of Europe.
4   Captivity.

to take up such blackamoors as he shall find within this realm with consent of their masters, who we doubt not considering her majesty's good pleasure to have those kinds of people sent out of the land and the good deserving of the stranger towards her majesty's subjects, and that they shall do charitable and like Christians rather to be served by their own countrymen than with those kind of people, will yield those in their possession to him. (20–21)

3. FROM ROBERT CLEAVER, *A GODLY FORM OF HOUSEHOLD GOVERNMENT FOR THE ORDERING OF PRIVATE FAMILIES, ACCORDING TO THE DIRECTION OF GOD'S WORD*, REVISED AND EXPANDED BY CLEAVER AND JOHN DOD (LONDON, 1598); SPELLING MODERNIZED

[Books offering advice on how to run a successful home were very popular among early-modern readers. Like the self-help paperbacks that crowd bookstore shelves today, these guides treat such subjects as how to find a suitable wife or husband, how to have a happy marriage, how to manage an efficient household, and how to raise well-behaved children. Unlike the secular emphasis of most modern manuals, however, those published in the sixteenth and seventeenth centuries emphasize the importance of Christian duty, and many were written by clerics. Typically these books uphold an ideal of gendered hierarchy and endorse a doctrine of wifely submission, though most also emphasize the need for some division of authority within the household, and many stress mutual respect, patience, and humility as essential traits for both partners in a successful marriage. *A Godly Form of Household Government*, written by Robert Cleaver (c. 1561–c. 1625), and later revised and expanded by him with the help of fellow Puritan minister John Dod (c. 1549–1645), sold so well that it underwent nine editions in the period. It is of particular interest to readers of *Othello* for the analogy it develops between the right ordering of the patriarchal family and the state, for its discussion of the potential dangers of friendship, for the details of the marital advice it offers to wives and husbands, for its assessment of the relative duties owed to spouses and parents, and for its comments on the proper response to infidelity.]

A household is as it were a little commonwealth, by the good government whereof God's glory may be advanced, the commonwealth which standeth of several families benefited, and all that live in that family may receive much comfort and commodity. But this government of a family is not very common in the world, for it is not a thing that men can stumble on by chance, but wisdom must lead us unto it.[1] (13)

The governors of a family be such as have authority in the family by God's ordinance, as the father and mother, master and mistress.[2] To whom, as God hath given authority over their children and servants, so he would have them to use it to the wise government of them, not only for their own private profit, credit, or pleasure, but also for the good of those whom they are to govern.[3] For by a wise government much good cometh to the parties governed. If masters then or parents do not govern but let servants and children do as they list, they do not only disobey God and disadvantage themselves but also hurt those whom they should rule. For when any have such liberty to do as they list, it make them grow out of order, to the provoking of God's displeasure, and curse against themselves, whereas if they had been held in by the bridle of government they might be brought to walk so as the blessing of God should follow them in their courses.

All government of a family must be in comeliness or decency; that is, it must be such as is meet and convenient both for the governor and for the person governed.[4] And therefore it is impossible for a man to understand to govern the commonwealth that doth not know to rule his own house or order his own person, so that he that knoweth not to govern, deserveth not to reign.

Lordliness[5] is unmeet[6] in a household government, and yet familiarity with such as are under government breedeth contempt. Again for the persons governed, all in the family are not to be governed alike.

---

1   [Cleaver's note:] The rule of good government is wisdom. Prov. 24.3–4.
2   [Cleaver's note:] The first sort are such as have authority in the family.
3   [Cleaver's note:] Who must use their authority. If the governor be charged with weighty affairs, he may appoint one to govern his house, as Abraham and Potiphar did. Gen. 24.2 & Gen. 39.4.
4   [Cleaver's note:] A property of good government. 1 Tim. 2.3.
5   Imperiousness.
6   Inappropriate.

There is one rule to govern the wife by, another for children, another for servants. One rule for young ones, another for old folks. (15–17)

As to have a faithful friend is a matter available to thrift, so by his friends a man may be endamaged. There is a friendship which is very costly and chargeable to maintain. He that desireth familiarity with great[1] men must have other things suitable, as costly apparel, well-trimmed houses, often invitings to banquets to recompense their kindness; he must follow their humors and not stick[2] to neglect his affairs to have their company when he may. This will cost a man sweetly, but what shall be his gain? A friendly countenance before his face, and perhaps a dry flout[3] behind his back, especially if things go not well with him for the world; then oh, it is pity a frank-hearted man, nobody's foe but his own, and such like. Solomon giveth thee warning of this kind of friendship.[4]

There is another man's friendship which Solomon would have thee to avoid as hurtful unto thee:[5] "Make no friendship with an angry man, neither go with the furious."[6] The choleric[7] man, though never so good a fellow while he is pleased, yet is soon turned to hate thee. And no heavier foe than he that was a friend, which Solomon declareth: "A brother offended is harder to win than a strong city, and their contentions are like the bar of a palace."[8] If a man could always keep in with the angry man—which cannot be done without putting up [with] many injuries—yet may that be hurtful. For the wise man addeth, "Lest thou learn his ways," that is, become like to him in furiousness. And that is as hurtful on the other side, for "the furious man aboundeth in transgressions,"[9] which do often cost him the setting on even from men who, being by his rage hurt, work him some woe. Whereupon we say in a common proverb, "The angry man never wanteth[10] woe." There be

---

1   Wealthy.
2   Linger.
3   Caustic jeer.
4   [Cleaver's note:] Prov. 23.1–3.
5   [Cleaver's note:] Prov. 22.24.
6   [Cleaver's note:] Prov. 18.19.
7   Having a predominance of the bodily humor choler; irascible.
8   [Cleaver's note:] [Prov. 18:]20.
9   [Cleaver's note:] Prov. 29.25.
10 Lacks.

also trencher-friends,[1] who to win favor and goodwill will smooth it in words, fawn, and glaver;[2] they will say as you say, and bring you tales of your enemy so to feed your humor that he may wind within you, a beast that biteth sorest of all tame beasts. For while a simple-hearted man suspecteth no hurt, he watcheth his occasions to speed himself of a booty, a matter that by the counsel of the Holy Ghost oft repeated in the Proverbs is as carefully to be avoided as it is hurtful to a man's estate. If he can do none of these, yet he hath not lost his labor for he had many a good welcome for his fair talk. And by often resorting to thy house, he hath furnished himself with something to discredit thee, except thou hast walked marvelous warily, which a man can hardly do before flatterers.

To end this matter of friendship, have some near friends but not many. Choose the best natured and best graced, that is, such as besides single-heartedness and plain simplicity are by grace brought to have conscience of the dealing. And lest under a show of simplicity, wiliness should be hid, try before you trust, and grow into familiarity not all at a push, but by steps. Tell things of no great secrecy as secrets to try their taciturnity. Be not over-credulous upon sight of a little kindness to account them amongst thy nearest friends. Many have been wiped of their commodities by falsehood in fellowship. Some have been betrayed by untrusty[3] friends and brought into great troubles. Many, opening their minds to blabs that can keep nothing,[4] have their purposes openly known and scanned before they can compass them, and so are oftentimes prevented through the malice of their enviers.[5] (81–83)

The Duty of the Husband towards His Wife

This duty consisteth severally in these three points. First, that he live with his wife discreetly, according unto knowledge. Secondly, that he be not bitter, fierce, and cruel unto her. Thirdly, that he love, cherish, and nourish his wife even as his own body and as Christ loved his

---

1 Hangers-on who exploit someone's hospitality and earn welcome by flattery. A trencher is a wooden platter for serving food.
2 Deceive with flattery.
3 Untrustworthy.
4 I.e., cannot keep a confidence.
5 Those who envy.

church and gave himself for it to sanctify it. But before we shall speak of these three points, we will a little touch the original and beginning of holy wedlock: what it is, when, where, how, and of whom it was instituted and ordained.

Wedlock or matrimony is a lawful knot and unto God an acceptable yoking and joining together of one man and one woman with the good consent of them both to the end that they may dwell together in friendship and honesty, one helping and comforting the other, eschewing whoredom and all uncleanliness, bringing up their children in the fear of God;[1] or it is a coupling together of two persons into one flesh, not to be broken according to the ordinance of God, so to continue during the life of either of them.[2]

By yoking, joining, or coupling is meant not only outward dwelling together of the married folks as to be ordinarily in a dwelling place for the better performance of each other mutual duties,[3] but also a uniform agreement of mind and a common participation of body and goods, for as much as the Lord saith that "they too shall be one flesh," that is, one body.[4] This is to be remembered: that matrimony or wedlock must not only be a coupling together but also it must be such a coupling together as cometh of God and is not contrary to his word and will. For there be some marriages made whom God coupleth not together but carnal lust, beauty, riches, goods and lands, flattery, and friendship; in such marriages God is not thought upon, and therefore they sin the more against him. These and such like marriages be disliked and condemned in the scripture.[5] God did appoint and ordain matrimony himself in paradise so that he is the author of the same.[6] Yea, and our savior Christ himself, who being the very natural son of God was born in wedlock although of a pure virgin, did honor and commend matrimony while he did vouchsafe to show his first miracle at a marriage,[7] whereby he did declare that the Lord is able to make the bitterness of marriage sweet and the scarcity thereof to abound with plenty. (97–99)

---

1   [Cleaver's note:] What wedlock is. Matt. 19.5–6, Gen. 1.27, 1 Cor. 6.16, Ephes. 5.31, Prov. 5.18–20.

2   [Cleaver's note:] Gen. 2.24, Mal. 2.14, Rom. 7.3.

3   [Cleaver's note:] Yoking and dwelling together, what it is. Matt. 1.18, 1 Cor. 7.10–13, 1 Pet. 3.7, Ruth 4.11–12.

4   [Cleaver's note:] Gen. 1.2–23.

5   [Cleaver's note:] Gen. 6.12, Ezek. 10.1 etc., Matt. 24.38–39.

6   [Cleaver's note:] Gen. 2.20.

7   [Cleaver's note:] John 2.1.

The husband, his duty is first to love his wife as his own flesh. Then to govern her in all duties that properly concern the state of marriage in knowledge, in wisdom, judgment, and justice. Thirdly, to dwell with her. Fourthly, to use her in all due benevolence, honestly, soberly, chastely.[1]

The wife, her duty is in all reverence and humility to submit and subject herself to her husband in all such duties as properly belong to marriage. Secondly, therein to be an help unto him according to God's ordinance. Thirdly, to obey his commandments in all things which he may command by the authority of a husband. Fourthly and lastly, to give him mutual benevolence. (118–19)

What the Duty of a Wife Is towards Her Husband

This duty is comprehended in these three points. First, that she reverence her husband. Secondly, that she submit herself and be obedient to him. And lastly, that she do not wear gorgeous apparel beyond her degree and place, but her attire must be comely and sober according to her calling. The first point is proved by the apostles Peter and Paul, whereby they set forth the wives' duties to their husbands, commanding them to be obedient unto them although they be profane and irreligious, and that they ought to do so much the more that by their honest life and conversation they might win them to the obedience of the Lord.[2]

Now for so much as the apostle would have Christian wives that are matched with ungodly husbands and such as are not yet good Christians to reverence and obey them much more they should show themselves thankful to God, and willingly and dutifully perform their obedience and subjection when they are coupled in marriage with godly, wise, discreet, learned, gentle, loving, quiet, patient, honest, and thrifty husbands. And therefore they ought evermore to reverence them and to endeavor with true obedience and love to serve them, to be loath in any wise to offend them; yea, rather to be careful and diligent to please them that their soul may bless them.[3] And if at any time it shall happen that the wife shall anger or displease her husband by doing or speaking anything that shall grieve him, she ought never to rest until she hath

---

1   [Cleaver's note:] 1 Pet. 13.7, 1 Cor. 7.45.

2   [Cleaver's note:] 1 Pet. 3.1, Eph. 5.22, Col. 3.18, 1 Cor. 7.3.

3   [Cleaver's note:] Wives must be serviceable and obedient unto their husbands, and stand in a reverend awe of them. Eph. 5.33.

pacified him and gotten his favor again. And if he shall chance to blame her without cause and for that which she could not help or remedy, which thing sometimes happeneth even of the best men, yet she must bear it patiently and give him no uncomely or unkind words for it but evermore look upon him with a loving and cheerful countenance, and so rather let her take the fault upon her than seem to be displeased.[1] Let her be always merry and cheerful in his company, but yet not with too much lightness. She must beware in any wise of swelling,[2] pouting, lowering, or frowning, for that is a token of a cruel and unloving heart except it be in respect of sin or in time of sickness. She may not be sorrowful for any adversity that God sendeth, but always to be careful that nothing be spilled or go to waste through her negligence. In any wise, see that she be quick and cleanly about her husband's meat and drink, and to prepare him the same according to his diet in due season.[3] Let her show herself in word and deed wise, humble, courteous, gentle, and loving towards her husband, and also towards such as he doth love, and then shall she lead a blessed life. Let her show herself not only to love no man so well as her husband, but also to love no other at all but him unless it be for her husband's sake.

Wherefore let the wife remember that, as the scripture reporteth, she is one body with her husband so that she ought to love him none otherwise than herself,[4] for this is the greatest virtue of a married woman; this is the thing that wedlock signifieth and commandeth, that the wife should reckon to have her husband for both father, mother, brother, and sister, like as Adam was unto Eve,[5] and as the most noble and chaste woman Andromache[6] said her Hector was unto her: "Thou art unto me both father and mother, / Mine own dear husband, and well beloved brother."

And if it be true that men do say that friendship maketh one heart of two, much more truly and effectually ought wedlock to do the same, which far passeth all manner both friendship and kindred. Therefore it is not said that marriage doth make one man, or one mind, or one

---

1 [Cleaver's note:] Cheerful in countenance.
2 Behaving arrogantly.
3 [Cleaver's note:] Gen. 27.9.
4 [Cleaver's note:] Gen. 2.23–24, Matt. 19.5, 1 Cor. 6.16, Eph. 5.31.
5 [Cleaver's note:] How the wife ought to behave herself unto her husband.
6 In Homer's Iliad, Andromache is portrayed as the ideal wife and mother, virtuously obedient while her husband is alive and patiently enduring after his death in the Trojan War.

body of two, but clearly one person. Wherefore matrimony requireth a greater duty of the husband towards his wife and the wife towards her husband than otherwise they are bound to show to their parents. The apostle biddeth, "to rejoice with them that rejoice, and weep with them that weep."[1] With whom should the wife rejoice rather than with her loving husband? Or with whom should she weep and mourn rather than with her own flesh? "I will not leave thee," saith Elisha to Elijah,[2] so she should say, "I will never leave him till death."[3] "Bear one another's burthen," saith Paul.[4] Who shall bear one another's burden if the wife do not bear the husband's burden? Wicked Jezebel comforted her husband in his sickness,[5] and Jeroboam's wife fought for his health, though she was as bad[6] as he.[7] God did not bid Sarah leave her father and country as he did bid her husband, yet because he bade Abraham leave his, she left hers too,[8] showing that she was content not only to be his playfellow, but his yokefellow too.[9]

Beside[10] a yokefellow, she is called a helper, to help him in his labors, to help him in his troubles, to help him in his sickness like a woman physician, sometime with her strength and sometime with her counsel. For sometime as God confoundeth the wise by the foolish and the strong by the weak,[11] so he teacheth the wise by the foolish and helpeth the strong by the weak. Therefore, Peter saith, "Husbands are won by the conversation of their wives,"[12] as if he should say sometime the weaker vessel is the stronger vessel, and Abraham may take counsel of Sarah, as Naaman was advised by his servant.[13] The Shunammite's counsel made her husband receive a prophet into his house,[14] and Esther's counsel[15]

---

1   [Cleaver's note:] Rom. 12.15.
2   [Cleaver's note:] 2 Kings 2.1–5.
3   The biblical account of Elisha's devotion to the prophet Elijah is often presented as emblematic of selfless loyalty.
4   [Cleaver's note:] Gal. 6.2.
5   [Cleaver's note:] 1 Kings 21.5.
6   Just as ill.
7   [Cleaver's note:] 1 Kings 14.4.
8   [Cleaver's note:] Gen. 12.1.
9   [Cleaver's note:] Gen. 2.18.
10 In addition to.
11 [Cleaver's note:] 1 Cor. 1.27.
12 [Cleaver's note:] 1 Pet. 3.1.
13 [Cleaver's note:] 2 Kings 5.3.
14 [Cleaver's note:] 2 Kings 4.9.
15 [Cleaver's note:] Esth. 7.3.

made her husband spare the church of the Jews.[1] So some have been better help to their husbands than their husbands have been to them, for it pleaseth God to provoke the wise with the foolish, as he did the Jews with the Gentiles.[2]

Besides a helper, she is called a comforter too,[3] and therefore the man is bid to rejoice in his wife, which is as much to say that wives must be the rejoicing of their husbands even like David's harp to comfort Saul.[4] A good wife, therefore, is known when her words, and deeds, and countenance are such as her husband loveth. She must not examine whether he be wise or simple but that she is his wife, and therefore they that are bound must obey as Abigail loved her husband though he were a fool, churlish, and evil conditioned,[5] for the wife is as much despised for taking rule over her husband as he for yielding it unto her.[6] Therefore one saith that a mankind woman is a monster, that is, half a woman and half a man. It beseemeth not the mistress to be master no more than it becometh the master to be mistress, but both must sail with their own wind and both keep their standing.

Lastly, we call the wife "huswife," that is, "house-wife."[7] Not a "street-wife," one that gaddeth[8] up and down like Tamar,[9] nor a "field-wife" like Dinah,[10] but a "house-wife," to show that a good wife keeps her house.[11]

---

1   In each of the biblical stories cited here, a strong-minded woman behaves bravely in the face of patriarchal authority and effects meaningful change as a result. In the first, a childless woman from Shunem convinces her husband to provide a guestroom for the prophet Elisha and is rewarded, first by the birth of a child, and again years later when the prophet heals her son from a deadly illness. In the second, Esther, wife of Ahasuerus, King of Persia, hosts a dinner at which she reveals that she is Jewish, denounces her husband's most trusted adviser for attempts to destroy her people, and convinces the king to issue a decree affirming the right of the Jews to defend themselves.

2   [Cleaver's note:] Deut. 32.21, Rom. 10.19.

3   [Cleaver's note:] Prov. 5.18, 19.

4   [Cleaver's note:] 1 Sam. 16.23.

5   [Cleaver's note:] 1 Sam. 25.3.

6   1 Samuel 25 presents Abigail as beautiful and intelligent, her husband, Nabal, as rude and foolish. Cleaver neglects to mention that Abigail is notable for acting without her husband's permission to save him when he offends David.

7   [Cleaver's note:] Why wives are called huswives.

8   Wanders.

9   [Cleaver's note:] Gen. 38.14.

10   [Cleaver's note:] Gen. 34.1.

11   Tamar is mistaken for a prostitute by her father-in-law when he encounters her, disguised, when they are both away from home. Dinah is raped when she leaves her father's tent to go visiting.

And therefore Paul biddeth Titus to exhort women that they be chaste and keeping at home,[1] presently after "chaste" he saith "keeping at home," as though home were chastity's keeper.[2] And there Solomon, depainting and describing the qualities of a whore setteth her at the door, now sitting upon her stall, now walking in the streets, now looking out of the window[3] like cursed Jezebel,[4] as if she held forth the glass of temptation for vanity to gaze upon.[5] But chastity careth to please but one, and therefore she keeps her closet as if she were still at prayer.

The angel asked Abraham, "Where is thy wife?" Abraham answered, "She is in the tent."[6] The angel knew where she was but he asked that he might see how women in old time did keep their tents and houses. It is recorded of the Shunammite that she did ask her husband leave to go unto the prophet, though she went to a prophet and went of a good errand and for his cause as much as her own, yet she thought it not meet to go far abroad without her husband's leave.[7]

The second point is that wives submit themselves and be obedient unto their own husbands as to the Lord, because the husband is by God's ordinance the wife's head, that is, her defender, teacher, and comforter,[8] and therefore she oweth her subjection to her husband like as the church doth to Christ, and because the example of Sarah, the mother of the faithful which obeyed Abraham and called him lord, moveth them thereunto.[9] This point is partly handled before in this first point, as in the duty of the husband to the wife.

As the church should depend upon the wisdom and will of Christ and not follow what itself listeth, so must the wife also submit and apply herself to the discretion and will of her husband even as the government and conduct of everything resteth in the head not in the body.[10] Moses writeth that the serpent was wise above all beasts of the field and that he did declare in assaulting the woman that when he had seduced her

---

1 [Cleaver's note:] Tit. 2.5.

2 Titus 2:5.

3 [Cleaver's note:] Prov. 7.12.

4 [Cleaver's note:] 2 Kings 9.30.

5 Proverbs 7 recounts a virtuous young man's seduction by a married woman; 2 Kings 9:30 describes Jezebel dressing up and appearing at a window to face Jehu, who orders her to be thrown down to her death.

6 [Cleaver's note:] Gen. 18.9.

7 [Cleaver's note:] 2 Kings 4.22.

8 [Cleaver's note:] Eph. 5.22, 23; 1 Cor. 11.3, 14.34.

9 [Cleaver's note:] Gen. 18.12., 1 Pet. 3.6.

10 [Cleaver's note:] Eph. 5.24.

she might also seduce and deceive her husband.[1] Saint Paul, noting this among other the causes of the woman's subjection, doth sufficiently show that for the avoiding of the like inconvenience it is God's will that she should be subject to her husband so that she shall have no other discretion or will but what may depend upon her head.[2] As also the same Moses saith, "Thy desire shall be subject to thy husband, and he shall rule over thee."[3] This dominion over the wife's will doth manifestly appear in this, that God in old time ordained that if the woman had vowed anything unto God it should notwithstanding rest in her husband to disavow it.[4] So much is the wife's will subject to her husband, yet it is not meant that the wife should not employ her knowledge and discretion which God hath given her in the help and for the good of her husband. But always it must be with condition to submit herself unto him, acknowledging him to be her head that finally they may so agree in one, as the conjunction of marriage doth require.

Yet, as when in a lute or other musical instrument two strings concurring in one tune the sound nevertheless is imputed to the strongest and the highest, so in a well ordered household there must be a communication and consent of the counsel and will between the husband and the wife, yet such as the counsel and commandment may rest in the husband. True it is that some women are wiser and more discreet than their husbands, as Abigail, the wife of Nabal,[5] and others. Whereupon Solomon saith, "A wise woman buildeth up the house," and "blessed is the man that hath a different wife."[6] Yet still a great part of the discretion of such women shall rest in acknowledging their husbands to be their heads and so using the graces that they have received of the Lord that their husbands may be honored not condemned, neither of them nor of others, which falleth out contrary when the wife will seem wiser than her husband. So that this modesty and government ought to be in a wife: namely that she should not speak but to her husband or by her husband. And as the voice of him that soundeth a trumpet is not so loud as the sound that it yieldeth, so is the wisdom and word of a woman of greater virtue and efficacy when all that she knoweth

---

1   [Cleaver's note:] Gen. 3.1.
2   [Cleaver's note:] 1 Tim. 2.14.
3   [Cleaver's note:] Gen. 3.16.
4   [Cleaver's note:] Num. 30.7.
5   1 Samuel 25.
6   [Cleaver's note:] Prov. 16.1, 18.22, 19.14, 31.

and can do is as if it were said and done by her husband. The obedience that the wife oweth to her husband dependeth upon this subjection of her will and wisdom unto him.[1] So that women may not provoke their husbands by disobedience in matters that may be performed without offense to God, neither to presume over him either in kindred or wealth, or obstinately to refuse in a matter than may trouble household peace and quiet. For disobedience begetteth contempt of the husband, and contempt wrath, and is many times the cause of troubles between the man and the wife. If the obedience importeth any difficulty, she may for her excuse gently propound the same, yet upon condition to obey in the case the husband should persist in his intent so long as the discommodity importeth no wickedness. For it is better to continue peace by obedience than to break it by resistance. And indeed it is natural in the members to obey the conduct and government of the head. Yet must not this obedience so far extend as that the husband should command anything contrary to her honor, credit, salvation, but as it is comely in the Lord.[2] Therefore, as it were a monstrous matter and the means to overthrow the person that the body should, in refusing all subjection and obedience to the head, take upon it to guide itself and to command the head, so were it for the wife to rebel against the husband. Let her then beware of disordering and perverting the course which God in his wisdom hath established, and with all let her understand that going about it she riseth not so much against her husband as against God, and that it is her good and honor to obey God in her subjection and obedience to her husband. If in the practice of this duty she find any difficulty or trouble, through the inconsiderate course of her husband or otherwise, let her remember that the same proceedeth not of the order established by the Lord, but through some sin afterward crept in which hath mixed gall[3] among the honey of the subjection and obedience that the woman should have enjoyed in that estate wherein together with Adam she was created after the image of God. And so let her humble herself in the sight of God and be well assured that her subjection and obedience is acceptable unto him. Likewise, that the more that the image of God is restored in her and her husband through the regeneration of the Holy Ghost, the less difficulty shall she find in

---

1 [Cleaver's note:] As 1 Pet. 3.6, Eph. 5.3, Esther 1.1, 2–12.
2 [Cleaver's note:] Col. 3.1, Eph. 5.22.
3 Bitterness.

that subjection and obedience, as many in their marriage have indeed tried to their great contentment and consolation.

Further, there is a certain discretion and desire of women to please the nature, inclination, and manners of their husbands, so long as the same imports no wickedness. For as the looking glass, however fair and beautifully adorned, is nothing worth if it show that countenance sad which is pleasant, so the woman deserveth no commendation that, as it were, contrarying her husband when he is merry showeth herself sad or in his sadness uttereth her mirth; for as men should obey the laws of their cities, so women the manners of their husbands. To some women, a beck[1] of her husband is sufficient to declare that there is somewhat amiss that displeaseth him, and specially if she bear her husband any reverence. For an honest matron hath no need of any greater staff but of one word or one sour countenance. Moreover, a modest and chaste woman that loveth her husband must also love her house, as remembering that the husband that loveth his wife cannot so well like of the sight of any tapestry as to see his wife in his house. For the woman that gaddeth from house to house to prate confoundeth herself, her husband, and family.[2] But there are four reasons why the woman is to go abroad: first, to come to holy meetings according to the duty of godliness; the second, to visit such as stand in need as the duty of love and charity do require; the third, for employment and provision in household affairs committed to her charge; and lastly, with her husband when he shall require her.[3]

The evil and unquiet life that some women have and pass with their husbands is not so much for that they commit with and in their persons as it is for that they speak with their tongues.[4] If the wife would keep silence when her husband beginneth to chide, he should not have so unquiet dinners, neither she the worse supper,[5] which surely is so for at the same time that the husband beginneth to utter his grief, the wife then beginneth to scold and chafe, whereof doth follow that now and then most unnaturally they come to handy gripes more beastlike than Christianlike, which their so doing is both a great shame and soul

---

1   A slight indication of will.
2   [Cleaver's note:] Tit. 2.5.
3   [Cleaver's note:] Gen. 20.1 etc.
4   [Cleaver's note:] The wife must keep a good tongue.
5   [Cleaver's note:] When the wife doth hold her peace, she keepeth the peace.

discredit to them both.[1] The best means, therefore, that a wife can use to obtain and maintain the love and good liking of her husband is to be silent,[2] obedient, peaceable, patient, studious to appease his choler if he be angry, painful[3] and diligent in looking to her business to be solitary and honest. The chief and special cause why most women do fail in not performing this duty to their husbands is because they be ignorant of the word of God,[4] which teacheth the same and all other duties, and therefore, their souls and consciences not being brought into subjection to God and his word, they can never until then yield and perform true subjection and obedience to their husbands and behave themselves so every way as Christian wives are in duty bound to do. But if wives be not so dutiful, serviceable, and subject to their husbands as in conscience they ought, the only cause thereof, for the most part, is through the want and neglect of the wise, discreet, and good government that should be in the husbands, besides the want of good example that they should give unto their wives both in word and deed. For as the common saying is, "such a husband, such a wife; a good Jack maketh a good Jill." For so much as marriage maketh of two persons one,[5] therefore the love of the husband and wife may the better be kept and increased[6] and so continued if they remember the duties last spoken of, as also not to forget these three points following.

They must be one of heart, will, and mind, and neither to upbraid or cast the other in the teeth[7] with their wants and imperfections any ways, or to pride themselves in their gifts, but rather the one to endeavor to supply the other's wants that so they both helping and doing their best together may be one perfect body.

It doth greatly increase love when the one faithfully serveth the other, when in things concerning marriage the one hideth no secrets nor privities[8] from the other, and the one doth not utter or publish the frailties

---

1   [Cleaver's note:] The cause of domestical combats.
2   [Cleaver's note:] Silence becometh a woman.
3   Painstaking.
4   [Cleaver's note:] Lack of knowledge of God's word is the principal cause of why wives do not their duty to their husbands.
5   [Cleaver's note:] One heart and one will.
6   [Cleaver's note:] How the love, faithfulness, and duty of married folks may be kept and increased.
7   To reproach the other.
8   Private thoughts.

or infirmities of the other, and when of all that ever they obtain or get they have but one common purse together, the one locking up nothing from the other, and also when the one is faithful to the other in eating, drinking, and so in all their necessaries and affairs. Likewise, when the one hearkeneth to the other, and when the one thinketh not scorn of the other, and when in matters concerning the government of the house the one will be counseled and advised by the other, and always the one to be loving, kind, courteous, plain, and gentle in words, manner, and deeds.

Let the one learn ever to be obsequious, diligent, and serviceable to the other in all other things. And this will the sooner come to pass if the one observe and mark what thing the other can away withal or cannot away withal, and what pleaseth or displeaseth them. And so from thenceforth to do the one and to love the other undone. And if one of them be angry and offended with other, then let the party grieved open and make known to the other their grief in due time and with discretion, for the longer a displeasure or evil will rageth in secret the worse will be the discord.[1] And this must be observed that it be done in a fit and convenient time because there is some season in the which if griefs were showed it should make greater debate. As if the wife should go about to tell or admonish her husband when he is out of patience or moved with anger it should then be not fit time to talk with him. Therefore Abigail, perceiving Nabal, her husband, to be drunk, would not speak to him until the morning.[2]

Both the husband and wife must remember that the one be not so offended and displeased with the manners of the other that they should thereupon forsake the company one of the other,[3] for that were like to one that stung with the bees would therefore forsake the honey. And therefore no man must put away[4] his wife for any cause except for whoredom, which must be duly proved before a lawful judge.[5] But all godly and faithful married folks are to commend their state and marriage to God by humble and fervent prayer that he for his beloved son's sake would so bless them and their marriage that they may so

---

1 [Cleaver's note:] They must secretly keep no evil will in their minds but tell their grief.
2 [Cleaver's note:] 1 Sam. 25.36, 37.
3 [Cleaver's note:] 1 Cor. 7.10–16, Matt. 19.6.
4 Reject.
5 [Cleaver's note:] Matt. 9, Matt. 5, Luke 16.18.

Christianly and dutifully agree between themselves that they may have no cause of any separation or divorcement. For like as all manner of medicines, and specially as they that go nighest death as to cut off whole members,[1] etc., are very loathsome and terrible; even so is divorcement indeed a medicine, but a perilous and terrible medicine. Therefore every good Christian husband and wife ought, with all care and heedfulness, so to live in marriage that they have no need of such medicine. As the holy scripture maketh mention of many wives and women that were wicked and ungodly ... and whosoever shall observe it in the reading of the word of God shall find that it speaketh of the praise of as many and more good women as men; yea, and we are persuaded that if at this day a due survey should be taken of all men and women throughout her majesty's dominions that there would be found in number more women that are faithful, religious, and virtuous than men.

Now if a wife be desirous to know how far she is bound to obey her husband, the apostle resolveth this doubt where, saith Ephesians 5.22, saying, "Wives submit yourselves unto your husbands as to the Lord."[2] As if he had said wives cannot be disobedient to their husbands but they must resist God also who is the author of this subjection, and that she must regard her husband's will as the Lord commandeth one that which is good and right, or else she doth not obey him as the Lord but as the tempter. The first subjection of the woman began at sin, for when God cursed her for seducing her husband when the serpent had deceived her, he said, "He shall have authority over thee."[3] And therefore as the man named all other creatures in sign that they should be subject to him as a servant which cometh when his master calleth him by his name, so he did name the woman also in token that she should be subject to him likewise, and therefore Ahasuerus made a law that every man should bear rule in his own house and not the woman because she sinned first, therefore she is humbled most.[4] And ever since, the daughters of Sarah are bound to call their husbands lord, as Sarah called her husband, that is, to take them for heads and governors.[5] (218–35)

---

1 Limbs.

2 [Cleaver's note:] The wife ought to obey her husband in all things that be honest and agreeable to God's word.

3 [Cleaver's note:] Gen. 3.16.

4 [Cleaver's note:] Esth. 1.20–22, Num. 30.7–9.

5 [Cleaver's note:] 1 Pet. 3.6, Judg. 19.26.

4. FROM THOMAS WRIGHT, *THE PASSIONS OF THE MIND IN GENERAL* (LONDON, 1604); EDITED IN MODERN SPELLING BY SARAH MILLIGAN AND JESSICA SLIGHTS

[Published first as *Passions of the Mind* in 1601 and three years later in revised and expanded form as *The Passions of the Mind in General*, Thomas Wright's (c. 1561–c. 1624) influential moral treatise argues that learning how to moderate "inordinate" emotions will allow all Christians to live quiet, prosperous, godly lives, and will enable the "civil gentleman and prudent politician" to "winneth a gracious carriage of himself, and rendereth his conversation most grateful to men" (5–6). The excerpts below are of interest to readers of *Othello* as they trace Wright's general understanding of the nature and function of the emotions, his argument for their use in the "service of virtue" (17), and his claims about how they affect people differently based on gender, nationality, and temperament.]

What we understand by passions and affections

Three sorts of actions proceed from men's souls: some are internal and immaterial, as the acts of our wits and wills; others be mere external and material, as the acts of our senses: seeing, hearing, moving, etc.; others stand betwixt these two extremes and border upon them both, the which we may best discover in children because they lack the use of reason and are guided by an internal imagination, following nothing else but that pleaseth their senses, even after the same manner as brute beasts do. For as we see beasts hate, love, fear, and hope, so do children. Those actions, then, which are common with us and beasts we call passions and affections, or perturbations of the mind. *Motus*, saith Saint Augustine, *animae quos Graeci* παθη *appelant ex Latinis quidam ut Cicero 3. Tuscul.*[1] *pertubationes dixerunt, alii affectiones, alii affectus, alii expressas passiones vocaverunt.* (The motions of the soul, called of the Greeks παθη, some Latins, as Cicero, called them "perturbations," others "affections," others "affects," others more expressly name them "passions.") They are called passions, although

---

1 *Tusculan Disputations.*

indeed they be acts of the sensitive power or faculty of our soul and are defined of Damascene:[1] *Motio sensualis appetetivae virtutis, ob boni vel mali imaginationem*: (a sensual motion of our appetitive faculty through imagination of some good or ill thing), because when these affections are stirring in our minds they alter the humors of our bodies, causing some passion or alteration in them. They are called perturbations for that—as afterwards shall be declared—they trouble wonderfully the soul, corrupting the judgment and seducing the will, inducing for the most part to vice and commonly withdrawing from virtue, and therefore some call them maladies or sores of the soul. They be also named affections because the soul by them either affecteth some good or, for the affection of some good, detesteth some ill. These passions, then, be certain internal acts or operations of the soul bordering upon reason and sense, prosecuting some good thing or flying[2] some ill thing, causing therewithal some alteration in the body.

Here must be noted that albeit these passions inhabit the confines both of sense and reason, yet they keep not equal friendship with both. For passions and sense are like two naughty servants who oft-times bear more love to one another than they are obedient to their master; and the reason of this amity betwixt the passions and sense I take to be the greater conformity and likeness betwixt them than there is betwixt passions and reason. For passions are drowned in corporal organs and instruments as well as sense; reason dependeth of no corporal subject, but, as a princess in her throne, considereth the state of her kingdom. Passions and sense are determined to one thing, and as soon as they perceive their object sense presently receives it and the passions love or hate it. But reason, after she perceiveth her object, she stands in deliberation, whether it be convenient she should accept it or refuse it. Besides, sense and passions, as they have a league the longer,[3] so their friendship is stronger; for all the time of our infancy and childhood, our senses were joint friends in such sort with passions that whatsoever delighted sense, pleased the passions, and whatsoever was hurtful to the one, was an enemy to the other. And so, by long agreement and familiarity the passions had so engaged themselves to sense, and with such bonds

1   After John of Damascus (c. 675–749), a Syrian monk and theologian considered one of the fathers of the Eastern Orthodox Church.
2   Fleeing.
3   I.e., the longer they work together.

and seals of sensual habits confirmed their friendship, that as soon as reason came to possession of her kingdom, they began presently to make rebellion; for right reason oftentimes deprived sense of those pleasures he had of long time enjoyed, as by commanding continency[1] and fasting, which sense most abhorred. Then passions repugned[2] and very often haled[3] her by force to condescend to that they demanded, which combat and captivity well perceived by him, who said, *Video aliam legem in membris meis repugnantem legi mentis meae et captivantem me in lege peccati.* (I see another law in my members, repugning to the law of my mind and leading me captive in the law of sin.) Whereupon Saint Cyprian said, *Cum Avaritia*, etc. (We must content with avarice, with uncleanness, with anger, with ambition; we have a continual and molestful battle with carnal vices and worldly enticements.)

Moreover, after that men, by reason, take possession over their souls and bodies, feeling this war so mighty, so continual, so near, so domestical[4] that either they must consent to do their enemies' will or still be in conflict. And withal, foreseeing by making peace with them they were to receive great pleasures and delights, the most part of men resolve themselves never to displease their sense or passions, but to grant them whatsoever they demand. What dainty meats the tongue will taste, they never deny it; what savors the nose will smell, they never resist it; what music the ears will hear, they accept it; and finally, whatsoever by importunity, prayer, or suggestion sensuality requesteth, no sooner to reason the supplication is presented, but the petition is granted. Yet if the matter here were ended and reason yielded but only to the suits of sensuality, it were without doubt a great disorder to see the lord attend so basely upon his servants. But reason, once being entered into league with passions and sense, becometh a better friend to sensuality than the passions were before. For reason straightaways inventeth ten thousand sorts of new delights which the passions never could have imagined. And therefore, if you ask now, who procured such exquisite arts of cookery, so many sauces, so many broths, so many dishes? No better answer can be given than reason, to please sensuality. Who found first such gorgeous attire, such variety of

---

1 Self-restraint.
2 Resisted.
3 Drew.
4 Familiar.

garments, such decking, trimming and adorning of the body that tailors must every year learn a new trade? But reason to please sensuality. Who devised such stately palaces, such delicious gardens, such precious canopies and embroidered beds? But reason to feed sensuality. In fine,[1] discourse over all arts and occupations and you shall find men laboring night and day, spending their wit and reason to excogitate[2] some new invention to delight our sensuality. In such sort, as a religious man once lamenting this ignominious industry of reason employed in the service of sense wished with all his heart that godly men were but half so industrious to please God as worldly men to please their inordinate appetites. By this we may gather how passions stand so confined with sense and reason that for the friendship they bear to the one, they draw the other to be their mate and companion. (7–11)

How the passions may be well directed and made profitable

… By this discourse may be gathered that passions are not only not wholly to be extinguished as the Stoics seemed to affirm, but sometimes to be moved and stirred up for the service of virtue as learnedly Plutarch teacheth, for mercy and compassion will move us often to pity as it did Job: *Quia ab infantia mea mecum crevit miseratio.* (Compassion grew with me from my infancy and it came with me out of my mother's womb.) Therefore he declareth what succor he gave to the poor (Job 31.18). Ire and indignation will prick forward the friends of God to take his quarrel in hand and revenge him of his enemies. So Christ, moved with zeal—which is a passion of love bordering upon anger—cast the buyers and sellers out of the Temple of Jerusalem because *Zelus domus tuae commedit me.* (The zeal of thy house did eat me.) The passions of shamefastness[3] brideleth us of many loose affections which would otherwise be ranging abroad. The appetite of honor which followeth, yea, and is due unto virtue, encourageth often noble spirits to attempt most dangerous exploits for the benefit of their country: fear expelleth sin; sadness bringeth repentance; delight pricketh forward to keep God's commandments; and, to be brief, passions are spurs that stir up sluggish and idle souls from slothfulness

---

1   In conclusion.
2   Devise.
3   Modesty, propriety; feeling of shame.

to diligence, from carelessness to consideration. Some questionless[1] they, almost by force, draw to goodness, and others withdraw from vice. For if that many noble captains had not possessed by nature such vehement passions of glory and honor, they would never have achieved such excellent victories for the good of the commonwealth. If many rare wits had not been pressed with the same affections, we should never have seen Homer's poetry, nor Plato's divinities, nor Aristotle's philosophy, nor Pliny's history, not Tully's[2] eloquence, for honor they aimed at. And although perhaps they took their aim too high, affecting more glory than their labor deserved, or compleasing[3] themselves more in the opinions and fancies of men than reason required, yet no doubt but if they had leveled right and at no more than their works merited, nor more prized the opinions and honors given by men, then they in very deed had obtained more renown and their passions had been occasion of great good to all their posterity, as now they profit them although they proceeded from their authors' vanity. I take it that shamefastness in women restraineth them from many shameful offenses, and fear of punishment restraineth from theft, and the remorse of conscience calleth many sinners to the grace of God.

Hereby we may conclude that passions well used may consist with wisdom, against the Stoics, and if they be moderated, to be very serviceable to virtue; if they be abused and overruled by sin, to be the nursery of vices and pathway to all wickedness. And as I think the Stoics were of this opinion, for they said that fear and heaviness was *Aegritudo quaedam*[4] or *animi adversante ratione contractio*.[5] (17–19)

What sort of persons be most passionate

... I am not of Seneca's opinion that *Mulier amat aut odit, nihil est tertium* (a woman loveth or hateth, and nothing is third). For although in some sort of women I hold it very probable, yet I cannot allow it to be common to all, for only women that be of a hot complexion, and for the most part those that be black and brown, I take to be of that

---

1 Undoubtedly.
2 I.e., Marcus Tullius Cicero.
3 Gratifying.
4 Some illness.
5 Heart opposed to reason.

constitution, and indeed those have their affections most vehement, and perhaps little women have a smack[1] therefore according to our English proverb:

> *Fair and foolish, little and loud,*
> *Long and lazy, black and proud.*
> *Fat and merry, lean and sad,*
> *Pale and pettish, red and bad.*[2]

By which saying we may gather that howbeit women commonly be subject to the aforesaid passions, yet because divers women have sundry complexions, so they be subject to sundry passions. Even as in like sort, I could say of men, for some are more prone to one passion than another, according to the Italian proverb:

> *Se l'huomini piccoli fufferi patienti*
> *Et l'huomini grandi fuffero valenti*
> *Et li rossi leali*
> *Tutto il mondo sarebbe uquale.*

That is,

> *If little men were patient,*
> *And great men were valiant,*
> *And red men were loyal,*
> *All the world would be equal.*

To this seemeth not unlike another old saying of theirs:

> *From a white Spaniard,*
> *A black German,*
> *And a red Italian,*
> *Libera nos Domine.*[3]

---

1 Taste, small amount.
2 Compare with Iago's sexist jokes, beginning at 2.1.99 (TLN 869), especially his rhymes about women's temperaments and coloring beginning at line 127 (TLN 903).
3 Deliver us, O Lord.

And we in English:

> To a red man read thy reed:[1]
> With a brown man break thy bread:
> At a pale man draw thy knife:
> From a black man keep thy wife.

The which we explicate after this sort:

> The red is wise,
> The brown is trusty,
> The pale is peevish,
> The black lusty.

By which ancient proverbs may be collected the verity of the assertion set down that divers complexions are inclined to divers passions, and in general I take them to be very true and verified in the most part, for that the same causes which concur to the framing of such a constitution serve also to the stirring up of such a passion. As for example, a little man having his heat so united and compacted together, and not dispersed into so vast a carcass as the great man, therefore he, by temperature, posesseth more spirits, and by them becometh more nimble, lively, choleric, hasty and impatient. (42–44)

How passions seduce the will

Without any great difficulty may be declared how passions seduce the will because the wit being the guide, the eye the stirrer and director of the will, which of itself, being blind and without knowledge, followeth that the wit representeth, propoundeth, and approveth as good, and as the sensitive appetite followeth the direction of imagination, so the will affecteth, for the most part, that the understanding persuadeth to be best. Wherefore the waves and billows of apparent reasons so shake the sandy shelf of a weak will that they mingle it with them and make all one. Besides, the sensitive appetite being rooted in the same

---

1   Take advice from. Ophelia uses a version of this proverbial phrase in *Hamlet* when she warns Laertes not to behave like an "ungracious pastor" who "recks not his own rede"—that is, who fails to take his own advice (1.3.51).

soul with the will, if it be drawn or flieth from any object, consequently the other must follow. Even so, the object that haleth the sensitive appetite draweth withal the will, and, inclining her more to one part than another, diminisheth her liberty and freedom.

Moreover, the will, by yielding to the passion, receiveth some little bribe of pleasure, the which moveth her to let the bridle loose unto inordinate appetites, because she hath ingrafted in her two inclinations: the one to follow reason, the other to content the senses—and this inclination, the other being blinded by the corrupt judgment caused by inordinate passions, here she feeleth satisfied. Finally, the will being the governess of the soul, and loathing to be troubled with much dissension among her subjects as an uncareful magistrate neglecteth the good of the commonwealth to avoid some particular men's displeasure, so the will, being afraid to displease sense, neglecteth the care she ought to have over it, especially perceiving that the soul thereby receiveth some interest of pleasure or escheweth some pain.

By this alteration which passions work in the wit and the will, we may understand the admirable metamorphosis and change of a man from himself when his affects are pacified and when they are troubled. Plutarch said they changed like Circe's potions from men into beasts.[1] Or we may compare the soul without passions to a calm sea with sweet, pleasant, and crispling streams, but the passionate to the raging gulf swelling with waves, surging by tempests, menacing the stony rocks, and endeavoring to overthrow mountains. Even so, passions make the soul to swell with pride and pleasure; they threaten wounds, death, and destruction by audacious boldness and ire; they undermine the mountains of virtue with hope and fear; and in sum, never let the soul be in quietness, but ever either flowing with pleasure or ebbing with pain. (57–59)

---

1   In Greek mythology, Circe is a temptress and sorceress whose magical potions transform those who cross her into animals.

The fourth effect of passions, which is disquietness of the mind

He that should see Hercules raging,[1] Orestes trembling,[2] Cain ranging,[3] Amon pining,[4] Dido consuming,[5] Archimedes running naked[6] would little doubt that passions mightily change and alter the quiet temper and disposition of the mind. For if peace be a concord or consort of our sensual soul with reason, if then the mind be quiet when the will ruled by prudence overruleth, moderateth, and governeth passions questionless, then the soul is troubled when passions arise up and oppose themselves against reason. Inordinate affections, as experience teacheth, many ways disquiet the mind and trouble the peaceable state of this petty commonwealth of our soul, but specially by five: by contradiction, by contrariety, by insatiability, by importunity, by impossibility.

1. Contradiction

By two ways the subjects of every commonwealth usually disturb the state and breed civil broils therein: the first is when they rise up and rebel against their king; the second is when they brawl one with another and so cause riots and tumults. The former is called rebellion, the latter sedition. After the same manner, passions either rebel

---

1   In Greek and Roman mythology, Heracles or Hercules is driven mad and kills his own children (and in some versions, his wife Megara) in a fit of rage. In penance, he must carry out twelve (in some versions, ten) labors in order to be purified and receive immortality.
2   In Greek mythology, Orestes avenges the murder of his father, Agamemnon, by murdering his mother, Clytemnestra. Afterwards, he goes mad and is pursued by the Furies, spirits of vengeance.
3   In Genesis 4, Cain kills his brother Abel in a fit of anger and jealousy. God punishes Cain by banishing him to wander the earth.
4   Wright probably means to refer to Amnon, eldest son of King David, who, in 2 Samuel 13, falls in love with his half-sister Tamar and then rapes her. Tamar's full brother, Absalom, later kills Amnon in vengeance.
5   In Virgil's *Aeneid*, Dido, the queen of Carthage, is consumed by love for the Roman hero Aeneas. When he leaves her to fulfill his mission of traveling to Italy, Dido kills herself on a pyre.
6   In a famous anecdote, the Greek mathematician and physicist Archimedes (c. 287–c. 212 BCE) has a sudden realization while in the bath that he can determine the volume of irregular objects by measuring the water they displace. He is so excited about his breakthrough that he runs naked through the streets.

against reason their lord and king, or oppose themselves one against another, that I call "contradiction," this "contrariety." The former be well understood, that said *Spiritus concupiscit adversus carnem, et caro adverdus Spiritum.* (The spirit affects against the flesh, and the flesh against the spirit.) This internal combat and spiritual contradiction every spiritual man daily perceiveth, for inordinate passions, willy-nilly,[1] cease not almost hourly to rise up against reason and so molest him, troubling the rest and quietness of his soul. It is related in the life of St. Anselm, our archbishop of Canterbury, that walking into the fields he saw a shepherd's little boy who had caught a bird and tied a stone to her leg with a thread, and ever as the bird mounted up to soar aloft, the stone drew her down again. The venerable old man, much moved at this sight, fell presently a-weeping, lamenting thereby the miserable condition of men who no sooner did endeavor to ascend to heaven by contemplation, but the flesh and passions haled the heart back again and drew it down to earth, enforcing the soul to lie there like a beast which should have soared in the heavens like an angel. For these rebellious passions are like crafty pioneers[2] who, while soldiers live carelessly within their castle, or at least not much suspect, they undermine it and break so upon them that they can hardly escape. In like manner, these affections undermine the under-standings of men. For while the wits are either careless or employed in other affairs, there creepeth up into their hearts some one or other perverse passion which transporteth the soul clean another way, in so much as that with extreme difficulty she can recall herself again and reduce her affections unto their former quietness and peaceable tem-per. Who seeth and feeleth not that oftentimes while reason attendeth to contemplation, a villainous passion of love withdraweth the atten-tion and with an attoxicated[3] delight imprisoneth the affections? Who perceiveth not that divers times reason would pardon all injuries and ire, opposeth itself, importuning revenge who experimenteth not; that reason would willingly fast and abstain from delicacies, but inordinate delight will feast and endure no austerities; who knoweth not that reason often prescribeth, yea, urgeth to labor and pain for the service of God or to perform the affairs of the world, and sensuality would

---

1   Whether he likes it or not.
2   Soldiers who dig mines under a castle during a siege.
3   Intoxicated.

pass her time idly; and after this sort almost continually inordinate passions contradict right reason.

2. Contrariety of Passions

The Egyptians fought against the Egyptians, the east wind riseth often against the west, the south against the north, the wind against the tide, and one passion fighteth with another. The choleric cavalier would with death revenge an injury but fear of killing or hanging opposeth itself against this passion. Gluttony would have dainties, but covetousness prescribeth parsimony. Lechery would reign and domineer, but dreadfulness of infamy and fear of disease draw in the reins of this inordinate affection. By which opposition we may easily perceive how unquiet is the heart of a passionate man tossed like the sea with contrary winds even at the same time and moment. Another disquietness there is also, which to many happeneth and that well nigh upon a sudden, for sometimes a man will be in the prime of his joy and presently a sea of grief overwhelmeth him. In what a world of joy lived Balthazar when, sitting at his supper with his minions and concubines, he caused in a triumph to be set before him for a glimpse of his glory, the golden vessel which his father had by conquest brought from the Temple of Jerusalem and yet the hand which appeared writing upon the wall drowned all his pleasure in a gulf of fear and woe.[1] Potiphar's wife was inflamed with love when she allured chaste Joseph to violate both her and his fidelity unto her husband, and presently the passion of hatred as vehemently vexed her as the passion of love had formerly tormented her.[2]

3. Insatiability of Passions

Hell, earth, and a woman's womb, saith Solomon, are insatiable, and with these he might have numbered a number of passions. How

---

1   In Daniel 5, Belshazzar, son of Nebuchadnezzar, is king of Babylon. During a feast, Belshazzar has the gold vessels that were taken from the Temple of Jerusalem brought to be used for wine. A disembodied hand suddenly appears and writes on the wall. Daniel interprets the writing, which foretells Belshazzar's death. Belshazzar is deposed and killed that night by the Medo-Persian armies.
2   In Genesis 39, Joseph is a slave to the Egyptian captain Potiphar. Potiphar's wife attempts to seduce Joseph, but he refuses her. She falsely accuses him of rape and Joseph is thrown into prison.

insatiable was the lust of Solomon, who had no less queens and concubines than a thousand? How increaseth the passion of covetousness with the increase of riches? *Crescit amor nummi quantum ipsa pecunia crescit.* (As riches flow, so love doth grow.) And herein we may resemble our passions to men affected with the dropsy,[1] who the more they drink, the more they thirst, for drink causeth such a desire and increaseth it. Even so, a vehement inordinate passion inclineth vehemently the soul to embrace or fly the object propounded, and a stronger passion causeth a stronger propension and inclination, and consequently an insatiable desire of pleasure or an exorbitant abomination of pain. It is well known in Scotland how insatiable is the passion of ire and the appetite of revenge, for their deadly feud will never be quenched but with the blood of all their enemies and their adherents. In the city of Naples not many years since, the base passionate people wanting corn[2] and imputing the dearth[3] either to the negligence or avarice of a certain magistrate, came and beset his house, killed divers of his servants, and finally caught the master and by main force brought him into the marketplace, ripped his belly, pulled out his heart, and there, in the presence of all the city, ate it with salt. How the passions of pride and ambition, how insatiable they be in women and courtiers, all the world knoweth, and no man is ignorant but that knoweth nothing.

4. Importunity of Passions

Inordinate passions either prevent reason or are stirred up by a corrupt judgment, and therefore neither observe time nor place, but upon every occasion would be leaping into action, importuning execution. Let a man fall a-praying and studying, or be busy in any negotiation [of] importance, and very often he shall feel a headless passion rush in upon him, importuning him even then to leave all and prosecute revenge, lust, gluttony, or some other unbridled desire. It is well known how in the sack of sundry cities, when the unruly and passionate soldiers should have attended and employed all their forces to keep the gates, or win the marketplaces, or defend the common passages, contrariwise by the importunity of passions, either distracted with

---

1 Now known as edema, this condition is characterized by swelling of tissue due to excessive accumulation of fluid.
2 Lacking grain.
3 Scarcity.

desire of spoil and riches, or drawn with appetite of private revenge, or haled with lust to violate virgins or honest matrons, leese[1] in a moment all they won with extreme loss and labor, and perhaps also their lives withal. Sometimes you shall have a number of greedy passions like so many young crows, half starved, gaping and crying for food, every one more earnest than another to be satiated; to content them all is impossible, to content none is intolerable, to prosecute one and abandon the rest is to carry so many hungry vipers gnawing upon the heartstrings of the soul. Saint Basil saith that inordinate passions rise up in a drunkard like a swarm of bees, buzzing on every side, or like wild horses drawing a coach, running with it headlong shaking, hurrying and hurling their master at their pleasure. For in such men a multitude of passions most apparently discover themselves, and in regard that reason in them is buried and cannot hold the reins of such savage and unreasonable beasts, therefore they break out deboistly,[2] and never cease to range and revel till reason rise out of her Cimmerian darkness,[3] grave of oblivion, and puddle of ignorance and senseless beastliness.

5. Impossibility of Passions

There is no man in this life which followeth the stream of his passions but expecteth and verily believeth to get at last a firm rest, contentation,[4] and full satiety of all his appetites, the which is as possible as to quench fire with fuel, extinguish a burning ague[5] with hot wines, drown an eel with water. Rachel well declared the impossible petitions of her passions when so importunely she demanded children of Jacob, or else that she would die, as though it lay in his power to have children at his pleasure. That epicure who wished his throat as long as a crane (yet rather deserved a nose as long as a woodcock[6]) that his dainty fare might longer feed his gluttonous taste and not pass away almost in a

---

1 Lose.
2 Debauchedly.
3 The Cimmerians were an ancient people said to have lived in perpetual darkness.
4 The state of being content.
5 Fever.
6 A common bird with a long bill; associated with gullibility due to the ease with which they are snared.

moment, well declared that passion's suits were not only senseless but also impossible to be granted. It is wonderful what passionate appetites reign in women when they be with child. I have heard it credibly reported that there was a woman in Spain which longest almost till death to have a mouth full of flesh out of an extreme fat man's neck. I will not here condemn all women who labor with such frantic fits, yet I cannot but approve a sage philosopher's sentence, who was my master of philosophy, that most of these appetites proceeded from women extremely addicted to follow their own desires, and of such a froward[1] disposition, as in very deed, if they were crossed of their wills, their passions were so strong as they undoubtable would miscarry of their children. For vehement passions alter vehemently the temper and constitution of the body, which cannot but greatly prejudice the tender infant lying in the womb. And the rather I am persuaded to this opinion, for that I never knew any woman very virtuous or well mortified[2] subject to these fancies. Nevertheless, by these preposterous desires and sundry appetites for things impossible, or almost impossible to be accomplished, we may well conclude that passion's desires keep neither sense, order, nor measure. (68–75)

Policy in Passion

Since men by nature are addicted to conversation, and one dependeth upon another, therefore it importeth much to know how to second or cross other men's affections, how we may please or displease them, make them our friends or foes. But because this subject is infinite, I will only set down certain general rules whereby some small light may be had, how to live and deal with men to the intent that love, peace, and charity be conserved. For good Christians ought not only to procure an union with God, but also an amity with men. And the world being green in malice and withered in goodness, men more guided by passions than ruled by reason, therefore the wiser ought to provide a salve proportionated to the sore, and means to prevent malice, lest the children of darkness in prudence surpass the children of light,

---

1 Perverse.
2 Having appetites in check.

seeing our master taught us how the eye of a dove adorneth best the serpent's head.

The first rule may be this: all men, commonly, are pleased with them whom they see affected with those passions whereunto they are subject and inclined. This rule both experience teacheth and reason proveth. We see that lions, tigers, and leopards, whose inclinations are most cruel, whose passions most fierce, yet one affecteth another and liveth in quiet society for the similitude of inclinations and likeness of passions. Alexander[1] asked a pirate that was taken and brought before him how he durst be so bold to infest the seas and spoil the commerceries.[2] He answered that he played the pirate but with one ship, and his majesty with a huge navy; the which saying so pleased Alexander that he pardoned his life and granted him liberty, so much could the similitude of action transport the king's affection. The reason also of this rule may easily be delivered: because all likeliness causeth love, and as every one judgeth he doth the best, or at least approveth well, even so, he cannot disprove,[3] but allow the same in others. Hereupon followeth that if thou wilt please thy master or friend, thou must apparel thyself with his affections, and love where he loveth, and hate where he hateth. And universally, to soothe other men's humors plaineth the way to friendship and amity, and as this mean fostereth flattery if it be abused, so it nourisheth charity if it be well used.

Out of this rule we may deduce the second, which ought no less to be observed in conversation than the former: that men commonly hate those whom they know to be of contrary passions. Whereupon proceedeth that common proverb: he that hateth whom I love, how can he love me? For as fire with fire do never jar, so fire and water can never agree. But in the next book, which shall be of love, I pretend[4] to discuss better this rule, because as similitude causeth love, so dissimilitude breedeth hatred. Therefore I omit to declare how sometimes likeliness of passions engendreth contention, as we say, *figulus figulum odit* (one potter hateth another) and *inter superbos semper sunt jurgia* (among proud men there are ever brawlings). For if similitude of passions prejudicateth profit, then likeliness of affections causeth dissension.

---

1   Alexander the Great (356–323 BCE).
2   Commercial trading.
3   Disapprove.
4   Intend.

The third rule: be not too credulous to men in their own causes. For as self-love for the most part conceives what appertaineth to ourselves with a greater show of good and honesty that indeed the thing carrieth with it, so men moved therewith declare the matter as they conceive it. For words spring from conceits; these are the tree, those the flowers and leaves, which do follow by just proportion. Wherefore Alexander did wisely, as Plutarch recounteth, at the beginning of his reign, by shutting one of his ears with his hand when he heard any accuser in criminal causes, thereby reserving, as he said, audience for the defendant. Contrariwise, others men's matters, which hinder our profit or cross our designs, for the most part we extenuate[1] and abase. As in Italy once befell to a number of wise men who heard an oration wherein they were all well nigh persuaded, but the next day came up another orator and told a contrary tale, and changed their minds, persuading them all to the other part; for which cause we may adjoin the fourth rule.

The fourth rule: when you are induced to anything by act, that is, by a tale well told in rhetorical manner, flexibility of voice, gestures, actions, or other oratorical persuasions, good I hold it a while for a man to suspend his judgment and not to permit his will follow too far his motion, more artificial than natural, grounded upon affection rather than reason. For that saying of Isocrates[2] ought well to be weighed, who, being demanded what was rhetoric, answered: to make great things little and little great. Wherefore, after Aeschines[3] was banished from Athens, coming to Rhodes he made an oration to the people in declaration of his cause of exile, they wondered at the Athenians who had banished him so undeservedly. "Oh," quoth he, "you did not hear what Demosthenes[4] answered to my reasons," ascribing wholly the cause of his exile to the force and eloquence of Demosthenes's oration. By this example we see proved that commonly wise rhetoricians affirm that rhetoric in an ill cause is a two-edged sword in the hand of a furious man. Yet I would not by this condemn the faculty of eloquence, which I confess, if it be well used, to be most profitable for the church and commonwealth. But because at this present it is sophisticated[5] by

---

1   Diminish.
2   Ancient Greek rhetorician and orator (436–338 BCE).
3   Ancient Greek statesman and orator (389–314 BCE).
4   Ancient Greek statesman and orator (384–322 BCE).
5   Adulterated.

many who cover stinking matters with fragrant flowers, and with a few sugared words temper the gall of their pernicious objects, therefore every wise man ought rather to examine the orator's reasons than to follow his intent with seduced affection. (96–99)

Sowers of Dissension

Other men more maliciously pretend friendship and use strange dealing, either to make friends or to breed dissension. Some I have found of such an humor that if they see two converse familiarly together and one to affect much another, they, under color of amity, will go secretly and reveal to the one of them what they know, or hear, or that the other person, his friend, secretly spoke or wrought to his discredit; yea, divers things they will relate by their own malice invented as by his friend discovered. Yet this they will not deliver but under oath that he should not detect them to the other. Whereby he of simplicity often revealeth all he knew of his friend because he believed his friend in very deed had betrayed him; whereas, for the most part, all was but a bait forged to catch the seely[1] simple soul. Presently, after they convent[2] the other, whom in secret they tell all they had fished out of his friend in his dispraise, and so learn what they can of the other, charging him withal in no case to manifest that he heard to the other. This stratagem I know many politic superiors to have frequented, and some persons of great policy but of most small conscience. Because this wicked invention proceeded from a most malicious, uncharitable, and envious mind, which hateth the peace and concord of friends, it argueth also a crafty politic wit apt to sift out other men's actions. For he casteth the poor man into an inextricable labyrinth for forcing him to swear, he cannot examine whether his friend spoke so ill of him or no, left by the notice thereof he should incur the crime of perjury. Neither can he tolerate in his mind that his friend should so notoriously abuse him. Wherefore he resolveth himself either wholly to break friendship, or at least not to use his friend so familiarly as before.

But how shall a man behave himself in such a case? At the beginning when he telleth thee thy friend's defects, excuse them, supposing the relator to be ill-informed or that he mistook thy friend. For true

---

1 Innocent, helpless.
2 Meet with.

friendship requireth that a friend should, in all cases, when evidently the contrary is not convinced, defend the good name and estimation of his friend, and thereby the sower of dissension shall be frustrated of his intention.

Much more I could deliver about this subject, but to wise men it sufficeth to show the way, and they will follow further than I can direct them. Simple men, for as much as I can see, must first try and then trust; for their rule lieth in experience and practice more than in reason and speculation, because their own harms or their neighbors' must school them; for few are capable for practical rules in universal, or at least, they cannot apply them to particular subjects. (122–24)

5. FROM STE[PHEN?] B., *COUNSEL TO THE HUSBAND: TO THE WIFE INSTRUCTION. A SHORT AND PITHY TREATISE OF SEVERAL AND JOINT DUTIES BELONGING UNTO MAN AND WIFE* (LONDON, 1608); TRANSCRIBED IN MODERN SPELLING AND EDITED BY SARAH MILLIGAN AND JESSICA SLIGHTS

[Among the many books offering lifestyle advice to the early moderns, those like *Counsel to the Husband: To the Wife Instruction* that focus on the nature of marriage proved particularly popular. Many scholars suggest that it is productive to read *Othello* in the context of such discussions of the obligations of husbands and wives, though they are divided in their conclusions.]

The whole estate of man's happiness may be easily disposed into the consideration of two times: the state of this life present and the glory of the life to come. This life, being the first, is both the image to resemble and the foundation wherein to lay or work that eternal happiness. Neither is there any estate wherein we may more lively behold or sensibly taste and feel any sparkle or jot of the Lord our God, his eternal love to us, than in that united estate of man and wife wherein two persons become but one,[1] which still are two, and mutually owe to other several duty. The union whereof, as it is unspeakable where there is indeed an holy union,[2] so hath it pleased the Lord, not seldom

---

1 [Author's note:] Eph. 5.13.
2 A double union.

but often in his word, and especially in the Song of Songs, called Solomon's Canticles, under the title of a husband rejoicing with his wife to set forth his love unto us, what it is in Christ Jesus. Whose mutual kindness expressed, in that song I mean, in terms, in duties, in wanting each other, in seeking, in sorrowing, in finding, in enjoying, in solacing and embracing, in unwillingness to leave and depart each from other, may well show the conjunction to be unspeakable between man and wife rightly conjoined and yoked equally, and be a lively pattern of more heavenly things. Howbeit, I say it is not in all conjunctions that this image of spiritual happiness doth appear, for in some it beareth rather a type of hellish sorrows,[1] wherein our Savior saith shall be weeping and gnashing of teeth when the judgment shall be pronounced upon the reprobate. "Go away ye cursed ones into everlasting fire."[2] Even so, where the match is unmeet, the conjunction unequal, the united in body disunited in spirit, of contrary affections, hearts, and religions, duties unperformed, each crossing other, or any of the twain unwise that will not be admonished, what are the fruits there but wrath, bitterness, contention, controlling, contradiction, taking all things in the evil part, jealousy, upbraiding, discontentment, false dealing, secret juggling, conspiring, wants without pitying each other, toil without helping each other, seeking each one his credit with discredit unto both, with many other as grievous to be spoken of as any part? All which no doubt made Solomon so to speak as his proverbs[3] do bear witness, namely, that it were better to dwell in the corner of an housetop, yea in the wilderness most desolate and solitary, and as another saith, with dragons and bears or other cruel beasts than with the contentious and froward[4] wife. So that as I said this image of God's love and of our eternal and most happy conjunction with Christ—he the head and we the members; he the husband, we the wife; he our well-beloved one, and we his as-well-beloved—is not to be found in every conjunction, as woeful experience giveth cause of complaint to many, but only in the godly united match, in the well-ordered and governed match.[5] So that how necessarily doth it behoove them that would live perfectly happy by enjoying the one and avoiding the other

---

1 [Author's note:] All marriages do not resemble heavenly happiness.
2 [Author's note:] Matt. 25.30, 41.
3 [Author's note:] Prov. 21.9, 19.
4 Unreasonable and ungovernable.
5 [Author's note:] A necessary caveat.

to be instructed in the means which lead hereunto? That is, seeing this happiness is in the right ordering of man and wife themselves, each towards other, and then both in the joint governing of their family to know, therefore, both their several works and conjoined duties. And whereas I called this estate before a foundation, wherein to lay the work of eternal happiness, I spake not without advisement, for that as the Church generally is the school of God's kingdom,[1] a place to make men fit before they can enjoy his kingdom, understanding me of such as come to the state of discretion and judgment, as also the word of God is called the gospel of this kingdom because that in this life is fitteth men thereunto, so is every man's house rightly ordered and governed by the rules of godliness not unjustly or without cause by the holy ghost called a church,[2] the governors, kings,[3] priests, and prophets unto God. Kings to rule, priests to offer sacrifice, and prophets to instruct or see instructed. The husband first and principally as the head and high priest, the wife in his absence or upon just cause he shall require her. (1–6)

The rule that you must level by, both concerning yourself and others that shall be your charge, is the most blessed word of God;[4] a young man's rule, an old man's rule, every man's rule, the prince must rule by it, the subject obey by it; the husband must govern his wife by it; the wife must yield her subjection thereby as it prescribeth. In it there is for every condition, state, and degree most perfect instruction to be taught and learned. (28)

There must be further building in the work and government of a family. For as the sweetness of music consisteth in the orderly concent[5] and tuning of the strings without which be he never so skillful that playeth, the instrument never so good, the strings never so true, there will be no sound of music;[6] even so, if the strings and members of a family be set in tune, every string in his due and proper place, every string in his place keeping his note and height, then, as David saith, is there

---

1 [Author's note:] The church is the school of God's kingdom.
2 [Author's note:] Rom. 16.5.
3 [Author's note:] Rev. 1.6.
4 [Author's note:] Ps. 119.
5 Playing in harmony.
6 Simile.

the comeliness, goodness, and well agreement, which he resembled to Hermon's pleasant and precious dews with that most sweet and sacred savor which from the priestly anointing of Aaron did arise and smell.[1] To this, naturally, we are not by birth apt, no more than the strings of an instrument will of their own nature without art or skill fall into tune. (38–39)

A family may be compared unto a commonwealth[2] wherein there are divers societies and degrees, reciprocally relating and mutually depending one upon another. The highest degree or society is between the husband and the wife, and this is as the first wheel of a clock that turneth about all the rest in order.[3] The next society is between the parents and the children. The third between the servants one with another and towards all other superiors in the family. Into these three societies may a family be disposed.[4] As touching the first and principal society, wherein also principally I purpose to insist, which is between yourself and your loving hind and roe,[5] whom many a time I have blessed and shall bless by God's grace unto your use and comfort, give me leave as one that can speak by the surest learning to power forth my mind mutually to you both, who can tell you that the canker unto happiness and danger of confusion to a family is the contention and disagreement of man and wife.

You will say, how may this be avoided? I answer very easily if in time true regard be had unto mutual duty, without which there can be no comfort nor that blessing of happiness which before we spoke of.[6] Nay, which is more, to have the blessing of God which is the foundation and cause of all happiness. It standeth not in what man and wife shall conclude upon that there may be peace and quietness, but what order God hath prescribed them, to be obeyed in their places,[7] so that they must look unto God's wisdom, order, and polity[8] for economical government, and not what may seem right and good in their own eyes. And that if

---

1 [Author's note:] [Psalms 133:]2–3.
2 [Author's note:] A family like to a commonwealth.
3 [Author's note:] Simile.
4 [Author's note:] Three societies of a family.
5 A female and male deer, respectively.
6 [Author's note:] The means to avoid contention in a family.
7 [Author's note:] God's ordinance must be preferred before unmeet conditions of peace.
8 Management.

the man may not wear woman's apparel, nor the woman man's,[1] how much less may the one usurp the other's dignity, or the other, to wit the husband, resign or give over his sovereignty unto his wife? But each must keep their place, their order and heavenly polity whereto God hath called them. The husband is made the head and the wife resembled to the body.[2] May the head of a body, natural, be turned downward? Can the whole person so continue and live well in that state? How unseemly is it? No more can the body politic be in peaceable or blessed condition if order be inverted. A most monstrous thing it was that the prophet Isaiah complained of when he said, "children are extortioners of my people, and women rule over them."[3] You will say the prophet speaketh of another case, I know it well; yet it doth, and very well may it, serve in any case that is contrary to God's word to show deformity, but in his right case most notoriously.[4]

You will say, shall the wife have no government? Shall she do nothing but be idle in the family? I answer, my words yet tend unto no such thing. Then, why was she taken for a yokefellow? Why is her help required and she called an helper?[5] Nay, I will say more, a glorious spectacle it may be where the wife hath the whole government. But with these cautions: that is, where the wife manageth household affairs, providently fore-seeing, carefully disposing, and religiously governing to the honor of her husband. Else would not Solomon have said, in the description of a virtuous wife, "Give her the fruit of her hands, and let her own works praise her in the gates."[6] Having before so notably set forth the qualities of a virtuous wife, first of her grace and obedient faithfulness, "she will do him good," saith Solomon,[7] though I know the words of his mother, Bathsheba, "and not evil all the days of her life."[8] No marvel though he said her price was above the pearls. Mark ye, wives, the pattern of a wife, and ye husbands that are to choose, learn ye to choose a wife. She will do him good. Good shall be the object and subject of her labor; so, you will say, will many, but, saith he, "she will do him good, and not

---

1   [Author's note:] Deut. 22.5.
2   [Author's note:] The husband the head, the wife the body. 1 Cor. 11.3.
3   [Author's note:] Isa. 3.12.
4   [Author's note:] Which is, when men being effeminate are led, as was Ahab and such like, to provoke the Lord.
5   [Author's note:] Gen. 2.18.
6   [Author's note:] Prov. 31.31.
7   [Author's note:] [Prov. 31:]12.
8   [Author's note:] [Prov. 31:]10.

evil," that is, good without intermixing it with evil, good wholly, good absolutely, good and no evil with it to distain or corrupt it.[1] (40–45)

In such a case, how great an honor is the wife's godly government unto the husband,[2] while he, as king to command yet with love as a husband, shall go in and out in the midst of his family? Not fearing spoil whether he be at home or abroad, nor needing unlawful spoils to maintain his state. As also how honorable a service is it in the wife to depend upon his beck, to advise with her head, to lean upon his breast, and yet to have the authority to do what she will? That is, whilst her will is honest, lawful, and to her husband's good, as hath been spoken of.

Can this be counted slavery or servile subjection? Must there not be in some subjection? Can all in a nation be kings? Can all in a family be fathers? Can all be wives? Can all be everything? "If the whole body," saith the apostle,[3] "were an eye, where were the hearing? Or if all were the ear, where were the smelling?"[4] If, therefore, in a kingdom or a family there must of necessity be these degrees, and that we see men so subject to princes that they contentedly delight therein and neither count it slavishness nor affect above their state, though some wicked do otherwise, should not the wife look unto the hand of God, which made her the wife, and not the husband, the weaker vessel and not the stronger, the body and not the head, to obey and not to rule?[5] That is, not to rule without obedience. To grudge here at is not against the husband but against God withal; to govern otherwise is not to rule but to usurp. (49–50)

Hitherto, you will say, I have wholly as it were entreated of the duty of the wife. And you will further say I have laid load upon their shoulders who are the weaker vessels, longing, it may be, to hear the duty of the husband in like sort set forth, to see what bonds he is to be tied withal in his conversation to his wife. (79–80)

---

1 [Author's note:] A perfect good.
2 [Author's note:] The wife governing well becometh an honor to her husband.
3 Saint Paul.
4 [Author's note:] 1. Cor. 12.17.
5 [Author's note:] The wife must consider that it is God who hath assigned her unto her subjection.

But that I have somewhat tarried upon this point of the cause of contention between man and wife, or laid forth the wife's duty of subjection and obedience somewhat largely, hath not been to oppress the wife or put a sword into the hand of the husband to upbraid his wife with her duty, but partly to inform all godly and virtuous wives what is honorable and dishonorable in them, which none that are virtuous but do desire to see,[1] and principally to lay a sound foundation for the husband to build upon. Which being thus laid, you shall now see what the building will arise to be. (82)

The husband also must not disdain to be counseled by his wife, to hear her reasons, and to weigh her words. For she is given for a helper, two are better than one,[2] and God many times reveals that to the wife that he doth not to the husband. Abraham hearkened to Sarah in the matter of Hagar and Ishmael; he was bid of the Lord to give ear unto her.[3] And did not Manoah's wife strengthen him, after the sight of the angel and the sacrifice which he had offered, who feared that they should die because they had seen the Lord? Which fear she put away with a most wise reason, saying, "If the Lord will kill us, he would not have received a burnt offering, and a meat offering at our hands; neither would he have showed us all those things, nor would have told us any such, etc."[4] And what is that honor that St. Peter speaketh of, which the husband, being a man of understanding, should give unto his wife, but, amongst other things, regard unto her advice?[5] Always provided that she counsel not as did Job's wife, to bless God and die.[6] Nor with Michal disdain at his zeal and godliness,[7] but counseling wisely she is as a counselor to be heard and honored. Neither cometh Solomon's counsel short of this when he biddeth the husband to give his virtuous

---

1   [Author's note:] All good wives desire to know their duties to the uttermost.
2   [Author's note:] Eccles. 4.9.
3   [Author's note:] Gen. 21.12. [Abraham's wife Sarah advises him to send away her maidservant, Hagar, and Hagar's son by Abraham, Ishmael.]
4   [Author's note:] Judg. 13.23. [An angel appears to Manoah's wife, and later to both husband and wife, telling them they will have a son who will be a Nazirite (one who vows to be set apart for God, to follow a restricted diet, and refrain from cutting his hair). Manoah's wife later gives birth to Samson.]
5   [Author's note:] 1 Pet. 3.7.
6   [Author's note:] Job. 2.9. [When Job is tested by God and loses everything, his wife advises him to bless God and die.]
7   When King David's first wife, Michal, sees her husband worshipping God and dancing half-naked in the streets, she despises and criticizes him (2 Samuel 6).

wife the fruit of her hands, that is, being wise, virtuous, and provident let her be commended and trusted for such a wife. And put case there be not to be found all those absolute qualities of that virtuous wife, in her whom thou has chosen to be thy wife, but some infirmities, yea many infirmities, to bear with hers as it becometh the wise husband to do, consider thine own that she must and doth bear within thee.[1] If thine be more than hers, thou canst not be grieved to bear hers; if hers be more than thine, she is said to be the weaker vessel and thou the stronger that the bigger horse might bear the heavier load. Why hath God made thee the stronger but to bear the frailties and infirmities of thy wife?[2] For a man the wife's, or the wife the husband's, for either I mean, to discourse other's infirmities by way of reproach is the greatest reproach that can fall to either. Except it be in such a case as wherein Solomon saith her corruptions cannot be hid, "but he that would hide them, hideth the wind, and she is as oil in his right hand that uttereth itself."[3] The husband must dwell with his wife, as a man of understanding,[4] that is, as one that hath understanding to govern that he give not occasion by foolishness to be disposed, nor by overmuch severity to be hated or feared. (85–88)

It is certainly a great encouraging of the wife where the husband maketh his love to appear by sound effects,[5] showing that he regardeth her duty, observeth her labor, pitieth her pains, considereth her weakness, and would lighten her yoke and burden by any means he could; that he trusteth her, and is not lightly or unjustly jealous of her, not exacting too narrow an account of her domestical affairs, but as if she were himself, who is indeed become one with himself, his half or other self, even so to be persuaded of her truth and faithfulness. "Many daughters have done virtuously, but thou," saith Solomon, "surmountest them all."[6] There the husband observeth the labors, travails, night-watchings, and early risings of his wife, which were spoken of before, and lastly doth crown and commend them in her. The contrary

---

1 [Author's note:] A rule for the husband to bear with the wife's infirmities.
2 [Author's note:] Bear with the homeliness of the similitude.
3 [Author's note:] Prov. 27.16.
4 [Author's note:] 1 Pet. 3.7.
5 [Author's note:] A special duty of the husband.
6 [Author's note:] Prov. 31.29.

neglecting of all the poor wife's travail taketh away her heart, breedeth discontentmnent, and maketh weak her hands. And for either the wife over the husband or the husband over the wife to be attainted with the filthy sin of jealousy is the next way to cause either to fall into the sin.[1] (90–91)

Our most precious vessels, whether glass or gold, are commonly the weakest by reason either of nature or workmanship, and those we most precisely order, not roughly or carelessly. To a virtuous woman there is no vessel, no jewel comparable. Count her therefore the chiefest vessel in your house that must contain your self and all your treasures. Her price, saith Solomon, is above the pearls.[2] Show not your rough and manlike courage, like Lamech, to your wife,[3] but to your enemy. You are both but one, therefore be both but as one. Look not so much what is required of her, as what is due to her from yourself. You are the covering of her eyes,[4] which must defend her, not oppress her. (95)

6. FROM NICHOLAS COEFFETEAU, "OF JEALOUSY, WHETHER IT BE AN EFFECT AND SIGN OF LOVE" (1621); TRANSCRIBED IN MODERN SPELLING BY DANIKA SIHOTA AND EDITED BY JESSICA SLIGHTS

[Nicholas Coeffeteau (1574–1623) was a prominent French theologian who acted as vicar general of the French congregation from 1606 to 1609, served as preacher to the king under Henri IV in 1608, and later held the titles of Bishop of Dardania (1621–23) and Bishop of Marseille (1623). He was celebrated during his lifetime as a particularly beautiful prose stylist and an articulate critic of the Protestant Reformation. In addition to a number of religious pamphlets, he wrote a major history of Rome and a book on human emotions from

---

1 [Author's note:] Beware of causeless jealousy.
2 [Author's note:] Prov. 31.10.
3 In Genesis 4, Lamech boasts to his wives that he has killed a man who injured him. Compare with Desdemona listening to Othello's recounting of his martial feats (1.3.146–47, TLN 491–92).
4 [Author's note:] Gen. 20.16.

which the following excerpt is drawn. In 1621, just a year after it first appeared in France, Coeffeteau's *Tableau des passions humaines, de leurs causes et de leurs effets* was translated into English as *A Table of Human Passions. With Their Causes and Effects* by the English historian Edward Grimston. Coeffeteau's discussion is engaging on its own account, but it is also a useful point of comparison for the explorations of jealousy and love in *Othello*.]

The vulgar sort think that as the sun runs not his course without light, so love cannot be without jealousy; and they add that as lightning is an infallible sign of thunder, which breaks forth, so jealousy is a certain sign of love, which desires to show itself powerfully. But they that have a more exact and particular knowledge of human passions maintain that as the sun being come to the south—which is the point of the perfection of his light—casts no shadow but spreads his beams all pure upon the earth, so a true and perfect love is not subject to the inclinations of jealousy.

And they say, moreover, that this unjust passion is not more a sign of love than storm and tempests are shows of fair weather. This opinion is more probable: for to begin with the proofs: How can jealousy subsist and remain with love unless we will overthrow the laws of nature, which suffer not two contraries to subsist in one subject? Is there anything more contrary to love than jealousy? Can the world see a greater antipathy than that which is observed in these two qualities, whereof the one doth participate with the condition of monsters, and the other is the very idea of perfection? Love unites the wills and makes that the desires of them that love strive to take, as it were, the same tincture,[1] to the end they may resemble one another. And contrariwise, what doth so much distract the wills and divide the hearts as jealousy? Love binds us to interpret favorably of all the actions of the party beloved, and to take in good part[2] that which we ought to believe she hath done with reason, whereas jealousy makes bad interpretations not only of her actions but even of her very thoughts. Is there any innocence that can be sheltered from the outrages of this inhuman fury? If the party beloved hath any joy, it then presupposeth[3] a rival; if she be pensive, they are

---

1   Color.
2   View positively.
3   Assumes the existence of.

The rivalrous passions jealousy and envy were often allegorized as women in the early modern period. A common variant of this figuration shows Envy as a repulsive old woman with sagging breasts and Gorgon-like snakes for hair. In this image, by the Dutch engraver Jacob Matham (1571–1631), she appears literally eating her heart out of her hand.

Jacob Matham, *Envy* (c. 1587). Wikimedia Commons, https://commons.wikimedia.org.

suspicions of contempt; if she speaks to another, it is infidelity; if she have wit, they apprehend practices;[1] if she be advised, they imagine subtleties;[2] if she be plain, they call it simplicity;[3] if she be well spoken, it is affectedness; if she be courteous, it is with a design. So as jealousy is like unto those counterfeit glasses,[4] which never represent the true proportion of the face—and what more sinister judgments could the most cruel enemy in the world give of the party beloved?—but not content thus to blemish the particular perfections of that she seems to love, she seeks to deprive it of the sweetest content in this life, which is by communication with men of honor and merit who do not visit her but for the esteem they make of her virtues. So as many times to please an importune,[5] who is himself a great burden to them that suffer him, she must forbear[6] all good company. What justice can force a soul well bred to endure this brutish rigor? Love is a lively fountain of joy and contentment, which banisheth all cares and melancholy; but jealousy, what is it else but a nursery of griefs and waywardness, whereas we see thorns of despair and rage to grow up among the sweetest and most pleasing flowers that nature can produce? How then can any man believe that these two contrary passions can subsist in one subject? If they oppose hereunto experience and the testimony of many persons worthy of credit which protest that they have loved sincerely and yet were never without jealousy, and will thereby infer that, at the least, jealousy is a sign of love, which is the second thing we must encounter, to satisfy that which hath been formerly propounded:[7] it sufficeth to answer that although for respect we yield to those personages what they publish[8] of their passions, yet as one swallow[9] makes no spring, so that which happens to particulars cannot prescribe a law to the general. But to contain ourselves within the bounds of our first proposition, we say that these persons are much deceived in this subject, and their error

---

1   Conspiracies.
2   Cunning tricks.
3   Lack of perceptiveness or judgment.
4   Mirrors.
5   One who pesters.
6   Do without.
7   Proposed.
8   Report.
9   Migratory bird whose appearance is traditionally and proverbially associated with the arrival of spring.

grows for that they cannot give proper names to things, for that of a respective[1] fear compatible with love, whereof it is full, they make an unjust jealousy, with the which love can no more subsist than water with fire. They that love entirely are, in truth, full of respect to the party beloved, honor her with all the passions of their souls, fight for her honor, and hold it a punishment to offend her. But these are not the effects of jealousy, which contrariwise violates the honor which is due to the party beloved, and, by a prodigious manner to blind the world, will have her favor by wronging her, treading her merits underfoot. We must then put a difference betwixt a respective fear, which always doth accompany those that love perfectly, and jealousy, which is never found but with an imperfect passion, which cannot judge of the perfections of the party beloved. They which know that these things are diverse,[2] and as remote one from another as the earth is from heaven, will easily pass on this side and yield that jealousy is neither compatible with love, nor is any sign thereof. Yet if we shall yield anything to the opinion of the vulgar, we may freely confess that jealousy in truth is a sign of love but as the fever is an argument of life. It is unquestionable that a fever is a sign of life seeing the dead are not susceptible of this bad quality. But as a fever showing that there are some relics[3] of life in the patient that is tormented accompanies him to his grave, so jealousy is I know not what sign of love, seeing they which love not cannot have any jealousy. But it is certain that if we expel it not, it will in the end ruin love, like unto a thick smoke which smothers the brightest flame. This is all we can yield unto the vulgar, so as according to this opinion which we have held the most probable, jealousy is to love as thick mists are to flowers, hail to harvest, storms to fruits, and poison to our lives.

---

1 Appropriate; respectful.
2 Distinct.
3 Remnants.

WORKS CITED AND BIBLIOGRAPHY

EDITIONS OF *OTHELLO*

Bevington, David, ed. *Othello. The Complete Works of Shakespeare.* 7th ed. New York: Pearson, 2014. 1150–1200.

Capell, Edward, ed. *Othello. Mr. William Shakespeare His Comedies, Histories, and Tragedies.* Vol. 10. London: J. and R. Tonson, 1768.

Evans, G. Blackmore, et al., eds. *Othello. The Riverside Shakespeare.* 2nd ed. Boston: Houghton Mifflin, 1997. 1251–96.

Furness, Horace Howard, ed. *Othello.* New Variorum. J.B. Lippincott, 1886; New York: Dover, 1963.

Harbage, Alfred, ed. *Othello. William Shakespeare: The Complete Works.* Baltimore: Penguin, 1969. 1021–59.

Honigmann, E.A.J., ed. *Othello.* Arden 3 Shakespeare. Surrey: Nelson, 1997.

Johnson, Samuel, ed. *Othello. The Plays of William Shakespeare.* Vol. 8. London: J. and R. Tonson, 1765.

Malone, Edmond, ed. *Othello. The Plays and Poems of William Shakespeare.* Vol. 9. London: J. Rivington, et al. 1790; rpt. New York: AMS, 1968.

McDonald, Russ, ed. *Othello.* Pelican Shakespeare. New York: Penguin, 2001.

Mowat, Barbara A., and Paul Werstine, eds. *Othello.* New Folger Library Shakespeare. New York: Simon & Schuster, 1993.

Muir, Kenneth, ed. *Othello.* London: Penguin, 1968.

Neill, Michael, ed. *Othello.* Oxford: Oxford UP, 2006.

Pechter, Edward, ed. *Othello.* New York: Norton, 2004.

Pope, Alexander, ed. *Othello. The Works of Mr. William Shakespeare.* Vol. 6. London: Jacob Tonson, 1723–25; rpt. New York: AMS, 1969.

Potter, Lois, ed. *Othello.* Shakespeare in Performance. Manchester: Manchester UP, 2002.

Ridley, M.R., ed. *Othello.* Arden 2 Shakesepeare. Rev. ed. London: Methuen, 1962.

Rowe, Nicholas, ed. *Othello. The Works of Mr. William Shakespear.* Vol. 5. London: Jacob Tonson, 1709–10; rpt. New York: AMS, 1967.

Sanders, Norman, ed. *Othello. The New Cambridge Shakespeare.* Cambridge: Cambridge UP, 1984, rev. ed. 2003.

Steevens, George, ed. *Othello. Twenty Plays of Shakespeare.* Vol. 4. London: J. and R. Tonson, 1766; rpt. New York: AMS, 1968.

Theobald, Lewis, ed. *Othello. The Works of Shakespeare.* Vol. 7. London: A. Bettesworth and C. Hitch, et al. 1733; rpt. New York: AMS, 1968.

Wells, Stanley, and Gary Taylor, eds. *Othello. The Oxford Shakespeare: The Complete Works.* 2nd ed. Oxford: Clarendon, 2005. 873–907.

OTHER REFERENCES

Alexander, Catherine M.S., and Stanley Wells, ed. *Shakespeare and Race.* Cambridge: Cambridge UP, 2000.

Alger, William. *The Life of Edwin Forrest: The American Tragedian.* Vol. 2. Philadelphia: J.B. Lippincott, 1877.

Altman, Joel. *The Improbability of Othello: Rhetorical Anthropology and Shakespearean Selfhood.* Chicago: U of Chicago P, 2010.

The Art of Falconry: Being the De Arte Venandi Cum Avibus of Frederick II of Hohenstaufen. Ed. and trans. Casey A. Wood and F. Marjorie Fyfe. Stanford, CA: Stanford UP, 1943.

Bartels, Emily C. *Speaking of the Moor: From "Alcazar" to "Othello."* Philadelphia: U of Pennsylvania P, 2008.

Barthelemy, Anthony Gerard. *Black Face, Maligned Race: The Representation of Blacks in English Drama from Shakespeare to Swinburne.* Baton Rouge: Louisiana State UP, 1987.

Boaden, James. *Memoirs of the Life of John Philip Kemble.* Vol. 1. London, 1825.

Boorde, Andrew. *The Fyrst Boke of the Introduction of Knowledge.* 1547. Ed. F.J. Furnivall. Early English Text Society. Vol.10. London: N. Trübner, 1870.

Boose, Lynda E. "Othello's 'Chrysolite' and the Song of Songs Tradition." *Philological Quarterly* 60 (1981): 427–37.

———. "Othello's Handkerchief: 'The Recognizance and Pledge of Love.'" *English Literary Renaissance* 5.3 (1975): 360–74.

Bradley, A.C. *Shakespearean Tragedy.* 1904. 4th ed. London: Palgrave Macmillan, 2007.

Bristol, Michael. "Charivari and the Comedy of Abjection in *Othello.*" *Renaissance Drama* 21 (1990): 3–21.

Britton, Dennis Austin. "Re-'turning' *Othello*: Transformative and Restorative Romance." *ELH* 78.1 (2011): 27–50.

Bullough, Geoffrey. *Narrative and Dramatic Sources of Shakespeare*. Vol. 7. New York: Columbia UP, 1957–75.

Burton, Jonathan. *Traffic and Turning: Islam and English Drama, 1579–1624*. Newark: U of Delaware P, 2005.

Callaghan, Dympna. *Shakespeare without Women: Representing Gender and Race on the Stage*. New York: Routledge, 2000.

Cavell, Stanley. "Othello and the Stake of the Other." *Disowning Knowledge in Seven Plays by Shakespeare*. 2nd ed. Cambridge: Cambridge UP, 2003.

Coleridge, S.T. *Coleridge's Shakespeare Criticism*. Ed. Thomas Middleton Raysor. 2 vols. Cambridge, MA: Harvard UP, 1930.

Cowhig, Ruth. "Blacks in English Renaissance Drama and the Role of Shakespeare's Othello." *The Black Presence in English Literature*. Ed. David Dabydeen. Manchester: Manchester UP, 1985. 1–25.

Culianu, Ioan P. *Eros and Magic in the Renaissance*. Trans. Margaret Cook. Chicago: U of Chicago P, 1987.

Cunningham, J.V. *The Collected Essays of J.V. Cunningham*. Chicago: Swallow, 1976.

Daileader, Celia R. *Racism, Misogyny, and the Othello Myth: Inter-racial Couples from Shakespeare to Spike Lee*. Cambridge: Cambridge UP, 2005.

D'Amico, Jack. *The Moor in English Renaissance Drama*. Gainesville: UP of Florida, 1991.

Dash, Irene. *Wooing, Wedding, and Power: Women in Shakespeare*. New York: Columbia UP, 1981.

Davidson, Nicholas. "Theology, Nature and the Law: Sexual Sin and Sexual Crime in Italy from the Fourteenth to the Seventeenth Century." *Crime, Society and the Law in Renaissance Italy*. Ed. Trevor Dean and K.J.P. Lowe. Cambridge: Cambridge UP, 1994. 74–98.

Deats, Sara Munson. "'Truly, an obedient lady': Desdemona, Emilia, and the Doctrine of Obedience in *Othello*." Othello: *New Critical Essays*. Ed. Philip C. Kolin. New York: Routledge, 2002. 233–54.

Dent, R.W. *Shakespeare's Proverbial Language: An Index*. Berkeley: U of California P, 1981.

Dessen, Alan C. *Recovering Shakespeare's Theatrical Vocabulary*. Cambridge, Cambridge UP, 1995.

————, and Leslie Thompson. *A Dictionary of Stage Directions in English Drama, 1580–1642.* Cambridge: Cambridge UP, 1999.

Distiller, Natasha. "Authentic Protest, Authentic Shakespeare, Authentic Africans: Performing *Othello* in South Africa." *Comparative Drama* 46.3 (2012): 339–54.

Elizabeth I. "Letter permitting deportation of blackmoors from England." 11 July 1596. *Acts of the Privy Council.* Vol. 26. Ed. John Roche Dasent. London: Eyre and Spottiswoode, 1902. 16–17.

————. "Letter permitting deportation of blackamoors from England." 18 July 1596. *Acts of the Privy Council.* Vol. 26. Ed. John Roche Dasent. London: Eyre and Spottiswoode, 1902. 20–21.

————. "Proclamation requiring transportation of negroes and blackamoors by Casper van Senden." *Tudor Royal Proclamations.* Vol. 3. Ed. Paul L. Hughes and James F. Larkin. New Haven, CT: Yale UP, 1969. 221–22.

Empson, William. "Honest in *Othello.*" *The Structure of Complex Words.* 1951. 3rd ed. London: Chatto and Windus, 1977. 218–49.

Farjeon, Herbert. *The Shakespearean Scene.* London: Hutchinson, 1949.

Floyd-Wilson, Mary. *English Ethnicity and Race in Early Modern Drama.* Cambridge: Cambridge UP, 2003.

Greenblatt, Stephen. *Renaissance Self-Fashioning: From More to Shakespeare.* 1980. Chicago: U of Chicago P, 2005.

Habib, Imtiaz, and Duncan Salkeld. "The Resonables of Boroughside, Southwark: An Elizabethan Black Family Near the Rose Theatre/Alienating Laughter in *The Merchant of Venice*: A Reply to Imtiaz Habib." *Shakespeare* 11.2 (2015): 135–56.

Hadfield, Andrew. *A Routledge Literary Sourcebook on William Shakespeare's* Othello. London: Routledge, 2003.

Hall, Edward. "The Politique Gouernaunce of Kyng Henry the VII." *The Vnion of the Two Noble and Illustrate Famelies of Lancastre & Yorke.* London, 1548.

Hall, Kim F. "*Othello* and the Problem of Blackness." *A Companion to Shakespeare's Works: The Tragedies.* Ed. Richard Dutton and Jean E. Howard. Malden, MA: Blackwell, 2003. 357–74.

————. "'These Bastard Signs of Fair': Literary Whiteness in Shakespeare's Sonnets." *Post-Colonial Shakespeares.* Ed. A. Loomba and M. Orkin. London: Routledge, 1998. 64–83.

————. *Things of Darkness: Economies of Race and Gender in Early Modern England*. Ithaca, NY: Cornell UP, 1995.

Hankey, Julie. *Othello*. Shakespeare in Production. 2nd ed. Cambridge: Cambridge UP, 2005.

Hart, Alfred. "The Date of *Othello*." *Times Literary Supplement* 10 October 1935: 631.

Heilman, Robert. *Magic in the Web: Action and Language in* Othello. Lexington: U of Kentucky P, 1956.

Honigmann, E.A.J. "The First Quarto of *Hamlet* and the Date of *Othello*." *Review of English Studies* 44 (1993): 211–19.

Hunt, Leigh. "Theatrical Examiner." *Examiner* 4 Oct. 1818: 632.

Hunter, G.K. "Othello and Colour Prejudice." *Proceedings of the British Academy* 53 (1967); rpt. *Dramatic Identities and Cultural Tradition: Studies in Shakespeare and His Contemporaries*. Liverpool: Liverpool UP, 1978, 31–59.

Jackson, Henry. "Letter of 1610." Trans. Dana F. Sutton. The Philological Museum, The Shakespeare Institute of the University of Birmingham. http://www.philological.bham.ac.uk/jackson/text.html.

Jameson, Anna Murphy. *Shakespeare's Heroines: Characteristics of Women, Moral, Poetical, and Historical*. Ed. Cheri L. Larsen Hoeckley. Peterborough, ON: Broadview, 2005.

Jardine, Lisa. "'Why should he call her whore?': Defamation and Desdemona's Case." *Reading Shakespeare Historically*. London: Routledge, 1996. 18–33.

Jones, Eldred. *Othello's Countrymen: The African in English Renaissance Drama*. Oxford: Oxford UP, 1965.

Kahn, Coppélia. *Man's Estate: Masculine Identity in Shakespeare*. Berkeley: U of California P, 1981.

Knight, G. Wilson. "The Othello Music." *The Wheel of Fire: Interpretations of Shakespearian Tragedy*. 1930; rev. and enl. London: Methuen, 1949. 109–35.

Knights, L.C. *How Many Children Had Lady Macbeth? An Essay in the Theory and Practice of Shakespeare Criticism*. Cambridge: Gordon Fraser, 1933.

Kolin, Philip C. "Blackness Made Visible: A Survey of *Othello* in Criticism, on Stage, and on Screen." *Othello: New Critical Essays*. Ed. Philip C. Kolin. London: Routledge, 2002. 1–87.

Kugler, Emily M.N. *Sway of the Ottoman Empire on English Identity in the Long Eighteenth Century.* Brill's Studies in Intellectual History 209. Leiden: Koninklijke Brill, 2012.

Leavis, F.R. "Diabolical Intellect and the Noble Hero; or The Sentimentalist Othello." *Scrutiny* 6 (1937); rpt. in *The Common Pursuit.* London: Chatto & Windus, 1952; rpt. London: Faber, 2008. 136–59.

Loomba, Ania. "Sexuality and Racial Difference." *Critical Essays on Shakespeare's* Othello. Ed. Anthony Gerard Barthelemy. New York: G.K. Hall, 1994. 162–86.

———. *Shakespeare, Race, and Colonialism.* Oxford: Oxford UP, 2002.

Lupton, Julia Reinhard. *Citizen-Saints: Shakespeare and Political Theology.* Chicago: U of Chicago P, 2005.

MacDonald, Joyce Green. "Acting Black: 'Othello,' 'Othello' Burlesques, and the Performance of Blackness." *Theatre Journal* 46 (1994): 231–49.

Mallett, M.E., and J.R. Hale. *The Military Organization of a Renaissance State: Venice c. 1400 to 1617.* Cambridge: Cambridge UP, 1984.

Martyr, Peter. *The Decades of the New World.* Trans. Richard Eden. London, 1555.

Massai, Sonia, ed. *World-wide Shakespeares: Local Appropriations in Film and Performance.* New York: Routledge, 2005.

Matteo, Gino J. *Shakespeare's Othello: The Study and the Stage 1604–1904.* Salzburg: Institut für Englische Sprache und Literatur, 1974.

Maxwell, J.C. "*Othello* and the Bad Quarto of *Hamlet.*" *Notes and Queries* 21 (1974): 130.

Minear, Erin. "Music and the Crisis of Meaning in *Othello.*" *SEL* 49.2 (2009): 355–70.

Nares, Robert. *A Glossary or Collection of Words, Phrases, Names, and Allusions to Customs, Proverbs, etc.* London, 1822.

Neely, Carol Thomas. *Broken Nuptials in Shakespeare's Plays.* New Haven, CT: Yale UP, 1985.

———. "Women and Men in *Othello.*" *Critical Essays on Shakespeare's* Othello. Ed. Anthony Gerard Barthelemy. New York: G.K. Hall, 1994. 68–90.

Neill, Michael. "'Unproper Beds': Race, Adultery, and the Hideous in *Othello*." *Shakespeare Quarterly* 40 (1989): 383–412.

Newman, Karen. "'And wash the Ethiop white': Femininity and the Monstrous in *Othello*." *Shakespeare Reproduced: The Text in History and Ideology*. Ed. Jean E. Howard and Marion F. O'Connor. New York: Methuen, 1987; rpt. *Essaying Shakespeare*. Minneapolis: U of Minnesota P, 2009. 38–58.

Novy, Marianne L. *Love's Argument: Gender Relations in Shakespeare*. Chapel Hill: U of North Carolina P, 1984.

Nucius, Nicander. *The Second Book of the Travels of Nicander Nucius, of Corcyra*. Ed. and trans. J.A. Cramer. London, 1941.

Orkin, Martin. "*Othello* and the 'plain face' of Racism." *Shakespeare Quarterly* 38.2 (1987): 166–88.

Orlin, Lena Cowen, ed. *New Casebooks: Othello*. Basingstoke: Palgrave Macmillan, 2004.

————, ed. *Othello: The State of Play*. London: Bloomsbury, 2014.

Parker, Patricia. "Fantasies of 'Race' and 'Gender': Africa, *Othello*, and Bringing to Light." *Women, "Race," and Writing in the Early Modern Period*. Ed. Margo Hendricks and Patricia Parker. New York: Routledge, 1994. 84–100.

————. "Shakespeare and Rhetoric: 'Dilation' and 'Delation' in *Othello*." *Shakespeare and the Question of Theory*. Ed. Patricia Parker and Geoffrey Hartman. New York: Methuen, 1985. 54–74.

Partridge, Eric. *Shakespeare's Bawdy*. 1947; rpt. London: Routledge, 1996.

Paster, Gail Kern. *Humoring the Body: Emotions and the Shakespearean Stage*. Chicago: U of Chicago P, 2004.

————, ed. *Reading the Early Modern Passions: Essays in the Cultural History of Emotions*. Philadelphia: U of Pennsylvania P, 2004.

Pechter, Edward. Othello *and Interpretive Traditions*. Iowa City: U of Iowa P, 1999.

————. "'Why Should We Call Her Whore?' Bianca in *Othello*." *Shakespeare and the Twentieth Century: The Selected Proceedings of the International Shakespeare Association World Congress, Los Angeles, 1996*. Ed. Jonathan Bate, Jill L. Levenson, and Dieter Mehl. Cranbury, NJ: Associated University Presses, 1998.

Pennacchia, Maddalena. "Female Marginalia: Handkerchiefs at the Border of Tudor History." *Textus: English Studies in Italy* 22.3 (2009): 699–713.

Pliny. *The Historie of the World. Commonly called, The Naturall Histories of C. Plinius Secundus*. Trans. Philemon Holland. London, 1601.

Pye, Christopher. "'To Throw Out Our Eyes for Brave Othello': Shakespeare and Aesthetic Ideology." *Shakespeare Quarterly* 60.4 (2009): 425–47.

Rosenberg, Marvin. *The Masks of Othello*. Berkeley: U of California P, 1961.

Ross, Lawrence J. "The Meaning of Strawberries in Shakespeare." *Studies in the Renaissance* 7 (1960): 225–40.

Rowe, Katherine. *Dead Hands: Fictions of Agency, Renaissance to Modern*. Stanford, CA: Stanford UP, 1999.

Rutter, Carol Chillington. "Unpinning Desdemona (Again) or 'Who Would Be Toll'd with Wenches in a Shew?'" *Shakespeare Bulletin* 28.1 (2010): 111–32.

Rymer, Thomas. *A Short View of Tragedy*. London, 1693.

Schlegel, August Wilhelm. *A Course of Lectures on Dramatic Art and Literature*. Trans. John Black and A.J.W. Morrison. London, 1815.

Shattuck, Charles H., ed. *John Philip Kemble Promptbooks*. Vol. 1. The Folger Facsimiles. Charlottesville: UP of Virginia, 1974.

Skura, Meredith Anne. "Reading Othello's Skin: Contexts and Pretexts." *Philological Quarterly* 87.3–4 (2008): 299–334.

Slights, Camille Wells. "Slaves and Subjects in *Othello*." *Shakespeare Quarterly* 48.4 (1997): 377–90.

Slights, William W.E. *The Heart in the Age of Shakespeare*. Cambridge: Cambridge UP, 2008.

Smith, Bruce. *Homosexual Desire in Shakespeare's England*. Chicago: U of Chicago P. 1991.

Smith, Gordon Ross. "Iago: The Paranoiac." *American Imago: Studies in Psychoanalysis and Culture* 16 (1959); rpt. *The Design Within: Psychoanalytic Approaches to Shakespeare*. Ed. M.D. Faber. New York: Science House, 1970. 170–82.

Smith, Ian. "Othello's Black Handkerchief." *Shakespeare Quarterly* 64.1 (2013): 1–25.

Snow, Edward. A. "Sexual Anxiety and the Male Order of Things in *Othello*." *English Literary Renaissance* 10.3 (1980): 384–412.

Snyder, Susan. *The Comic Matrix of Shakespeare's Tragedies:* Romeo and Juliet, Hamlet, Othello, *and* King Lear. Princeton, NJ: Princeton UP, 1979.

————. Othello: *Critical Essays.* New York: Garland, 1988.

Spivak, Bernard. *Shakespeare and the Allegory of Evil.* New York: Columbia UP, 1958.

Swift, Daniel. *Shakespeare's Common Prayers: The Book of Common Prayer and the Elizabethan Age.* Oxford: Oxford UP, 2013.

Thompson, Ayanna, ed. *Colorblind Shakespeare: New Perspectives on Race and Performance.* New York: Routledge, 2006.

Tilley, Morris Palmer. *A Dictionary of Proverbs in England in the Sixteenth and Seventeenth Centuries.* Ann Arbor: U of Michigan P, 1950.

Tokson, Elliot. *The Popular Image of the Black Man in English Drama, 1550–1688.* Boston: G.K. Hall, 1982.

Turner, David M. "Adulterous Kisses and the Meanings of Familiarity in Early Modern Britain." *The Kiss in History.* Ed. Karen Harvey. Manchester: Manchester UP, 2005. 80–97.

Vanita, Ruth. "'Proper' Men and 'Fallen' Women: The Unprotectedness of Wives in *Othello.*" *SEL* 34 (1994): 341–56.

Vaughan, Virginia Mason. Othello: *A Contextual History.* Cambridge: Cambridge UP, 1994.

Vitkus, Daniel. *Turning Turk: English Theater and the Multicultural Mediterranean, 1570–1630.* New York: Palgrave Macmillan, 2003.

Walen, Denise. "Unpinning Desdemona." *Shakespeare Quarterly* 58.4 (2007): 487–508.

Wangh, Martin. "*Othello:* The Tragedy of Iago." *Psychoanalytic Quarterly* 19 (1950): 202–12; rpt. *The Design Within: Psychoanalytic Approaches to Shakespeare.* Ed. M.D. Faber. New York: Science House, 1970. 157–68.

Wells, Stanley, et al. *William Shakespeare: A Textual Companion.* Oxford: Clarendon, 1987.

Wilder, Lina Perkins. *Shakespeare's Memory Theatre: Recollection, Properties, and Character.* Cambridge: Cambridge UP, 2010.

Williams, Gordon. *A Dictionary of Sexual Language and Imagery in Shakespearean and Stuart Literature.* 2 vols. London: Athlone, 1994.

————. *A Glossary of Shakespeare's Sexual Language.* London: Athlone, 1997.

Wood, Sam. "Where Iago Lies: Home, Honesty and the Turk in *Othello*." *Early Modern Literary Studies* 14.3 (2009). http://purl.oclc.org/emls/14-3/Woodiago.html.

From the Publisher

A name never says it all, but the word "Broadview" expresses a good deal of the philosophy behind our company. We are open to a broad range of academic approaches and political viewpoints. We pay attention to the broad impact book publishing and book printing has in the wider world; for some years now we have used 100% recycled paper for most titles. Our publishing program is internationally oriented and broad-ranging. Our individual titles often appeal to a broad readership too; many are of interest as much to general readers as to academics and students.

Founded in 1985, Broadview remains a fully independent company owned by its shareholders—not an imprint or subsidiary of a larger multinational.

For the most accurate information on our books (including information on pricing, editions, and formats) please visit our website at www.broadviewpress.com. Our print books and ebooks are also available for sale on our site.

broadview press
www.broadviewpress.com

This book is made of paper from well-managed FSC® - certified forests, recycled materials, and other controlled sources.